Praise for Amy Chua's

DAY OF EMPIRE

"Amy Chua smartly condenses the complex histories of the Persian, Mughal, Dutch, and other empires into an irresistible argument: that empires expand through toleration and contract through closed-mindedness. As with any shrewd and elaborate argument, the getting there is half the fun."
—Robert D. Kaplan, *Atlantic Monthly* correspondent and author of *Balkan Ghosts* and *Imperial Grunts*

"Absorbing." —*The New York Times*

"Informative and charming. . . . Chua's thesis is ingenious and thought-provoking." —*The Baltimore Sun*

"Brilliant." —*National Review*

"Ambitious and challenging. . . . [Chua] has at once shifted and in some ways elevated the interpretive terrain."
—*Chicago Tribune*

"Fascinating. . . . A lively read, full of intriguing factoids."
—*Salon*

"From ancient Achaemenid Persia to the modern United States, by way of Rome, Tang China, and the Spanish, Dutch, and British Empires, Amy Chua tells the story of the world's hyperpowers—that elite of empires which, in their heyday, were truly without equal. Not everyone will be persuaded by her ingenious thesis that religious and racial tolerance was a prerequisite for global dominance, but also the slow solvent of that cultural 'glue' which holds a great nation together. But few readers will fail to be impressed by the height of this book's ambition and by the breadth of scholarship on which it is based."

—Niall Ferguson, Laurence A. Tisch Professor of History, Harvard University, and author of *Empire: The Rise and Demise of the British World Order and the Lessons for Global Power*

"Scintillating history, breathtaking in scope and chock-full of insight. Amy Chua argues persuasively that the real key to acquiring and maintaining great power lies in the ability to attract and assimilate, rather than to coerce or intimidate."

—Andrew J. Bacevich, author of *The New American Militarism: How Americans Are Seduced by War*

"Amy Chua is a law professor, but in this book she writes as a sage historian. She draws lessons from the past that one who cares about the future cannot afford to ignore."

—Amitai Etzioni, author of *Security First: For a Muscular, Moral Foreign Policy*

AMY CHUA

DAY OF EMPIRE

Amy Chua is the John Duff, Jr. Professor of Law at Yale Law School. She is the author of *World on Fire* and a noted expert in the fields of international business, ethnic conflict, and globalization. She lives in New Haven, Connecticut, with her husband, daughters Sophia and Louisa, and their Samoyeds Coco and Pushkin.

ALSO BY AMY CHUA

World on Fire

DAY OF EMPIRE

HOW HYPERPOWERS RISE TO GLOBAL DOMINANCE—

AND WHY THEY FALL

AMY CHUA

Anchor Books
A Division of Random House, Inc.
New York

FIRST ANCHOR BOOKS EDITION, JANUARY 2009

The Library of Congress has cataloged the Doubleday edition as follows:
Chua, Amy.
Day of empire : how hyperpowers rise to global dominance—
and why they fall /
Amy Chua. — 1st ed.
p. cm.
Includes bibliographical references and index.
1. Imperialism—History. 2. Hegemony—History. I. Title.
JC539.C58 2008
327.1'12—dc22
2007015116

Anchor ISBN: 978-1-4000-7741-0

Author photograph © Peter Mahakian
Book design by Caroline Cunningham

www.anchorbooks.com

Printed in the United States of America
10 9 8 7 6 5 4 3 2 1

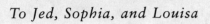

To Jed, Sophia, and Louisa

CONTENTS

PREFACE

I think of my father as the quintessential American. Both he and my mother were Chinese, but grew up in the Philippines. They were children during World War II and lived under Japanese Occupation until General Douglas MacArthur liberated the Philippines in 1945. My father remembers running after American jeeps, cheering wildly, as U.S. troops tossed out free cans of Spam.

My father was the black sheep in his family. Brilliant at math, in love with astronomy and philosophy, he hated the small, backstabbing world of his family's aluminum-can business and defied every plan they had for him. Even as a boy, he was desperate to get to America, so it was a dream come true when the Massachusetts Institute of Technology accepted his application. My parents arrived in Boston in 1961, knowing not a soul in the country. With only their student scholarships to live on, they couldn't afford heat their first two winters and wrapped blankets around themselves to keep warm.

Growing up in the Midwest, my three younger sisters and I always knew that we were different from everyone else. Mortifyingly, we brought Chinese food in thermoses to school; how I wished I could have a bologna sandwich like everyone else! We were required to speak Chinese at home—the punishment was one whack of the chopsticks for every English word accidentally uttered. We drilled math and piano every afternoon, and we were never allowed to sleep over at our friends' houses. Every evening when my father came home from work, I took off his shoes and brought him his slippers. Our report cards had to be perfect; while our friends were rewarded for Bs, for us getting an A-minus was unthinkable. In eighth grade, I won second place in a history contest and took my family to the awards ceremony. Somebody else had won the Kiwanis prize for best all-around student. Afterward, my father said to me: "Never, never disgrace me like that again."

When my friends hear these stories, they often imagine that I had a horrible childhood. But that's not true at all; I found strength and confidence in my peculiar family. We started off as outsiders together, and we discovered America together, becoming Americans in the process. I remember my father working until three in the morning every night, so driven he wouldn't even notice us entering the room. But I also remember how excited he was when he introduced us to tacos, sloppy joes, Dairy Queen, and "all-you-can-eat" buffets, not to mention sledding, skiing, crabbing, and camping. I remember a boy in grade school making slanty-eyed gestures at me, guffawing as he mimicked the way I pronounced *restaurant*; I vowed at that moment to rid myself of my Chinese accent. But I also remember Girl Scouts and hula hoops; poetry contests and public libraries; winning a Daughters of the American Revolution essay contest; and the proud, momentous day my parents were naturalized.

Like many other immigrant groups, Asians weren't always welcome in the United States. In 1882, the U.S. Congress passed the Chinese Exclusion Act, banning Chinese—along with prostitutes, criminals, and lepers—from entering the country. As late as World War II, while my father was cheering on American troops in Manila, the U.S. Supreme Court upheld the government's policy of evacuating Japanese Americans from their homes into internment camps.

By the late 1960s, however, legal reforms had lifted many barriers for immigrants. For my father, as for many other newcomers who arrived during that period, determination and hard work translated directly into success. My father got his Ph.D. in less than two years, became a tenured professor at the age of thirty-one, and won a series of national engineering awards. In 1971 my father accepted an offer from the University of California at Berkeley, and we packed up and moved West. My father grew his hair long and wore jackets with peace signs on them. Then he got interested in wine collecting and built himself a thousand-bottle cellar. As he became internationally known for his work on chaos theory, we began traveling around the world. I spent my junior year in high school studying in London, Munich, and Lausanne, and my father took us to the Arctic Circle.

And yet there were always contradictions: about who we were, who we weren't, and what we were supposed to be. Even as we were thriving in the American melting pot, and indeed representing the United States abroad, my parents never let us forget that we were Chinese—not just by heritage, but by blood.

As a child, one of the first things I learned was the difference between a Chinese person, a *Han*, and everyone else. The definition of a Chinese person, whether in modern times or thousands of years ago, has always been contrasted against the "foreign barbarian." Moreover, it went without saying in my family that being Han was not something that could be learned or acquired through acculturation. A white person—no matter how fluent in Chinese, no matter how long he had lived in China—could never be Han. My mother spoke frequently of the magnificence of China's five-thousand-year history and the superiority of Chinese culture. She also talked about the "purity" of Chinese blood and what a shame it would be to dilute it. In my native Hokkien dialect, the height of insult is to describe someone as *tzup jeng*—literally, "of ten breeds"; the closest English equivalent is probably *mongrel*.

In fact, the idea that there is a "pure" Han bloodline defining a "pure" Han people is not only a great myth, but a relatively recent one. Who has counted as Chinese throughout China's long history is far more complicated than is usually acknowledged. But I didn't know any of this as a child. Still, I always had trouble applying the concept of "foreign barbarian mongrel" in America. Everyone seemed to be of mixed ancestry; my best friend in Indiana was Scottish-Irish-English-Dutch-German. And what about the heroic GIs who liberated the Philippines? Were they barbarians? If so, perhaps being a barbarian wasn't so bad.

Conveniently, there was no time for analyzing these questions. Instead, my father issued edicts, such as "You will marry a non-Chinese over my dead body," which he declared when I was four. When it came time to apply to college, my father announced that I was going to live at home and attend Berkeley (where I had already been accepted), and that was that—no visiting campuses and agonizing choices for me. Disobeying him, as he had disobeyed his family, I forged his signature and secretly applied to a school on the East Coast I had heard people talking about. When I told him what I had done—and that Harvard had accepted me—my father's reaction surprised me. He went from anger to pride literally overnight. He was equally proud when I later graduated from Harvard Law School and when his next daughter graduated from Yale College and Yale Law School. He was proudest of all (but perhaps also a little heartbroken) when his third daughter left home for Harvard, eventually earning her M.D./Ph.D. there.

Just before entering college, I visited China for the first time. My family and I spent the summer of 1980 in Chengdu, the capital of Sichuan province. At that time, China was a backward Communist country, reeling from decades of xenophobic isolation and the anti-intellectual purges of the Cultural Revolution. Chengdu, once known as The Brocade City for its magnificent silks, was a concrete, Mao-suited eyesore. Our host, the president of the Engineering and Technology Institute, appeared to be an uneducated peasant. At our welcome banquet, he sprayed a fusillade of watermelon seeds from his mouth directly onto the sticky restaurant floor. Afterward, my mother wept. Was this all that remained of the Middle Kingdom's magnificent civilization?

A lot has happened in the last quarter century—to the world, to China, to the United States, to my family. Despite my father's draconian injunction, I ended up marrying a Jewish American. Today, my father and my husband are the best of friends, and my parents could not dote more on their mixed-blooded, Mandarin-speaking American grandchildren.

First and foremost, this book is a tribute to America's tolerance, which, for all its imperfection, drew my parents to this country and allowed my family to flourish, to change on our own terms, and to become Americans. At the same time, it is a study of power—colossal power—and the conditions that allow some societies to attain and maintain it. At yet a different level, this book is about the contest between ethnic "purity" and ethnic pluralism, each of which has its own allure and its own potency. Finally, this book is a warning. Tolerance, I will argue, has always been the true secret to America's success, and today, more than ever before, we are in danger of losing our way.

INTRODUCTION

THE SECRET TO WORLD DOMINANCE

How fast the world changes. In the 1980s, the United States was a mere superpower, with an easy-to-hate authoritarian rival. Ten years later, it was the world's undisputed hyperpower, and American global dominance seemed almost boundless. Today, after the debacles of Iraq and Hurricane Katrina, people are already talking about America's decline.

When the term *hyperpower* was first applied to the United States, it was not intended favorably. The word was coined by France's foreign minister Hubert Vedrine, one of the most outspoken critics of the United States, when he declared that France "cannot accept a politically unipolar world, nor a culturally uniform world, nor the unilateralism of a single hyperpower." Although he meant "hyperpower" reproachfully, Vedrine captured a historical development of fundamental importance. As Vedrine described it, the United States had become "dominant or predominant in all categories": America had attained not only economic, military, and technological preeminence, but also a "domination of attitudes, concepts, language and modes of life."[1]

Today, the idea of an America "dominant in all categories" does not ring quite as true. America remains the world's economic and military powerhouse, but it is beleaguered on many fronts, its confidence shaken, its reputation bruised, its fisc depleted by hundreds of billions poured into a war it may not win. Meanwhile, other emerging powers are shifting and jockeying for position. The European Union has not only a larger population but a gross domestic product already almost equal to that of the United States. China, with a fifth of the world's people, is exploding after centuries of stagnation. Could China, the EU, or perhaps some other contender—such as India—overtake the United States, or at least gain sufficient strength to reestablish a multipolar world order?

Whether America retains or falls from its hyperpower status is a question of immense consequence for both the world and the United States. Does the twenty-first century need an "American Empire," as the British historian Niall Ferguson argues, to deal with genocide, rogue states, and "terrorist organizations committed to wrecking a liberal world order"?[2] Or is an American hyperpower a threat to world peace and global stability, as others believe?[3] From the U.S. point of view, would American decline mean unemployment, reduced standards of living, and increased vulnerability to attack? Or is America's role as hyperpower paradoxically leading the nation to bankrupt its future, incur the world's wrath, and make itself even more of a terrorist target?

———

This book is about hyperpowers—not great powers, not even superpowers, but *hyper*powers. Many have written about empires, ancient and modern, despotic and beneficent.[4] Explaining the rise and fall of empires has been a particularly venerable pastime, dating back to the Greeks. Thucydides hinted that democracy was to blame for the fall of Athens.[5] Edward Gibbon singled out Christianity as a primary cause of Rome's decline.[6] In recent times, Paul Kennedy attributed the fall of great powers more sweepingly to "imperial overstretch," while Jared Diamond in *Collapse* identified "environmental damage" as a chief culprit.[7] After 9/11 and the invasions of Afghanistan and Iraq, writing about empires and imperialism, whether hopefully or condemningly, has practically become an industry.[8]

To date, however, no one has systematically analyzed the far rarer phenomenon of hyperpowers, the remarkably few societies—barely more than a handful in history—that amassed such extraordinary military and economic might that they essentially dominated the world. This is a special category, acutely relevant to the present day, the hidden dynamics of which have yet to be laid bare. How does a society come to be not merely a great power but a *world-dominant power*? And once a society has achieved such dominance, what can bring it down? In the rise and fall of hyperpowers past, there are crucial lessons to be learned, reflecting both the similarities and the differences between the United States and its predecessors, with far-reaching implications for the twenty-first century.

The thesis of this book is as follows. For all their enormous differences, every single world hyperpower in history—every society that could even arguably be described as having achieved global hegemony—was, at least by the standards of its time, extraordinarily pluralistic and tolerant during its rise to preeminence. Indeed, in every case tolerance was indispensable to the achievement of hegemony. Just as strikingly, the decline of empire has repeatedly coincided with intolerance, xenophobia, and calls for racial, religious, or ethnic "purity." But here's the catch: It was also tolerance that sowed the seeds of decline. In virtually every case, tolerance eventually hit a tipping point, triggering conflict, hatred, and violence.

Let me begin by clarifying what I mean by a "world-dominant power." Defining this term is tricky, especially given that the world was so much larger two thousand, or even five hundred, years ago, before ships, planes, and technology drastically shrank it. Rome in its heyday, for example, was clearly a world-dominant power—if it wasn't, then no one was—even though halfway across the globe there existed another great empire, Han dynasty China, with which Rome had virtually no contact. If the point is that Rome was dominant in *its* world—the world it knew and inhabited—then weren't the Aztecs dominant in their world, the Egyptians in theirs, and so on? Isn't Tahiti a hyperpower in its own little world?

Any definition that includes Tahiti as a global hegemon is clearly too broad. But what is the right definition? What exactly differentiates Rome from, say, the Aztecs, who at one time dominated Central America but who could never have been considered a world-dominant power? Several factors are obvious: the sheer size of the Roman Empire (2 million square miles, as compared to estimates of between 11,000 and 77,000 square miles for the Aztecs); the immense population ruled by Rome (roughly 60 million, as compared to estimates of between 1 and 6 million for the Aztecs)[9]; the fact that no power on earth (including Han China) was economically or militarily superior to Rome during the High Empire; and the fact that Rome competed with and overpowered societies on the then cutting edge of world technological development. In short, the critical difference is that Rome did not merely achieve dominance in *its* world; it achieved dominance in *the* world.

Accordingly, for the purposes of this book, I will consider a nation or empire a world-dominant power only if it satisfies all three of the following conditions: Its power clearly surpasses that of all its known contemporaneous rivals; it is not clearly inferior in economic or military strength to any other power on the planet, known to it or not; and it projects its power over so immense an area of the globe and over so immense a population that it breaks the bounds of mere local or even regional preeminence. Under this definition, Louis XIV's France was not a world-dominant power; neither was the Hapsburg Empire, or the United States during the Cold War. Each of these great powers failed condition one: They each had formidable rivals of roughly comparable might.

Much of this book will be devoted to discussing the societies that *do* qualify as hyperpowers and to showing how in every case tolerance was critical to their rise to world dominance. But let me first say something about why tolerance has been so vital. This claim might initially seem surprising, but in fact there is a very simple, intuitive explanation.

To be world dominant—not just locally or regionally dominant—a society must be at the forefront of the *world*'s technological, military, and economic development. And at any given historical moment, the most valuable human capital the world has to offer—whether in the form of intelligence, physical strength, skill, knowledge, creativity, networks, commercial innovation, or technological invention—is never to be found in any one locale or within any one ethnic or religious group. To pull away from its rivals on a global scale, a society must pull into itself and motivate the world's best and brightest, regardless of ethnicity, religion, or background. This is what every hyperpower in history has done, from Achaemenid Persia to the Great Mongol Empire to the British Empire, and the way they have done it is through tolerance.

But wait—the *Mongols* were tolerant? Genghis Khan's ravaging hordes razed entire villages, then used the corpses as moat-fill. Persia's King Darius sliced off the ears and noses of his enemies before impaling them. (One of Darius's predecessors, King Cambyses, skinned a corrupt official, turning him into chair upholstery.) The British Empire, according to the entire field of postcolonial studies, was built on the racism and condescension of the White Man's Burden. Can these empires possibly be described as tolerant?

I'm going to suggest that the answer, surprisingly, is yes. But that's because I'm not talking about tolerance in the modern, human-rights sense.[10] By tolerance, I don't mean political or cultural equality. Rather, as I will use the term, tolerance simply means letting very different kinds of people live, work, and prosper in your society—even if only for instrumental or strategic reasons. To define the term a little more formally, tolerance in this book will refer to the degree of freedom with which individuals or groups of different ethnic, religious, racial, linguistic, or other backgrounds are permitted to coexist, participate, and rise in society.

Tolerance in this sense does not imply respect. The Romans, while recruiting warriors from all backgrounds to build their massive military, also saw themselves as favored by the gods and constantly expressed contempt for the "completely savage" Celts, the "the unclad Caledonii" who "lived for days on end in marshy bogs," and the "vast and beastly" northern Europeans with their "huge limbs."[11] Tolerance, moreover, can be selectively deployed. Groups perceived as useful may be tolerated even while others are excluded or violently oppressed. By the late eighteenth century, the English were learning to accept Protestant Scots as fellow Britons—particularly since the Scots were seen as assets for empire building—but this new British tolerance hardly extended to Irish Catholics.[12]

Finally, the key concept is *relative* tolerance. In the race for world dominance, what matters most is not whether a society is tolerant according to some absolute, timeless standard, but whether it is more tolerant than its competitors. Because tolerance is a relative matter, even the tolerated groups may be subject to harshly inequitable treatment. Russian Jews in the late nineteenth century found America a haven compared to the pogroms they were fleeing, but were still subjected to anti-Semitism and anti-Jewish quotas in the United States.

I am not arguing that tolerance is a sufficient condition for world dominance. No matter how tolerant, the Kingdom of Bhutan is unlikely ever to become a global hegemon. It is always a confluence of additional factors—geography, population, natural resources, and leadership, to name just a few—that leads to the rare emergence of a world-dominant power. Pure luck plays a part, too. Even in the most propitious circumstances, a society's ability to achieve and maintain global dominance will also depend, for example, on the state of the competition.

Rather, I am arguing that tolerance is a *necessary* condition for world dominance. Conversely, I am also arguing that intolerance is starkly associated with the decline of hyperpowers. Here, however, separating cause from effect is more problematic. It is often difficult to say whether intolerance leads to decline, or whether intolerance is a by-product of decline. In most cases, both propositions are probably true.

Finally, my thesis is not that more tolerance always leads to more prosperity, nor that tolerance is necessary for prosperity. Plenty of intolerant societies have become rich and powerful; Nazi

Germany is a case in point. But throughout history, no society based on racial purity, religious zealotry, or ethnic cleansing has ever become a world-dominant power. To attain and maintain dominance on a global scale, coercion is simply too inefficient, persecution too costly, and ethnic or religious homogeneity, like inbreeding, too unproductive.

———————

The United States is perhaps the quintessential example of a society that rose to global dominance through tolerance. Of course, for much of its history the United States was no more an exemplar of human rights than were the Romans or the Mongols. Americans kept slaves; they brutally displaced and occasionally massacred indigenous peoples. Nevertheless, from the beginning, through a genuinely revolutionary commitment to religious freedom as well as a market system unusually open to individuals of all classes and diverse nationalities, the United States attracted, rewarded, and harnessed the energies and ingenuities of tens of millions of immigrants.

This immigrant manpower and talent propelled the country's growth and success from westward expansion to industrial explosion to victory in World War II. Indeed, America's winning the race for the atomic bomb—an event of unfathomable historical importance—was a direct result of its ability to attract immigrant scientists fleeing persecution in Europe. In the decades after the war, with *Brown v. Board of Education* and the civil rights movement, the United States at last began, however fitfully and imperfectly, to develop into one of the most ethnically and racially open societies in world history. Not coincidentally, this was also the period in which the United States achieved world dominance.

America's emergence as a hyperpower in the last decade of the twentieth century was in part the consequence of the Soviet Union's collapse. But it also reflected the United States' staggering technological and economic dominance in the burgeoning Computer Age, and this dominance once again stemmed directly from America's superior ability to pull in talented and enterprising individuals from all over the world. Silicon Valley, which catalyzed the greatest explosion of wealth in the history of man, was to an astonishing extent an immigrant creation.

But while America is like every past hyperpower in the fundamental respect that it owes its world dominance to tolerance, it also differs radically from its predecessors. America is the first mature, universal-suffrage democracy to become a hyperpower. It is the first hyperpower to inhabit a world where human rights and the right of all nations to self-determination are almost universally recognized. Finally, America is the first hyperpower to confront the threat of global terrorist networks potentially wielding weapons of mass destruction.

This unprecedented constellation of factors leaves many Americans today profoundly uncertain about the proper role of the United States in the world. How should America use its military might? How can the threat of terrorism be met? Should America try to remain a hyperpower, or would a return to a multipolar global order be better for the world and even for the United States itself?

No such uncertainty was in the air in the first years after the fall of the Berlin Wall—a period of almost euphoric global optimism. Communism had been defeated, authoritarianism discredited. Francis Fukuyama announced the "end of history." There seemed to be a consensus, not just in Washington but to a considerable extent all around the world, that the spread of markets and democracy would "turn all friends and enemies into 'competitors,' " permitting "more people everywhere to turn their aspirations into achievements," erasing "not just geographical borders but human ones."[15] Free market democracy was the only game in town, and the United States was the natural leader of an increasingly globalizing, marketizing, democratizing world.

In retrospect, perhaps the most striking feature of this period was the widespread assumption that the United States would *not* get into the business of warmaking or military coercion. Here was a country with unrivaled military might and the most devastating arsenal of weapons known to man. Yet in the 1990s many both inside and outside the United States simply assumed that the world's new hyperpower would not use its military aggressively for expansionist, empire-building purposes. Instead, when it came to U.S. military power, the most debated questions were whether the use of force for purely humanitarian purposes was permissible (as in Bosnia or Rwanda), and what America should do with its "peace dividend"—the billions of dollars it would no longer have to spend on defense. America was, it seemed, the world's first hyperpower that was *not* an empire, the first hyperpower with no militaristic imperial designs.

But September 11, 2001, changed everything. Within a month, the hyperpower was at war. A year later, the United States issued a new National Security Strategy, emphasizing "the essential role of American military strength," asserting the right to "act preemptively," and declaring a commitment to maintaining American unipolar military superiority. Suddenly, talk of an American empire was everywhere. Articles appeared—not only in such publications as the *Wall Street Journal* and *Weekly Standard*, but also in the *New York Times* and *Christian Science Monitor*—openly championing American imperialism. "Afghanistan and other troubled lands today cry out," wrote Max Boot in his much-quoted "The Case for American Empire," "for the sort of enlightened foreign administration once provided by self-confident Englishmen in jodhpurs and pith helmets." The "answer to terrorism," asserted historian Paul Johnson, is "colonialism." Early in 2003, Harvard human rights scholar Michael Ignatieff asked, "[W]hat word but 'empire' describes the awesome thing America is becoming?" and argued that American imperialism was "in a place like Iraq, the last hope for democracy and stability alike." Around the same time, Niall Ferguson called on Americans to shed their fear of "the 'e' word" and to take up Great Britain's former imperial mantle.[14]

What exactly did these proponents of an American empire have in mind? Obviously, no one was calling for President George W. Bush to be named Emperor of the Middle East as Queen Victoria was once named Empress of India. Rather, for most of its advocates, the idea of an American empire refers to the aggressive, interventionist use of U.S. military force, with or without international approval, to effect regime change and nation building—to replace dictatorships, rogue states, and other threatening regimes with pro-market, pro-democratic, pro-American governments. As one commentator put it, America's "twenty-first-century imperium" is one "whose grace notes are free markets, human rights, and democracy, enforced by the most awesome military power the world has ever known."[15]

So understood, the calls for an American empire after 9/11 were not unreasonable. After all, following World War II, the United States army had taken advantage of a moment of unparalleled military might to occupy and reconstruct Germany and Japan. If America had succeeded then, how could it *not*, in the face of the incalculable threat of terrorism, do the same for the post–9/11 world? How could it not pick up the reins of Rome or Britain and undertake to civilize, modernize, and pacify the world?

After 9/11 this position was supported by a wide range of voices in the United States, including many who never embraced the term *empire* and who would probably describe themselves as intensely anti-imperialist. *New York Times* columnist Thomas Friedman may be the most notable example. While presciently skeptical of the Bush Administration's claims of weapons of mass destruction and deeply suspicious of the role of U.S. oil interests, Friedman nevertheless defended the war in Iraq in order to "oust Saddam Hussein" and "to partner with the Iraqi people" in building a much-needed stable, democratic society with "freedom, women's empowerment, and modern education." Similarly, Michael Ignatieff, "arguably the most prominent liberal supporter of the U.S. invasion of Iraq," wrote that "[i]t remains a fact—as disagreeable to those left wingers who regard American imperialism as the root of all evil as it is to the right-wing isolationists"—"that there are many peoples who owe their freedom to an exercise of American military power."[16]

But what all these writers overlooked—whether they used the term *empire* or preferred to call it *democratization* and *nation building*—was history. In a new form, America today faces a problem as old as empire itself, a problem so fundamental that it brought down most of history's past world-dominant powers. For lack of a better term, I will refer to this as the problem of "glue."

———————

This problem is the subject of Samuel Huntington's controversial book *Who Are We? The Challenges to America's National Identity*. With an anti–politically correct vengeance, Samuel Huntington argues that continued immigration—particularly from Spanish-speaking regions like Mexico—threatens to destroy America's core "Anglo-Protestant" values of "individualism," "the work ethic," and "rule of law." Unless America reasserts its identity, Huntington warns, it may "evolve into a loose confederation of ethnic, racial, cultural, and political groups, with little or nothing in common apart from their location in the territory of what had been the United States of America."[17]

Huntington has been much maligned. The truth is that he almost goes out of his way to be inflammatory and insulting—suggesting, for example, that Mexican Americans are multiplying like rabbits and that they may try to take back California, Utah, and Texas. Nevertheless, I think Huntington is correct to worry about whether American society has sufficient "glue" to hold together its many different subcommunities. Many of history's past hyperpowers, including Achaemenid Persia and the Great Mongol Empire, fell because they lacked an overarching political identity capable of holding their ethnically and religiously diverse subjects together.

But Huntington makes two critical mistakes. First, as I will show, hyperpowers have fallen prey to fragmentation and disintegration precisely when their core group turns intolerant, reasserting their "true" identity, adopting nativist or chauvinist policies, and attempting to expel or exclude "aliens" and "unassimilable" groups. From this point of view, the surest path to the destruction of America's social fabric lies in efforts to tie American identity to a single, original ethnic or religious group. Perversely, this is just what Huntington is doing when he identifies America's true identity with WASP culture and WASP civic values, notwithstanding his insistence that people of any race or background (except apparently Latinos) can adopt these WASP virtues.

Even more fundamentally, Huntington fails to see that America's real problem of glue lies abroad, rather than at home. Inside its borders, the United States has been uniquely successful in creating an ethnically and religiously neutral political identity strong and capacious enough to bind together as Americans individuals of all ethnicities, religions, and backgrounds. But here's the problem: America does not exert power over only Americans. Through its unrivaled military might (including military bases in more than sixty countries, widely seen as "intrusions on national sovereignty"), its extraordinary economic leverage, and its omnipresent multinationals, consumer brands, and culture, America's dominance is felt in every corner of the world. And outside its borders, there is little if any glue binding the United States to the billions of people around the world it dominates.

History shows that hyperpowers can survive only if they find ways to command the allegiance or at least the acquiescence of the foreign populations they dominate, and for this, military force alone has never been sufficient. Imperial Rome offers perhaps the best example of a world-dominant power that succeeded in winning over key sectors of conquered populations, pulling them into Rome's orbit more effectively than mere force of arms could have done. Unique among the empires of antiquity, Rome offered a political affiliation and cultural package that was enormously appealing to far-flung, vastly different peoples. Similarly, the United States today offers a cultural package—supermodels and Starbucks, Disney and double cheeseburgers, Coca-Cola and SUVs— that holds infuriating allure for millions, if not billions, around the world.

But ancient Rome had an advantage: It could make the people it conquered and dominated part of the Roman Empire. Defeated peoples from Britain to Eastern Europe to West Africa all became subjects—and in the case of male elites, citizens—of the greatest power on earth. During the Italian Renaissance, Niccolò Machiavelli admiringly observed that Rome had "ruined her neighbors" and created a world empire by "freely admitting strangers to her privileges and honours."[18]

The United States is not Rome. The first mature democracy to become a world-dominant power, the United States does not try or want to make foreign populations its subjects—and certainly not its citizens. When the U.S. government speaks of bringing democracy to the Middle East, it is not contemplating Iraqis or Syrians voting in the next U.S. presidential election. The ironic result of the United States' dual role as global hyperpower and self-proclaimed beacon of freedom and democracy is rampant anti-Americanism. Today, the United States faces billions of people around the world, most of them poor, who want to be like Americans but don't want to be under America's thumb; who want to dress and live like Americans but are denied visas by the U.S. embassy; who are told over and over that America stands for freedom but see only the American pursuit of self-interest.

Those calling for an American empire constantly invoke the glory and enduring success of the Pax Romana. But as I hope to show, in its relationship to the world it dominates, modern America is perversely far more like the "barbaric" Mongol Empire than it is like Rome.

———

Social scientists have a concept called selection bias, which basically means "proving" one's thesis by picking out cases that support it and ignoring the ones that don't. I tried to avoid selection bias by casting the widest possible net and considering every society in history that could even arguably have qualified as a world-dominant power.

As a result, some of my examples of world-dominant powers—the Dutch Republic, for example—were not as clearly world-dominant as others, or arguably were not world-dominant at all. To reiterate, however, in my selection of world-dominant powers, I have consciously tried to be overinclusive rather than underinclusive, and it actually supports my thesis that the empires that came closest to world dominance also track the pattern I describe: tolerance on the rise to power and intolerance in decline.

The rest of this book is organized as follows. Part One addresses the premodern hyperpowers. Chapter One begins with Achaemenid Persia and ends with Alexander the Great. Chapter Two is about Imperial Rome. Chapter Three discusses China's Tang Empire, which in its heyday was by far the greatest power in the world and, unlike the better-known Ming dynasty, had openly hegemonic ambitions. Chapter Four examines the Great Mongol Empire.

Between antiquity and the modern era came the rise of the great religious empires: those of Christendom and Islam. Unlike the syncretic religions of antiquity, which assumed that different peoples would worship different gods, both Christianity and Islam insisted that there was one—and only one—true faith. In this sense, Christianity and Islam were inherently intolerant in a way that ancient religions were not. Whether or not sanctioned by scripture, the result was a millennium of religious strife, bloodshed, and war.

Part Two is about the enlightening of tolerance. In the West, the era of religious wars slowly gave way to the Enlightenment. For the Enlightenment thinkers, tolerance was not merely instrumental; it was a moral virtue, even a duty. Persecution was not only bad strategy; it violated the freedom of conscience. Thus was born the modern ideal of tolerance: no longer merely the prerogative of calculating monarchs, but a fundamental element of the "rights of man." The Enlightenment ended up both underwriting and undermining a new age of empires. On one hand, the new toleration would make possible the first hyperpowers Europe had seen in over a thousand years; on the other hand, with its principles of universal equality, fundamental rights, and individual liberty, the Enlightenment would make all future empires profoundly problematic.

Chapter Five takes a short look at medieval Spain as a representative pre-Enlightenment European power. Spain was remarkable for its religious diversity, including in its population significant numbers of Muslims and Jews. Yet Spain could not resist the zealotry of the time; religious pogroms, expulsions, and inquisitorial persecution wracked Spanish society, undercutting its prosperity and making Spain a vivid illustration of how Christian intolerance prohibited the great European powers of the medieval era from attaining global dominance.

Chapter Six is about the unlikely rise of the tiny Dutch Republic, the first European state to embrace the new tolerance. In 1579, while the rest of Europe was still engulfed in fanaticism, the Dutch Republic enshrined the principle of religious freedom in its founding charter. Almost overnight, it became a magnet for religious refugees, not just from Spain but from all over Europe. As a direct result, it became far and away the richest nation on earth, with by far the most upward mobility, enjoying "productive, commercial, and financial superiority" and the "rare condition" of global "hegemony."[19]

Chapter Seven turns away from the West, for a comparative glimpse at three empires that never achieved world dominance: China's Ming empire, as well as two great Islamic empires, the Ottomans and the Mughals. Returning to the West, Chapter Eight discusses Great Britain, which succeeded the Dutch Republic as Europe's most tolerant society and came to rule "a vaster Empire than has ever been"[20]—an empire that, if one includes the oceans dominated by the British navy, covered an astonishing 70 percent of the earth's surface. But as they encountered Africans, Asians, and other nonwhites, the British hit the limit of their tolerance. However "enlightened" the British imagined themselves to be, they never overcame their colonial racism, which proved to be a profoundly destructive force throughout the empire.

Part Three takes us from the fall of the British Empire to the modern day. Chapter Nine discusses the role of tolerance in the transformation of the United States from upstart colony to global hyperpower. Chapter Ten discusses two great powers built on principles of intolerance and ethnic purity: Nazi Germany and imperial Japan. Chapter Eleven analyzes the United States' main rivals today.

Chapter Twelve applies the lessons of the past to the twenty-first century, specifically addressing the debate about an American empire. For two and a half millennia, every hyperpower in history has faced the same two formidable challenges: maintaining the tolerance that fueled its rise and forging common bonds capable of securing the loyalty or at least quiescence of the peoples it dominates. Over the last several years, America's efforts to assert its world-dominant power abroad have exacerbated both these challenges. Ironically, it may be that America can remain a hyperpower only if it stops trying to be one.

PART ONE

THE TOLERANCE
OF BARBARIANS

THE FIRST HEGEMON

The Great Persian Empire from Cyrus
to Alexander

When Cyrus entered Babylon in 539 B.C., the world was old.
More significant, the world knew its antiquity. Its scholars had
compiled long dynastic lists, and simple addition appeared to
prove that kings whose monuments were still visible had ruled
more than four millenniums before.
— A. T. OLMSTEAD, *History of the Persian Empire*, 1948

I should be glad, Onesicritus, to come back to life for a little
while after my death to discover how men read these present
events then.
— ALEXANDER THE GREAT, QUOTED BY LUCIEN IN
How to Write History, CIRCA AD 40

The word *paradise* is Persian in origin. Old Persian had a
term *pairidaeza*, which the Greeks rendered as *paradeisos*,
referring to the fabulous royal parks and pleasure gardens
of the Achaemenids—the kings of the mighty Persian Empire who
ruled from roughly 559 to 330 BC. Indeed, the earliest Greek
translators of the Old Testament used this term for the Garden of

Eden and the afterlife, as if to suggest that the Achaemenid paradises were as close as man had come to replicating heaven on earth.[1]

The Achaemenid paradises were famous throughout the ancient world. Their riches, it was said, included every tree bearing every fruit known to man, the most fragrant and dazzling flowers that grew anywhere from Libya to India, and exotic animals from the farthest reaches of an empire covering more than two million square miles. There were Parthian camels, Assyrian rams, Armenian horses, Cappadocian mules, Nubian giraffes, Indian elephants, Lydian ibex, Babylonian buffalo, and the most ferocious lions, bulls, and wild beasts from throughout the kingdom. Not just formal gardens, the paradises were also centers for horticultural experimentation, zoological parks, and hunting reserves. A royal hunt in a single paradise could yield four thousand head.[2]

In this respect, the Achaemenid paradises were a living metaphor for the Achaemenid Empire as a whole. Founded around 559 BC by Cyrus the Great and spanning more than two centuries, the Achaemenid Persian Empire was, even by today's standards, one of the most culturally diverse and religiously open empires in history. The Achaemenid kings actively recruited the most talented artisans, craftsmen, laborers, and warriors from throughout the empire. In 500 BC, Persepolis was home to Greek doctors, Elamite scribes, Lydian woodworkers, Ionian stonecutters, and Sardian smiths. Similarly, the Achaemenid military drew its colossal strength from Median commanders, Phoenician sailors, Libyan charioteers, Cissian cavalrymen, and hundreds of thousands of foot soldiers from Ethiopia, Bactria, Sogdiana, and elsewhere in the empire.[3]

For most Westerners, antiquity refers solely to classical Greece and Rome. But the Achaemenid Empire was the first hyperpower in world history, governing a territory larger than all the ancient empires, including even Rome's. Achaemenid Persia dwarfed—in fact conquered and annexed—the great kingdoms of Assyria, Babylonia, and Egypt, ruling at its peak as many as 42 million people, nearly a third of the world's total population.[4] How could a relatively small number of Persians govern so vast a territory and population? This chapter will suggest that tolerance was critical: first in allowing the Persians to establish their world-dominant empire, then in helping them maintain it.

WHERE IS BACTRIA, AND SHOULD WE BELIEVE HERODOTUS?

As early as 5000 BC, the great plateau that is now modern Iran was already populated. Its early inhabitants had some curious family practices:

> [A]mong the Derbices, men older than seventy were killed and eaten by their kinsfolk, and old women were strangled and buried. . . . Among the Caspians, who gave their name to the sea formerly called Hyrcanian, those over seventy were starved. Corpses were exposed in a desert place and observed. If carried from the bier by vultures, the dead were considered most fortunate, less so if taken by wild beasts or dogs; but it was the height of misfortune if the bodies remained untouched. . . . [F]arther east, equally disgusting practices continued until Alexander's invasion. The sick and aged were thrown while still alive to waiting dogs.[5]

Starting in the second millennium BC, these friendly peoples succumbed to the Aryan conquest. The term "Aryan," despite the Nazis' later twisting, is essentially a linguistic designation referring to a variety of peoples who spoke eastern Indo-European languages or dialects and migrated from southern Russia and central Asia into India, Mesopotamia, and the Iranian plateau. How the Aryans overpowered the preexisting societies is unclear, but within a few hundred years they had established kingdoms in eponymous territories throughout the region: for example, the Medes in Media, the Bactrians in Bactria, and the Persians in Persis or Parsa.[6]

The Persians themselves consisted of a number of tribes and clans, of which the Achaemenids were one. In time, the Achaemenids would extend Persian rule to the other Aryan kingdoms. Indeed the name *Iran* derives from the Persian word *Ērānšahr*, meaning "Empire of the Aryans." The Achaemenid Empire was, however, far larger than modern-day Iran. Its provinces or satrapies, with their archaic names, correspond to some modern headline-making regions in the Middle East and central Asia. Babylon, for example, which the Achaemenids conquered in 539 BC, stood in what is now Iraq, approximately sixty miles from Baghdad. Sogdiana was located in modern Uzbekistan. And Bactria, so significant in the Achaemenid Empire, maps roughly onto present-day Afghanistan.[7]

A note about sources: The Achaemenid rulers left virtually no written histories of their own empire. The ancient Persians transmitted the triumphs and deeds of their kings primarily through oral traditions. The few written records we have from the Achaemenid kings consist principally of royal inscriptions—for example, Cyrus's cylinder or Darius's trilingual engravings on the cliffs of Behistun. Unfortunately, these inscriptions are not narrative accounts of actual events. Rather, they are abstract exaltations of royal power and virtue and more than a little propagandistic. Cyrus's cylinder, for example, proclaims, "I am Cyrus, king of the universe, great king, mighty king, king of Babylon, king of Sumer and Akkad, king of the world quarters."[8]

As a result, most of what we know about the Achaemenid Empire comes from a very limited number of Greek sources, including Xenophon's *Anabasis*, Aeschylus's *Persians*, and, most important, Herodotus's *Histories*. Most of these classical authors lived in the latter half of the Achaemenid period and presumably based their accounts in part on oral testimonies and Persian legends passed on over the years; here again, it may be difficult to separate historical fact from political propaganda.

Additionally, depending on the era, the Greeks were the enemies, subjects, or conquerors of the Persians. Thus, Greek authors were not necessarily the most impartial expositors of Persian history—imagine Saddam Hussein writing *A History of the United States, 1990–2006*. As a result, Greek references to Persians as "barbarians of Asia," or the frequent Greek portrayals of the Achaemenid kings as decadent and gluttonous, should be taken with a grain of salt. An exceptional case may be Herodotus, who wrote about the Persians with such little hostility, relative to that of his contemporaries, that Plutarch accused him of being a "friend of the barbarians" (*philobarbaros*).[9]

In general, there are enough corroborating sources from different perspectives, often supported by archaeological evidence, to feel comfortable with most of the basic facts about the Achaemenid Empire. Where there are doubts, discrepancies, or differing interpretations among historians, I will point them out.

TOLERANCE AND THE RISE OF THE ACHAEMENID EMPIRE

The story of the Achaemenid Empire begins with Cyrus the Great. Cyrus's origins are shrouded in legend. According to the version favored by Herodotus, Cyrus was the grandson of Astyages, the weak final ruler of the powerful kingdom of Media. When Cyrus was born—to Astyages's daughter and her husband, Cambyses, a Persian from the Achaemenid clan—Astyages ordered his newborn grandson killed, after an ominous dream suggesting that Cyrus would one day depose him.

The plan failed, as these types of plans always do. Harpagos, whom Astyages had ordered to kill Cyrus, gave the baby instead to a shepherd, who raised Cyrus as his own. Astyages eventually discovered that Harpagos had deceived him and that Cyrus was alive, but his magi advisors reinterpreted his dream so that Astyages feared Cyrus no longer. Cyrus was sent to Persia, where he rejoined his Achaemenid family. Harpagos, however, did not fare as well: Astyages invited him to a banquet, where he served him the flesh of his own son mixed with lamb.[10]

A different version of the Cyrus legend has him abandoned by the shepherd but saved and suckled in the wild by a female dog. Yet another says that his mother was a goatherd and his father a Persian bandit. However he got there, Cyrus had by 559 BC become a vassal king under Astyages in Persia. A few years later, Cyrus led a rebellion against Astyages. Assisting him were a number of Persian tribes and clans, most prominently the Achaemenids, as well as the same Harpagos who had been served the unappetizing dinner.

In 550 BC, Cyrus defeated Astyages and took over the Median kingdom and its claims to Assyria, Mesopotamia, Syria, Armenia, and Cappadocia. By 539, Cyrus had conquered both the Lydian kingdom (located in modern-day Turkey) and the formidable neo-Babylonian kingdom. He was now ruler of the largest empire that had ever existed.[11]

The strategy Cyrus employed was essentially "decapitation"—but of leadership, not of the leader's head. After conquering each new kingdom, Cyrus simply removed the local ruler, typically sparing his life and allowing him to live in luxury, and replaced him with a satrap who governed the territory, or satrapy. The satrap was almost always a member of the Persian aristocracy. Beneath the satrap, however, Cyrus interfered very little with the daily lives of his subject peoples, leaving them their gods and their disparate cultures. He embraced linguistic diversity, including as languages used for official administrative purposes in the empire Aramaic, Elamite, Babylonian, Egyptian, Greek, Lydian, and Lycian. He codified and enforced local laws, keeping in place local authority structures. It was not unusual for high-ranking officials in conquered territories to retain their official positions under Achaemenid rule. Babylonian records also show that the same families often dominated business before and after Cyrus's conquest.[12]

Perhaps most striking was Cyrus's religious tolerance—his legendary willingness to honor the temples, cults, and local gods of the peoples he conquered. In a sense, it was easier in the ancient world for rulers to allow the worship of multiple deities. Unlike Judaism or Christianity, the religions of the ancient Near East were syncretic. They assumed the existence of many gods, each guarding its own city, people, or aspects of life. But this syncretic worldview did not necessarily imply that one people had to respect or tolerate the religious beliefs of others. On the contrary, many con-

quering kings of antiquity liked to demonstrate the superiority of
their own gods—and assert their own power—precisely by sup-
pressing and destroying rival cults.

For example, not long before the fall of the Assyrian Empire,
the Assyrian king Ashurbanipal conquered the country of Elam.
He ravaged the entire kingdom, leveling major cities, desecrating
temples, and dragging off sacred cult objects. He also ordered his
troops to destroy the royal tombs of the Elamite kings because
they, in Ashurbanipal's own words, "had not revered the deities
Ashur and Ishtar," his "lords." Assyrian kings similarly razed the
cities of Jerusalem and Thebes and left many other districts a
wilderness stripped of human and animal population.[13]

Nabunidus, the king of Babylonia when it fell to Cyrus, is also
famous for his religious intolerance. He suppressed popular worship of the god Marduk, forcing adherence instead to the deity of
his own cult, the moon-god Sin. If we can believe the inscriptions
on the Cyrus cylinder, now in the British Museum, Nabunidus
"did evil" to his subjects, tormenting them by imposing "a cult
that was not proper to them." By contrast, Cyrus took just the opposite approach.

Entering the city of Babylon with his army, Cyrus prostrated
himself before the god Marduk in order to win over the local people. He presented himself as the liberator of the Babylonians, di-
vinely chosen and assisted by their own great deity. In his own
words from the Cyrus cylinder:

> When I made my gracious entry into Babylon, with rejoicing
> and pleasure I took up my lordly residence in the royal palace.
> Marduk, the great lord, turned the noble race of the Babylo-
> nians toward me, and I gave daily care to his worship.
>
> I did not allow anybody to terrorize [any place] of the
> [country of Sumer] and Akkad. I strove for peace in Babylon
> and in all his [other] sacred cities. As to the inhabitants of
> Babylon . . . I abolished forced labour. . . . From Nineveh, As-
> sur and Susa, Akkad, Eshnunna, Zamban, Me-Turnu and Der
> until the region of Gutium, I returned to these sacred cities on

the other side of the Tigris, the sanctuaries of which have been ruins for a long time.[14]

Although this account is in part self-glorifying propaganda, it is nonetheless instructive of how Cyrus wished to be perceived by his subjects.

Classical sources consistently attest to Cyrus's tolerance and magnanimity. In his romanticized *Cyropaedia*, for example, Xenophon writes:

> Believing this man [Cyrus] to be deserving of all admiration, we have therefore investigated who he was in his origin, what natural endowments he possessed, and what sort of education he had enjoyed, that he so greatly excelled in governing. . . . That Cyrus's empire was the greatest and most glorious of all the kingdoms in Asia—of that it may bear its own witness. . . . And although it was of such magnitude, it was governed by the single will of Cyrus; and he honoured his subjects and cared for them as if they were his own children; and they, on their part, revered Cyrus as a father.[15]

As a side note, Xenophon also writes admiringly of Cyrus's skill in cultivating his public image. At a parade in Persepolis, Cyrus "appeared so great and so goodly to look upon," evidently in part because he chose to wear the physique-flattering Median native costume:

> [Cyrus] thought that if anyone had any personal defect [the Median] dress would help to conceal it, and that it made the wearer look very tall and very handsome. For they have shoes of such a form that without being detected the wearer can easily put something into the soles so as to make him look taller than he is. He encouraged also the fashion of pencilling the eyes, that they might seem more lustrous than they are, and of using cosmetics to make the complexion look better than their nature made it. He trained his associates also not to spit or wipe the nose in public.[16]

The biblical accounts of Cyrus are even more exalting. After conquering Babylon, Cyrus freed the Jews from their Babylonian captivity and allowed them to return to Jerusalem. For this benevolence, Jewish prophets hailed him as a savior. The book of Isaiah describes Cyrus as "anointed" by Yahweh, the Jewish name for God:

> Thus says Yahweh to his anointed, to Cyrus, whom he has taken by his right hand to subdue nations before him and strip the loins of kings, to force gateways before him that their gates be closed no more: I will go before you levelling the heights. I will shatter the bronze gateways, smash the iron bars. I will give you the hidden treasures, the secret hoards, that you may know that I am Yahweh.

According to the book of Ezra, Cyrus not only freed the Jews but he restored to Jerusalem "the vessels of gold and silver" that Nebuchadnezzar had taken to Babylon. Cyrus also rebuilt the Jewish Temple in Jerusalem, apparently at his own expense.[17]

There is no question: Cyrus the Great has had good press. From the classical Greek accounts to the Cyrus cylinder to the Old Testament, the first Achaemenid king comes off as so tolerant that some modern fans have called him the founder of "human rights." This portrayal is both anachronistic and misleading. Cyrus's conquests were almost certainly bloodier and harder fought than some of the ancient sources suggest; it is implausible that the Persians were welcomed with open arms from Media to Babylonia.[18]

More fundamentally, most modern historians agree that Cyrus's tolerance was a matter of strategy and expediency, not a matter of principle. Embracing local deities—whether Marduk for the Babylonians or Yahweh for the Jews—gave Cyrus legitimacy. Respecting local traditions and practices decreased the likelihood of resistance and rebellion among conquered peoples. The modern concept of freedom of religion as a "human right" was foreign to Cyrus and his successors. For the Achaemenids, tolerance was simply good politics.[19]

THE MADMAN AND HIS CHAIR

Cyrus left the massive empire he established to his son Cambyses, who ruled for just eight years (roughly 530–522 BC). According to Greek sources, Cambyses did not share his father's even temperament. Indeed, Herodotus opined: "I have no doubt whatever that Cambyses was completely out of his mind." Herodotus recorded a particularly charming episode involving Cambyses's efforts to enforce the rule of law: "One judge, Sisamnes, had given an unjust judgment in return for a bribe; Cambyses slaughtered him like a sheep and flayed him. Then from the skin he caused leather strips to be tanned and with them covered the judgment seat of the son Otanes, who was appointed to the father's office with the grim admonition to remember on what he sat."[20]

If Cambyses was a madman, he was an effective one. He invaded Egypt soon after becoming king, and by 525 had captured Heliopolis, where he continued his father's policy of respecting local customs and religions.

In Egypt, Cambyses declared himself a "son of Ra" and "beloved of [the goddess] Wajet." At the urging of his Egyptian advisor Udjahorresnet, Cambyses went to the town of Sais and prostrated himself at the altar of Neith, an Egyptian goddess. He embraced the rites and rituals of Egyptian tradition, made offerings to the local gods, and helped restore their temples. In the famous Serapeum stele, excavated in Egypt in 1851, Cambyses is dressed in Egyptian royal garb, with uraeus—the sacred Egyptian rearing cobra—around his neck. As the historian Pierre Briant puts it, Cambyses permitted himself to be "Egyptianized" in Egypt. Rather than imposing Persian culture on his subjects, Cambyses presented himself as a devotee of the Egyptian deities and the legitimate successor to the Egyptian pharaohs.[21]

In addition to Egypt, Cambyses also subjugated Phoenicia, Libya, and many Greek cities in Asia Minor. With these conquests, the Achaemenid Empire not only had swallowed every major kingdom in the Near East and central Asia, but also, by incorporating the Phoenician and Egyptian fleets, had become the world's greatest naval power, controlling a vast maritime front from the Mediterranean to the Persian Gulf. Cambyses died in 522 BC, of gangrene or suicide, depending on the source. Later that year, a distant relative of his named Darius took the throne.[22]

DARIUS THE GREAT

The Achaemenid Empire reached its zenith under Darius the Great, who ruled for nearly forty years (roughly 522–486 BC). Darius expanded Persian dominion into India, strengthened its foothold in Greece, and even made forays into eastern Europe, marching past the Danube in a failed effort to conquer the Scythian peoples. (The Scythians were helmeted, expert horseback riders from the steppes of southern Russia, who, as part of their funerary rituals, toasted marijuana seeds on red-hot stones and inhaled the fumes.) At the outset of his reign, Darius also had to contend with a rash of opportunistic rebellions brought about by the questionable nature of his ascent to the throne. He suppressed all of them, some quite ruthlessly, "smother[ing] them in a sea of blood," in his own words.[23]

Darius was by all accounts an exceptional administrator. When not engaged in his many military campaigns, he occupied himself ensuring that the Achaemenid Empire would take its place in history as one of the most glorious and sophisticated the world had ever seen. He oversaw the construction of new regional capitals; Persepolis became one of the architectural wonders of the ancient world. He introduced a standard currency and extended the empire's fabulous network of roads and its communications system, which included royal mail service, express messengers, and fire signals.[24]

To finance his ambitious projects, Darius formalized the system of imperial taxation and tribute, requiring each satrapy to pay a fixed annual amount, usually in talents of gold or silver. Herodotus reports that both Bactria and India were assessed 360 talents a year. Egypt had to pay 700 talents and the "income from the fish of Lake Moeris." Babylonia was assessed 1,000 talents and

"500 young eunuchs." In addition, for reasons still debated, some peoples did not have to pay taxes but made their contributions in the form of "gifts." For example, Colchis (a kingdom in the Caucasus) sent a "gift" of "a hundred boys and a hundred girls," and the Ethiopians, "about two quarts of unrefined gold, two hundred logs of ebony, [five Ethiopian boys,] and twenty elephant tusks." According to Plutarch, Darius also mastered the art of the fictitious tax cut. After setting the amount of taxes for a particular satrapy, Darius would "consult" with local leaders, asking if the amounts were too heavy, then magnanimously announce that the taxes were to be cut in half.[25]

Throughout his reign, Darius continued the Achaemenid tradition of cultural and religious tolerance; indeed, he carried it further. Darius apparently took pride in the extraordinary diversity of his empire. He described himself with a title that has been translated as "king of the countries containing all races" or "king of the peoples of every origin." He respected his empire's multilingualism: His royal inscriptions were translated into several languages; satrapal orders were proclaimed in Greek, Babylonian, Lycian, or Demotic, and interpreters operated throughout the kingdom. Interestingly, Darius himself was almost certainly monolingual—and probably could not read.[26]

In some of his royal inscriptions, Darius refers to the divinity Ahura Mazda as the "greatest of gods" and "god of the Aryans." Historians continue to debate these passages: What was the religion of the Achaemenids? Did Darius and Cyrus favor the same gods? Were the Achaemenids Zoroastrians? But on one point there is consensus: Like Cyrus, Darius did not impose Persian gods on his subjects. On the contrary, Darius and the satraps under him exhibited great reverence for local cults and divinities. Darius also left local social structures largely intact. "The great majority of the elites of subject peoples, with the possible exception of Egypt, saw the Persian king not as a foreign ruler or tyrant, but as the guarantor of political stability, social order, economic prosperity, and hence ultimately of their own position."[27] Darius famously codified and enforced local laws. For example, the Persian king upheld and even guaranteed decisions of Egyptian judges. Similarly, Darius reportedly recognized and sanctioned the Torah as the law of Israel.[28]

From these policies of tolerance, Darius reaped tremendous benefits. Instead of wasting resources destroying conquered populations or trying to "Persianize" them, Darius harnessed their different skills, talents, and resources. In this way, Darius built some of the most splendid imperial capitals the world had ever seen.

For example, in constructing the grand royal residence at Susa, Darius employed the finest materials and best artisans from his empire, drawing on the labors of at least sixteen different peoples. In Susa's trilingual "foundation charter," Darius says:

> The palace of Susa, it is I who made it; its materials were brought from afar. . . . That which [was made] of molded bricks, people who [were] Babylonians made it themselves. And the beams which [were] cedar, them, from a mountain call[ed] Lebanon, from down there they were brought. . . . And the ivory which was worked here, it, from Ethiopia and India and Arachosia were brought. . . . The craftsmen who worked the stone, they, [were] Ionians and Sardians. And the goldchasers who worked this gold, they [were] Sardians and Egyptians. And the men who baked the brick, they [were] Babylonians. And the men who decorated the terrace, they [were] Medes and Egyptians.

As the historian Richard Frye puts it, this was likely "the most cosmopolitan crew of workers ever assembled up to that time."[29]

Recruiting the best from the empire's diverse peoples was the hallmark strategy of not only Darius but all the Achaemenid kings. The imperial court welcomed Egyptian doctors, Greek scientists, and Babylonian astronomers. According to Greek sources, the Achaemenid kings constantly tried to lure prominent Greek thinkers into their service with promises of great rewards. In 513 BC, when Darius needed a bridge built over the Bosporus to cross into Europe, he chose for the job a Samian architect (from the Greek island of Samos). Three decades later, the Achaemenid king

Xerxes ordered two bridges built across the Hellespont (today, the Dardanelles Straits). Xerxes employed specialists from several countries, including "Phoenicians, who spun cables of white linen; and Egyptians, who brought cables made of papyrus."[30]

Most crucially, it was only through tolerance that the Achaemenids were able to amass the greatest war machine yet known to man. Under Cyrus the Great, the Persian army initially consisted primarily of Persians and Medes. (The Medes and the Persians were apparently closely related. Indeed, the ancient Greeks and Egyptians often used the terms "Persians" and "Medes" interchangeably.[31]) At the core of the army were the Ten Thousand Immortals, so named because their numbers never dropped below ten thousand, "a substitute being always ready when one fell sick or was killed." According to Herodotus, not only were the Immortals "gorgeously clad in gold-decked raiment, but on the march they were permitted to take with them their concubines and servants on wagons, while special food was brought on camels and other baggage animals." Nine thousand of the Immortals carried spears adorned with silver pomegranates; the remaining thousand, who constituted the king's royal guard, had pomegranates of gold.[32]

With each new conquest, however, the Achaemenid military engulfed additional units, including entire cavalries, phalanxes, and navies. By the time of Darius, the army was an amazingly diverse multinational force, commanded principally by Persians. Each satrapy supplied its own contingent, which in turn was divided into squads of tens, companies of hundreds, regiments of thousands, and so on. Soldiers wore armor and headdresses, and bore weapons distinctive to their nationality. The Persian infantry carried long bows, short swords, and wicker shields. They wore multicolored tunics over armor, topped with loose felt hats and tiaras. By contrast, the Alarodians wore "wooden helmets"; the Paphlagonians, "plaited helmets"; and the Pisidians, "crested bronze helmets with horns and ears of an ox." Perhaps in a fashion faux pas, the latter also wore "purple leggings," giving them "an extraordinary appearance."[33]

Every attempt was made to match skill with role. The Achaemenid navy, for example—the source of Persia's tremendous sea power—was dominated by Phoenicians, expert sailors whose ships formed the core of the Persian fleet. The Persians, while not themselves seafaring people, fostered maritime trade and commerce, and Phoenician merchants flourished under Achaemenid rule. So did the Achaemenid rulers, who siphoned off a good share of the commercial profits through customs duties and tolls.[34]

The Persians drew also on the naval strength of the Egyptians and Greeks. Under Darius, the Ionian admiral Scylax famously sailed down the Indus River to the Indian Ocean and then to Egypt. Darius likely sent out other expeditionary ships as well, perhaps even circumnavigating Africa. In addition, the Persians recruited large numbers of Greek mercenaries, renowned for their tactical capabilities. At least according to Greek historians, these mercenaries eventually became the cream of the Achaemenid army.[35]

As always, there is a danger of anachronism when discussing ancient empires in modern terms. Although the Achaemenids "recruited" the best craftsmen and warriors from throughout the empire, we are not talking about recruitment in the modern sense of recruiting college basketball players. Many craftsmen and warriors were probably conscripted; individual liberty and freedom of contract were not organizing principles of ancient Persia. It also bears noting that Darius was fond of impaling anyone who defied him. When the Sagartian rebel Cicantakhma was captured, Darius, in his own words, "cut off both his nose and ears," "put out one eye," and kept him "bound at [the] palace entrance," where "all the people saw him." "Afterwards," he continued, "I impaled him at Arbela." As for Fravartis the Mede, Darius had a similar treatment: "I cut off his nose, ears, and tongue and plucked out an eye; he was chained under guard at the gate of my palace and everyone could see him there. Then I impaled him at Ecbatana."

Nor was Achaemenid tolerance accompanied by any modern sense of equality. On the contrary, Achaemenid Persia was a hierarchy, with Persians unmistakably on top. Power was concentrated in the Great King. The center of authority was wherever he happened to be, whether at Susa, Persepolis, or Memphis (depending on the season, the Achaemenid rulers moved from one capital to another, accompanied by massive entourages). Below the king, the satraps who ruled over their mini-kingdoms were exclusively Persian. Below the satraps, the highest-ranking positions throughout the empire were also held by members of the Persian aristocracy. Herodotus wrote of the Persians: "Themselves they consider in every way superior to everyone else in the world, and allow other nations a share of good qualities decreasing according to distance, the furthest off being in their view the worst."[36]

Nevertheless, for two centuries the Achaemenid kings successfully ruled over an empire of unprecedented territorial scale, and policies of tolerance made it possible for them to do so. By embracing local laws and traditions, and by allowing local languages, religions, and rituals to flourish, the Achaemenids minimized the likelihood of opposition and revolt among conquered peoples. By drawing on the specialized talents of the empire's best artists, thinkers, workers, and fighters regardless of ethnicity or religion, the Achaemenid kings turned cultural diversity into a source of synergy and strength.

———

Achaemenid culture was dazzlingly cosmopolitan. Just as their paradise gardens boasted the rarest, most valuable flora and fauna from all over the empire, the Achaemenid kings' royal tables overflowed with the choicest, most exotic foodstuffs that subjugated countries had to offer: Arabian ostrich, "acanthus oil from Carmania," fish from the Persian Gulf, grain from "the wheatfields of Assos in Aeolis," and "dates from Babylon, exclusively from the gardens of Bagôas." According to Xenophon, "The Persian king has vintners scouring every land to find some drink that will tickle his palate." Royal cooks traveled vast distances, searching for new recipes, and prizes were given to anyone who brought the king new culinary delights.[37]

The Greeks would later disparage the excess and sumptuousness of Persian meals. On birthdays, wrote Herodotus, rich Persians would have "an ox or a horse or a camel or a donkey baked whole in the oven." (Poor Persians got only sheep and goats.) Herodotus also stressed the great variety of Persian dishes, contrasting it with Greek restraint: "They have many sorts of dessert, the various courses being served separately. It is this custom that has made them say that the Greeks leave the table hungry, because we never have anything worth mentioning after the first course: they think that if we did, we should go on eating."

Royal banquets were on a different order of magnitude. According to Heraclidis, "One thousand animals are slaughtered daily for the king." (This figure seems so incredible that at least one historian believes it refers to soldiers' rations.) Dishes and cups were of silver and gold. Over three hundred royal concubine musicians were available to play the harp or sing throughout the banquet.[38]

The magnificent Achaemenid palaces—which fused architectural styles from conquered kingdoms—were also metaphors for the empire as a whole. By incorporating Assyrian, Babylonian, Egyptian, and other foreign elements into their buildings and monuments, the Achaemenid kings announced their continuity with earlier empires and demonstrated their ascendance over them. For the Achaemenids, power was most effectively demonstrated not by homogenizing and "Persianizing" subject peoples, but by preserving, incorporating, and exploiting the empire's tremendous ethnocultural diversity.[39]

THE FALL OF THE FIRST HEGEMON

Achaemenid Persia was the first world-dominant power in history. Cyrus and Darius had mastered the secret of strategic tolerance, which enabled them to build an empire that included "the whole of the known world and a good deal of territory till then unknown," stretching "from the burning sands of Africa to the icebound border of China."[40] But if history has glorified Cyrus and Darius, so it has villainized Darius's son Xerxes. Indeed, the beginning of the end of the Achaemenid Empire is usually traced to

Xerxes' "despotic" reign (485–465 BC), which was marked by a number of major military setbacks for the Persians and the first hints of Greek ascendancy.

Our knowledge of Xerxes largely comes from the Greeks, who tell us that he brutally crushed rebellions across the empire—desecrating temples and sanctuaries, killing priests, even enslaving subjects in the process. In addition to being cruel and intolerant, Xerxes is also reputed to have been decadent and licentious. Not content with his harems, it seems that Xerxes fell in love with many women, including his sister-in-law, his daughter-in-law, and his niece. (None of these relationships worked out.) Greek sources suggest that Xerxes also insisted more forcefully on the "Persian" character of the empire. He elevated the Persian god Ahura Mazda over all other deities in a way that none of the earlier Achaemenid kings did. In Egypt and Babylonia, where Cyrus and Darius had left the local population considerable autonomy and respected their local customs, Xerxes reduced these countries to a condition of "servitude."[41]

These classical Greek depictions of Xerxes may well be biased. After all, Xerxes mounted a massive military campaign against Greece and, in his brief capture of Athens, laid waste to the shrines of the Acropolis. But since it was common for ancient rulers to take such retributive measures in cases of rebellion, it is difficult to know whether Xerxes was actually more "despotic" than the earlier Achaemenid kings. According to some modern historians, Xerxes merely continued the Achaemenid tradition of tolerance when it was strategically possible and ruthless retaliation when it was not—the difference being that Xerxes faced much more serious and widespread threats to Persian rule.[42]

In any event, Xerxes managed to preserve the Persian Empire, although the latter half of the Achaemenid dynasty was marked by revolts throughout the land, especially in Asia Minor, often followed by harsh suppressions. Egypt was lost around 400 BC only to be retaken sixty years later by Artaxerxes III, the penultimate Achaemenid ruler. As a conqueror, Artaxerxes seems more a reflection of Xerxes than of Cyrus or Darius. According to Diodorus, after "demolishing the walls of the most important [Egyptian] cities, by plundering the shrines [Artaxerxes] gathered a vast quantity of silver and gold, and he carried off the inscribed records from the ancient temples." A court eunuch eventually poisoned Artaxerxes. In many ways, the Achaemenid dynasty in its death throes had come to mirror the empires that preceded it.[43]

Darius III, the last Achaemenid king, ascended the throne in 336 BC. Meanwhile, a new power was rising in Greece. Around 338, the Macedonian king Philip united the Greek city-states behind him. Within six years of Philip's death, his son Alexander the Great conquered the once invincible Persian empire.

Why did the Achaemenid Empire fall? Classical Greek accounts emphasize the increasing brutality and repression of the later Achaemenid kings, provoking violent uprisings among subject peoples and causing them to favor Alexander. According to classical historians, the Egyptians rejoiced at Alexander's arrival: "For since the Persians had committed impieties against the temples and had governed harshly, the Egyptians welcomed the Macedonians." In Phoenicia, "the inhabitants accepted him willingly." At Ephesus, after paying homage to the local sanctuary of Artemis, Alexander issued a proclamation to the Greek coastal cities: "He ordered the oligarchies everywhere to be overthrown and democracies to be established; he restored its own laws to each city. . . . Straightway [sic] all the cities sent missions and presented the king with golden crowns and promised to co-operate with him in everything."

Like the Cyrus cylinder, such accounts almost certainly contain a substantial dose of imperial propaganda. It is implausible that Alexander was universally hailed as a liberator. He was after all a conqueror and reputedly "the most brilliant (and ambitious) field-commander in history."[44] Nevertheless, it appears accurate that the later Achaemenid period was characterized by growing intolerance, unrest, and violence. This is consistent with the basic thesis of this book: As Persian rule grew more intolerant, it became increasingly difficult to maintain political stability across the vast Achaemenid domains or to harness the energies of diverse subject peoples in the service of the empire.

But here's the final and most important twist. Ironically, the very tolerance that enabled Cyrus and Darius to build their immense empire sowed the seeds of the intolerance that followed. As the world's first hyperpower, Achaemenid Persia faced—but never solved—the same fundamental problem that would confront every subsequent world-dominant power.

The Persians incorporated within their realm unprecedentedly large numbers of diverse peoples. This they accomplished because Cyrus and Darius had the shrewdness neither to try to Persianize their subjects nor to suppress their local religions, languages, social networks, and aspirations. Initially, some of these conquered peoples were so close to them—culturally, geographically, linguistically—that the Persians were able simply to absorb them. The Medes, for example, essentially merged with their Persian conquerors. But as the empire expanded, it came to include increasingly divergent peoples and cultures, which remained distinct communities under their Persian overlords.

Although militarily unified, the Achaemenid Empire had no overarching political identity, as modern nations do. No common religion, language, or culture bound the sprawling empire together. Precisely because of the legendarily tolerant policies of Cyrus the Great, "a Greek felt that he was a Greek and spoke Greek, an Egyptian felt that he was an Egyptian and spoke Egyptian, and so on." Achaemenid subjects generally did not feel any special allegiance to the empire or take any particular pride in belonging to it—as, for example, the subjects of the Roman Empire did by the fourth century AD. "[T]here was no Achaemenid identity that might have induced the peoples, in all of their diversity, to rise up and defend some common norms."[45]

As a result, powerful forces of disintegration lay at the heart of the empire. With increasing antagonism, the distinct peoples whose identities had been preserved and strengthened through Persian tolerance eventually turned on the empire itself. Lacking any strong ideological glue capable of holding the empire's disparate peoples together, the centralizing power eventually lost control. By the late Achaemenid period, separatist rebellions were constantly erupting. Nothing but military might held the empire together.

When Alexander of Macedon conquered their countries and made it clear to the local elites that their positions and lives would not change, Achaemenid subjects simply traded one overlord for another.

ALEXANDER THE GREAT

Classical writers give us a physical description of Alexander. At thirteen, he was not especially tall, but unusually muscular, compact, and fleet of foot. He was fair-skinned and had blond tousled hair resembling a lion's mane. His eyes were an unsettling mismatch, one gray-blue, the other dark brown. He had sharply pointed teeth—"like little pegs." His voice was slightly high-pitched, and his gait was fast and edgy. He held his head tilted upward and to the left, possibly an affectation. In the historian Peter Green's words, "There is something almost girlish about his earliest portraits, a hint of leashed hysteria behind the melting charm."

Alexander grew up believing that he was a blood descendant of heroes and divinities such as Achilles and Herakles, and this idea nourished his lifelong ambition. By his father's arrangement, and for a hefty honorarium, Alexander was tutored by Aristotle, who was warned that the boy was "a trifle unmanageable." Like most Greeks at the time, Aristotle was unrelentingly ethnocentric. He believed that all "barbarians"—non-Greeks—were born to be slaves and that it was just and fitting for Greeks to rule over them. It is said that Alexander relied on a version of the *Iliad* annotated by his teacher as a "handbook of warfare." Whether young Alexander originally shared and then later shed his tutor's contempt for "barbarians" is a matter of debate. In any event, immediately after his father's assassination in 336, Alexander ascended to the Macedonian throne, consolidated his military allies, and began his conquest of Persia.[46]

Was Alexander tolerant? In his recent biography of Alexander, the historian Guy MacLean Rogers cautions against applying modern concepts to a distinctly pre-modern figure: "[Alexander] cannot be resolved into an individual who was either gay or straight (as some have claimed), an ultranationalist or someone who went native, a mass murderer or a messiah. Rather, Alexander was an ambiguous genius who defeats our polarized and polarizing modern categories." At the same time (using some pretty modern concepts himself), Rogers describes Alexander as "a kind of unacknowledged proto-feminist, limited multi-culturalist, and religious visionary" who established an extraordinary empire ruled by the "best" among humankind. What is indisputable is this: As his power grew, Alexander increasingly followed the great Persian emperors before him, employing strategic tolerance to win favor with his conquered peoples and incorporating the most talented warriors and leaders of all ethnicities into his military and administration.[47]

When Alexander entered Persia, he presented himself not as a foreign conqueror but as the avenger of the murdered Darius—his former opponent—and as the legitimate successor to the Achaemenid throne. Alexander conspicuously honored Cyrus and reinstated a number of the Achaemenid satraps even though they had fought against him. He also married a Persian, encouraging other Greeks to do the same. Although these policies baffled and frustrated many of his Greek subjects, they succeeded in winning the support of the Persian aristocracy and much of the local population.

After conquering Babylon, Alexander ordered the rebuilding of temples that Xerxes had allegedly destroyed, including the temple of Baal, the powerful storm god. Alexander pointedly made sacrifices to Baal, following the precise instructions of the Babylonian priests. Whether the Babylonians actually saw Alexander as their deliverer from Persian oppression or merely feared his wrath, they welcomed him with open arms. They also gave his Macedonian troops the time of their lives. For an entire month, Alexander's men were feted and lodged in the city's poshest private homes and given unlimited access to wine, food, and women, including the wives and daughters of prominent citizens. Professional courtesans offered their expert services; after-dinner striptease was apparently a favorite entertainment. The soldiers were also shown the city's most popular sites, including the marvelous Hanging Gardens.

Alexander engaged in similar crowd-pleasing religious rituals after conquering Egypt. Writing about Alexander's success with the Egyptians, Peter Green adds a fascinating psychological gloss:

> [Alexander] got rather more than he bargained for. What had been conceived as a piece of political diplomacy turned into a profoundly felt emotional and spiritual experience. . . . The Persian kings had been, *ex officio*, Pharaohs of Egypt, by right of conquest over the native dynasty. Alexander had put down Darius: in the priests' eyes he now became their legitimate ruler. So, on 14 November 332, the young Macedonian was solemnly instated as Pharaoh. They placed the double crown on his head, and the crook and flail in his hands. He became simultaneously god and king, incarnation and son of Ra and Osiris. . . . There [were earlier] signs that . . . Alexander [had begun] to lose touch with his Macedonians. . . . Now, amid the ancient splendours of Egypt—a civilization which invariably bred semi-mystical awe in the Greek mind—he learnt that he was in truth a god, and the son of a god.[48]

Around 330 BC, Alexander heard that a Persian rival was organizing an uprising against him. In response, Alexander went to Bactria and filled his court with Persian ushers and bodyguards, including Oxathres, Darius's brother. He put on a Persian diadem, dressed himself in the traditional Persian white robes and sash, and even outfitted his horses in Persian harnesses. Several ancient writers criticized Alexander's adoption of Persian dress and customs as a decline into luxury and "orientalism." But once again, it was more likely part of a shrewd strategy of instrumental tolerance—a strategy that reached a spectacular high point in the mass marriage Alexander organized at Susa.

In 324 BC, Alexander and (on his orders) roughly ninety of his Greek and Macedonian officers took Persian or Median brides, all from royal or noble families. Scholars debate Alexander's motives, but it appears that he wanted both to establish himself as the legitimate heir to the Achaemenid Empire and to create a mixed-blooded ruling class. In any case, Alexander married two women at Susa: Barsine, the oldest daughter of the dead king Darius, and another daughter of the Persian royal family. Unlike Alexander's first marriage (to a Bactrian woman named Roxane), which had been in the Macedonian style, the mass wedding was extravagantly Persian. Following a simple ceremony, a lavish five-day wedding bacchanalia ensued. According to an ancient source, Alexander had a special pavilion constructed with one hundred bridal chambers,

> furnished in the most costly and magnificent manner, with sumptuous garments and cloths, and beneath them were other cloths of purple, and scarlet, and gold. . . . [P]illars supported the tent, each twenty cubits long, plated all over with gold and silver, and inlaid with precious stones; and all around these were spread costly curtains embroidered with figures of animals, and with gold, having gold and silver curtain-rods.[49]

Like the Achaemenids, Alexander raised the largest army on earth through his ability and willingness to incorporate men from every part of his empire. Thirty thousand young Persians, chosen for their strength and grace, were taught Greek, trained in Macedonian military techniques, and made part of the army. His cavalry included not just Persians but Bactrians, Sogdians, Arachotians, Zarangians, Areians, and Parthians. His navy was similarly diverse. With a massive fleet of nearly two thousand ships, he propelled 120,000 troops down the Indus into India. Working on the ships were Phoenicians, Cypriots, and Egyptians, as well as mainly Greek and Persian commanders. Alexander's six-month campaign on the Indus was notoriously brutal. Encountering intense resistance, his army killed at least 80,000 Indians and enslaved many more.

Many Greeks, including a good number of Alexander's soldiers, scorned and resented their king's reliance on foreigners and his ostentatious adoption of foreign customs. Concerns that Alexander had become "barbarianized" led to an attempted mutiny at Opis. Alexander prevailed, and in victory, he hosted a celebratory feast for nine thousand people. To reconcile himself to the Greeks, Alexander segregated the guests according to ethnicity and merit. Alexander sat with the Greeks, who sat next to the Persians, who sat next to soldiers from other ethnic groups, with no intermingling across peoples.

Thus, if Alexander harbored hopes for the eventual "unity of mankind," as some have suggested, he did not let these hopes get in the way of his overriding ambition. As Peter Green writes, Alexander's "all-absorbing obsession" was "war and conquest. It is idle . . . to pretend that he dreamed, in some mysterious fashion, of wading through rivers of blood and violence to achieve the Brotherhood of Man by raping an entire continent. He spent his life, with legendary success, in the pursuit of personal glory." The fact remains that in his achievement of glory, tolerance played an indispensable role.

By 324 BC, world dominance had passed from the Persians to the Greeks. Alexander was, and remains, the ruler of the largest empire in Greek or Macedonian history. Indeed, he was arguably "the richest and most powerful man in the history of the world up to that point in time." He held court on a throne of pure gold, and his retinue included five hundred Persian "Apple Bearer" guards clad in purple and yellow; a thousand bowmen wearing mantles of crimson and dark blue; and five hundred "Silver Shields," elite Greek infantry warriors.[50]

With Alexander's conquests, the Greek language and Greek literature, art, architecture, and philosophy spread across the Mediterranean, across the continents—and ultimately across the centuries. At the same time, in the city-states Alexander established from Egypt to India, "barbarian" ideas were translated into Greek and absorbed into the empire, creating a cultural hybrid—known as Hellenism—that would profoundly influence Christianity and the Western world. For all his military feats, Alexander's greatest legacy was a degree of transcontinental cultural unity that the Persian kings never achieved.

But political unity of the region died with Alexander. Before he could conquer his next targets—Arabia, the western Mediterranean, and Europe—Alexander, at the age of just thirty-two, succumbed to a mysterious fatal fever. Alexander's empire immediately fragmented into warring kingdoms torn by internal rebellions. Tellingly, after his death, all but one of Alexander's co-bridegrooms from Susa divorced their Persian wives.[51]

Reunification would have to await the coming of Rome.

TWO

TOLERANCE IN ROME'S HIGH EMPIRE

Gladiators, Togas, and Imperial "Glue"

[Rome] alone received the conquered to her bosom and cherished the human race with a common name, in the fashion of a mother, not of an empress; and she called "citizens" those whom she subdued and bound with her far-reaching and pious embrace. To her pacifying customs we owe everything: ... that we are all of us one race.

—CLAUDIAN, FOURTH-CENTURY POET

They are all right, they no longer wear trousers.

—EMPEROR CLAUDIUS, CIRCA AD 48, REFERRING
TO THE CONQUERED GAULS

I f there is an iconic empire in the West, it is Rome. Territorially, it fell just short of the Achaemenid Empire. But the Roman hyperpower outshone its predecessor in virtually every other way. Whereas Achaemenid Persia was essentially just a war machine, Rome was also an idea.[1] Inhabitants from the farthest reaches of the empire wanted to be—and became—"Roman."

Along the empire's remarkable 53,000-mile network of paved roads and bridges that linked Britons to Berbers, one could find thousands of Roman baths, amphitheaters, and temples, built roughly to the same specifications and filled with toga-clad Roman citizens. Two languages, Greek and Latin, sufficed to allow communication among hundreds of thousands of merchants, legionnaires, and imperial officials throughout the *orbis terrarum*, or "the world," as the Roman Empire was known to its inhabitants.

At its height, the Roman Empire counted perhaps 60 million inhabitants within its borders. The empire was so vast that Romans liked to believe that it stretched to the limits of the inhabitable world. Terminus, the god of boundaries, had supposedly been absent at Rome's birth.[2]

According to the historian Anthony Pagden, the Romans consciously "aimed at world domination." As early as 75 BC, the republic struck coins "with images of a sceptre, a globe, a wreath, and a rudder"—symbols of Rome's hegemony over all the world. The empire's global reach was evident even to the average citizen, who saw lions from Syria, bulls from Greece, leopards from Tunisia, and bears from England all compete against gladiators in the empire's great amphitheaters such as the Colosseum in Rome, which packed in nearly 50,000 people for regular events. In the words of Seneca, playwright and philosopher of the first century, "[Romans] measure the boundaries of our nation by the sun." In the mid-second century, the emperor Antoninus Pius took the title *Dominus Totius Orbis*—Lord of All the World.[3]

More than just an immense military power, Rome represented a new pinnacle of Western civilization, achieving heights in science, literature, and the arts that would not be surpassed for more than a thousand years. In addition to classical poets and philosophers such as Virgil and Seneca, Roman civilization produced Galen, doctor to the gladiators, whose medical textbooks were widely used in Europe until the fifteenth century, and the astronomer Ptolemy. Pliny the Elder, who died in the eruption of Mount Vesuvius in AD 79, wrote *Natural History*, one of the world's first encyclopedias, and the ten books by the Roman architect Vitruvius inspired the builders of the Italian Renaissance more than a millennium after their author died. Rome also set new global standards of representative government. In the year AD 212, Emperor Caracalla extended citizenship to every freeborn male inhabitant of the Roman Empire. This mass enfranchisement catapulted Rome far beyond Greece or any other ancient civilization in terms of individual participation in the political process.

The "glory of Rome" spanned more than two millennia, from the city's fabled founding by Romulus in 753 BC to the fall of Constantinople to the Ottoman Turks in AD 1453. Rome's rulers are among the most famous in history, whether for their conquests or cruelty. The names of Julius and Augustus Caesar give us two of the months of the calendar; the name of Caligula is practically synonymous with despotism and depravity. But most historians agree that the High Empire, from AD 70–192, represented the apogee of Roman civilization.

The High Empire roughly tracks the reign of four successive emperors: Trajan, Hadrian, Antoninus Pius, and Marcus Aurelius, each of whom followed the Roman practice of adopting a son whom they molded into the next emperor. During this period, the Pax Romana, or Roman Peace, prevailed, and Roman provinces from southern Scotland to the agricultural towns of West Africa actively traded with each other. The nineteenth-century German historian Theodor Mommsen captured the essence of the period, writing, "Seldom has the government of the world been conducted for so long a term in an orderly sequence."[4]

This chapter will not even remotely try to offer a history of the Roman Empire. Instead, focusing on its second-century golden age, I will explore the way in which tolerance enabled Rome to pull away from its rivals on a global scale and grow into the hyperpower of its time. I will also highlight the factors underlying the Roman Empire's extraordinary staying power—a subject of special relevance for the United States, which has been a global hegemon for less than two decades.

COSMOPOLITAN ROME: "THE SINGLE NATIVE LAND
OF ALL THE PEOPLES IN THE WORLD"

Like Achaemenid Persia, imperial Rome incorporated conquered
nations by making them "provinces" of the Roman Empire. During the High Empire, there were roughly forty such provinces. Also
like the Achaemenids, the Romans marshaled the services of local
elites to help rule their vast empire. They kept local governments
largely intact, allowing them to continue ruling the day-to-day life
of their subjects.

But unlike in Achaemenid Persia or perhaps any other ancient
empire, there was no ceiling on the power that elites from the
provinces could achieve in the Roman Empire. Whereas all
the Achaemenid Persian kings and virtually all of its governors
were Persians, not so in Rome. Rome's highest power holders—
all the way up to emperor himself—came from every corner of
the empire. As the historian Cornelius Tacitus wrote, "Emperors
could be made elsewhere than at Rome." The emperor Trajan,
who ruled from AD 98 to 117, was born in Spain. His top advi-
sory included a Greek, a Moor, and Gaius Julius Alexander Bereni-
cianus, a descendant of the Israelite king Herod the Great.

Trajan, whose mother was Spanish, was the first Roman emperor to come from a province, and his rise announced that the
empire's highest offices were now "open to all educated men, regardless of race and nationality." Trajan's successor, Hadrian, also
hailed from Spain, and Hadrian's successor, Antoninus Pius, descended from a family of Gallic origin. The father of the next emperor, Marcus Aurelius, was Andalusian, and Septimius Severus,
who ruled from AD 193 to 211, was an African with a Syrian wife.
People of all colors, backgrounds, and cultural traditions coexisted
in the "Eternal City" of Rome.

The provinces produced Roman elites in every walk of life. The
playwright and poet Seneca was Spanish. Tacitus was probably
from Gaul. Fronto, the orator and tutor of Marcus Aurelius,
was an African. During the height of the empire, "Roman" was a
cultural identity that allowed citizens—even those, in Cicero's

words, from "savage and barbarous nations"—to participate in the political process and share in the power and prestige of the empire.[5]

In adopting this tolerant outlook, Rome learned from the history of ancient Greece, where bigotry and ethnic division often caused resentment that led to war. The logic of Roman toleration was best explained by Emperor Claudius, who argued in a speech to the Roman Senate in AD 48 that the recently defeated tribes of Gaul should be allowed to stand for public office. Speaking to the Senate, Claudius reflected:

> What else was the downfall of Sparta and Athens, than that they held the conquered in contempt as foreigners? But our founder Romulus' wisdom made him on several occasions both fight against and naturalize a people on the same day! We have had strangers as kings; granting high offices on sons of freedmen is not a rarity, as is commonly and mistakenly thought, but rather a commonplace in the old Roman state. . . . And yet, if you examine the whole of our wars, none was finished in a shorter time than that against the Gauls; from then on there has been continuous and loyal peace. Now that customs, culture, and marriage ties have blended them with us, let them also bring their gold and riches instead of holding them apart.

The Senate was convinced. Thereafter, as Edward Gibbon put it, "the grandsons of the Gauls, who had besieged Julius Caesar in Alesia, commanded legions, governed provinces, and were admitted into the senate of Rome. Their ambition, instead of disturbing the tranquility of the State, was intimately connected with its safety and greatness."

The Roman Empire set a new standard for toleration. As the U.S. Supreme Court justice James Wilson, one of the drafters of the Constitution, observed in 1790, "It might be said, not that the Romans extended themselves over the whole globe, but that the inhabitants of the globe poured themselves upon the Romans." For

Wilson, Rome's strategic tolerance was plainly "the most secure method of enlarging an empire."[6]

Of course, there were limits to Rome's famed toleration and inclusion. Women were almost entirely excluded from public life; they were not allowed to vote, hold office, or wear the toga. Moreover, even when citizenship was extended to nearly every freeborn male in the empire, only a tiny fraction of the population qualified as citizens. Slaves were far more numerous, often condemned to labor in the fields to feed the great Roman cities.

The avenues to slavery were many. Among those who found themselves being auctioned off were prisoners of war, wives and children of prisoners of war, victims of pirates and kidnappers, children of slaves, children whose parents had sold them into slavery, men seized for debt by tax collectors, and even free adults who put themselves up for sale. The plight of slaves varied as well. Some were purchased to herd cattle. Others performed sexual services. Still others worked in households, where they were carefully trained and taught Latin. The unluckiest of the lot were sent to the gladiator games—and not as spectators. Along with common criminals, thousands of slaves were shredded by wild beasts as roaring crowds watched with glee. "So many victims were tied to stakes and then cut open that doctors used to attend the games in order to study anatomy." Men and women alike were beaten, skewered, flogged, and gutted. Children were strung up by their feet while hyenas were unleashed upon them.

Still, it would be wrong to suggest that the benefits of the Roman Empire never extended beyond the base of Roman citizens. As long as subjects paid their taxes, which were relatively light, Rome essentially left local communities with their local customs alone. Imperial subjects from Britain to Mesopotamia benefited from the Pax Romana and the spread of Roman law, which brought order and stability on a scale never before seen.[7]

HOW TO GROW AN EMPIRE

According to the Roman myth, the twin brothers Romulus and Remus founded Rome in 753 BC on the site near the Tiber River where they had been found in a basket and suckled by a she-wolf. Romulus was apparently a little defensive; he supposedly killed Remus for joking that the city walls Romulus had built were too short. Nevertheless, Rome became known for its generosity, particularly toward refugees from all across Italy. According to historical legend, the early Romans agreed to incorporate the neighboring Sabines into the city in order to avoid a conflict over Roman abduction of Sabine women. The orator Cicero wrote in 56 BC, "What is most responsible for the establishment of the Roman Empire and the fame of the Roman people is that Romulus, the founder of the city, instructed us by his treaty with the Sabines that the state should be increased even by the admission of enemies to the Roman citizenship. Our ancestors through his authority and example never ceased to grant and bestow the citizenship."

Over the following centuries, the Romans adopted similar tactics to incorporate other Italian tribes such as the Etruscans and the Umbrians under the umbrella of Rome. Rather than pillaging or looting the cities of defeated foes, Rome offered them treaties of peace that were rarely refused. In most cases, the basic terms of these treaties were simple. The conquered cities could continue to be ruled by their own leaders under their own laws, with two conditions. First, each could trade freely with Rome but not with each other; in this way, the smaller city-states quickly became economically dependent on Rome. Second, each was required to provide Rome with troops.[8]

These alliances helped Rome grow dramatically in military and economic strength. By 275 BC, Rome had become the largest state in Europe, covering 50,000 square miles from the Rubicon in northern Italy to the Straits of Messina off Italy's southern coast. A decade later, Rome began consolidating its control of the entire western Mediterranean. The Punic Wars, which lasted more than a century, resulted in Rome's conquest of Sicily, Sardinia, and Corsica. The wars culminated with Rome's defeat of Hannibal's legendary elephant corps at Zama in modern Tunisia in 202 BC.

The Punic Wars demonstrated the success of Rome's strategic tolerance. Hannibal's military strategy was based on the belief that after several Carthaginian victories, Rome's Italian allies would rush to defect. To Hannibal's surprise, however, despite a number of hard-fought battles, every one of Rome's alliances held firm and Rome prevailed.

Of course, Rome was also prepared to deal brutally with enemy cities that would not yield. For example, with Carthage itself, Cato famously declared, "Carthage must be destroyed." Three years after the Third Punic War began in 149 BC, the city of Carthage was razed, most of its population slaughtered, and Carthage's territory annexed as a new Roman province.[9]

The conquest of Carthage marked a significant shift in Roman policy that would permanently change the direction of the empire. For most of its early expansion, Rome refrained from direct annexations. Instead, the early Roman emperors expanded the empire by establishing dependent states and spheres of influence and by using offensive armies to intimidate potential enemies. Thus, at the time of the Punic Wars, it would have been difficult to determine the exact borders of the Roman Empire with any precision.

Around the first century AD, however, Roman strategy changed. Emperors like Augustus and Trajan led military campaigns to annex already conquered territories—from Wales to Armenia, from Switzerland to Jordan—gradually bringing them all under Rome's direct rule. Rome's borders came to be clearly defined, usually tracking major waterways. Once the empire's boundaries were set, Rome's emperors poured enormous resources into building border fortifications like Hadrian's Wall in northern England. At the same time, they dramatically expanded the Roman network of paved roads, allowing imperial legions to move quickly when there were revolts to be suppressed or barbarian invaders to be repelled.

Even under direct control, however, the Roman emperors interfered very little with the lives of their subjects, imposing virtually no major economic or social reforms. Indeed, one source describes the Roman Empire as "government without bureaucracy." Certainly, it was undergoverned by comparison to the contemporaneous Han Chinese Empire, which, proportionately, employed a bureaucracy perhaps twenty times as large.

From 150 BC to AD 70, Rome expanded at a startling pace, engulfing most of continental Europe, Asia Minor (now Turkey), and much of the Middle East, including Palestine, Syria, and Egypt. Throughout these military campaigns, Rome extended the right of citizenship to defeated elites while harshly punishing states that resisted Roman rule. Six centuries after its founding, Rome had grown from a tiny city-state to a global empire that surrounded the Mediterranean on all sides, turning the famed sea into a Roman lake.[10]

THE GOLDEN AGE OF ROME

Historians disagree about the exact timing of Rome's golden age or High Empire, but the general consensus is that it stretched roughly over the reign of four emperors, beginning with Trajan, who ruled from AD 98 to 117 and was known as the *optimus princeps* (best ruler) by later generations of Romans.[11] Charismatic, popular, and remarkably accessible for an emperor, Trajan is equally famous for his spectacular military conquests and the excellence of his governance. Under Trajan, the borders of the empire expanded all the way to the Persian Gulf; no other Roman commander ever marched so far. He apparently returned from conquered Dacia (now Romania) with millions of pounds of gold and silver—the last time Rome's treasury would reap large profits from a war.

At the same time, Trajan also implemented one of the few examples of social legislation in the ancient world, creating the famous *alimenta* program that lent money to farmers, with the interest going to support poor children. Trajan's legacy as a just and fair ruler formed the basis of the Senate's fourth-century prayer that the new emperor might be "better than Trajan." In the Middle Ages, Dante imagined him as one of the pagans who would be released from hell through the prayer of Pope Gregory.

Trajan's successor, Hadrian, who ruled from 117 to 138, was a cosmopolitan with a passion for Greek culture and one of the greatest administrators in Roman history. Hadrian halted Rome's offensive wars, focusing his attention instead on the consolidation, defense, and embellishment of the empire. In addition to the eighty-mile-long Hadrian's Wall, he oversaw the construction of new cities, temples, baths, harbors, aqueducts, arches, and amphitheaters throughout the empire. A hands-on commander, and evidently an ardent sightseer, Hadrian spent more than half of his twenty-one-year reign outside Italy, touring Rome's provinces and checking on the constant readiness of his soldiers, at one point even living and training with them.

Despite Hadrian's reputation for tolerance, he is also known for an act seen by many as quintessentially intolerant. Heavily influenced by the Greek ideal of the human body, Hadrian banned circumcision, the ritual procedure required for male infants under Jewish law. (The philhellenic Hadrian probably saw circumcision as an offensive mutilation of the human body; he also cracked down on the practice of castration.) This ban, together with Hadrian's decision to build a Roman colony in Jerusalem, exploded into the Jewish rebellion of AD 131–135, led by Simon Bar Kochba. After the rebellion, according to several ancient sources, Hadrian expelled the Jews from Jerusalem, built a temple to Jupiter over the site of a former Jewish temple, and placed a statue of himself inside the temple. To add further insult to injury, a large marble pig was erected on the temple grounds. (The pig was evidently the symbol of a Roman legion that had fought against the Jews.)[12]

Such intolerance was the exception, not the rule, during Rome's golden age. After Hadrian died, Jews were once again allowed to practice their religion and even granted exemptions from Roman laws that conflicted with their religious duties. During the reign of Hadrian's successor, Antoninus Pius (138–161), the security and prosperity of the Pax Romana reached their peak. Unlike Trajan and Hadrian, who were known for their extensive travels throughout the empire, Antoninus Pius never left Italy after becoming emperor. Although he launched a few small wars in Scotland and North Africa to secure the empire's borders, he preferred to use diplomacy and threats of force to deter potential enemies. His successor, Marcus Aurelius, later described Antoninus Pius as follows:

"His attitude to the gods was not superstitious and he did not court the favour of men—he did not try to cultivate people by gifts or flattery, but was temperate in every respect, without any mean behaviour or love of novelty for its own sake."

More than any other emperor, Marcus Aurelius, who ruled from 161 to 180, represents the incarnation of the philosopher-king. Born into a powerful senatorial family, Marcus Aurelius caught the eye of Hadrian, who named the boy an "equestrian" at age five, and ensured that he received the best education available. When he was twelve, Marcus Aurelius opted for the life of the stoic philosopher. He wore a rough cloak and slept on the ground, until his mother finally persuaded him "to sleep on a little bed strewn with skins." Marcus Aurelius successfully steered his empire through a variety of challenges, including a terrible plague that struck in 169 and the Germanic invasions later in his rule. When he died in 180, the Roman Empire was still in its full glory, more powerful than any empire in Western history.[13]

And Rome's economy? Writing in the mid-second century AD, the Greek rhetorician Aelius Aristides gives us a glimpse:

> So many merchant ships arrive here, conveying every kind of goods from every people every hour and every day, that the city is like a factory common to the whole earth. . . . Hesiod said about the limits of the Ocean that it is a place where everything has been channeled into one beginning and end. So everything comes together here—trade, seafaring, farming, the scourings of the mines, all the crafts that exist or have existed, all that is produced and grown. Whatever one does not see here is not a thing which has existed or exists.

Rome's High Empire was a pre-modern model of economic globalization, free trade, and open markets that would make a Chicago economist proud. Import taxes and earlier limits on trade between city-states fell away as Rome consolidated its power. As the borders of the empire solidified, Rome became an enormous free-trade zone, with African olive oil and the highly prized Spanish fish sauce *garum* being traded in markets from Scotland to Cyprus. Commerce boomed as never before, supported by the Pax Romana and an exceptional transportation network consisting of European rivers, Mediterranean seaways, and the famous Roman roads.

Rome's "global economy" extended even to the Far East. Roman merchants sailed the Indian Ocean and traveled the Silk Road to bring back exotic spices, fragrant perfumes, and all kinds of silk and luxurious cloth to the markets of Alexandria, Rome, and London. In return, Rome traded glassware, gold coins, and other goods, which have been found as far away as Vietnam and Malaysia. As early as 289 BC, the Romans had developed bronze coins to meet the commercial needs of the empire, adding a common currency to the mix of factors that made Rome an economic hyperpower.[14]

But it was not only goods that flowed with ease. Rome also attracted skilled and talented people from the farthest-flung reaches of the empire. It was perfectly common for a Roman military force to include "Cretan archers, Balearic slingers," Spanish swordsmen, and sailors from the Greek isle of Rhodes. Merchants and traders—particularly Syrians, Jews, Arameans—streamed in and out of Rome, importing "gold, ivory, and precious woods" from Africa, spices from Arabia, "pearls and precious stones" from India, silks from China, "furs from central Asia and Russia, amber from Germany and Scandinavia." With the exception of slaves and serfs, who were bound to their masters and to the land, Roman subjects across the empire enjoyed an unprecedented level of freedom of movement.

At the same time, Rome offered extraordinary opportunities for upward mobility, even to distant regions. One remarkable story of this kind is told by an inscription found in the tiny North African town of Tiddis (now in Algeria), describing the life of the second or third son of a local Berber landowner. This boy, who became known as Quintus Lollius Urbicus, left North Africa for Asia, Judea, the Danube, and the lower Rhine, rising steadily through the imperial ranks. Eventually he became governor of Britain, where he led imperial troops into Scotland, expanding the empire's borders. By the end of his life, Quintus had become the city prefect of Rome.[15]

"GOD'S OWN PEOPLE"

Racism in the modern sense did not exist in Rome. There is little evidence that the Romans saw light skin as superior to dark skin, or vice versa. But lest there be misunderstanding, one point must be made: The Romans were snobs. They did not consider other peoples their equals. On the contrary, the Romans saw themselves as favored by the gods, as "Heaven's representatives among mankind." They also had an extensive array of largely unflattering stereotypes about the populations they conquered.

Thus, Ireland's inhabitants "were completely savage and led a miserable life because of the cold." Their neighbors in Scotland, "the unclad Caledonii and Maeatae," "lived for days on end in marshy bogs, only their heads protruding above the surface, kept alive by a diet of marsh weeds." At the other extreme, in torrid Africa, the Ethiopians, Numidians, and Mauretanians were small, "wooly-haired," "shrill-voiced, strong-legged," and "burnt black by the sun." The sun drew the blood to their heads, so they were "quick-witted," but their resulting blood deficiency made them terrified of getting wounded and thus poor warriors.

Africans were also said to be "fickle" and "over-sexed." Their women were unusually fertile and thus prone to bearing twins. Egyptian women tended to produce triplets—the effect of drinking water from the Nile.

The supposed anatomical peculiarities of foreign peoples were a frequent theme in the Roman imagination. In India, for example, it was said that there were "people who slept in their ears." At the same time, the Romans appeared to have considerable respect for the highest caste of Indians, the Brahmans, who were said to be "vegetarians, wearing no wool or leather, indeed often no clothes at all, men of immense physical self-control, completely celibate for thirty-seven years (after which they married as many wives as they could)."

In general, Easterners, including Syrians and the people of Asia Minor, were "sissies" in battle, clad in feminine cloaks and fighting with "unmanly" bows and arrows. Corrupted by luxury, gems, and exotic foods, these Easterners were soft, decadent, sycophantic, and overly subservient to their kings. By contrast, the peoples to the west of Rome were generally crude, uncultured, and warlike, while the Sardinians were "ferocious, unattractive brigands and congenital liars."

The Spaniards were admired for their extraordinary military prowess. Compared to, say, the "particularly barbarous" Thracians, Armenians, and Parthians, the Spaniards were relatively civilized. Apart from "the infestation of their country by rabbits," they had just one peculiar characteristic: "They cleaned their teeth in urine, and even bathed in it."

Interestingly, the Romans had particular distaste for peoples of excessive size and height. In general, northerners were "vast and beastly" with ghastly "huge limbs." The Britons and Caledonians were of "atrocious size." The Germans, like the Celts and Gauls, were a "race of giants." But their "abnormal" height was accompanied by inferior intelligence and only hindered these barbarians in battle.

Even on his own turf, the oversized northerner "did not know how to husband his strength." He was even worse in a warm climate, where "he ate too much and, parched by thirst, he drank too much, particularly of the wine which was not easy to obtain in his own country; and so he quickly put on weight. He could not stand the heat or the dust, but ran for shelter in the shade." The Alpine Gauls, in particular, were "superhuman in size, with the spirit of wild beasts." "At their first attack," a Roman explained, "they are supermen but, after that, like women. With some resemblance to the snow on their own Alps, at the first heat of battle they break into sweat and after slight action they are, as it were, melted by the sun."

In short, the Romans regarded their own stature as a kind of golden mean. It was a blessing that their soldiers were on average probably between three and six inches shorter than the Gallic and

German soldiers. "Romans were superior to northerners in intelligence, to southerners in physical strength."[16]

Yet, despite such prejudices, Romans were able to draw into the empire all these diverse "barbarians," enlisting their talents, allowing them to rise within Rome's ranks, and in general coexisting peacefully with them. According to Gibbon, Rome in the second century AD was "the period in the history of the world, during which the condition of the human race was the most happy and prosperous."[17] How did Rome bind its different peoples together and induce them all to work for the benefit of the empire?

THE ALLURE OF ROMAN CULTURE AND CITIZENSHIP

Perhaps the most intriguing aspect of the Roman Empire was the attraction that people felt toward it. Conquered subjects from Britannia to Arabia wanted to be a part of it—to be "Roman." As Gibbon observed, Roman magistrates seldom "required the aid of a military force" because "the vanquished nations, blended into one great people, resigned the hope, nay even the wish, of resuming their independence, and scarcely considered their own existence as distinct from the existence of Rome." But what was Rome's allure?

More than any other ancient power, Rome represented a *communis patria*, a common fatherland, for its diverse subjects. True, Roman civilization was understood (at least by Romans) to be superior to all others, but rather than being spurned or subjugated, the elites of defeated powers were enticed to embrace Roman culture as a means to power and privilege. Once subdued, conquered peoples went on, often within two generations, to build Roman towns and amphitheaters and embrace Roman values and lifestyles. Local elites sent their children to schools in Rome, and these children grew up to be full members of the community of Roman citizens.[18]

Moreover, Romans were surprisingly willing to absorb the traditions, knowledge, and practices of other peoples if they found them useful. "The main reason for the Romans becoming masters of the world was that, having fought successively against all peoples, they always gave up their own practices as soon as they found better ones." This attitude was particularly evident when it came to the Greeks, whose cultural superiority the Roman elites generally acknowledged. Having conquered the Mediterranean, Rome proclaimed itself the cultural heir of ancient Greece. Rather than encouraging Roman nationalism or ideas of Roman uniqueness, emperors such as Hadrian would often talk of membership in an overarching Greco-Roman civilization.

Like the Greek civilization on which Rome modeled itself, the Roman Empire was centered around the city, or polis. Everywhere the empire expanded, Romans built new cities, many of them with Roman names and Roman architecture. While drawing heavily from Greek literature, painting, sculpture, and architecture, Roman culture also created some popular features of its own, such as gladiatorial shows and wild beast hunts. Roman civilization was a cultural fusion—typically combining not just Greco-Roman but provincial and local elements as well—that proved deeply attractive to the elites from across the empire.

All educated Romans were fluent in Greek as well as Latin and grew up reading the great Greco-Roman epicurean and stoic philosophers. As a result of this shared education, by the second century AD the upper classes of Africa, Italy, and Spain had much more in common with each other than they did with the slaves and peasants who farmed their food and tended their flocks. Over time, the empire ceased to be stratified across ethnic lines; cultural and ethnic divisions were replaced by socioeconomic ones.[19]

Significantly, while successfully exporting Greco-Roman culture, Rome did not try to extinguish local languages or traditions. On the contrary, the reality on the ground was enormous linguistic and cultural diversity. Although Latin was the official language throughout the empire, Greek, Coptic, Aramaic, Celtic, and Berber dialects all continued to be spoken. In Africa, Punic could still be heard until the time of St. Augustine. The empire's great cities, such as Rome or Alexandria, were as polyglot and pluralistic as New York or London today.[20]

A critical piece of Rome's cultural formula was the enticement of Roman citizenship. To pacify its defeated enemies, Rome held out the olive branch of citizenship, and for centuries this strategy helped hold the empire together, allowing it to expand to the edge of the known world.

At its core, citizenship signified that someone was a member of the elite, and it guaranteed a certain level of protection, both from imperial officials above and from the masses below. The rights accorded citizens changed over time, but in general Roman citizenship meant the right to vote; the right to hold property and make contracts; freedom from torture; special protections from the death penalty; and equal treatment under Roman law. The Greek orator Aelius Aristides observed, "[Y]ou have divided into two parts all the men in your empire . . . and everywhere you have made [Roman] citizens all those who are the most accomplished, noble, and powerful people, . . . while the remainder you have made subjects and the governed."

One telling story about Roman citizenship comes from the New Testament. As recounted in the Book of Acts, Roman magistrates ordered the flogging of the apostle Paul in Macedonia. After Paul revealed that he was a Roman citizen, the magistrates "feared" and released him, issuing him an official apology. Later, in Jerusalem, when he was again arrested, Paul declared, "Can you legally flog a man who is a Roman citizen, and moreover has not been found guilty?" Although Paul was eventually executed by Roman officials, his citizenship apparently earned him the "right" to be beheaded (rather than tortured or crucified).[21]

The Romanization of local communities began with the aristocracy. Public officeholders were typically granted Roman citizenship as a matter of course, regardless of their race or ethnicity. This citizenship grant resulted in the gradual Romanization of the local elite, who came to identify themselves with Roman rule and to see their interests as aligned with the preservation of the empire. As Aristides wrote, "There is no need for garrisons to hold their citadels, but the men of greatest standing and influence in every city guard their fatherlands for you."

Roman citizenship was not limited to the upper classes. Many among the lower classes were incorporated into the ranks of citizens through service in the army. Both tradition and Roman religion decreed that the legions of the Roman army—its prestigious core—had to be composed of Roman citizens. When the legions were low on recruits, the commanders would accept foreigners and simply grant them citizenship. This happened en masse in extreme circumstances, as when Caesar created his famous Gallic legion, and even in ordinary times, especially in the East, when numbers were low and citizens were not turning out for the army.

It was much more common, however, to become a Roman citizen by joining the auxiliary forces. Although these forces were mainly comprised of noncitizens, twenty-five years of service in the auxiliary army entitled one to citizenship. Ten thousand people annually became citizens via this route. Soldiers in the Roman army were generally not allowed to contract into marriage during their tenure; it was thought that this would distract them from their duties and reduce their ferocity. Nonetheless, most soldiers did have relationships that resulted in offspring, and those children were granted citizenship at the end of their father's service. This practice contributed greatly to the Romanization of the lower classes.

In other cases, a whole community could be granted the prestigious—and usually materially beneficial—status of "Roman colony." When this happened, the entire free male population became citizens. Over time, the ranks of Roman citizens throughout the empire steadily increased, culminating in Emperor Caracalla's mass enfranchisement of AD 212, granting citizenship to every freeborn male in the empire.

Rome's color-blind and surprisingly class-blind approach to citizenship was instrumental in spreading Roman culture and values. Across the empire, Roman citizens eagerly donned the Roman toga and adopted the *tria nomina*, the Roman three-part name, in order to convey their elite status.[22]

"TO SEE THE WHOLE POPULATION
OF THE WORLD IN TOGAS"

In incorporating different peoples, Rome's ideal was emphatically not multicultural diversity. It was assimilation. Rome was tolerant in the sense that any group willing to adopt Roman customs, manners, and ethos could be fully incorporated into the empire, regardless of ethnic origins. But the Romans had no interest in preserving, respecting, or honoring the practices they found barbaric.

They were disgusted, for instance, by the unkempt appearance of the Irish Celts, who wore their hair long and sported trousers instead of togas. They criticized the Britons, who had access to milk, but—unfathomably—did not use it to make cheese. They spurned the Lusitanians, in today's Portugal, who slept on the ground, made bread out of acorn meal, preferred water to wine, and cooked with butter instead of olive oil.

For the Romans, however, these coarse traits were remediable. Roman contempt for barbarian subjects evaporated as soon as they adopted the Roman way of life. Barbarians were not thought to lie forever outside the pale of civilization; they had only to live by Roman practice to be considered part of the empire. Thus, in AD 48, when his opponents argued that the barbarous Gauls were too uncivilized to be included in the Roman Senate, the emperor Claudius famously replied, "They are all right, they no longer wear trousers."[23]

Claudius's point was clear: Barbarism could be shed. And the sooner it was shed, the better. Like the British nearly two millennia later, the Romans believed firmly in their civilizing mission. As described by Pliny the Elder, the goal was "to soften people's ways, *ritus molliret*, to bring the clashing wild speech of infinite different peoples to a common conversation through a common tongue, and to supply civilization, *humanitas*, to men, that all races might, in a word, belong to a single *patria*." Claudius thus hoped "to see the whole population of the world in togas—Greeks, Gauls, Spaniards, Britons, the lot."

Similarly, the historian Tacitus described how his father-in-law,

Agricola, the governor of Britain, sought to create "Britons in to-gas" by encouraging his subjects to build Roman-style houses and temples and by educating the sons of the leading men in the liberal arts. According to Tacitus, the Britons, who initially lived in "primitive settlements" and were "inclined to war," eventually grew "accustomed to peace and quiet by the provision of ameni-ties." "Even our style of dress came into favour and the toga was everywhere to be seen," he said. As time went on, the Britons were seduced by "the allurement of evil ways, colonnades and warm baths and elegant banquets. The Britons, who had no experience of this, called it 'civilization,' *humanitas,* although it was part of their enslavement."[24]

In other words, the Romans were not cultural relativists. Ro-man officials encouraged subjugated elites to accept the Roman cultural formula, creating a political and economic system that re-warded assimilation. What was remarkable was that nationality and ethnicity did not affect one's ability to be Roman. It was Rome's willingness and ability to incorporate and assimilate an endless stream of new peoples into its empire that held the secret to its greatness.

RELIGIOUS TOLERANCE IN THE HIGH EMPIRE

One of the most striking features of Rome's golden age was its cos-mopolitan approach to religion. As Gibbon shrewdly observed, "The various modes of worship, which prevailed in the Roman world, were all considered by the people, as equally true; by the philosopher, as equally false; and by the magistrate, as equally use-ful. And thus tolerance produced not only mutual indulgence, but even religious concord."[25] The only requirement Rome imposed on local religions was that they pay sufficient respect to Roman au-thority and official rituals.

In some ways, Rome's religious tolerance is not surprising. Like the Persians, the Romans were polytheists and believed that differ-ent peoples would naturally worship different gods. Moreover, Rome's system of multiple gods was based almost entirely on

Greek mythology—with Zeus, Athena, and Aphrodite reincarnated as Jupiter, Minerva, and Venus. According to the Greco-Roman worldview, there were gods for almost everything. If other people worshipped new gods, what was wrong with that?

By the second century AD, it was virtually impossible to isolate a "pure" Roman religion. As the Roman legions marched across Europe and North Africa, they "captured" new gods nearly as often as they conquered foreign cities and cultures. After the conclusion of a battle, Roman generals often would adopt the defeated enemy's deity in order to steal the source of their enemy's power. Far from desecrating these local gods, enterprising legionnaires would carry them back to Rome, frequently incorporating them in their hometown temples.

In addition to "capturing" foreign deities, Rome often "summoned" a prestigious foreign god to come to Rome to help the city cope with a natural emergency such as an epidemic or invasion. If a drought or famine was particularly bad, the Roman gods must be either angry or otherwise engaged. The answer was to find new gods to solve the problem.

For the most part, Roman religion coexisted with native local cults in the new regions of the empire. In some places this took the form of layered religious recognition. In Mauretania, for example, a local market was known to be protected by Jupiter (a god in the Roman pantheon), Juba (a deified local king), and Genius Vanisnesi (the local guardian spirit). Elsewhere, locals fused gods together. For example, Saturn and Jupiter were treated almost as one in Northern Africa; the Celtic god Lug was subsumed into Mercury; and Minerva was associated with a number of local goddesses such as Sulis, the water goddess of Bath.[26]

But Rome's inclusive treatment of religion also had its limits. To begin with, cults or customs that were deemed "un-Roman" or morally repugnant were forbidden. Thus the Roman Senate banned the Druid practice of human sacrifice, as well as the rite of self-castration followed by worshippers of the Phrygian goddess Cybele. Other deities fell victim to politics. The Egyptian gods Isis and Serapis—widely identified with Antony and Cleopatra—

were banned by Emperor Augustus when he emerged victorious in Egypt. It was not until two centuries later that the emperor Caracalla received Isis and Serapis into the Roman pantheon.[27]

————

On the whole, the Romans were remarkably successful at incorporating local gods into the empire's religious system. But the monotheistic religions of Judaism and Christianity—with their refusal to acquiesce in Roman pagan rituals—presented more serious challenges.

The Jews of antiquity lived mainly in their ancestral homeland in Palestine and the coastal cities of Egypt and the eastern Mediterranean, including Alexandria, which was home to the largest community of Greek-speaking Jews. The Jews posed a unique problem for the Roman empire. In the "happy melting pot" of Rome's major cities, the Jews often built separate Jewish quarters centered around their own synagogues and courts and resisted attempts to replace Hebrew with Greek or Latin. Although there was also a large number of Greek-speaking "Hellenized" Jews, the Jewish tendency to live separately led many Romans to consider the Jews to be "internal barbarians."

At first the Jews thrived in the empire, enjoying the same strategically motivated tolerance that Rome extended to other groups. Around 161 BC, the Jews approached the Romans after being harshly attacked by the Syrian king Antiochus IV. Eager to weaken Syria, Rome made a declaration of friendship with the Jews. As the century progressed, the relationship strengthened. Julius Caesar granted the Jews freedom of worship and legal autonomy throughout the empire. In return, the Jews provided Caesar with military support; after Caesar's assassination, Roman Jews returned night after night to the funeral pyre, mourning his death.

Caesar's successor, Augustus, also treated the Jews favorably, even making exceptions to ensure that the Roman government's grain collection and distribution schedule did not interfere with the Jewish Sabbath. The Jewish philosopher Philo of Alexandria wrote glowingly of Augustus' tolerance:

Augustus knew that much of the city of Rome on the Tiber's farther side was inhabited by Jews. Many were freedmen who now had become Roman citizens. . . . [H]e did not banish them from Rome or strip them of their Roman citizenship just because they took pains to preserve their identities as Jews. He did not compel them to abandon their places of worship, or forbid them to gather or receive instruction in the laws. . . . He respected our interests so piously that with the support of nearly his whole household he adorned our temple through the magnificence of his dedications, and he ordered that forever more whole burnt offerings should be sacrificed every day as a tribute at his own expense to the most high God.

Other emperors were far less accommodating. Hadrian banned circumcision and the teaching of Jewish law. Caligula forced the Jews of Alexandria to eat pork. Such provocations, in addition to a long-simmering conflict over control of Jerusalem, exploded into three major revolts, beginning in AD 66–73, when the emperor Titus destroyed the Jewish temple in Jerusalem, then recurring in 115 and 131, when Jews revolted against oppressive laws and the perceived influx of Greek and other settlers into Jewish areas. These revolts led to enormous bloodshed, both on the Roman and Jewish sides.

Some historians have argued that the conflict between the Romans and Jews was primarily political in nature. Others stress religious and cultural factors. In any event, the Jews' fortunes varied widely over time, often turning on the opinions of the particular emperor in power.[28]

Christianity presented a different set of challenges to Roman tolerance. Like the Jews, Christians denied the gods of Rome and refused to swear oaths to the emperor. The Jews, however, were essentially exempted from these requirements because of the "ancient cult" status extended to them when they were first conquered by the Roman legions. Christianity, a "new cult" with growing adherents from all over the empire, had no such status and thus no right to violate the implicit bargain that the Romans would tolerate other religions unless they publicly disrespected the Roman authorities.

As a result, there were sporadic clashes between the early Christians and local Roman officials. Christians also faced hostility from Jews, who viewed them as heretics within their own faith. Nevertheless, as a practical matter, Christians during the High Empire were largely left alone. As Gibbon wrote, "The indifference of some princes and the indulgences of others, permitted the Christians to enjoy, though not perhaps a legal, yet an actual and public, toleration of their religion."[29]

INTOLERANCE, CHRISTIANITY, AND THE FALL OF ROME

When did the Roman Empire begin to decline? Historians disagree widely, depending on the particular theory of decline they champion—and there have been dozens of these theories. Imperial overstretch, economic crisis, barbarian invasions, and military weakness are frequently cited and no doubt all played a role. More idiosyncratic explanations include lead poisoning; moral corruption; soil exhaustion; a proliferation of hermits, monks, nuns, and other "drop-outs"; and dilution of the "pure" Roman stock.[30] Assessing the totality of the causes of Rome's collapse is beyond the scope of this chapter. But two points are clear, and both exemplify the thesis of this book.

First, while tolerance was essential to both Rome's rise to world power and its maintenance of the Pax Romana, it also sowed the seeds of Rome's eventual disintegration. As we have seen, Rome was far more successful than Achaemenid Persia in assimilating diverse conquered peoples through the inducements of citizenship, participation in the empire, and the appeal of Roman culture. Whereas most of the peoples under Achaemenid rule never "Persianized," stunning numbers of Roman subjects "Romanized."

But not all. Particularly in the Hellenic east and the "barbarian" north, the empire sought to absorb peoples whose varying traditions and cultures were, for one reason or another, more at odds with Rome's and more resistant. The great early emperors tolerated this heterogeneity, and their tolerance undoubtedly worked to Rome's advantage throughout the High Empire. But precisely because of Roman toleration, the peoples of the east and north were permitted to remain socially intact, relatively autonomous, and relatively un-Roman; over time, they chafed at imperial rule and began agitating for independence.

The historian Anthony Pagden explains, "As the empire grew and the diversity of the peoples it included increased, so its sheer heterogeneity became more difficult to handle." In the fourth century, the divide between the Latin-speaking west and the Greek-speaking east deepened, and in 395 the empire was permanently split in two. At the same time, the empire "began slowly but inexorably to be hollowed out from within as long-quiescent subject peoples revolted and once-loyal subjects seized the opportunity to carve out independent states for themselves."[31]

But "too much diversity" was only part of the problem. Far more devastating, after the golden age Rome descended into an era of intensifying religious persecution and ethnic bigotry. This is my second point: Although not the only cause of Roman decline, intolerance helped tear the empire apart.

Christianity was deeply implicated in the new intolerance, first as a target and later as its primary source. Over the course of the third century AD, Christianity spread to every corner of the empire, representing by the year 300 approximately one-tenth of the total population. The early Christians were not popular among their fellow subjects. Not only did they deny the gods of Rome, they were also accused of incest and cannibalism, the Eucharist taken literally to be the consumption of human bodies and blood. Because of their refusal to participate in the official rites of sacrifice to the deities, Christians were often held responsible for military defeats as well as natural disasters like plagues, earthquakes, and famines.[32]

In AD 303 the emperor Diocletian launched the so-called Great Persecution against Christianity. At the time, the Pax Romana was breaking down, with Germanic tribes invading from the north and Persians attacking in the east. Seeking to restore the glory of the High Empire—ironically through measures antithetical to the values of the golden age—Diocletian decided to extirpate the "un-Roman" Christians. For nearly ten years, Christians were systematically persecuted. Imperial officials stripped Christians of public office and purged the army. In 304, an imperial edict ordered the arrest of every Christian who would not make sacrifice to Rome's gods. Churches were destroyed, scriptures burned, and thousands killed.

Amazingly, in the battle between mighty Rome and the fledgling Christian church, the church won. After a brief but intense war of succession, Constantine the Great emerged as emperor and, for reasons opaque to this day, converted to Christianity in AD 312. With his conversion, the persecution of Rome's millions of Christians abruptly ended, but for the rest of the empire's inhabitants, the era of persecution was just beginning.

The role of Christianity in Rome's fall has been debated for centuries. Gibbon believed that Christianity was a major factor—perhaps *the* major factor.[33] Although tempered by various qualifications, Gibbon's view was that Christianity's emphasis on "a future life," "passive obedience," and "pusillanimity" fatally corrupted Rome's traditional manly, martial, and worldly virtues. My emphasis is different. Rome's official embrace of Christianity introduced into imperial policy a virulent strain of intolerance that undermined those strategies of assimilation and incorporation that had so successfully held together the empire's diverse populations.

At first, paganism was far too widespread to be simply banned. Instead, Constantine stripped Roman temples of their riches while erecting lavish Christian basilicas. But as the empire became more and more Christian, intolerance intensified. Particularly conspicuous "sects" such as Stoicism, Manichaeism (an ancient religion of Persian origin), and Judaism were aggressively repressed. By the late fourth century, Rome had embarked on a systemic campaign to weed out paganism—and indeed all dissenters, including "heretic" Christians who deviated from the official orthodoxy. For the first time, Europe had an established church: "[T]he closed Christian society of the Middle Ages was now in existence."

Undoubtedly, Constantine and his successors believed that religious uniformity would reinvigorate the empire and strengthen it against increasing barbarian attacks. In fact, the opposite occurred. The attacks on pagans and heretics proved deeply self-destructive, actually facilitating barbarian encroachments. In North Africa, for example, the shutdown of pagan temples provoked bitter rioting, and the persecution of heresy threw popular support behind the Vandal king Genseric—himself a heretic Christian—helping him to sweep into power as a liberator. Elsewhere, pogroms led to an exodus of Jews, who resettled in Persian territory, damaging imperial trade and allying themselves with Rome's enemies. As Montesquieu later wrote, "Whereas the ancient Romans fortified their empire by tolerating every cult, their successors reduced it to nothing by cutting out, one after another, every sect but the dominant one."[34]

Worse still, a plague of intensifying ethnic conflict swept over Rome beginning in the late fourth century AD. By this time, hundreds of thousands of principally Germanic "barbarians" had immigrated into Roman territory. These Germans—many of whom were refugees fleeing the Huns—included the Goths, Vandals, Burgundians, and Lombards from the northeast and the Franks, Alamanni, Saxons, and Frisians from the northwest.

These Germanic immigrants occupied a highly precarious position within the Roman Empire. On the one hand, they represented potentially fearsome enemies—invaders who had pushed their way across the Danube through the empire's collapsing frontier defenses. On the other hand, they represented potential allies, offering desperately needed manpower for the badly depleted Roman military.

At first, Rome's traditional strategy of tolerance and uncoerced assimilation appeared to be succeeding with the various Germanic tribes. They were allowed to live under their own rulers, following their own customs and laws. Their men filled the ranks of Rome's armies. The sons of their chiefs were classically educated and allowed to rise, in some cases to the highest positions of military command. They were given ample land and converted in large numbers to Christianity. Far from planning to sack and pillage Rome (as they would eventually do), the Germanic chiefs initially embraced the idea of contributing to and being part of the great Roman Empire. The Visigoth leader Ataulf spoke of "restoring the fame of Rome in all its integrity, and of increasing it by means of the Gothic strength."[35]

But the assimilation of the Germanic immigrants was never complete and always turbulent. From early on, the Germans were subjected to periodic Roman abuse and contempt. Their sons were sometimes taken as hostages to ensure obedience. Their wives and daughters were taken as slaves. At the same time, the usually starving Germans—although given land, they were ignorant of agriculture—often pillaged and attacked their more prosperous Roman neighbors. Revolts broke out as some Germanic tribes sought more autonomy. Distrust and hostility intensified on both sides.

Essentially, the famous Roman tradition of tolerance had hit a limit it could not cross. The Germans disgusted the native Roman people, who complained of the Germans' "nauseous smell" and the repulsive rancid butter they smeared in their yellow hair. Even highly literate Romans who argued for coexistence with the "noble savages" described "the Alamanni as drunkards, the Saxons, Franks, and Heruli as wantonly brutal, and the Alans as rapacious lechers."

In the late fourth century, Rome for the first time adopted policies of apartheid against one of its subject peoples, barring intermarriage, forbidding Romans from wearing trousers and other barbarian clothing (as opposed to togas or tunics), and condemning the barbarians' form of Christianity as heretical. Officers of German heritage were accused of disloyalty, denied posts, and persecuted. Mob lynchings of Goth soldiers grew common. In the worst cases, there were pogroms and massacres, fueling the fire that would eventually lead to the sacking of Rome.

A famous victim of this strife was the mixed-blooded Stilicho, son of a "barbarian" father—actually a Roman cavalry officer of Vandal descent—and a Roman mother. Stilicho was a towering example of the ability of men of non-Roman stock to rise through the imperial ranks. By 400, he was one of the most powerful men in the empire: a general in the Roman army and father-in-law of the western emperor, Honorius. But Stilicho, to fill his desperate needs for military manpower, had recruited thousands of barbarian troops into the Roman army, and a rumor spread that he planned to overthrow the eastern emperor and put his own barbarian son in control. Although the historical evidence suggests that Stilicho was a loyal Roman to the end, the rumor was believed. Honorius divorced Stilicho's daughter. Roman soldiers mutinied, killing Stilicho's supporters and launching a series of pogroms against his barbarian troops, whose families were massacred in cold blood and whose property was confiscated. In August of 408, Stilicho himself was decapitated.

Enmity escalated, and the destruction of Rome came with astonishing rapidity. "[D]isliked and despised," the Germans "retaliated by hating the people whose glories they had once hoped to share." Outraged Germans once loyal to the empire turned against the Romans, throwing their lot in with rebellious forces. Stilicho's barbarian soldiers joined forces with the Gothic king Alaric, who laid siege to Rome itself in the autumn of 408 and sacked it in 410. In 419 the Visigoths overran Gaul. In 439, the Vandals took Carthage and much of Roman North Africa; in 455 they sacked Rome again.

By 476 the western Roman Empire was no more. In its place was an assortment of warlike "barbarian" kingdoms, the distant precursors of the modern European nations. The eastern Roman Empire, with its capital at Constantinople, lasted another thousand years. But this Byzantine Empire—fervently intolerant of religious dissent, riven by ecclesiastical infighting, and continually besieged by Persians, Slavs, and later Muslims—never approached the grandeur of ancient Rome.[36]

———————

A century ago, when racial theories were more in vogue, some historians argued that Rome fell because the "pure" Roman stock had been polluted and diluted by the blood of Rome's conquered peoples. If I am right, just the opposite is true.

Rome thrived so long as it was able to enlist, absorb, reward, and intermix peoples of diverse ethnicities, religions, and backgrounds. At the Roman Empire's peak, Africans, Spaniards, Britons, and Gauls alike could rise to the highest echelons of power—indeed, could even become emperor—as long as they assimilated. The empire sank when it let in peoples that it failed to assimilate, either because they were unassimilable or because their culture and habits exceeded the limits of Roman tolerance. Out of a mixture of religious and ethnic intolerance, Rome sparked wars and internal rebellions it could not win. It was precisely when the empire sought to maintain the "purity" of Roman blood, culture, and religion—replicating the mistake that Claudius and later Gibbon imputed to ancient Athens and Sparta—that Rome spiraled downward into disintegration and oblivion.

THREE

CHINA'S GOLDEN AGE

The Mixed-Blooded Tang Dynasty

W hen I was a girl in West Lafayette, Indiana, my father told me that I was descended from a demigod. This may sound hard to believe, but it turns out that my great-grandfather was a revered statesman and philanthropist in the Fujian province of China. After his death, when tiny ghost sprites—or in my father's words, Chinese leprechauns—were sighted dancing on his grave, his fellow villagers declared him a deity (*lo-han*).

Thirty years later, I repeated this story to my own daughters, and in the summer of 1999 my husband and I took them to China to visit Tangdong, where my great-grandfather had lived. Based on my father's descriptions, I was expecting a worn but graceful mansion on the South China Sea, overlooking acres of white sand. On a clear day, supposedly, one could see all the way to Taiwan.

After a sweltering two-hour taxi ride from the city of Xiamen, we arrived at Tangdong. It was indeed a seaside village, and there was white sand—but no mansion. Instead, scattered all over the beach were huge piles of stinking oyster shells, rising up thirty or forty feet in the air. Except for a few scrawny chickens, the village seemed completely deserted. Whatever its past glories, Tangdong in 1999 was, at least to the disappointed eye, little more than an impoverished ghost town.

I eventually found a local villager. He was sitting on a stoop on the town's long, dusty main street. He stared at us with his mouth open, his four front teeth missing. In the local dialect, I told him my last name and asked if he knew where the Chuas had lived.

The villager blinked at me a few times. Then, he turned and waved his arm. "Everyone on this side of the street is named Chua," he grunted. "Everyone on the other side is named Lao."

The sudden discovery of two hundred new, inbred relatives complicated matters, and the search for my family's house ultimately proved futile. There was, however, solace. We found my great-grandfather's tomb, which, amazingly, and for reasons probably long forgotten, is still regarded as sacred by the townspeople—even if it is now next to some municipal drainpipes.

In addition to my great-grandfather, I have obsessively tried to track down every other remotely impressive ancestor I have in China. A fifth cousin by marriage, thrice removed, collected great works of nineteenth-century calligraphy; his collection is now in the Shanghai Museum. My great "uncle" Chua Ge Kun, possibly unrelated by blood, was a renowned symphony conductor and the founder of the Fuzhou Music School. Finally, my family's most prized heirloom—in fact, our only heirloom—is an original 2,000-page treatise from 1655, handwritten by a direct ancestor named Chua Wu Neng, who was the royal astronomer to Emperor Shen Zong of the Ming dynasty. Also a philosopher and poet, Wu Neng was appointed by the emperor to be the chief of military staff in 1644, when China faced a Manchu invasion. A leather-bound copy of Wu Neng's treatise sits prominently on my living room coffee table.

Like many others who can trace their roots to great fallen empires—whether China, Greece, Persia, Turkey, or Rome—I cling for my identity to ethereal strands of history and high culture.

China's long traditions of calligraphy, science, poetry, opera, philosophy, naturalism, and Confucian discipline have always fascinated me, perhaps because they contrasted so sharply with the
dismal third world reality of the China that confronted me as a
child.

For Westerners, the best known of the Chinese dynasties may
be the Ming, famous for its blue and white porcelain and recently
the subject of Gavin Menzies' *1421: The Year China Discovered
America*. But for ethnic Chinese around the world, it is the Tang
dynasty that represents China's golden age—not only a period of
unprecedented prosperity and political power, but the pinnacle of
Chinese literary and artistic achievement, setting a standard to
which every subsequent dynasty aspired.[1] In terms of population
under its control, the Tang dynasty towered over every other contemporaneous empire, including the powerful Arab caliphates. The
Tang was also, not coincidentally, more open, cosmopolitan, and
ethnically and religiously tolerant than any other empire of its day,
and perhaps than any other period in Chinese history.

INTOLERANCE AND "BARBARIANS" IN CHINESE HISTORY

For centuries prior to 221 BC central China's Yellow River plains
had consisted of numerous vying kingdoms, tribes, and states engaged in perpetual warfare. Known as the "Spring and Autumn"
and "Warring States" eras, this period of disunity and constant
strife was also characterized by tremendous intellectual ferment.
All of China's major schools of philosophy—including Confucianism, Taoism, and Legalism—emerged during this period. As Chinese historians would later note, it was a time when "one hundred
schools of thought" contended.[2]

The Warring States era was brought to an end by the First Emperor of the Qin (Qin Shi huangdi), who unified China politically
for the first time in 221 BC. ("Qin," pronounced "chin," is the
source of the Western name "China.") Like other great nation
builders, he imposed a standard currency and a uniform written
script, undertaking construction projects of unprecedented scale,

including the 1,500-mile-long Great Wall of China, said to have cost a million lives, and the emperor's own royal tomb, containing the famous 7,000-strong terra-cotta army.

Even among his admirers, the First Emperor is known for his cruelty and intolerance. He prohibited philosophical debate, burning thousands of "subversive" books and forbidding any praise of the past or criticism of the present. In 212 BC, the emperor reportedly executed 460 scholars, burying them all in a single grave. Those who defied the emperor were buried alive, boiled to death, or ripped to pieces by chariots tied to their four limbs.[3]

The First Emperor's oppressive policies sparked widespread rebellions and at least three assassination attempts against him. Although the emperor survived these attempts, he became obsessed with finding an elixir of immortality, and he died traveling in search of it. His son was a weakling, and only fifteen years after its founding, the house of Qin was overthrown, succeeded by the Han dynasty, which would remain in power for four hundred years.

Despite the brevity of his reign, the First Emperor had laid down a powerful principle that—with only a few striking exceptions, including the Tang dynasty—would reappear throughout Chinese history: that the ruthless suppression of diversity could be required to unify China. During the Qin dynasty, it was principally intellectual diversity that was quashed. Over the next two thousand years, China's intolerance would take the form of sporadic ethnic and religious oppressions, cultural "purification," rejection of foreigners and foreign ideas, and, most fundamentally, Chinese ethnocentrism and the assertion of Chinese cultural supremacy.

Perhaps all societies practice a degree of ethnocentrism, but special circumstances in China encouraged such attitudes to an unusual degree. Hemmed in by natural barriers, China for centuries experienced only the most limited contact with the developed civilizations of Europe, India, and the Middle East. China's neighbors were principally scattered, nomadic, and tribal. The Chinese were thus for centuries the largest unified population in the region, the most urbanized, the most literate, and consequently by far the most advanced technologically and culturally.

At the same time, the Chinese had good reason to fear their

neighbors. The Chinese were far superior in numbers and technology, but the nomads had one thing that the Chinese did not: horses. The nomads alone possessed the vast grasslands necessary for grazing large numbers of specially bred horses that for centuries provided a critical military advantage. These horses, along with superb riding and archery skills derived from the hunt, allowed the northern barbarians to conduct raids into the settled lands to their south to seize the Chinese food and other goods they depended on to survive, and then to retreat into the limitless steppe. This constant threat of slaughter and pillage by mounted raiders, a problem that defied permanent solution, shaped the ancient Chinese notion of barbarism. The taint of barbarity was not limited to the steppe peoples. Some foreigners were more dangerous than others, some more civilized than others, but all non-Chinese were, to some degree, barbarians.[4]

Even today, in the newly "open" China, the idea of mixing with foreigners retains a hint of the unnatural and taboo for many Chinese. People of mixed racial heritage are regarded as exotic specimens. My two daughters, for example, are half Chinese. They both have brown hair, brown eyes, and vaguely Asian features, and they both speak fluent Mandarin. Yet on a trip to China as recently as 2004, everywhere they went—even in sophisticated Shanghai—my daughters drew curious local crowds, who stared, giggled, and pointed at the "two little foreigners who speak Chinese" as if they were visitors from outer space. Indeed, at the Chengdu Panda Breeding Center, while we were taking pictures of newborn giant pandas—pink, squirming, larva-like creatures that rarely survive—the Chinese tourists were taking pictures of us.

The First Emperor bequeathed more than one legacy to the nation named after him. The Great Wall he constructed remains China's greatest historical monument. It has long been a symbol of China itself—of the country's unity, territorial integrity, exclusivity, and constant need to insulate and protect its superior civilization from the "barbarians," whether the fierce nomads from the central Asian steppes or "imperialists" from Europe, Japan, and most recently the United States.

It is especially ironic, therefore, that the dynasty hailed as

China's golden age was founded by a mixed-blooded man of part barbarian ancestry and that the Tang period was characterized above all by cosmopolitanism, embrace of cultural diversity, and an openness to foreigners unsurpassed in Chinese history.

THE RISE OF THE TANG DYNASTY (AD 618-907)

After the collapse of the Han dynasty in AD 220, China fell into three hundred years of fragmentation. By the late sixth century, northern China was dominated by rival warlords and aristocratic clans, often of mixed Chinese and Turkic heritage, while southern China was dominated by clans of "purer" Chinese stock.

In 581, the Sui clan succeeded in reuniting China, but their rule was short-lived. Constantly attacked by Turkic tribes from the steppe, racked by internal rebellion, and overextended militarily, the Sui dynasty collapsed after only thirty years. In 618, Li Yuan, a general belonging to the northern mixed Chinese-Turkic aristocracy, renounced his loyalty to the Sui, marched on the capital city of Changan (now Xian), and declared himself emperor of China, with the imperial title Gaozu ("High Ancestor"). Thus was founded the Tang dynasty, which would rule China for the next three hundred years.

How Gaozu conquered the Sui is extremely telling: He entered into a military alliance with the barbarian Eastern Turks. Moreover, in his letter to the Turkic ruler, Gaozu used the character qi— which is used by an inferior addressing a superior. For a would-be Chinese emperor to address a barbarian as an equal or, worse, as a superior amounted to sacrilege. In response to the objections of his horrified Confucian advisors, Gaozu explained: "The men of ancient times had a saying, 'To bend before one man and stand above ten thousand.' What do the barbarians beyond the frontier amount to in terms of this analogy? They merely amount to one ordinary person. Moreover, the word qi is not worth a thousand measures of gold. Even that I am willing to give away. Why should one worry about one word?"

Gaozu's shrewd diplomacy reflected the new realities of

seventh-century China. China was now threatened on all sides by numerous powerful non-Chinese groups, including the Eastern and Western Turks, the Uighurs, the Khitan, and the Xi, all from the steppe lands north of China, as well as the Tibetans, the Nanzhao, and the Koguryŏ from the Korean peninsula. Maintaining a unified China in the face of these threats would require not just a Great Wall but complex relationships and alliances with different barbarian groups.[5]

Moreover, China's religious landscape had completely transformed since the fall of the Han dynasty. By the time the Tang emperors took power in 618, Buddhism—founded in India and brought to China by merchants and missionaries—had become China's predominant religion, with more followers than indigenous Taoism. Buddhism adapted itself to China by accommodating and absorbing local elements. While Buddhist and Taoist priests often fought bitterly, most ordinary Chinese had no problem worshipping Buddhist, Taoist, and local deities simultaneously. For the layman, Buddhism's promise of paradise was also far more appealing than the traditional Chinese view of the afterlife, in which a tiny few achieved immortality, with everyone else relegated to gloomy underworld jails.[6]

Finally, at least in northern China, the sharp line between Chinese and barbarians had blurred. During the centuries of anarchy between 220 and 581, a number of "barbarian" rulers conquered parts of northern China and established independent kingdoms. Many of these rulers adopted Chinese customs and intermarried with socially powerful Chinese families, giving rise to a mixed-blooded aristocracy who rode on horseback, supported Buddhism, and spoke both Chinese and Turkic languages. (Because most nomads had no written language, mastery of Chinese was crucial for any official position.) The control of the north by sinicized, often highly cultured former nomads and the prevalence of intermarriage complicated the traditional view in which Chinese were civilized and barbarians were not. Indeed, the Tang emperors themselves, while claiming descent from the famous Han general Li Guangli as well as the Taoist philosopher Lao Tzu, hailed from north China's mixed aristocracy and were probably no more than half Chinese.[7]

These and other factors converged to produce a dynasty more tolerant of foreign cultures, religions, and influences than any other in Chinese history. This tolerance was exemplified in the person of Taizong, the second Tang emperor, whom many regard as the wisest and most heroic of China's rulers. Historians often describe Taizong as "the real founder" of the Tang dynasty, although his ascension to the throne involves a surprisingly grim story.

THE EMPIRE BUILDER

Taizong was born Li Shimin, one of several sons of Gaozu. It was Li Shimin who, as a youth of seventeen, provoked his father into rebelling against the Sui rulers in 617. After his father's taking of Changan, the emerging Tang regime faced hundreds of rebellious movements as well as challenges from powerful rival clans. Over the next seven years, Li Shimin led troops to one decisive victory after another, outmaneuvering far larger armies while keeping the Turks neutralized on the northern border. By 624, the Li family had consolidated power in both north and south China. Absolutely critical to Tang military success was the use of foreigners. The Li family built its conquering forces by incorporating foreign armies whose leaders were allowed to continue to command their troops and govern the territory they brought with them into the empire.[8]

From the moment the Tang dynasty was established, Li Shimin and his brothers contended for power. In 626 Li Shimin murdered his older brother, the heir apparent, and stood by as one of his officers killed another brother. He then deposed his own father and went on to rule as Emperor Taizong for more than two decades (626–649). Despite his brutal treatment of his family, Taizong is a revered figure in Chinese history—noted, surprisingly, for his benevolence.

Taizong's goal was to establish a universal empire in which Chinese and barbarians would be equals and in which he would rule over all, both as emperor and as Turkish khan. In Taizong's own words: "The emperors from ancient times all appreciated the Chinese and depreciated the barbarians. Only I view them as equal. That is why they look upon me as their parent." Like his father, Taizong incorporated submitted peoples into the empire, making particular use of Turkic and other foreign leaders as generals, granting them Chinese titles, marriage alliances, and even the royal surname Li. His claim that the Turks looked upon him as a parent was no empty boast. Taizong was adept in both Chinese and Turkish customs. Even as a child, he formed close friendships with a Western Turkic prince and an Eastern Turkic khan. Such relationships later helped make him acceptable as ruler of the nomads.

Taizong was a brilliant military strategist, and vast lands were brought under Middle Kingdom control during his reign. Whereas the Han emperors had been content to leave the northern steppes beyond China's Great Wall to the nomads, ruled by their own "khan," Taizong was even more ambitious. In 630, through a combination of "personal charisma, bluff, nomadic ceremonies, and battle tactics," Taizong so impressed the Mongolian Turks that their chieftains offered him the title of Heavenly Khan. Taizong accepted, becoming the first Chinese ruler to establish dominion over the steppes.[9]

Taizong's simultaneous accession to the titles Son of Heaven and Heavenly Khan was unprecedented. The Turkish title Heavenly Khan, with its deep roots in nomadic tradition, legitimized Taizong's authority beyond the Great Wall. Just as striking was Taizong's surprisingly modern rhetoric of tolerance. "The Yi and Di [peoples of the steppe] are also just human beings," he argued, "and their natures are not different from those of the Chinese. A ruler's concern is that the beneficence of his virtue may not extend to them, and he should not suspect them because of racial differences."[10]

Taizong's egalitarian rhetoric should not, of course, be taken entirely at face value. It was probably more propaganda than a true description of policy, intended more for the Turks than for the

Chinese. Still, it is important to keep in mind that Taizong's pro-nouncements ran directly counter to imperial precedent and the Chinese worldview at the time (and, arguably, the Chinese world-view even today).

By combining Turkic and Chinese forces, Taizong extended Tang control throughout central Asia and across the Pamir Moun-tains into modern-day Afghanistan. Samarkand, Bukhara, and Tashkent all became Chinese administrative districts. Tibet and Turkic tribes as far west as the Caspian Sea submitted to Chinese suzerainty. Without the nomadic forces behind him, these con-quests would not have been possible. Taizong's successors further extended Tang rule, engulfing Manchuria, most of the Korean peninsula, central Vietnam, and parts of present-day Iran. During Taizong's reign, no other empire in the world came close to the Tang in size, population, or military power.

From the start of his reign, Taizong recognized the potential benefits of trade. Early on, while his empire was still recovering from extended warfare, Taizong emptied the coffers of the state to renovate the Silk Road. Simultaneously, he worked to wrest con-trol of the western regions and oasis states from the Western Turks, completing his conquest of that empire in 658. With the Silk Road made safer than ever by greater Tang control and protection, for-eigners and their goods poured into Changan, the eastern terminus of the Silk Road, from central and south Asia. Foreign goods and fashions flowed to the rest of China from there. Embassies came from as far west as the Byzantine and Sassanid Persian empires.

Tang China eventually had official contacts with more than three hundred countries and regions. Diplomacy and commerce in-termeshed, often indistinguishable: Much exchange of goods re-sulted from the tribute system, and foreign missionaries and merchants often traveled in single convoys. A complex bureau-cracy worked to manage every aspect of foreign relations: corre-sponding with foreign envoys; arranging emissaries' travel and accommodations within China; bestowing Chinese titles on for-eign kings; registering tribute goods and gifts to the emperor; em-ploying translators; compiling information on foreign customs, geography, and products. All Chinese foreign officials, bureaucrats, and even Chinese princesses married to foreign rulers were expected to report back with information about foreign states.

The massive increase in foreign interaction corresponded with a broad love of foreign things: "The Chinese taste for the exotic permeated every social class and every part of daily life." Chinese in Changan and Luoyang wore Turkish and Persian clothing, men and women both favoring barbarian hats, especially when going riding. The fashionability of Turkish things even led some Chinese in the bustle of the capital to live in tents. South Asian forests were denuded for exotic timbers to go into Chinese gaming boards, furniture, decorative and religious carvings, mansions and palaces, temples and monasteries. Chinese cherished foreign drugs, foods, and spices for their medicinal and magical properties. Powerful Indian aromatics were highly coveted. Court ladies were so heavily scented that a procession could reportedly be detected several miles away.

Foreign animals delighted the ruling classes and the common people alike. Lions, rhinoceroses, and elephants were all presented to Tang emperors by foreign emissaries as gifts. Foreigners themselves were often cherished "goods." Wealthy Chinese families bought foreign slaves to serve in their households, and foreign musicians, dancers, dwarfs, and courtesans were sent to the Tang court as gifts from foreign rulers. Though there were periodic attempts to wean themselves from corrupting foreign exotics, the Chinese simply could not get enough foreign goods.[11]

Love of foreign things, however, should not be confused with love of foreigners. Among most Chinese, suspicion and hatred of foreigners always coexisted with love of their products. Indeed, Taizong's alliances with barbarian tribes were deeply opposed by his own largely Confucian court, which remained stubbornly committed to the idea of inherent Chinese superiority.

This ethnocentric worldview was reflected in the enormously influential Tang Code, promulgated by Taizong's legal advisors and later adopted, sometimes in its entirety, by subsequent dynasties, as well as by rulers in Japan, Korea, and Vietnam. At least on paper, the Tang Code called for the segregation of Chinese and non-Chinese. Under the code, foreign settlements were generally limited to the trade centers of Changan, Luoyang, Canton, and Yangzhou, and to the corridors along the land trade routes. Moreover, foreigners were not supposed to talk to Chinese unless they had business with them, and Chinese who married foreigners were to be exiled to a distance of 2,000 *li* (roughly 400 miles).

These provisions, however, were not strictly enforced. Indeed, it is difficult to square the segregationist Tang Code with the realities of the Tang imperial family. Taizong himself was the product of Chinese-barbarian intermarriage, and strategic marriages with the ruling families of the steppe were a common Tang device for cementing critical alliances. In addition, Taizong was extraordinarily receptive to foreigners and foreign influences. For example, Taizong relocated 70,000 people from Korea into China; Korean aristocrats and officials who settled in China were given honorific titles. At another point, over the intense objections of some advisors, Taizong brought a hundred Turkic families to Changan, to test whether they could be assimilated into Chinese culture. He also ensured that Chinese and non-Chinese soldiers served together in integrated military units.

Moreover, Taizong was conspicuously open to foreign religions. Around 645, China's most famous Buddhist monk, Xuanzang, returned to Changan after a sixteen-year pilgrimage in central Asia and India, bringing with him more than 650 Indian texts and 150 "authentic" relics of Buddha. Emperor Taizong received the home-coming monk with great honor, showering him with gifts and granting him a title. At the emperor's request, Xuanzang recorded his travels, describing in colorful detail his adventures in Bactria, Persia, Afghanistan, Kashmir, and eventually India, where he had been warmly received by the great Hindu king Siladitya.[12]

With Emperor Taizong as his patron, Xuanzang devoted the rest of his life to translating the Sanskrit texts he had brought back. The emperor was deeply influenced by the monk. The year before he died, when poor health led him to seek Buddhist longevity drugs, Taizong declared Buddhism superior to Chinese religions.

(Some historians now believe that the Buddhist drugs, administered by an Indian doctor claiming to be two hundred years old, unfortunately may have poisoned the emperor.)[13]

In fact, Taizong's reign was one of the most religiously pluralistic in Chinese history. Taizong welcomed not only Buddhism but the new, unfamiliar religions that foreigners from even farther west brought with them to Tang China. During his reign, Zoroastrianism, Manichaeism, Judaism, Islam, and Christianity—all introduced to China by travelers along the Silk Road—were freely practiced by their largely foreign followers. In Changan's Western Market, where the foreign population clustered, Persian merchants sacrificed live animals at Zoroastrian fire altars, while in the mornings and evenings muezzins atop minarets summoned the Muslim faithful to prayer. Today, a great mosque complex with both Chinese and Arabic inscriptions still stands in Changan.[14]

Nestorian Christianity, a mixture of Christian and Near Eastern religions, also came to China under Taizong. In 635, a Nestorian monk known by the Chinese as O Lo Pen (possibly a translation of "Ruben") arrived at the imperial court. Taizong granted him several audiences, pressing the monk each time with questions about his beliefs and at one point ordering the translation of his sacred books. Favorably impressed, Taizong not only authorized the construction of a Nestorian temple in Changan but issued the following edict:

The Way has more than one name. There is more than one Sage. Doctrines vary in different lands, their benefits reach all mankind. O Lo Pen, a man of great virtue from [the Roman Empire] has brought his images and books from afar to present them in our capital. After examining his doctrines we find them profound and pacific. After studying his principles we find that they stress what is good and important. His teaching is not diffuse and his reasoning is sound. This religion does good to all men. Let it be preached freely in Our Empire.[15]

Taizong's rule had unsettling effects on China's traditional social hierarchy. In 632, Taizong ordered that a genealogy be compiled of the empire's most important families. This proved humiliating. While intermarriage between Chinese and non-Chinese was not uncommon during the Tang period, China's most aristocratic clans remained "pure-blooded" Chinese, who looked down on the "semi-barbarian" clans of the northwest no matter how sinicized they were. To Taizong's fury, the report ranked the emperor's own family in lowly third place. Taizong rejected the draft, with instructions for its revision. Needless to say, the second edition of the report came back with the imperial family ranked first.

The new genealogy also did something else, of great import. It raised the status of the families of Taizong's highest ministers—whom the emperor selected on the basis of ability and Confucian learning—over China's most powerful hereditary clans. This change had two significant implications. First, it elevated the scholar-official over mere aristocratic lineage. Second, it foreshadowed the rise of meritocracy in Chinese government through the civil service examination system. The latter institution, which would transform not only Chinese but much of East Asian society, was not established by Taizong himself. The person principally responsible for its development was the extraordinary Empress Wu, a former concubine who became the first and only woman officially to rule China.[16]

THE EMPRESS AND THE APHRODISIACS

The son chosen by Taizong as his heir was an unusual personality, perhaps mentally disturbed. He refused to speak Chinese, insisting instead on speaking Turkish, following Turkish customs, and wearing Turkish dress. His homosexual affair with a court entertainer infuriated his father, who ordered the lover killed. Eventually the heir-prince himself was killed, and another of Taizong's sons ascended the throne as Emperor Gaozong. But Gaozong was weak and indolent, and for most of his long reign (649–683) he ruled as the puppet of his wife, the Empress Wu.

Wu Zhao was a woman of exceptional beauty and intelligence and ruthless political opportunism. At the age of twelve, she be-

came a concubine in the elderly Emperor Taizong's court. According to custom, after Taizong's death in 649, Wu Zhao should have
shaved her head and become a Buddhist nun, along with all the
other concubines who had not borne children. Whether she did or
not is the subject of debate, but in any event, Wu Zhao quickly in-
fatuated the new Emperor Gaozong, becoming his favorite consort
and giving birth to his son in 652. In 655 she was elevated to the
status of empress. Shortly afterward, to remove any threat to her
power, she reputedly disposed of Gaozong's first wife and a rival
concubine by ordering their arms and legs cut off and then dump-
ing both women in a wine vat. When her husband suffered a par-
alyzing stroke in 660, she became the de facto ruler of China. In
690, seven years after Gaozong's death, Wu Zhao officially seized
the throne, adopting the title of emperor and proclaiming a new
dynasty called Zhou. For the first and only time in Chinese history,
a woman assumed the Mandate of Heaven.[17]

A woman openly ruling as emperor of China violated the Confucian order, in which women obeyed men. (Not surprisingly, traditional historians, most of whom were Confucianists, did not
treat Empress Wu kindly.) Empress Wu, however, shrewdly used
Buddhism to legitimize her rule. With the help of one of her
lovers—a cosmetics and aphrodisiac peddler turned monk—
Empress Wu in 694 declared herself the reincarnation of the
Maitreya Buddha, a messiah who would one day rule over a future
paradise. Empress Wu also funded fantastic monuments such as
the giant Longmen Cave Buddha, carved out of solid stone and rising fifty-five feet high. Under the empress's rule, Buddhism in
China, already a powerful economic and political force, grew increasingly sinicized, branching off into new, highly influential Chinese sects and schools. In the eighth century China became a
leading source of Buddhist dissemination, with foreign pilgrims
and even monks from India traveling to China to honor Chinese
bodhisattvas.[18]

Empress Wu further transformed China's traditional social
structure. She removed from government positions members of the
northwestern aristocracy, who had monopolized power in China

for centuries. At one point she ordered hundreds of these aristocrats executed. The empress also systematized and expanded the
civil service examination system, creating a new class of government officials selected by competition, not bloodline. The result
was by no means a pure meritocracy: Only people from well-
placed families had access to the Confucian education necessary to
prepare for the examinations. Nevertheless, the empress's innovations marked a turning point in Chinese history. The newly established state examination system reflected the radical new principle
that government officials should be recruited solely on the basis
of their education and literary talent, as opposed to hereditary
privilege.[19]

Empress Wu, however, did not always follow this principle herself. Although her administration included many respected scholar-
officials, she also appointed a number of her own undistinguished
favorites to the court. She had her own secret police, many of them
her relatives, who eliminated her enemies in grisly ways. Amazing
rumors circulated about the empress's personal life, including tales
about the wild sexual adventures she had with two half brothers
when she was nearly eighty. Supposedly, the empress took so many
aphrodisiacs that she "sprouted new teeth and eyebrows."[20]

In 705, Empress Wu was finally deposed. After seven years of
internecine struggle, the Li family returned to the throne, and in
712 the Tang dynasty was restored. The new emperor, called Ming
Huang, or Brilliant Monarch, ruled over the most magnificent cultural flowering that China would ever see.

THE ZENITH OF TANG POWER

Along with Taizong, Ming Huang is considered one of the Tang
dynasty's greatest emperors. Upon ascending the throne, he purged
the court of Empress Wu's worst extravagances, abolished capital
punishment, and embarked on reforms throughout the empire. His
reign was the longest in Tang history, spanning nearly half a century (712–756). Like Taizong, Ming Huang combined military aggression with vigorous foreign diplomacy. Under his rule, China's

foreign influence reached its zenith, with non-Chinese peoples from Kashmir to Korea, from Iran to Vietnam, acknowledging Tang overlordship.

At the center of the vast Tang Empire was the imperial capital Changan, the most populous city on earth at the time, as well as the most cosmopolitan. As much as one-third of the city's population may have been foreign: emissaries from Arabia; merchants from India, Persia, and Syria; monks and students from Korea and Japan; tribal leaders from Nepal, Tibet, and Siberia; artists and performers from Bukhara, Samarkand, and Tashkent.

Among the Chinese residents of Changan, foreign music, fashions, and flavors were all the rage. The game of polo, almost certainly from Persia, became one of the favorite sports of Tang high society. On special occasions, female musical troupes from central Asia, seated on platforms carried by camels, played strange new instruments such as the *pipa* (a pear-shaped lute) to the delight of imperial officials. Aristocratic Chinese women wore tight-fitting dresses and shawls in the central Asian style. Other times, they wore loose trousers and rode horseback, in stark contrast to upper-class women of later periods in Chinese history, who could barely walk because of their bound feet.[21]

Changan was not just stylish and eclectic. It was a center of learning and high art. Under Ming Huang, literature, painting, historical and aesthetic theory, and especially poetry flourished as never before. The most celebrated poets in Chinese history, including Li Po, Tu Fu, and Wang Wei, lived during this period. In one historian's words, "Ch'ang-an was more than the functioning capital of a great empire: it was a cosmopolis, the greatest city in the world; it was the radiating center of civilization for the whole of Eastern Asia."[22]

Like Taizong, Emperor Ming Huang was famous for his openness to foreigners and tolerance of cultural and religious differences. In 713, Ming Huang received an Arab delegation of ambassadors from the Umayyad caliph Walid seeking China's military cooperation. In violation of Chinese imperial etiquette, the Arabs refused to perform the ceremonial kowtow—a forehead-to-ground prostration—before the emperor. The strangers asserted that Muslims prostrated themselves only to God and would merely bow for a king on earth. Displaying surprising restraint, Ming Huang waived the requirement, declaring, "Court etiquette is not the same in all countries." (A thousand years later, China's Manchu rulers would make the opposite decision. When the English ambassador Lord Amherst similarly refused to kowtow, he was turned away and the diplomatic mission was ended.) During the Tang Empire's golden age, foreign merchants and missionaries—whether Muslim, Buddhist, Jewish, Christian, Zoroastrian, or Manichaean—worshipped freely at their own temples, without fear of persecution, and sometimes even with imperial military protection.[23]

The tolerance of the Tang is all the more striking when compared to the conduct of the two other major empires of the time: the Umayyad caliphate and the Byzantine Empire, both far more religiously dogmatic.

The Umayyad Empire (661–750) was built around Islamic orthodoxy, rejecting all other religions as heresy. Although persecution of non-Muslims was relatively mild under the early Umayyad rulers, in 704–5 the same Caliph Walid just mentioned rounded up the Christian nobles of Armenia and burned them to death in their own churches. Others were crucified or decapitated. A few years later, Caliph Umar II issued the following pronouncement: "O ye who believe! The non-Moslems are nothing but dirt. Allah has created them to be partisans of Satan; most treacherous in regard to all they do; whose whole endeavor in this nether life is useless, though they themselves imagine that they are doing fine work. Upon them rests the curse of Allah, of the Angels and of man collectively." Non-Muslims were not allowed to hold public office. (By contrast, when the Sassanian prince of Persia, defeated by the Arabs, fled to China in 674, he was welcomed at Changan and made a general of the Imperial Guard.)[24]

The Christian Byzantine Empire was even more extreme in its persecution of heretics. In the seventh century, paganism was essentially eradicated, through forced conversions, torture, starvation, and brutal massacres. Anti-Semitism pervaded the empire, and various Byzantine rulers from Heraclius to Leo III ordered the forced baptism of Jews. Under Justinian II (685–695, 705–711), waves of vicious persecutions continued, and members of the rival Armenian Orthodox Church were condemned to death by burning. Justinian's excesses were so egregious—Gibbon claims he let his own mother be scourged by one of his chief advisors—that his nose was cut off after he was deposed, earning him the name Justinian Rhinotmetus, meaning "slit-nose." By the mid-eighth century, the Byzantine Empire was a shadow of its former self, most of its lands having been conquered by the Arabs.

The rise of the great religious empires of Christendom and Islam—along with the costs of their monotheistic zeal—will be discussed in Part Two. For now, however, suffice it to say that the largest powers of Europe and the Middle East from 600 to 800 were organized around their respective orthodoxies, "each secure in the conviction that unbelievers could offer nothing of importance to followers of the true faith." The rigidity of these societies contrasted sharply with the far "looser-textured" and less dogmatic Tang dynasty, in which "China attained perhaps the most vigorous and variegated cultural efflorescence of her long history."[25]

––––––––––

Unlike virtually every other Chinese dynasty, the Tang rulers took a keen interest in contemporaneous empires and sought to inform themselves about daily life in foreign cities. Tang imperial documents include surprisingly detailed descriptions of Byzantium, called Fu Lin by the Chinese:

> Fu Lin is the ancient [Roman Empire]. It is situated on the Western Sea. To the south-east it borders Persia, to the north-east is the territory of the Western Turks. The land is very populous, and there are many towns. The walls of the capital are of dressed stone, and more than 100,000 families reside in the city. There is a gate 200 feet high, entirely covered with

bronze [the Golden Gate]. In the imperial palace there is a human figure of gold decorated with glass and crystal, gold, ivory, and rare woods. The roofs are made of cement, and are flat. In the heat of summer machines worked by water power carry up water to the roof, which is used to refresh the air by falling in showers in front of the windows.

Twelve ministers assist the King in the government. When the King leaves his palace he is attended by a man carrying a bag, into which any person is free to drop petitions. The men wear their hair cut short and are clothed in embroidered robes which leave the right arm bare. The women wear their hair in the form of a crown. The people of Fu Lin esteem wealth, and they are fond of wine and sweetmeats. On every seventh day [the Christian Sunday] no work is done.

From this country come byssus, coral, asbestos, and many other curious products. They have very skilled conjurers who can spit fire from their mouths, pour water out of their hands, and drop pearls from their feet. Also, they have skilled physicians who cure certain diseases by extracting worms from the head.

Similarly, Tang accounts describe Arabia and the origins of Islam as follows:

[Arabia] was formerly part of Persia. The men have large noses and black beards. They carry silver mounted swords on a silver girdle. They drink no wine and have no music. The women are white and veil the face when they leave the house. There are large halls for worship which can hold several hundreds of persons. Five times daily they worship the god of Heaven. Every seventh day [Friday] their King [the Caliph] seated on high, addresses his subjects, saying: "Those who die in battle will be reborn in Paradise. Those who fight bravely will obtain happiness." Therefore their men are very valiant soldiers. The land is poor and cannot grow cereals, they hunt and live on meat, and collect honey among the rocks. Their dwellings are formed like the hoods of a cart [tents]. They have grapes which are sometimes as big as a hen's egg.

In the Sui period . . . a man [Mohammed] of the western peoples (hu), a Persian subject, was guarding flocks in the mountains near Medina. A Lion-man [The Archangel Gabriel] said to him: "To the west of this mountain, in a cave there is a sword and a black stone [the black stone of Ka'aba] with white lettering. Whoever obtains these two objects will reign over mankind." The man went to the place and found everything as he had been told. . . . Afterwards the [Arabs] became very powerful. They destroyed Persia, defeated the King of Fu Lin, invaded northern India, attacked Samarkand and Tashkent. From the south-western sea their empire reached to the western borders of our territory.[26]

Whatever their imprecisions or caricatures, these accounts of Byzantium and Islam reflect the spirit of confident curiosity, as well as the effort to gain an understanding of foreign cultures, characteristic of the Tang. While these accounts may sound unsophisticated to the modern reader, they display far more knowledge about the outside world than, for example, the records of the Manchu Qing emperors, who ruled a thousand years later (1644–1912). Despite world advances in communication and technology, the Qing emperors were stunningly—almost willfully—ignorant about the rising European powers, whom they preferred to lump all together as "barbarians that send tribute." In an imperial text from the mid-eighteenth century, the following confusions can be found:

1. Italy presented tribute to China in 1667 (it was actually Holland), and the Pope came to do so in 1725 [not the case].
2. France is the same as Portugal.
3. Sweden is a dependency of Holland.
4. The Spanish in the Philippines are the Portuguese who took Malacca and Macau.
5. Sweden and England are shortened names for Holland.

As late as 1818, the powerful empires of Britain, Russia, and France—then on the verge of taking over China—were listed in Qing imperial records as Chinese "vassal states" alongside Kelantan, Trengganu, and other tiny kingdoms on the Malay peninsula. Indeed, some historians cite the Qing rulers' profound ignorance of the West as a factor contributing to China's inability to resist European domination.[27]

———

Was Tang China in its golden age world dominant—a hyperpower of the same magnitude as Achaemenid Persia or ancient Rome? What makes this question difficult is the fact that seventh- and eighth-century China was surrounded by kingdoms and tribal alliances much smaller than itself yet strong enough to pose serious military threats—indeed, strong enough even to defeat Tang forces when the latter were deployed at less than full strength, as was almost always the case in an empire so vast. In 678, a Tang army of some 180,000 was beaten by Tibetans at Lake Koko Nor in a contest for control of western lands. In 751, a much smaller Tang army lost the battle of Talas to the Abbasid caliphate near modern-day Samarkand—although the battle was probably no more than a border skirmish and the Arab troops far outnumbered the Tang contingent.

Complicating matters further is the frequently deployed Tang strategy of subduing rival kingdoms through shrewd diplomacy backed by the threat of force rather than by bloody conquest. This strategy was enormously successful, but it left the Tang vulnerable, its dominion dependent on the loyalty of foreign kings and subjects who were often held in contempt by the Chinese and who reciprocated these sentiments with undisguised hostility toward China.

Despite this vulnerability, the global preeminence of Tang China is hardly open to serious doubt. Indeed, the extent to which the Tang towered over its contemporaries is breathtaking. Consider the "great powers" of post-Roman Europe. The mighty Frankish Empire was arguably the greatest Western European power in the eighth and ninth centuries, boasting perhaps five to ten million subjects under the rule of the celebrated Charlemagne. Ming Huang ruled sixty million. At roughly the same time, the Byzantine Empire probably had a population of no more than ten to thirteen million. Even the Umayyad caliphate of the Middle East—by far the most populous and powerful empire after Tang China—ruled at most thirty-six million subjects. Taken altogether, the Tang army of roughly 500,000 to 750,000 professional soldiers dwarfed the Umayyad forces. In short, Tang China in its heyday starkly surpassed all other powers of the world in population, wealth, and total military might.[28]

THE TWILIGHT OF THE TANG AND THE RISE OF INTOLERANCE

As with the ancient Roman and Persian empires, the very tolerance that was indispensable to the extraordinary reach and influence of the Tang Empire also sowed the seeds of its decline. Ironically, the fall of the Tang can be traced to an attack by a foreigner who was allowed too much power. And once the Tang Empire began to decline, intolerance set in.

The Tang policy of strategic tolerance meant that the empire never tried to impose a Han Chinese identity on its non-Chinese subjects. As a result, no common political, linguistic, or cultural "glue" bound "barbarians" and Chinese together in the sprawling Tang Empire. On the contrary, even in the early eighth century Ming Huang found himself ruling over large numbers of distinct, fiercely independent communities with no loyalty or even goodwill toward their Chinese overlords.

To maintain order across the empire, Ming Huang had to rely on an ever-larger proportion of foreign forces, particularly Turkic peoples like the Xi and Khitan. The chiefs of these tribes were made military governors who commanded great permanent frontier armies and wielded virtually unchecked power over civil, economic, and military affairs. Between 712 and 733, the Tang established nine such military governorships. The military governors often acted on their own initiative to expand Tang borders.

Because successful aggression was rewarded, independent military actions grew more frequent. As a result, loss of central control and military dominance by foreigners grew more pronounced over the course of Ming Huang's reign.

In one sense, the power and autonomy granted to non-Chinese military commanders reflected the extraordinary success of the Tang effort to cross the divide between the Chinese and the "barbarian" peoples of the steppe. But the vast foreign armies enlisted by the Tang remained just that—foreign armies. When these Turks or Tibetans or Mongolians, led by their ambitious generals, began to feel used and manipulated by the Chinese, they quickly turned on the Tang. In the end, the great Tang dynasty was brought low by foreigners, who never really came to see themselves as part of the Middle Kingdom.

The fatal blow was the An Lushan Rebellion of 755. In the 740s, at around the age of sixty, Ming Huang fell hopelessly in love with one of his son's consorts, Yang Guifei. In a very short time, Yang Guifei had almost total control over the smitten emperor, and the imperial court was filled with her corrupt relatives and lackeys. It was through Yang Guifei's influence that An Lushan, an obese military man, acquired the power to organize a revolt that would forever change China.

Historians differ on the precise ethnic origins of An Lushan. According to one source, he was a Turk of the Khitan tribe; according to others, he was Turk-Sogdian. There is a consensus, however, that he was non-Chinese, grossly fat, illiterate, and of vulgar wit. It is also clear that An Lushan was a man of considerable cunning, adept at pleasing his superiors. By 750, he had attained the rank of general and become a court favorite, captivating the fancy of Yang Guifei and entertaining the emperor with his clownish buffoonery.[29]

Although others in the imperial family suspected An Lushan's motives, Yang Guifei took him under her protection, even adopting him as her son. As a result, he had the unheard-of privilege of visiting her in the inner palace, which suggests, as many historians have speculated, that the two had an affair. In any case, despite his low birth and alien heritage, An Lushan accumulated extraordinary power. In 754, to the horror of the emperor's relatives, An Lushan was appointed commissioner of the imperial stables, a strategically important post. On the eve of the An Lushan Rebellion, the general had sole military command over three critical northern regions, including modern-day Beijing, Shanxi, and Shandong, with some 200,000 men and 30,000 horses at his disposal.

Meanwhile, at the court, An Lushan continued to play the self-mocking bumpkin. At one point, rumors that An Lushan was planning a revolt reached the emperor. Summoned before him, An Lushan promptly fell weeping to the emperor's feet, swearing his loyalty and declaring slander by his detractors. The emperor was completely convinced, and lavished An Lushan with new honors.[30]

Shortly afterward, in 755, An Lushan rose in rebellion. Both Changan and the eastern capital of Luoyang fell instantly to An Lushan's forces. The emperor and Yang Guifei, along with a few troops, fled ignominiously to Sichuan. The emperor's troops then mutinied, demanding that he kill his consort, whom they blamed for their plight. Left with no choice, the heartbroken emperor ordered his chief eunuch to strangle his beloved concubine. Her corpse was thrown into a ditch, and the crushed emperor himself soon abdicated in favor of his son. It was not until eight years later, in 763, that the An Lushan Rebellion was finally suppressed and the Tang family restored to power.

The An Lushan Rebellion was a turning point in Chinese history, marking the beginning of the long Tang decline. Prior to the rebellion, the Tang emperors had tried to blur the divide between Chinese and non-Chinese, pursuing deliberate policies of ethnic and cultural intermingling. For years, this policy proved surprisingly successful. Even as the empire expanded its dominion over more and more territory, Tang China drew strength and vitality—economic, military, and cultural—from the participation of foreigners at all levels of Chinese society. All this was to change. By the late eighth century, the openness of the Tang to foreign peoples and foreign ideas had become a source not of power but of division, insecurity, and violence.[31]

Even before the An Lushan Rebellion, incursions and insurrections by non-Chinese peoples like the Tibetans, the Western Turks, and the Nanchao had occurred in the frontier regions of the Tang territories. With the An Lushan crisis, these military defeats intensified and the Tang frontiers began disintegrating. Tibetan power expanded into China's western regions, and the Tang rulers lost control over the lucrative Silk Road. At the same time, regional military commanders across China—almost all of foreign descent—grew increasingly defiant of the Tang central government. Islam spread rapidly throughout the Tang's central Asian lands, eventually replacing Buddhism as the dominant religion. But whereas in the past the Tang rulers had welcomed Islamic practitioners and mosques as part of their cosmopolitan society, Islam now became a rival force and a threat to Tang power.[32]

In the late eighth century, intolerance seized Tang China and spread like a cancer. Chinese high and low began blaming foreigners for all of China's problems. An uneducated Turk, after all, had nearly brought down the Tang Empire. It was humiliating, moreover, that Ming Huang's government had permitted barbarians to so dominate China's military leadership.

Perhaps the most reviled of the "barbarians" were the Uighurs. In exchange for their support during the An Lushan Rebellion, the desperate Tang emperors lavished the Uighurs with gifts, Chinese royal titles, marriages with Tang princesses, and a monopoly on horse imports into China. The latter arrangement worked as follows: Each year the Uighurs brought to China tens of thousands of horses, many of them weak and sickly, and demanded forty pieces of silk for each horse. This rate of exchange was extremely unfavorable to the Chinese, and before long the Tang imperial coffers were depleted. None of this stopped the Uighurs from routinely abusing Tang officials, raiding imperial courts, kidnapping Chinese children, and killing Chinese citizens.

In the end, Taizong's experiment with a "universal empire" proved a failure. Tang China ultimately could not overcome the deep-seated, centuries-old Chinese contempt for and fear of barbarians. Unlike Rome, China never developed a concept of political citizenship that could apply and appeal equally to Chinese and non-Chinese alike. Rather, the overarching political and social identity that united China remained essentially ethnic—with barbarians on the other side of the line. When cracks appeared in the empire and non-Chinese groups like the Uighurs and Tibetans became an increasingly aggressive threat, native Chinese intolerance surged.

In 760, thousands of Arab and Persian merchants were slaughtered by Chinese brigands in Yangchow. In 779, the Tang emperor Dezong banished foreign envoys and banned non-Chinese groups from wearing Chinese dress. Imperial policy toward the people of the steppe changed. There was no longer even a pretense that the northern nomads were "equal partners" with the Chinese. At best, the barbarians were the "claws and teeth" of the empire whose duty it was to defend the Tang frontiers for the benefit of the Chinese.

As xenophobia set in, Tang cosmopolitanism rapidly dissipated. Chinese scholar-officials from the southeast, who had risen through the examination system, spread the idea that China's moral standards and superior culture had been polluted by the decadent barbarian-blooded aristocrats from the north. Among the literati, a movement grew to reassert traditional Chinese values and ancient Chinese literary styles. Foreign influences and ideas were now seen as corrupting, and the roads to central Asia were literally closed. In a historical pattern that would reappear many times, China turned self-destructively inward, cutting itself off from the rest of the world, trying to achieve "purity" by ridding itself of foreign elements.[33]

Tang intolerance intensified in the ninth century. In 836, an imperial decree prohibited Chinese from interacting with "people of colour," referring to foreigners from Southeast Asia or beyond the Pamir Mountains, including Arabs, Persians, Indians, Malays, Sumatrans, and other groups. More striking still was the burst of religious persecution under Emperor Wuzong, an ardent Taoist. Manichaeism, the religion of many Uighurs, was first to be targeted. In 840, Wuzong ordered the execution of seventy Manichaean nuns, the destruction of Manichaean temples, and the confiscation of Manichaean lands. Five years later, in the great proscription of 845, the emperor struck at all foreign religions. Christian and Zoroastrian churches and temples were suppressed, and their priests forbidden from preaching, "in order that they may no longer corrupt" Chinese "simplicity and moral purity."

Buddhism, above all, despite its sinicization and popularity among the Chinese, came under attack. The Buddhist church had grown increasingly decadent in the late Tang period, and whereas the imperial government was financially strained, the Buddhist monasteries were scandalously wealthy. Some of this wealth was enjoyed by corrupt monks, who broke the Buddhist vow of poverty to live in open luxury. Most of the church's wealth took the form of large monastic estates and precious metals cast as statues, bells, and other religious objects. Emperor Wuzong's proscription decree specifically accused Buddhism, which it labeled a "foreign religion," of debilitating China, morally and economically.[34]

Partly to increase dwindling imperial revenues, Wuzong forcibly secularized 260,000 monks and nuns, returning them to the tax registers. More than 4,000 Buddhist monasteries and 40,000 smaller temples were shut down or converted to public use. Large properties belonging to the church were confiscated, and bronze statuaries melted down to make coins. But Wuzong's attempt to eradicate Buddhism proved unsuccessful. Many officials throughout the empire were sympathetic to Buddhism and quietly resisted the emperor's orders. Moreover, just two years after Wuzong's great proscription, a new emperor ascended the throne and reversed his predecessor's anti-Buddhist policies, restoring damaged temples and even building new monasteries. Although past its heyday, Buddhism in China would survive for centuries to come. By contrast, Manichaeism, Nestorian Christianity, and Zoroastrianism all eventually disappeared from China.[35]

The prestige and power of the Tang rulers declined throughout the ninth century. Regional warlords came to rule their own kingdoms, and the central government lost fiscal control. Between 875 and 884, another series of uprisings shattered the empire. The final collapse of the Tang dynasty was protracted and bloody. Changan was looted and ravaged. In Canton, rebels massacred 120,000 foreign merchants, including Muslims, Jews, Christians, and Zoroastrians. In 904, a regional commander named Zhu Wen captured the emperor, executing him along with his entire imperial entourage, including servants. The dismantled palaces of Changan were floated down the Wei River to Luoyang, where Zhu Wen had set up his own capital. The end of the Tang dynasty is usually dated as 907, when Zhu Wen slaughtered the last boy-emperor of the house of Tang.[36]

———————

After the fall of the Tang Empire, China turned increasingly insular and xenophobic. Chinese in staggering numbers migrated from the north, where the barbarian threat was greatest, to the south, which would henceforth be home to the great majority of China's enormous population. Ironically, it would be the barbarians who a few centuries later would be tolerating the Chinese and creating history's next world-dominant power.

FOUR

THE GREAT MONGOL EMPIRE

Cosmopolitan Barbarians

Just as God gave different fingers to the hand so has He given different ways to men.

—MONGKE KHAN, CIRCA 1250

By the arms of Zingis and his descendants the globe was shaken: the sultans were overthrown: the caliphs fell, and the Caesars trembled on their throne.

—EDWARD GIBBON, 1776

Seven and a half centuries ago, on a high plateau in the Mongolian steppe, where today there is nothing but wild grass, herders, and the occasional Canadian mining convoy, there stood the royal tent city of Karakorum. From their yak-felt yurts—circular white tents that the Mongols call *gers*—illiterate Mongol khans ruled over an empire far larger than the Romans ever conquered. The nomadic Mongols had no science, engineering, or written language of their own. They had no agriculture and could not even bake bread. Yet they ruled over half the known world, including the most magnificent cities of the time: Baghdad, Belgrade, Bukhara, Kiev, Moscow, Damascus, and Samarkand.[1]

In 1162, seventy years before Karakorum was erected, a boy named Temujin was born on a desolate hill in a harsh part of the steppe. At the time, the Mongols were a fragmented collection of kin-based tribes and clans, locked in cycles of attack and retribution, killing each other's men, kidnapping each other's women, and stealing each other's animals. Temujin's mother, Hoelun, was herself "stolen": Temujin's father had abducted her shortly after her marriage to a man from a rival tribe. When Temujin was nine, his father was killed, but not before betrothing Temujin to a girl named Borte. Shortly afterward, Hoelun and her five hungry children were abandoned by their clan. As the harsh winter set in, the family survived by eating berries and roots and wearing "the skins of dogs and mice." By the time he was sixteen, Temujin had killed his half brother, a taboo act under Mongol codes, and was a renegade on the run.[2]

How did this outcast, who became Genghis Khan, unite the warring tribes of the steppe and conquer more territory and people than any other man in history? How did the Mongols, lacking any sophisticated technology of their own, come to wield the massive siege engines—catapults, trebuchets, explosives, portable towers—that allowed them to defeat the great walled cities of medieval China, Persia, and eastern Europe? How did a relatively small band of nomads maintain and govern for 150 years an empire that stretched from the gates of Vienna to the Sea of Japan?

Undoubtedly, Genghis Khan was a brilliant military tactician. The Mongols were also utterly ruthless in battle. They poured molten silver into the eyes and ears of their enemies. They killed treacherous women by sewing up their orifices. Genghis Khan himself allegedly said that happiness was "to crush your enemies, to see them fall at your feet—to take their horses and goods and hear the lamentation of their women. That is best."[3]

At the same time, Genghis Khan pursued policies that were remarkably tolerant, even by modern standards and certainly by comparison to contemporary rulers. While Europe was burning heretics at the stake, Genghis Khan decreed religious freedom for everyone. He also embraced ethnic diversity, deliberately breaking down the tribal barriers that had previously divided the people of the steppe and drawing into his service the most talented and useful individuals of all his conquered populations. Two generations later, his grandsons Mongke, Hulegu, and Khubilai followed the same strategy on an even larger scale, ultimately building the largest continuous land empire that has ever existed. Far more than their bloodthirstiness, ethnic and religious tolerance allowed the Mongols to achieve and maintain world dominance.

CONQUERING THE STEPPE

The first European to enter the Mongolian steppe may have been the friar Giovanni Di Plano Carpini. In 1246, after a year of crossing Europe on horseback, the elderly friar arrived at the capital of the Mongol Empire in Karakorum. In fact, Carpini was acting as a spy for Pope Innocent IV, who commissioned the friar to learn as much as he could about the Mongols who had terrified and conquered so much of Europe. The unimpressed Carpini described the Gobi steppe as follows:

> Here are no towns or cities, but everywhere sandy barrens, not a hundredth part of the whole being fertile except where it is watered by rivers, which are very rare. . . . This land is nearly destitute of trees, although well adapted for the pasturage of cattle. Even the emperor and princes and all others warm themselves and cook their victuals with the fires of horse and cow dung. . . . The climate is very intemperate, as in the middle of summer there are terrible storms of thunder and lightning by which many people are killed, and even then there are great falls of snow and such tempests of cold winds blow that sometimes people can hardly sit on horseback. In one of these we had to throw ourselves down on the ground and could not see through the prodigious dust. There are often showers of hail, and sudden, intolerable heats followed by extreme cold.[4]

These were likely the same geographic conditions that faced the sixteen-year-old Temujin in 1178. The social conditions, however, were entirely different. In 1178, there was no Mongol Empire or capital—indeed, no Mongol nation. The steppe was inhabited by dozens of vaguely related, constantly warring tribes and clans. The Mongols' closest relations were the Tatars, Khitans, and Manchus to the east and the Turkic tribes of central Asia to the west. But whereas the Tatars and the central Asian tribes had consolidated themselves into powerful confederacies, the Mongols in 1178 were subdivided into scattered rival bands headed by local chieftains or khans.[5]

Among the peoples of the steppe, the Mongols were near the bottom of the heap, seen as "scavengers who competed with the wolves to hunt down the small animals." Nevertheless, among the Mongols themselves, some clans—for example, the Tayichiuds—claimed to be more "highborn" than others, and they asserted their dominance brashly. Later in his life, Temujin would break down the blood-based hierarchy of the steppe, replacing the entire kinship system with a new social order based on merit and personal loyalty. At age sixteen, however, Temujin was nothing and nobody. Moreover, the Tayichiuds sought to punish him for the killing of his half brother in their territory.[6]

The historical records get particularly murky at this point. It appears that Temujin was captured by the Tayichiuds, endured a period of enslavement, then escaped. Not long afterward, Temujin returned to the clan of his betrothed and claimed Borte as his bride. Although he knew of Temujin's problems with the Tayichiuds, Borte's father honored the promise he had made seven years earlier. One biographer speculates that Temujin at sixteen already had "some special attraction or ability" that impressed people. In any event, as a wedding present Borte's father gave Temujin a coat of black sable, the most valued fur on the steppe. This gift allowed Temujin to take his first step toward power.

Instead of keeping the coat, Temujin presented it as a gift to an influential elder named Torghil, also known as Ong Khan, leader of the powerful Kereyid tribal confederacy. Linked commercially with central Asia, the Kereyids, who were of Turkic origin, had a much more developed culture than the Mongols. The Kereyids also practiced a steppe variant of Nestorian Christianity, worshipping from their tents the powerful shaman Jesus, who had healed the sick and triumphed over death. More important for Temujin's purposes, the Kereyids were united and large in number, controlling a great expanse of the Gobi steppe. By giving Ong Khan his own wedding gift, Temujin symbolically acknowledged him as a father figure and established the first of many shrewd alliances.[7]

Over the next quarter century, this alliance would prove pivotal to Temujin's rise to dominance over the steppe. Early on, the Kereyids helped Temujin rescue his new wife, who was kidnapped shortly after their marriage by raiders from the Merkid tribe. By this time, Temujin had already acquired a small but loyal following. Together with Ong Khan's men, Temujin began to conquer various smaller tribes of the steppe, including most notably the Tayichiuds, the clan that had abandoned Temujin and his starving family when he was a boy. With each victory Temujin pursued the same basic strategy. He killed off the defeated tribal leaders, including most of the male "aristocracy," then incorporated the rest of the tribe into his own following—not as slaves but as equal members.

By consolidating forces, Temujin and Ong Khan also defeated the Tatars, a tribal confederacy much richer than the Kereyids. Temujin is said to have been deeply struck by the sumptuous possessions of the Tatars—silver cradles, pearl-embroidered blankets, satin and gold-threaded clothing even for children—the likes of which the Mongols had never seen. Further breaking down the traditional tribal bonds that long had divided the steppe, Temujin encouraged intermarriage, taking on for himself two Tatar sisters as additional wives. He also asked his mother to symbolically adopt as her own sons orphaned boys from each of the defeated tribes. Thus, Temujin's "brothers" included a Merkid, a Tayichiud, a Jurkin, a Tatar, and so on.[8]

Although still subordinate to Ong Khan, Temujin was now in command of a significant intertribal, interethnic army numbering as many as 80,000. In 1203, Temujin ordered a reform that would radically transform the steppe of central Asia. For generations, the people of the steppe had been bound by male kinship ties. The more closely related two men were by blood, the more loyal they were supposed to be to each other. To break down the traditional clan- and lineage-based divisions that fragmented the steppe, Temujin reorganized the Mongol army. He divided his warriors into interethnic squads of ten, who were ordered to live with and defend one another as brothers, regardless of their tribal origin. The eldest of the squad was designated the leader, unless the group decided otherwise. Ten squads in turn formed a company, ten companies formed a battalion, and ten battalions formed a *tumen*, or army of 10,000, the leader of which Temujin personally selected. This intertribal, interethnic decimal system eventually came to organize not just the military but all of Mongol society.[9]

Whereas traditional steppe leaders had always surrounded themselves with their closest relatives, Temujin selected his lieutenants and advisors on the basis of talent and proven loyalty. Many of Temujin's closest confidants and highest-ranking generals—for example, Boorchu, who commanded a *tumen* in the Altai Mountains, and Subodei, who eventually conquered Poland and Hungary—were not related to him at all. Conversely, Temujin had no problem excluding from his inner circle "blood" relations whom he did not trust. Indeed, in glaring violation of Mongol tradition, none of Temujin's uncles, brothers, or nephews was initially given a top military post. Because of Temujin's emphasis on merit rather than kinship, camel boys and cowherds became generals. So many Tatars rose to prominence in the Mongol Empire that over the centuries the names "Tatar" and "Mongol" sometimes became synonymous.

Temujin's judgment in selecting his generals was unerring and surprisingly subtle. He valued not just courage but cunning and patience. The brave but foolhardy were not allowed to lead others, but instead were assigned to the important task of protecting the military supplies. Reportedly, Temujin once refused to promote a warrior, offering the following explanation:

> No man is more valiant than Yessoutai; no one has rarer gifts. But, as the longest marches do not tire him, as he feels neither

hunger nor thirst, he believes that his officers and soldiers do not suffer from such things. That is why he is not fitted for high command. A general should think of hunger and thirst, so he may understand the suffering of those under him, and he should husband the strength of his men and beasts.[10]

In 1203, Temujin took the audacious step of requesting a marriage between his eldest son, Jochi, and Ong Khan's daughter. Ong Khan and Temujin had been allies for more than two decades. Under Ong Khan's overlordship, Temujin had conquered most of the steppe peoples, with the exception of the powerful Naiman confederation in the west. Nevertheless, despite Temujin's reputation as the greatest military commander on the steppe, Ong Khan saw Temujin and his family as unworthy of the aristocratic Kereyids. Ong Khan was also likely manipulated by rivals of Temujin, who were jealous of his influence over the aging Kereyid ruler. In any event, according to Marco Polo, writing a century later, Ong Khan's reaction was, essentially, "Is not [he] ashamed to seek my daughter in marriage? Does he not know that he is my vassal and my thrall? Go back to him and tell him that I would sooner commit my daughter to flames than give her to him as his wife."

Shortly afterward, however, he sent another message to Temujin, saying that he had changed his mind and would approve the marriage after all. En route to the ceremony, Temujin learned that the wedding was a ploy and that Ong Khan had ordered his army to ambush Temujin's camp and slay him in his tent. Far outnumbered, Temujin ordered the warriors with him to disperse. He and his closest officers fled for their lives, arriving eventually at the shores of Lake Baljuna. What happened next has become legendary in Mongol lore.

A wild horse appeared from nowhere. The men, on the verge of starvation, took this as a sign of divine intervention and slaughtered and skinned the horse. Relying on an ancient cooking technique,

they cut up the meat and made a large bag from the horsehide into which they put the meat and some water. They gathered

dried dung to make a fire, but they could not put the hide ket-
tle directly on the fire. Instead, they heated rocks in the fire
until glowing hot, then they dropped the hot rocks into the
mixture of meat and water . . . After a few hours, the starving
men feasted on boiled horseflesh.

The companions then swore eternal allegiance to one another
and to Temujin as their leader. Strikingly, these men, although just
twenty in number, hailed from nine different tribes and included
Buddhists, Christians, and Muslims, as well as animists like Temujin, who worshipped the Eternal Blue Sky and the God Mountain
of Burkhan Khaldun. This multiethnic, multicreedal oath of brotherhood would come to symbolize the new form of society that
Temujin, as Genghis Khan, would soon create.[11]

First, however, Temujin had to defeat Ong Khan. From Lake
Baljuna, Temujin sent word throughout the steppe of his plan for
counterattack. Over the next few days, his army reassembled in its
units of tens and hundreds all across the steppe. A few warriors
rode ahead to station fresh teams of horses at crucial points. Temujin and his reorganized army then raced back toward Ong Khan's
territory.

In the end, it was Temujin who ambushed the Kereyid leaders.
Temujin and his men descended on the Kereyids as they celebrated—quite drunkenly—their perceived victory over him. After
three days of hard battle, Temujin triumphed. Ong Khan fled with
his court, while much of his army deserted to Temujin's side. As
was always Temujin's policy, he accepted Ong Khan's followers as
long as they had not committed any previous act of treachery
against their former leader. Essentially folding the powerful
Kereyid forces into his own, Temujin went on to conquer the
Naimans, the last great steppe confederation not yet under his control. By 1204, Temujin had defeated every tribe on the steppe. His
territory extended from the Gobi Desert to Manchuria to the Arctic tundra. Much of this land, however, was sparsely populated. It
included perhaps twenty million animals but probably only around
a million people.

In 1206, to legitimize his rule, Temujin convened a great meeting, or *khuriltai*, of representatives from every part of the steppe. In a massive open-air ceremony that included days of solemnity alternating with days of festivities, sports, and music, hundreds of thousands saw Temujin installed as Genghis Khan—originally Chinggis Khan, from the Mongolian *chin*, meaning "strong, firm, unshakable, and fearless"—ruler of all the tribes. The official name he chose for his new empire was the Great Mongol Nation, but he made a point of calling his followers the People of the Felt Walls, referring to the material out of which all the nomads made their tents. Out of the many warring tribes, clans, and lineages of the steppe, Genghis Khan had created a "people."[12]

———

Once in power, Genghis Khan took a number of steps, some quite radical, to maintain unity in his new empire. He prohibited the stealing of animals and the kidnapping of women, two age-old sources of strife on the steppe. Punishments were severe: Any man who stole a horse or steer, for example, was "cut into two parts." Also condemned to death were adulteresses, spies, sorcerers, and "men given to infamous vices." More remarkably, Genghis Khan decreed absolute freedom of worship for everyone, whether they were Buddhists, Christians, Muslims, or shamanists. All religious leaders, monks, "criers of mosques," and "persons who are dedicated to religious practice" were exempted from taxation and public service. He himself remained an animist, worshipping the spiritual forces of nature.[13]

At the same time, Genghis Khan continued to annex different tribes and ethnicities, such as the Koreans and the forest tribes of Siberia, into the Great Mongol Nation. To overcome ethnic divisions, Genghis Khan absorbed their warriors into his army and arranged marriages between his own children and those of the submitting tribal leaders. He also recruited the most able of their men, bringing to the Mongols talents and skills they had never before possessed. This is how the Mongols acquired writing.

Tradition has it that when Genghis Khan conquered the Naimans in 1204, he was amazed to discover that their khan kept a Uighur scribe who memorialized his official pronouncements. The Uighur people, closely related to the Mongols, had obtained their script from Christian missionaries; the script was based on the Syriac alphabet and originally flowed horizontally, from right to left. Genghis Khan took the Naiman's Uighur scribe into his entourage. More important, he ordered the creation of a new writing system, essentially adapting the Uighur script to the Mongolian language. The new Uighur-Mongolian script was almost exactly like the old Uighur script, except that it flowed vertically, from top to bottom, the way Chinese characters do. Over the years, Genghis Khan continued to recruit and rely on Uighur scribes to facilitate communication throughout the empire.[14]

By 1206, the man who started off as Temujin—an outcast who supposedly feared dogs and cried easily as a boy—was at the age of forty-four ruler of all the steppe. But Genghis Khan was still just an emperor of nomads. He had yet to take on the civilized world.

CONQUERING EASTWARD

In the early thirteenth century, China was divided and decaying— "like an aged woman, sunk in meditation, clad perhaps in too elaborate garments, surrounded by many children, little heeded." But compared to the steppe, China was still magnificent, rich with pagodas and pleasure lakes, silver dragons with turquoise eyes, carved jade, ivory chess pieces, phoenix-eared vases. Whereas Genghis Khan's subjects were hunters or herders, China's population included mandarins and scholars, poets and calligraphers, bridge builders, beggars, bronze-casters, dukes, princes, and of course the emperor.[15]

At that point, however, China had more than one emperor. Northern China was dominated by the kingdom of the Jurchens, themselves originally a "barbarian" forest-dwelling people from Manchuria. From their capital, Zhongdu, now Beijing, the Jurchen emperor ruled more than 50 million subjects. Southern China was dominated by the even larger, more powerful Song dynasty, based in Hangzhou, where the Chinese Son of Heaven ruled some 60 million people. Both the Jurchen and Song emperors had far more military manpower than Genghis Khan, not to mention moats and walls protecting the major cities, massive fortifications, and sophisticated weaponry. Neither ruler paid much attention to the Mongol nomads—they were too busy warring with each other.

In 1210, a young, newly ascended Jurchen emperor sent a delegation to the Mongol steppe. The envoys demanded tribute and a display of submission from Genghis Khan, who, after all, was listed on the official rolls as "Commander Against Rebels" and a subject of the Jurchen emperor. Instead of kowtowing, Genghis Khan reportedly spat on the ground, called the Jurchen ruler an "imbecile," then mounted his horse and rode away. Such defiance by the Mongol leader was equivalent to a declaration of war.

Historians suspect that Genghis Khan wanted to invade the Jurchen kingdom anyway in order to seize control of the rich supply of trade goods that flowed through their territory. And Genghis Khan was no doubt emboldened by his recent subjugation of the Tanguts, who, while much less formidable than their Jurchen neighbors, also had walled fortifications. Genghis Khan had defeated the Tanguts despite a self-inflicted catastrophe. In an attempt to flood the Tangut capital, the Mongols diverted a section of the Yellow River, but, lacking in engineering skills, they flooded their own camp instead. Nevertheless, Genghis Khan managed to secure an alliance with the Tangut king, who provided him with famous Tangut camels (as reserves for the Mongol cavalry) as well as his daughter's hand in marriage.[16]

Meanwhile, the Jurchen emperor, although infuriated by Genghis Khan's insolence, apparently belittled the idea of a Mongol threat. "Our empire is like the sea; yours is but a handful of sand," he is said to have boasted. "How can we fear you?" His confidence was understandable. The massive city walls of the Jurchens seemed impregnable, particularly given the Mongols' primitive weapons. The Jurchen warriors also outnumbered the Mongol army by a ratio of more than two to one.

But Genghis Khan was, by all accounts, a brilliant commander. The Mongol military differed starkly from traditional armies. It consisted entirely of horsemen; the absence of foot soldiers gave the Mongol forces not only much greater mobility but a decisive ability to strike suddenly. Genghis Khan's men were hardy, disciplined, and resourceful. Marco Polo claimed that they could go for ten days without stopping to make a fire, surviving on dried meat and dried milk mixed with water. When nothing else was available, "they opened a vein in a horse, drank a small quantity of blood and closed the vein." Sometimes the warriors got fresh meat, either by slaughtering some of the reserve animals that always accompanied them or by hunting and looting.[17]

In the end, Genghis Khan defeated the Jurchens through trickery, psychological warfare, and, perhaps most important, by ruthlessly using the Jurchens' own population and technology against them. Before taking on the great Jurchen cities, the Mongols typically attacked the surrounding villages first, setting them on fire. The terrified peasants fled toward the cities for refuge, clogging the roads and cutting off the Jurchen supply convoys. The sudden influx of more than a million refugees overcrowded the walled cities, producing havoc and disease. Food supplies were quickly exhausted. As starvation set in, looting, rebellion, and cannibalism broke out. In one instance, Jurchen soldiers ended up slaughtering 30,000 of their own villagers. Meanwhile, outside the city walls, the Mongols conscripted thousands of peasants, who were forced to labor under the command of Mongol soldiers, hauling water, digging ditches, and maneuvering enormous wooden and stone battering rams. Often displaying utter disregard for their captives' lives, the Mongols also used them as human shields. When these human shields died, the Mongols would use their corpses as moat-fill.

At the same time, Genghis Khan eagerly recruited men with skills and technological expertise the Mongols themselves lacked. After every battle, the Mongols carefully examined their captives and impressed any engineers found. At the same time, they offered generous rewards to engineers who voluntarily defected. In these ways, Genghis Khan brought into his service numerous Chinese engineers who knew how to construct powerful siege engines—

portable towers, arrow-spraying ballistas, flame-hurling catapults, fire lances, trebuchets, explosives—that could bring down seemingly inviolable walled cities. These weapons became part of the Mongol arsenal, and the Chinese engineers who designed them were incorporated into the Mongol army. With each new victory, the Mongol war machinery grew more sophisticated and deadlier.[18]

Even so, conquering the heavily garrisoned Jurchen kingdom was no small feat. To make matters worse, northern China's hot, muggy summers were almost unbearable for the Mongols, who repeatedly fell ill in the densely populated urban areas. It took Genghis Khan's men many campaigns over a period of three years before they finally, in 1214, surrounded the imperial city of Zhongdu. Rather than fight the Mongols, the besieged Jurchen emperor agreed to a settlement proposed by Genghis Khan. In exchange for the Mongols' withdrawing, the Jurchens would acknowledge the supreme rule of Genghis Khan. As "gifts" of appeasement, the Jurchen emperor presented Genghis Khan with large quantities of gold, silver, and silk, three thousand horses, five hundred youths, five hundred slave girls, and the hand of a Jurchen princess in marriage.[19]

Genghis Khan kept his end of the bargain. He and his men headed back to the Mongolian steppe. As with the Uighur, Tangut, and Khitan kingdoms, he left the Jurchens with great autonomy, as long as they acknowledged their vassal status and continued to pay tribute. The truth was that the Mongols had neither the interest nor the wherewithal to govern the sedentary civilizations they had conquered. However, shortly after the Mongols withdrew, the Jurchen emperor fled south and set up a new court in the city of Kaifeng. Genghis Khan viewed this as an act of betrayal and immediately returned to China. This time, he had Zhongdu sacked, razed, burned, and plundered mercilessly. According to one contemporaneous source, "The bones of the slaughtered rose mountain-high, the earth was fat with human fat and the rotting corpses gave rise to a plague." According to another, "[S]ixty thousand Chinese maidens flung themselves down from the city walls . . . rather than fall into the hands of the Mongol soldiery."[20]

The conquest of northern China, finally completed in 1215, proved immensely lucrative for the Mongols. Genghis Khan's men returned to the steppe, their crude carts overflowing with some of the most exquisite artisanship then in existence: silk robes alive with embroidered gold peonies, jade bulls and bodhisattvas, celadon vases, lacquered furniture, tapestries, board games, hand-painted marionettes, and headdresses inlaid with coral, emeralds, diamonds, and lapis lazuli. To store these exotic goods, Genghis Khan ordered for the first time the construction of a few buildings on the Mongolian steppe. Although the complex was called the Yellow Palace, it served principally as a warehouse. Genghis Khan and his followers continued to live in their portable felt *gers*.

But the real bounty took the form of human capital. Along with engineers, Genghis Khan brought back from northern China entire regiments of soldiers and officers, many of whom had de-serted to the Mongols: acrobats, jugglers, contortionists, musi-cians, singers, and dancers, as well as skilled workers of every kind, including tailors, pharmacists, translators, potters, jewelers, astrologers, painters, smiths, and doctors. Despite—or perhaps be-cause of—his own illiteracy, Genghis Khan specifically recruited scholars of all ethnicities, like the erudite, polyglot Yelu Chucai, a member of the Khitan royal family, who would advise Genghis Khan wisely and loyally to the end.

Religious tolerance continued to be a hallmark of Genghis Khan's rule. It turned out to be a powerful tool of empire building as well. For example, not long after Genghis Khan returned to the steppe from China, Muslim envoys arrived from the central Asian city of Balasagun in modern-day Kyrgyzstan. The envoys ex-plained that the Muslims of Balasagun were suffering harsh reli-gious persecution under their Christian khan Guchlug, who had prohibited the Muslim call to prayer and the public worship of Is-lam. They sought protection from the great Mongol Khan, and he was happy to oblige. The Mongol army invaded Balasagun, be-heading Guchlug and incorporating his territory into the Mongol Empire. Shortly afterward, Genghis Khan proclaimed freedom of worship throughout Guchlug's lands. Thus it was that the man whom Europe later called the Scourge of God came to be known in the East, from Tibet to the Aral Sea, as a defender of religions—and even, according to the medieval Persian chronicler Juvaini, "one of the mercies of the Lord and one of the bounties of divine grace."[21]

CONQUERING WESTWARD

Perhaps Genghis Khan, who now controlled the entire Silk Road between China and Arabia, was sated with war. Perhaps, as historians often suggest, at nearly sixty he had accumulated enough bounty and wanted to live the rest of his life in tranquility on the steppe. Whatever the reason, in 1219 Genghis Khan proposed a peaceful trading relationship with the Muslim sultan Muhammad II of Khwarizm.

In the thirteenth century, the Muslim world was divided. The Seljuk Turks dominated Asia Minor, and there was an Arab caliph in Baghdad. But the sultan of Khwarizm, also a Turk, ruled the largest territory, a great empire stretching from India to the Volga River, including the magnificent cities of Nishapur, Bukhara, and Samarkand. The Muslim lands were the richest in the world, and their civilization in many ways the most advanced. No existing society had a higher literacy rate among the general population, or superior mathematics, linguistics, agronomy, astronomy, literature, and legal traditions. It is not surprising, then, that although the sultan of Khwarizm ostensibly accepted an offer of peace from Genghis Khan, within a year a 450-man Mongol trade delegation was slaughtered in Khwarizm territory. When the news reached Genghis Khan, he dispatched envoys to the sultan, demanding retribution. The sultan responded by killing the chief envoy and sending the others back to Genghis Khan with their faces disfigured. This proved to be a mistake that not only cost the sultan his empire and his life but "laid waste a whole world."[22]

Like the Jurchen emperor, the sultan of Khwarizm did not believe the Mongol forces posed a serious threat. Khwarizm's major cities were powerfully fortified; between the Mongol steppe and Khwarizm's borders were two thousand miles of treacherous mountain and desert terrain, which no army had ever breached. Counterintuitively, Genghis Khan waited until the winter to make the crossing. He knew there would be bone-chilling winds, snow, and icy gorges to contend with. But the Mongols preferred the cold, and a summer crossing of the parched, barren desert would have been deadlier still. To this day, Genghis Khan's march to central Asia, in which tens of thousands of warriors must have died, remains one of the most remarkable military feats in history.

But for all the tenacity and fortitude of Genghis Khan's men, the Mongols could never have overcome Khwarizm's mighty stone citadels without the great siege engines that Chinese engineers designed and constructed, practically right on the spot. Unlike traditional armies, the Mongol cavalry did not travel with heavy equipment, which would have slowed them down. Instead, they were accompanied by a corps of foreign engineers who simply built whatever instruments of attack were needed, using whatever resources were available. Thus, after their desert crossing, Genghis Khan's men felled the first trees they encountered; out of them the engineers constructed retractable ladders, giant crossbows mounted on wheels, rope-pulled mangonels (single-armed torsion catapults) that hurled stones and flaming liquids, and other sophisticated weapons of siege warfare that "barbarians" were not expected to have.[23]

The Khwarizm Empire's main defense lay in the great oasis cities of Bukhara and Samarkand, as well as a chain of smaller strongholds. Farther east they controlled the Persian cities of Nishapur, Tabriz, Qazvin, Hamadan, and Ardabil. One by one these cities collapsed before the Mongol juggernaut. Bukhara, with its awe-inspiring mosques and academies, and supposedly "a wall twelve leagues . . . in circuit," was stormed first, then methodically plundered. Next in line was Samarkand, lush with pleasure gardens and protected by an enormous wall with "twelve iron gates flanked by towers," "[t]wenty armored elephants and one hundred and ten thousand warriors, Turks and Persians." When the Mongols pulled up with their great fire-spewing machines, the people and army of Samarkand surrendered, terrified by reports of inhuman Mongol cruelty: rape, torture, dismemberment, and mass slaughter.

There is no question that the Mongols killed enormous numbers and wreaked incalculable destruction. After Genghis Khan's son-in-law was killed in battle at Nishapur, the city's entire population was reportedly wiped out. It was said that the severed heads of men, women, and children rose in three piles sky high and that "not even cats and dogs survived." Such reports of Mongol savagery were likely exaggerated, but Genghis Khan apparently encouraged their circulation as a form of wartime propaganda. Indeed, the Mongols themselves may have inflated the number of people they killed in order to terrorize their next target population.[24]

Although the details of each siege varied, Genghis Khan usually followed the same basic strategy. In central Asia as in northern China, he attacked and burned unfortified villages in the surrounding countryside first, taking captives, slaying many, and generating a flood of panicked refugees, who brought chaos, hunger, and tales of terror to the cities. The besieged citizens were then given a choice. Those who capitulated would be treated with leniency. Those who refused to yield, as at Nishapur, would die terrible deaths.

Not surprisingly, many civilian populations—for example, those of Bukhara and Samarkand—surrendered to the Mongols, opening the city gates. (It may also have helped that many of Khwarizm's subjects were Persians and Tajiks, with no particular loyalty to their Turkic sultan.) Aristocrats, governors, and resisting soldiers were typically executed. By contrast, religious clerics and personnel were placed under Genghis Khan's protection, and civilians of any skill were actively recruited, whether glassblowers, potters, carpenters, furniture makers, cooks, barbers, jewelers, leather workers, papermakers, dyers, physicians, merchants, or cameleers. Perhaps most important for his rapidly expanding empire, Genghis Khan absorbed Khwarizm's ethnically diverse literati: rabbis, imams, scholars, teachers, judges, and anyone who could read and write in different languages.[25]

By 1223, Genghis Khan's conquest of Khwarizm was complete. (The sultan, who fled the empire with Mongol hordes on his heels, is said to have died alone and impoverished on a remote island in the Caspian Sea.) Genghis Khan had once again done the impossible: crossed two thousand miles of glacier and desert, breached impregnable fortifications, crushed an army far larger than his own, and brought one of the greatest, richest, and most glorious civilizations on earth under the thumb of a man who ate yak and slept in a *ger*.

Now in his midsixties and ruler of the largest empire on earth, Genghis Khan returned to the Mongolian steppe. He died in 1227, surrounded by family and friends, all his generals still loyal to him. Following Mongol custom, he was given a secret burial in a secret location. (Legend has it that eight hundred horsemen were ordered to trample repeatedly over the area in order to remove any trace of Genghis Khan's grave. The horsemen were then killed by another set of soldiers, who were then slain by others, who were in turn slain as well.) According to Edward Gibbon, Genghis Khan "died in the fullness of years and glory, with his last breath, exhorting and instructing his sons to achieve the conquest of the Chinese empire."[26]

"THE SORROW OF EUROPE"

Genghis Khan's sons, however, were not up to the job, and their father knew it. In the last years of his life, Genghis Khan had grown increasingly concerned about the preservation of his empire. Although his earliest campaigns were primarily plunder-driven, as an older man he spoke about his desire "to unite the whole world." "Without the vision of a goal," he told his sons, "a man cannot manage his own life, much less the lives of others." Above all, Genghis Khan worried that his sons would fight among themselves, particularly over who would succeed him as Great Khan. His fears proved justified. None of his four sons had his wisdom, shrewdness, or ability to inspire loyalty. The elder two quarreled so bitterly—the second insinuating that the first was a bastard—

that in the end, as a compromise, Genghis Khan chose as his heir a third son: the jovial, drink-loving Ogodei.[27]

Extravagant and almost pathologically generous, Ogodei began spending the moment he took office. At his inauguration, he reportedly threw open the royal treasury and distributed its contents, including loads of pearls and gems, to his new subjects. He ordered the construction of a new capital with a palace and gardens designed by Chinese architects, decorated by Chinese craftsmen, and walled for the first time in steppe history. Karakorum, the name the capital acquired, means "black stones" or "black walls." For all its loftiness, the new palace was again principally a warehouse and a residence for craftsmen; the royal family continued to favor their *gers*. One-third of the capital city was set aside for the corps of foreign administrators—scribes and scholars from every conquered nation—who handled communications and essentially ran the empire for the illiterate ruling family. Ogodei also called lavishly for the building of new houses of worship for his diverse subjects, including mosques, churches, and Buddhist and Taoist temples, making simple Karakorum the most religiously pluralist capital in the world.

Ogodei's city was costly to operate, and his habits even more expensive to maintain. The Mongols themselves, still primarily herders and nomads, produced little of value. Tribute, the empire's sole source of income, had started to dwindle under Ogodei's more relaxed rule. Moreover, Ogodei was not a gifted businessman. In order to lure traders to his remote capital, he paid outrageous prices for goods he had no use for—"ivory tusks, pearls, hunting falcons, golden goblets, jeweled belts, willow whip handles, cheetahs"—then gave these goods away. By 1235, almost all the enormous wealth accumulated by Genghis Khan had been squandered. For the Mongols, there was only one solution: to conquer and plunder new lands.

To settle on a target, Ogodei convened a *khuriltai*, where he encountered intense disagreement. Some of the participants wanted to invade India. Others advocated a campaign against the great cities of Baghdad and Damascus. Still others, including Ogodei himself, wanted to take on China's ailing Song Empire, which had staved off Mongol conquest for thirty years. But the most experienced voice was that of the elderly Subodei, one of Genghis Khan's most trusted generals, who had played a key role in every one of the Mongols' major battlefield victories. Subodei urged the conquest of Europe—a land most of the other Mongols had barely heard of.

Subodei had accidentally come upon Europe twelve years earlier, when he and another general were pursuing the sultan of Khwarizm. After the sultan's death, Subodei received Genghis Khan's permission to explore the unknown lands north of the Caspian Sea. There he discovered and conquered the Christian kingdom of Georgia, which became a Mongol vassal state. Continuing north, Subodei came to what is now Russia and Ukraine, at that time ruled by rivaling dukes and princes, each with his own fiefdom and army. One by one, the Russian city-states fell as Subodei outmaneuvered their forces and slew their rulers. He was on the verge of crossing the Dnieper River into eastern Europe when he was recalled by Genghis Khan. Subodei now asked the *khuriltai* of 1235 to approve a campaign in the west, where there were vast pasturelands for the Mongol horses and surely great treasures to be had.[28]

Unable to overcome the difference of opinion within the *khuriltai*, Ogodei made a decision that would probably have horrified his father. Dividing the Mongol army, Ogodei ordered that Europe and China be attacked simultaneously. The campaign against the Song failed, and Ogodei's favorite son died commanding it; the Mongol conquest of China would have to wait another generation. In Europe, however, Subodei was victorious.

Despite Ogodei's shortcomings, the invasion of Europe in many ways showed the Mongol forces at their most formidable. The main army consisted of 150,000 horsemen, of whom 50,000 were Mongols. Subodei knew and deployed all the ingenious battle tactics that Genghis Khan had perfected over his lifetime. Also in command were two of Genghis Khan's most capable grandsons, Mongke and Batu. Most important, the Mongol army, incorporating the most advanced Islamic and Chinese technology, possessed fearsome weapons unknown in Europe. The Mongols attacked Europe's walled cities not only with catapults and battering rams—familiar to the Europeans—but also with grenades, exploding naphtha, primitive rocket launchers, and smoke bombs spewing chemicals with monstrous smells.

Russia and eastern Europe fell first. The destruction in 1240 of Kiev, the jewel and religious heart of the Slavic world, sent terrified rumors flying across Europe. The Mongols, it was said, were like a cloud of locusts, and their cavalry included fire-spitting dragons (probably a reference to the Mongol incendiaries). As far away as England, Matthew Paris, a Benedictine monk, recorded in 1240 that "an immense horde of that detestable race of Satan" had ravaged eastern Europe. "They clothe themselves in the skins of bulls, and are armed with iron lances; they are short in stature and thickset, compact in their bodies, and of great strength; invincible in battle, indefatigable in labour; they wear no armour on the back part of their bodies, but are protected by it in front; they drink the blood which flows from their flocks, and consider it a delicacy."[29]

Next, the Mongols poured into Germany, Poland, and Hungary. Their stunning defeat of "the flower" of European knighthood—as many as 100,000 soldiers died—foreshadowed the end of European feudalism. The Mongol assault on Hungary was infamous. According to a contemporaneous account, "The dead fell to the right and to the left; like leaves in winter, the slain bodies of these miserable men were strewn along the whole route; blood flowed like torrents of rain." There was also hysteria: Accounts of Mongols gobbling up old women and gang-raping Christian virgins—before eating them at banquets—are probably apocryphal.

Christian Europe responded to the Mongol attacks with a surge of vicious intolerance. Helpless in defeat, and at a loss to explain the sudden emergence of the Mongol hordes, Europe's clerics blamed—of all people—the Jews in their midst. The Mongols, they claimed, were in fact the missing Hebrew tribes from the time of Moses, whom God in vengeance had turned into cruel and irrational beasts. Moreover, these beasts were supported and sponsored by Europe's most influential Jewish leaders, who hoped, along with their Tatar brethren, to take over the world. Ominously, the year 1241 corresponded to the year 5000 in the Jewish calendar—what further proof was needed of "the enormous wickedness of the Jews" and their "hidden treachery and extraordinary deceit"? Preposterous as they were, these theories fueled tragic consequences. In York, Rome, and other major European cities, Christians took out their anger by persecuting their Jewish neighbors, burning their homes and massacring them—practically imitating the Mongols, only in the name of God.

In the thirteenth century, Christian Europe was fragmented and fanatic, consumed with the Crusades, sectarian rivalry, anti-Semitism, and the persecution of infidels. European division and intolerance worked to the Mongols' advantage. For all their ruthlessness in battle, the Mongols were not hampered by religious zeal or bigotry. As European princes were torturing and expelling some of their most skilled non-Christian subjects, the Mongols recruited freely and to tremendous profit from conquered populations, blind to ethnicity or religion. From Europe the Mongols acquired new ranks of scribes, translators, architects, and craftsmen, as well as miners from Saxony who knew how to bring forth unsuspected riches from the Mongolian steppe. When, on the eve of their own defeat, Hapsburg soldiers captured a Mongol officer, they were shocked to discover that he was a brilliant multilingual Englishman who, threatened with excommunication by the Roman Catholic Church, had opted to work for the Mongols. The Hapsburg soldiers killed him.[30]

Late in 1241, Ogodei died suddenly, inebriated as usual. Within a few months, his elder brother—the last of Genghis Khan's sons—died as well. Succession problems loomed once more, and Mongke and Batu quickly led their forces out of Europe in order to return to the steppe, bringing to a close the second wave of Mongol conquest. The Mongol Empire now stretched west nearly to Vienna. But it was to grow much vaster still.

MONGOL WORLD DOMINANCE

Genghis Khan's grandsons were far abler than his sons. Ogodei left no great heirs. Instead, following a series of lurid palace intrigues, the grandsons who emerged victorious were all from the line of Tuli, Genghis Khan's youngest son. Under the leadership of these new khans—Mongke, Hulegu, Arik Boke, and Khubilai—the third and greatest wave of Mongol conquest swept the earth.

Mongke, the eldest, was installed as Great Khan in 1251. Shortly afterward, he charged his brother Hulegu with the conquest of the Middle East and his brother Khubilai with the conquest of southern China. Khubilai, who was not an eager warrior, took his time. Aggressive Hulegu did not; over the next seven years his military triumphs in the Muslim world rivaled those of his grandfather, Genghis Khan.

For all Subodei's hopes, the European campaign had produced only meager booty. Europe in the Middle Ages was primitive, undeveloped, and poor compared to the great Islamic and Chinese civilizations. Baghdad, Damascus, and Cairo—Hulegu's main targets—were among the richest cities in the world. Baghdad, in particular, was the commercial, artistic, and cultural heart of Islam. With breathtaking palaces, mosques, and synagogues in every corner, along with teeming bazaars and gambling houses, the city of Scheherazade seemed to overflow with gold and treasure.

Baghdad was also the seat of the Abbasid caliphate, founded five hundred years earlier. The ruling caliph was the thirty-seventh—and arguably feeblest, vainest, and least worthy—successor to the Prophet Muhammad. In what must have seemed an astounding act of hubris, Hulegu issued a summons to the caliph, demanding that he surrender or perish. The caliph responded haughtily, declaring that all of the Islamic world, with God by their side, would rise up to slay the infidels. The caliph was mistaken.

The Abbasid caliphate was a theocracy, committed to Sunni Islamic orthodoxy. By the mid-thirteenth century, the Abbasid lands were filled with disaffected minorities, including Shiites, Jews, and especially Christians, who were eager to see the overthrow of their Sunni overlords. The Mongols shrewdly exploited these religious and sectarian divisions. Many among Baghdad's significant Shiite minority, most likely including the caliph's own vizier and chief minister, conspired with the Mongols, acting as informants and spies. Thousands of Baghdad's Christians simply joined the Mongol forces.[31]

By contrast, the Mongols were more religiously open than any other power in the world. Hulegu had Muslims and Christians of every sect in his army. One of his advisors was the brilliant Shiite astronomer Nasir ad-Din Tusi. Moreover, Hulegu's mother and two wives were Christian, making it easier for him to cultivate the Christians of the Middle East, many of whom hailed him as a savior. Hulegu marched on Baghdad in 1257. (He had left the steppe in 1253, but it took his men several years to overcome the hashish-smoking, fearless Order of the Assassins, a bizarre Muslim sect that controlled an extensive network of mountain fortresses stretching from Afghanistan to Syria.) On February 5, 1258, after a week of flooding and bombardment, they breached the eastern wall of Baghdad; the caliph capitulated days later. In falling to the Mongols, the Abbasid caliphate succumbed not to a nomadic horde but to the combined "human, financial, material, and technological resources of northern China, central Asia, Russia, the Caucasus, and Iran."[32]

Baghdad was sacked and looted; corpses piled up on the streets, producing a suffocating stench. Christians and Shiites were generally spared. Hulegu reportedly tried to force the caliph to eat pieces of his own gold. When that failed, Hulegu ordered the caliph and his male heirs rolled in carpets and stomped to death—a punishment apparently reserved for the very highborn.

By bringing down the caliphate, the Mongols had accomplished in two years what the Christian crusaders had not been able to do in two centuries. Baghdad's Christians celebrated by slaughtering Muslims and destroying mosques. Throughout the Middle East, Christians from Damascus to Aleppo hailed the Mongol advance with almost apocalyptic fervor. Above all, they prayed that the Mongols would liberate Jerusalem, and gleefully prepared to take vengeance on their former Muslim oppressors.[33]

For all their ruthlessness, there was no such religious venom or zealousness among the Mongols. On the contrary, back at Karakorum, the Mongol court's approach to religion was more like that of an Ivy League university. According to William of Rubruck, a Franciscan monk who visited Karakorum in 1254, Grand Khan Mongke presided over elaborate religious debates in which everyone had an equal voice and the finding of common ground was encouraged. Rubruck himself was a rigid Catholic, intolerant even of other Christians. When Rubruck informed the Great Khan that he had come "to spread the word of God," Mongke asked him to participate in a debate before three judges: a Buddhist, a Muslim, and a Christian. The debate was closely supervised, the most critical rule being that "no one shall dare to speak words of contention." The anthropologist Jack Weatherford vividly describes the events that followed:

> In the initial round, Rubruck faced a Buddhist from North China who began by asking how the world was made and what happened to the soul after death. Rubruck countered that the Buddhist monk was asking the wrong questions: the first issue should be about God from whom all things flow. The umpires awarded the first points to Rubruck.
>
> Their debate ranged back and forth over the topics of evil versus good, God's nature, what happens to the souls of animals, the existence of reincarnation, and whether God had created evil . . . after each round of the debate, the learned men paused to drink deeply in preparation for the next match.
>
> . . . [A]s the effects of the alcohol became stronger, the Christians gave up trying to persuade anyone with logical arguments, and resorted to singing. The Muslims, who did not sing, responded by loudly reciting the Koran in an effort to drown out the Christians, and the Buddhists retreated into silent meditation. At the end of the debate, unable to convert or kill one another, they concluded the way most Mongol celebrations concluded, with everyone too drunk to continue.[34]

Comic as they might seem in the twenty-first century, these debates were all the more remarkable given the contrasting treatment of religious dissent elsewhere in the thirteenth-century "civilized" world. In 1252, Pope Innocent IV issued his fateful bull *ad exstirpanda*, sanctioning the use of torture to root out heretics. Eager to comply, Dominican friars—"hounds of the Lord"—roamed from city to city, extracting confessions from suspects with ghoulish techniques. Across Europe, cross-bearing monarchs from Edward I to Frederick II took up the anti-Muslim sword; tongues were torn out and heads rolled in the name of Christ. In France, Rubruck's sponsor, Louis IX, was canonized for various acts of saintliness, including the burning of 12,000 handwritten Talmudic texts. "Soldiers of the Cross" unleashed their fury not only on Muslims but also on Orthodox Christians. In Constantinople, "Crusaders butchered everyone they met regardless of sex or age. . . . Nuns, maidens, and matrons were abused and violated. . . . Exquisite cruelties were inflicted on Orthodox priests."[35]

The "barbarian" Mongols, meanwhile, were deeply cosmopolitan in their openness to different cultures. At Mongke's court, Rubruck met not only religious thinkers, merchants, and diplomatic envoys from many lands but superb craftsmen from Syria, Russia, Hungary, Germany, and France, including the master Parisian goldsmith Guillaume Boucher. Though technically war captives, these artisans were treated with the greatest esteem. Assigned a team of fifty assistants, Boucher redecorated the Mongol capital in tony European style. To be sure, the Mongols were arrogant in their own way: Mongke, like Genghis Khan, believed that the Mongols were chosen by God and by nature—interchangeable in their view—to conquer the entire earth. But having little art, science, erudition, or administrative capability of their own, the Mongols, with seemingly no prejudice, simply took whatever was useful from the more civilized peoples they had conquered.

In the end, the Mongols did not take Jerusalem. On the contrary, the Mongol drive westward ended in 1260 in Palestine, at Ayn al-Jalut (Goliath's Well), where Hulegu's forces were defeated by the Egypt-based Mamluks. Not long before, Hulegu had received word of his brother Mongke's death. Hulegu, who himself had no ambition to be Great Khan, was apparently stricken with grief. Perhaps he sensed that Mongke's death also marked the end of the Mongol Empire's unity.[36]

THE MONGOL RULE OF CHINA

A few years before his death, Mongke, tired of his brother Khubilai's lack of progress and constant excuses, took the conquest of the Song dynasty China into his own hands, leaving the administration of the empire to his youngest brother, Arik Boke, in Karakorum. In May of 1258, employing the same tactics used by his grandfather, Genghis Khan, Mongke led his army across the Yellow River toward the heart of southern China. But the great Song—even in its twilight, the most formidable adversary the Mongols ever faced—battled back stubbornly. Mongke died almost two decades before the campaign was completed, probably from dysentery or cholera, in the province of Sichuan.

Mongke's death brought on a period of turbulent internecine warfare. Most dramatically, in 1260, Khubilai and Arik Boke each convened a *khuriltai*—Khubilai's in Xanadu, Arik Boke's in Karakorum—and had himself declared Great Khan. The struggle between them would permanently fracture the Mongol Empire.

Among his brothers, Khubilai was unquestionably the odd man out. The rest of his siblings clung to their steppe traditions. They were, above all, nomads and warriors, and like Genghis Khan they saw the luxuries of sedentary civilization as invidious temptations. By contrast, Khubilai preferred palaces and cities to the steppe. He loved comfort and feasting, and grew fat and gouty early on.

In the end, Khubilai triumphed over Arik Boke. His triumph was in part that of the farmer over the nomad. At the worst possible time for Arik Boke, Mongolia suffered a cold-induced famine that decimated much of the animal population on the steppe. With no food for his starving followers, Arik Boke found himself at the mercy of Khubilai, whose territory included agricultural lands and food supplies. In 1264, Arik Boke submitted to Khubilai, explaining his defeat with some telling words: "We were then, and you are today." Khubilai forgave his brother (who conveniently died of poisoning two years later) but destroyed Karakorum. For the new Mongol capital he chose the site of the former Jurchen capital of Zhongdu—sacked by Genghis Khan in 1214—which later became Beijing.

The reality, however, was that the Mongol Empire was now divided. The factions of the Mongol royal family that had wanted Arik Boke to be Great Khan refused to recognize Khubilai's legitimacy. Meanwhile, Hulegu and his descendants ruled the Arab and Persian lands, which became known as the Ilkhanate, while descendants of Genghis Khan's eldest son, Jochi, controlled Russia and eastern Europe, and also openly refused to recognize Khubilai as their Great Khan.[37]

But even without his family's full support, Khubilai accomplished what his famous grandfather had not been able to do: He conquered southern China and reunified the Middle Kingdom. In many ways, Khubilai's victory over the Song was less a military victory than the conquest of the proverbial hearts and minds of the Chinese people. In contrast to Genghis Khan's blitzkriegs, Khubilai's defeat of the Song occurred gradually, over almost forty years. Throughout this period, Khubilai worked patiently, through propaganda and shrewd public policies, to convince the Chinese that he, far more than the aloofly decadent Song leaders, embodied China's traditional virtues.

With each military victory over the Song, however small, Khubilai promoted the idea that the Mandate of Heaven had fallen to him. This was a hard case for a "barbarian" to make, but each year a growing number of Chinese peasants, students, soldiers, and even generals deserted to the Mongol side. More remarkable, the Mongols—famous for their cavalry—triumphed in naval warfare as well. Once again, Khubilai recruited experienced non-Mongols to build and man his fleet. He also secured the allegiance of powerful Chinese admirals, whose control of China's seaboard and internal waterways proved pivotal to the Mongol victory.[38]

Khubilai's reign (1260–94) was long and relatively peaceful.

When Hangzhou, the magnificent Song capital, finally succumbed to Mongol forces in 1276, Khubilai found himself in control of China's greatest treasures, richest cities, and most flourishing ports—some 200,000 trading boats plied the Yangtze River alone each year—as well as a massive, meticulously trained navy. Moreover, China, now reunited, was far and away the most populous nation in the world, with an estimated 110 to 120 million subjects.

Although their empire was now fragmented, the descendants of Genghis Khan dominated virtually the entire civilized world. Khubilai alone ruled over more people than perhaps any previous sovereign in history. To govern his Chinese subjects, who were not only vastly more numerous but also vastly more cultured than the Mongols, Khubilai pursued a curious combination of ethnic policies. On one side, he adopted a number of seemingly intolerant policies. Most notably, Khubilai banned intermarriage between the Mongols and the Chinese and forbade the Chinese from learning the Mongol language or carrying arms. In addition, Khubilai abolished the Confucian examination system as a mechanism for staffing China's bureaucracy, and he generally refused to appoint Chinese to the country's highest government posts. (This was not a universal Mongol policy; in Persia, for example, Persians were allowed to occupy such posts.)

Different theories have been proposed to explain Khubilai's exclusionary policies. It might be thought that he was simply an anti-Chinese Mongol supremacist. Nothing could be further from the truth. Having spent virtually his entire life in the Middle Kingdom, Khubilai unabashedly admired the refinement of Chinese culture, the beauty of Chinese architecture, and the order of Chinese society. In striking contrast to his predecessors' savage treatment of northern China, Khubilai destroyed almost nothing in southern China. On the contrary, he made a point of repairing temples, shrines, and other public buildings damaged by war. He surrounded himself with Chinese advisors and ruled with moderation and enlightenment. Khubilai's sympathetic approach to China angered many of his more traditional relatives, who, consistent with past Mongol practices, simply wanted to plunder and exploit China.

Moreover, Khubilai displayed what is arguably the ultimate form of ethnic tolerance. Not only did he refrain from imposing Mongol customs on the Chinese, but he embraced, at least on the surface, Chinese culture for himself, his court, and the ruling class. He adopted a Chinese title and posthumously assigned his ancestors Chinese names. He built a Chinese capital based on an ancient Chinese model, followed Chinese imperial rituals, and established a Chinese dynasty, known to this day as the Yuan, meaning "the origin" or "great beginnings." He eagerly promoted Chinese art, music, and drama, laying the groundwork for what became the Peking Opera. Although he probably remained illiterate, Khubilai also allowed Chinese literature and scholarship to flourish, building Chinese schools and reviving the Hanlin Academy, traditionally reserved for the brightest scholars in the Middle Kingdom. According to the historian David Morgan, "for literary artists there may well have been greater freedom of expression [under the Mongols] than under some more 'respectable' dynasties."[39]

Interestingly, having excluded the Chinese from the highest governmental posts, Khubilai filled these posts not with Mongols but principally with non-Chinese foreigners. Recognizing that the Mongols themselves lacked the experience and numbers necessary to govern a society as complex as China's, Khubilai recruited talented Uighurs, Khitans, Persians, central Asians, and Europeans as China's governors and top ministers. Thus, a (notoriously corrupt) native of Tashkent served as Khubilai's minister of finance for twenty years, and a Muslim father and son also from central Asia served as successive governors of the Yunnan Province. Even Marco Polo apparently served as a Yuan official, in the city of Yangzhou, near Nanjing. Marco Polo later boasted to his fellow Venetians that he had been Yangzhou's governor, but this was not true. More likely, he helped administer the government's salt monopoly—a position that just didn't have the same ring to it.

Below the highest, foreign-filled government posts, Chinese continued to occupy lower civil servant positions. Indeed, Khubilai kept much of the existing (and very effective) Chinese bureaucratic apparatus while creating new offices to address problems of special Mongol concern, such as the Section for Retrieving Lost Animals. Within each department, Khubilai systematically mixed Chinese and foreigners: Each office was staffed according to ethnic quotas, specifying the required number of northern Chinese, southern Chinese, and foreign bureaucrats. In at least some cases, Khubilai appointed two officers—one Chinese, one foreign—to the same important government post, requiring them to govern together.

In short, Khubilai's approach to governance reflected cosmopolitanism far more than intolerance. (He repeatedly sent envoys to the pope and the rulers of Europe, inviting them to send their best scholars, but the Europeans declined.) From this perspective, Khubilai's laws prohibiting the Chinese from marrying Mongols, learning the Mongol language, or occupying top government posts can be seen in a different light. Rather than driven by chauvinism, they were most likely political expedients designed to protect the tiny handful of ruling Mongols from being swallowed up or overthrown by the vast Chinese population. They may also have been, as some historians suggest, part of a larger strategy that allowed Khubilai to play different ethnic groups against one another.

In any event, the result of Khubilai's policies was a remarkable motley of different cultures, ethnicities, and religions. Within the walls of the imperial palace, the Mongol ruling family continued with their Mongol ways, speaking Mongolian, eating and drinking like Mongolians, and sleeping in *gers* on the palace floor. Outside the palace, the capital city—known as Dadu or "great capital" by the Chinese, and as Khan Balik or "city of the khan" by Europeans—overflowed with Arabs, Armenians, Tanguts, Turks, Tibetans, Persians, central Asians, and Europeans. These international sojourners filled every imaginable role: hawkers, physicians, prostitutes, chefs, hydraulic engineers, astrologers, sculptors, gatekeepers, scribes, translators, spiritual advisors, merchants, and traders.

Virtually every religion in the world was represented. On the thronging streets of Dadu, rabbis and Hindu sages mingled with their more numerous Buddhist, Muslim, Nestorian, and Catholic counterparts. Although Khubilai himself favored Buddhism, many in the royal family were Mass-attending Christians, while other Mongols in China continued to practice shamanism. Meanwhile, some of the Mongols' most esteemed advisors were Taoists and Confucians.[40]

Although the Confucian-trained upper classes of southern China probably always found barbarian rule loathsome and humiliating, the Mongols brought to China a peace and political unity not seen since the overthrow of the Tang in 907. China's port cities became leading centers of import and export, Hangzhou specializing in sugar, Yangzhou in rice, and Zaytun (modern-day Quanzhou) in pearls and precious stones.

The new Grand Canal cut by the Mongols, stretching 1,100 miles from Hangzhou to modern Beijing, linked north and south China economically. Chinese commercial vessels called frequently at Vietnam, Malaysia, Java, Ceylon, and south India, usually returning with heaps of sugar, ivory, cinnamon, and cotton. International trade, both overland and maritime, between China and Mongol-dominated Persia, central Asia, and Europe boomed as never before. Throughout the Middle Kingdom, merchants of every religion and ethnicity made fortunes under the Pax Mongolica.[41]

Meanwhile, China's peasantry, the bulk of the country's population, probably experienced little change in their daily lives. They simply paid taxes to a different imperial family and continued to be exploited by their landlords. (To win their support, Khubilai left the estates of southern China's great landowners essentially intact.) On the other hand, if imperial records are to be believed, Khubilai created more than 21,000 public schools designed to promote universal education. In addition, peasants likely benefited from Khubilai's reform of the Chinese penal code, which had been exceptionally harsh under the Song. Khubilai granted amnesty to minor criminals who demonstrated remorse, and in other cases substituted fines for corporal punishment. While his European counterparts were ordering more and more people stretched on the rack or crushed with huge wheels, Khubilai opposed torture. He also disfavored the death penalty; during his rule, executions fell dramatically, to annual rates lower than those of modern China and the United States.[42]

Some see in the centuries of Mongol world domination the first great wave of globalization. Under Mongol rule, Europe and the Far East were linked for the first time by trade routes as well as by the Yam: a network of relay stations, roughly thirty miles apart that stretched from one end of the empire to the other. According to Marco Polo, urgent messages could move through this courier system up to three hundred miles a day. The Yam also catered to international merchants by providing beds—sometimes with silk sheets—food, extra horses, fodder, even travel guides.

The Mongols, writes Weatherford, were "civilization's unrivaled cultural carriers." They built churches in China, Islamic schools in Russia, and Buddhist stupas in Persia. "Because they had no system of their own to impose upon their subjects, they were willing to adopt and combine systems from everywhere." The Mongols brought new strains of rice, millet, and other grains from China to Persia, while transporting new varieties of lemons and other citrus trees in the opposite direction. "An ever-expanding variety of peas, beans, grapes, lentils, nuts, carrots, turnips, melons, and diverse leaf vegetables" circulated the Mongol-dominated globe, as did new dyes, oils, spices, architectural styles, printing methods, card games, and fabrics such as satin, muslin, and damask silk. Muslim surgeons, supposedly the best in their day, now operated in China, while Chinese specialists in internal medicine and pharmacology cured diseases in central Asia and Mesopotamia. Russians were sent to north China, Genoese traders to the Black Sea, and Chinese merchants to Southeast Asia, where they built extensive commercial networks surviving to this day. From Arab mathematicians to Tajik carpets to Chinese acupuncturists, the Mongols "searched for what worked best; and when they found it, they spread it to other countries."[43]

Khubilai, the last of the great Mongol rulers, died peacefully in 1294 after a reign of thirty-four years. In many ways, he differed from Genghis Khan. He lacked his grandfather's knack and drive for military expansion. He was also much more humane. Even on the campaigns he did lead, Khubilai never committed the ruthless massacres that earned his predecessors their terrible name. But like his grandfather, Khubilai was unhampered by ethnic or religious chauvinism. He freely admired and shrewdly drew on the knowledge, ingenuities, and cultural achievements of his subject peoples. He allowed all creeds to flourish, and he treated Chinese civilization like a jewel, even while infusing it with learning and technology from India and the Muslim lands.

Perhaps more consciously than his grandfather, who remained at heart a steppe nomad, Khubilai was a globalizer, seeking to create one world system. By synthesizing Arab, Chinese, and Greek expertise, Khubilai's astronomers and cartographers produced the world's most sophisticated maps, nautical charts, and terrestrial globes, far outstripping their European counterparts. He embraced international commerce, religious coexistence, free communication, and cultural exchange. Fittingly, two of Khubilai's most passionate ambitions were to establish a universal alphabet, encompassing all the languages of the world, and a universal calendar unifying the lunar calendar of the Arabs, the solar calendar of the Europeans, and the twelve-year animal cycle of the Chinese.[44]

INTOLERANCE AND DECLINE

As is the case with every empire, the collapse of the Great Mongol Empire was fueled by many factors, among them incompetent leaders, corruption, revolts, decadence, factional struggles, assassinations, external attacks, and bad luck. Not all parts of the empire fell at the same time. Mongol rule in China ended in 1368, when the new Ming rulers—triumphantly ethnic Chinese—sent Genghis Khan's descendants fleeing back to the steppe. Mongol rule in the Persian Ilkhanate, long in disarray, had already collapsed three decades earlier. By contrast, the Mongols who ruled central Asia undertook a series of bloody new conquests in the late fourteenth century, eventually founding the Mughal Empire, which governed

India until the British took over in the nineteenth century. Mean-while, the Mongols of Russia, known as the Golden Horde, lost their power and territory gradually, breaking into smaller and smaller hordes over four centuries.

But throughout the Mongol-dominated lands, the decline of the empire was marked by one consistent feature: a stark turn toward intolerance, especially religious intolerance, both officially and among the general Mongol population. For a variety of rea-sons—most saliently, the spread of the bubonic plague, which killed seventy-five million people, extinguished international trade, and effectively cut off the four Mongol khanates from one an-other—the Mongol rulers of the fourteenth century aligned them-selves with powerful religious factions within their territory. Abandoning the principles of religious freedom established by Genghis Khan, they embarked on paths of zealotry, scapegoating, and, in some cases, mass murder.

Within each khanate, the details of intolerance differed. The Mongols of Russia were the first to convert to Islam. They soon joined the Egyptian Mamluks in their holy war against Christen-dom, at several points even attacking their fellow Mongols in Per-sia, who for their part were increasingly oppressing their Muslim subjects. Then, in 1295, Ghazan, the Mongol khan of Persia, also converted to Islam, the religion of most of his subjects. Unfortu-nately, one of Ghazan's most influential advisors was Nawruz, a Muslim general and fanatical bigot.

Nawruz purged the Ilkhanate of Buddhism, destroying its tem-ples and statues and forcing its adherents—only a tiny, mainly Mongol minority—to convert to Islam. Jews and Christians were ordered to wear special clothing so that Muslim mobs could harass and assault them. Religious riots broke out; churches were sacked and Christians arrested, beaten, or killed. Even shamanism, the original religion of the Mongols, was harshly suppressed. Nawruz eventually lost favor with Ghazan, who had the general cut in half. But the Mongols of Persia still ruled in the name of Islam, and re-ligious strife continued to debilitate the Ilkhanate until it ultimately collapsed in 1335.[45]

In China, Khubilai Khan's descendants, surrounded by rising popular discontent, decided that they had weakened themselves by becoming "too Chinese." Members of the imperial court recounted dreams in which Genghis Khan urged them to rule the Chinese more harshly. Whatever the cause, the late Yuan emperors increasingly defined themselves against their Chinese subjects, isolating themselves, stressing their Mongol identity, and rejecting the Chinese language and culture. Traditional Chinese storytelling and Chinese opera, once vigorously promoted by Khubilai, were prohibited. As in the other khanates, the Mongol rulers renounced their predecessors' religious neutrality. But in China, it was Buddhism, in its mystical Tibetan, Tantric form, that was elevated above all other religions.

The last decades of Mongol rule in China were sordid and chaotic. Rumors began circulating throughout the country that behind the palace walls the Mongol rulers were plotting to exterminate Chinese children and participating in bizarre sexual rituals. The latter rumor was at least partly true. At the urging of the Tibetan clergy, the Mongol ruling family engaged in lurid sexual dances, supposedly part of the path to Tantric enlightenment. Outside the Forbidden City, paranoia and xenophobia mounted. Along with other foreigners of influence, Tibetan monks, who received glaring imperial privileges, became objects of popular hatred. In 1333, Toghon Temur, a boy of thirteen, ascended the Mongol throne. Around the same time, the bubonic plague struck China, leaving 90 percent of the population dead in Hebei province. By 1351, as much as two-thirds of China's entire population had died. Meanwhile, trade and commerce dried up, hyperinflation set in, and peasant revolts broke out.

According to Bayan, one of Toghon Temur's ministers, the root cause of all these problems was excessive sinicization. As a solution, he reportedly proposed that all Chinese throughout the empire surnamed Chang, Wang, Liu, Li, and Chao be executed. This plan, which would have eliminated 90 percent of China's population, was never carried out, but it illustrates the intolerant atmosphere that marked the Yuan dynasty in its last years.

Toghon Temur was China's last Yuan emperor. Anti-Mongol uprisings erupted across southern China, and a charismatic ethnic Chinese rebel by the name of Zhu Yuanzhang asserted his claim to the Mandate of Heaven. In 1368, after his forces drove Toghon Temur's army from China, Zhu Yuanzhang founded the Ming dynasty.

Over the next three hundred years, China would sink ever deeper into ethnocentric isolationism. When it became clear to the Ming emperors that they could not subjugate the "barbarians" surrounding them, they built massive walls to seal the Chinese in. Foreign merchants were expelled, and travel abroad was prohibited. At the same time, there was a crackdown on non-Chinese customs, religions, and ideas. Foreign languages were banned, while traditional Confucianism and Taoism were reinstated as official orthodoxy. Not until the twenty-first century would China again be as open, cosmopolitan, and outward-reaching as it was during the Mongol era.[46]

It was Genghis Khan's genius to create a single people out of the warring tribes of the Mongolian steppe. Unlike the Achaemenid Persians, Genghis Khan succeeded in establishing a new political identity—the Great Mongol Nation, or "People of the Felt Walls"—but this identity embraced only the nomadic peoples of the steppe. It was not intended to include, and had no appeal whatsoever to, non-Mongol peoples and nations, who regarded their Mongol conquerors as the crudest of barbarians.

As Genghis Khan's descendants went on to annex huge swaths of Persia, China, India, Russia, and eastern Europe, the peoples of these lands never remotely saw themselves as Mongols, "People of the Felt Walls," or proud subjects of the Great Mongol Empire. On the contrary, a fascinating thing happened.

Instead of imposing a Mongol identity on their vast empire, the Mongol rulers increasingly took on the culture of their more "civilized" subjects. In China, Khubilai Khan adopted a Chinese title, established a Chinese dynasty, and surrounded himself with Chinese art, music, and drama. In central Asia, the Mongol khans became Muslim and made Persian their official language. No "glue" held these increasingly divergent kingdoms together. Within a short time, the once world-dominant Mongol empire broke into four large chunks, each turning increasingly intolerant and religiously fanatic. Before long, the Great Mongol Empire had disintegrated.

PART TWO

THE ENLIGHTENING OF TOLERANCE

FIVE

THE "PURIFICATION" OF
MEDIEVAL SPAIN

Inquisition, Expulsion, and the Price
of Intolerance

[W]e are informed by the inquisitors and many other people, religious, churchmen, and laymen, of the great harm suffered by
Christians from the contact, intercourse and communication
which they have with Jews, who always attempt in various ways
to seduce faithful Christians from our Holy Catholic Faith. . . .
[We] decree that all Jews male and female depart our kingdoms
and never return. . . . And if they do not observe this and are
found guilty of remaining in these realms or returning to them,
they will incur the death penalty.

—EXPULSION DECREE, MARCH 1492

On October 19, 1469, in a private ceremony shrouded in
secrecy and intrigue, the seventeen-year-old heir to the
crown of Aragon married the eighteen-year-old heiress
of Castile. From the union of Ferdinand and Isabella, who had first
met just four days earlier, a unified Spain would ascend to great
heights of glory. At the time of the wedding, and for much of

the preceding two hundred years, Spain was one of the most religiously diverse societies in Christian Europe. Ferdinand himself had Jewish ancestors on his mother's side.[1] Twenty-three years later, as Jewish-funded Spanish ships reached the shores of America, Ferdinand and Isabella would famously order the expulsion of Spain's Jews. Spain's turn to increasingly virulent intolerance—not just against Jews, but against converted Jews, Muslims, converted Muslims, Protestants, and eventually even Jesuits—fatally undermined its rise to power, destroying any chance for world domination.

Unlike any of its northern European neighbors, medieval Spain had a large Muslim minority, the result of centuries of earlier Islamic rule. In Aragon, some 35 percent of the total population of roughly 200,000 were Mudejars, the term for Muslims living in Christian lands. In some rural areas, Muslims were actually a majority. Spain was also home to the overwhelming majority of Christian Europe's Jews, who had been expelled at various points from England (1290) and France (1306, 1322, and 1394) and massacred repeatedly in Germany (1298, 1336–38, and 1348). As a result of this unusual coexistence of religious communities, Spaniards were worldlier about non-Christians than many of their fellow Europeans. "No Iberian writer fantasized, as the German Wolfram von Eschenbach did, that the offspring of a Christian-Muslim couple would be mottled white and black; they knew better."[2]

Of course, Spanish tolerance should not be overstated or confused with the "respect for difference" that tolerance implies in the twenty-first century. Jews and Muslims were often confined to separate quarters and required to wear special identifying emblems. Intermarriage with Christians was punishable by imprisonment, torture, or even execution. Although there was no fear of mottled offspring, Muslim women caught fornicating with Christian males were sometimes stripped naked and whipped in the streets. Popular anti-Semitism, frequently fomented by the clergy, periodically erupted in violence and waves of forced conversions. The latter created a significant class of so-called *conversos* (converted Jews), who would then be suspected—often correctly—of secretly continuing to practice Judaism. The spasms of anti-Semitic violence could be shockingly brutal. In June of 1391, Jews were massacred in Seville; the pogrom quickly spread to Córdoba, Toledo, Valencia, and Barcelona, resulting in mass throat-slitting and thousands of conversions.[3]

But once again, what matters is *relative* tolerance, and despite such bursts of horrific violence, Spain was for most of the fourteenth and fifteenth centuries the best place—sometimes the only place—for non-Christians to live and prosper in western Europe. Many of Spain's Muslims benefited from special treaties, granting them the right to practice their own religion and to be governed by their own laws. In places like Valencia, Mudejars lived largely autonomously, interacting only with other Muslims and speaking only Arabic. In other locales, Muslims were much more integrated into Christian society. In Aragon and Catalonia, for example, Muslims and Christians lived side by side, buying each other's goods and services. Mudejars came to dominate certain local industries, most prominently the building trades.[4]

The situation of the Jews was quite different. Whereas the great majority of Mudejars were agricultural laborers—most of the Muslim elite having emigrated to Islamic lands—Spanish Jews were principally urban and far more acculturated. All of Spain's Jews spoke a form of Spanish, typically in addition to Hebrew and Arabic. While most Muslims were vassals of feudal and ecclesiastical lords, Spain's Jews were under the immediate control and protection of the king, paying taxes directly to the royal treasury.

Jews in Spain participated in a striking range of economic activities. Jewish men were cobblers, grocers, tailors, shopkeepers, blacksmiths, silversmiths, butchers, chemists, beekeepers, dyers, and jewelers. Their clientele included many Christians and Muslims. Jewish women were weavers, spinners, and midwives. Some Jews were major sheepherders. Others were landowners, leasing property from small farms to large estates to great vineyards and orchards.

Though most Spanish Jews were, like most Spanish Christians, of modest means, a disproportionate number occupied positions of respect and influence, and a few rose to astonishing heights of wealth and power. Jews were among Spain's most celebrated court astronomers, philosophers, cartographers, and doctors. A Jewish physician attended every Castilian king of the fifteenth century. Jewish tax collectors were common throughout the country, and Jewish merchants were important in Spain's import-export trade. The wealthiest Jews were royal treasurers and financiers, advising, bankrolling, and even (as *conversos*) intermarrying with Spanish royalty and nobility. Jewish families in Castile were apparently instrumental in arranging Isabella's marriage to a prince with Jewish ancestry. During the first few decades of Ferdinand and Isabella's rule, the inner court circle included not only *conversos* but a number of practicing Jews, including Abraham Senior, the treasurer of the Santa Hermandad (the centralized militia) and one of the most powerful men in Spain.[5]

The benefits Spain reaped from its relative tolerance were vital to its territorial expansion and imperial rise. Besides the intangible rewards of cultural and intellectual invigoration, Spain gained two essential advantages from its non-Christian populations: manpower and money.

When the Spanish kings reconquered Muslim-held lands, they initially followed the same successful strategy pursued by Achaemenid Persia or ancient Rome: They allowed these communities to maintain their own customs, to practice their own faith, and in some cases to govern themselves. The immediate result was a considerable increase in the population under Spanish rule. For example, the crown of Aragon doubled in size through military conquest in the thirteenth century. By tolerating the Muslims who already lived there rather than attempting to expel or exterminate them, Spain was able both to secure its conquest and to obtain the labor it needed to farm the fertile soils of southern Spain. Indeed, the need for agricultural labor was a chief reason the Spanish kings entered into treaties with their conquered Muslim communities, allowing the latter to practice Islam.

At the same time, by opening itself to Jews, however grudgingly, medieval Spain reaped enormous financial gains. The Jews of this period had access to one of the most extensive commercial, trading, and lending networks in the world. They dominated the global diamond industry and were major players in the early development of international finance. From the thirteenth to the fifteenth century, Jews served as treasurers and revenue collectors for an astonishing number of Spanish kings, noble houses, bishops and archbishops—even cathedral chapters. Jewish money lending was critical to sustaining the royal fisc, both in the form of direct loans to the crown and as a major source of tax revenue. (In return for the privilege of lending at interest, all Jewish loans were taxed by the king.)

An example of the indispensability of Jewish financiers can be seen in the fourteenth-century civil war between King Peter "the Cruel" of Castile and his bastard half brother Henry of Trastámara. Peter's chief treasurer was the powerful Jewish financier Samuel Halevi, who built the stunning synagogue in Toledo that still stands today. As part of his strategy for usurping Peter, Henry painted his bid for the throne as a Christian crusade against the "evil presence" of Jewish financiers and tax collectors in the royal court. But after defeating Peter, Henry too found he could not do without Jewish capital and financial expertise; his chief royal financial officer would turn out to be a Jew, as would his private physician. A century later, it would be Jewish bankers' money that financed Spain's initial expeditions to the New World.[6]

INQUISITION AND INTOLERANCE

In 1478 the Spanish Inquisition was founded by papal bull. Thus ended the era of Spanish relative tolerance.

A church institution led by the Dominican order and vested with draconian powers, the Inquisition was charged with purifying the country of heretics. Interestingly, "heretics" referred not to openly practicing Jews or Muslims but rather to false Christians. Starting in 1480 the Inquisition began hunting down, trying, and often torturing and executing *conversos* who despite their professed Christianity were universally suspected of secretly practicing

Judaism. Soon, however, Spain would turn to the business of eliminating every Jew and every Muslim from its territory.

In 1492, Ferdinand and Isabella issued their famous decree giving Jews the choice either to convert to Catholicism or to leave Spain within four months. According to one estimate, 200,000 Jews left Spain, roughly 120,000 of them going to Portugal and the rest to Italy and the Ottoman lands. In 1502, the Muslims of Castile were ordered to convert or emigrate. Almost all chose to convert, creating a massive new group called Moriscos. A similar decree soon followed for the Muslims of Aragon. In 1526 the Inquisition began prosecuting Moriscos for failing to practice Christianity. The Spanish monarchy had officially embraced intolerance, and for an empire hoping to rise in global preeminence, this was a staggeringly bad move.[7]

The first wave of the Inquisition decimated Spain's *converso* population. In Valencia between 1494 and 1530, nearly one thousand *conversos* were convicted of "judaizing" and sentenced to death. In Seville over roughly the same period, an estimated four thousand *conversos* were burned at the stake. Terrified, tens of thousands of *converso* families fled.

The mass exodus of Spain's *conversos* and Jews left a catastrophic financial vacuum. Castilian culture did not favor finance or trade. There was a distinctly anti-entrepreneurial streak among Spain's Castilian elite, who exalted instead the warrior, the priest, and the aristocratic landowner. Nevertheless, before 1492, foreign bankers played virtually no role in Spain. As the Spaniards themselves saw it, "[O]ur kings . . . did not need bankers foreign to the kingdom. The Abrahams, Isaacs, and Samuels sufficed." This domination of finance by Jews and *conversos* was in many respects a healthy state of affairs: Jews had a powerful interest in maintaining the strength of the Spanish state, on which they depended for their protection. Throughout the fourteenth and fifteenth centuries, this symbiotic relationship served the Spanish kings well. By the end of the 1400s, the Spanish crown united under Ferdinand and Isabella was one of the richest in Europe, and Spain "the greatest power on earth."

But by attacking its Jews and *conversos*, Spain destroyed its own primary source of credit and thereafter became completely dependent on foreign bankers, including the Dutch, the Germans, the French, and especially the hated Genoese ("white Moors," as a resentful Spaniard called them). The price of capital increased. As early as 1509, the Genoese were making loans at such high rates of interest that the archbishop of Seville sought to ban them, but Ferdinand sanctioned them on grounds of necessity.

Within a few decades, Genoese bankers controlled the provisioning of the Spanish fleet, and "[f]oreign bankers ran the Crown's finances." This dependence on foreign financiers was particularly perilous because these were the years of Spain's most aggressive imperial expansion, particularly in the Americas, with naval expeditions and warfare calling for seemingly limitless sums of money. Hence the ironic emergence of an empire that was essentially insolvent even as it discovered and exploited the vastest reserves of precious metals yet encountered.[8]

The fantastic gold and silver mines of Central and South America poured their ore onto Spanish ships, but the ore was pledged in advance to foreign bankers who had financed the ships, the army, and the luxurious opulence of the Spanish crown. Royal bankruptcies occurred in 1557 and 1575. Suddenly, the crown reawakened to the utility of Jewish financiers.

In 1580, Spain absorbed the kingdom of Portugal and, desperate for capital, Philip II began to accept loans from Portuguese Jews and "New Christians" (the *conversos* of Portugal). Many of these New Christians attained great wealth, becoming important investors in Spanish international trade, making fortunes in Brazilian sugar, Asian spices, and African slaves. Some Portuguese New Christians emigrated to the Spanish American colonies, where, for example, they dominated the Pacific trade in and out of Lima. Others returned to Spain—the land their ancestors had fled a century before—believing that the period of persecution was over.[9]

They were mistaken. Perversely but predictably, a new paroxysm of religious intolerance surged through Spain. In the 1590s, the dormant Inquisition came back to life, starting with a relentless campaign of persecution, torture, and execution directed at New Christians in La Mancha, who were denounced as secret Jews by their debtors. *Limpieza de sangre*—or "purity of blood"—once again became a battle cry, as old statutes were resurrected banning anyone with Jewish blood from holding positions in government, universities and colleges, and military and religious institutions. In 1600, the Inquisition of Lima attacked Portuguese New Christians in Peru. In 1609, Spain commenced another mass expulsion, this time directed not at Jews but at Muslims and "secret" Muslims. By 1614, Spain had driven out about a quarter million Moriscos, destroying its own agricultural base in the south.[10]

With ebbs and flows, Spain persisted in this fanatical, self-destructive intolerance throughout the seventeenth century. In 1625, thirty-nine New Christians were executed at an *auto-da-fé* in Córdoba. In 1632, the Inquisition celebrated another act of faith in Madrid, burning seven "judaizers" to death before King Philip IV. At Granada in 1672, seventy-nine more were burned at the stake. And at Madrid again in 1680, twenty-one "perfidious Jews . . . God's worst enemies" were executed before Charles II and his court. All told, the Inquisition burned some 32,000 "heretics" at the stake. At the same time, the empire took on the mission of defender of the faith in Europe, spending fortunes on wars against Protestants in Germany, France, and the Netherlands. In 1767, King Charles III actually expelled Spain's *Jesuits*, supposedly because of "machinations" so "abominable" that the king had to keep "the most absolute silence on th[e] subject."[11]

———

Why sixteenth-century Spain declined has been a favorite topic of historians. Technological backwardness, entrenched feudal traditions, crushing foreign debt, the lack of a significant industrial and entrepreneurial sector, demographic decline, a weak state apparatus, and chronic budgetary crises are some of the contributing factors most often cited.[12] In fact, many of these factors can be traced, directly or indirectly, to the Spanish crown's official embrace of religious purging and burning beginning in the 1480s.

This is not to suggest that the Inquisition was the source of all of Spain's ills—a position mocked by one writer of the nineteenth century: "Why was there no industry in Spain? On account of the Inquisition. . . . Why are Spaniards lazy? On account of the Inquisition. Why are there bull-fights in Spain? On account of the Inquisition. Why do Spaniards take a siesta? On account of the Inquisition."[13]

Nevertheless, the fact remains that Spanish intolerance—the combination of the Inquisition, the expulsions, the *limpieza de sangre* statutes, and so on—inflicted catastrophic costs on the empire. Even putting aside the horrendous killing and human suffering, Spain's religious persecutions required a colossal waste of resources. For example, to expel its quarter-million-strong Morisco community, Spain had to put into service its entire navy and militia. The trials and torture chambers of the Inquisition were deadweight losses, generating no knowledge or wealth, only hatred and paranoia. Moreover, with each new round of violent fanaticism, Spain either destroyed or drove out its most valuable sources of human, financial, and social capital. Eventually, Spain's "purification" campaigns tore into every level of society: its rural population, its artisans, its doctors and scientists, its merchants and financiers, even its Catholic nobility, many (if not most) of whom had Jewish ancestry.

Perhaps he was just posturing, but Ferdinand himself seemed to be aware of the self-destructiveness of the Jewish expulsion he ordered. In a letter sent on the same day the decree was issued, Ferdinand wrote that he had been persuaded by the Holy Office of the Inquisition to expel the Jews "despite the great harm to ourselves, seeking and preferring the salvation of souls above our own profit and that of individuals."[14]

In any case, by 1640 Spain was on the brink of collapse, no longer even one of Europe's premier powers. It continued to decline thereafter, becoming increasingly marginal on the world stage. While it is by no means clear that a tolerant Spain could have become a hyperpower—to reiterate my thesis, tolerance is a necessary but not sufficient condition of world dominance—there is no question that imperial Spain's intolerance stymied its ascent and precipitated its downward spiral.

Although Spain "specialized in expulsions," it was certainly not the only European power consumed by religious zeal. On the contrary, in pre-Enlightenment Europe, religious persecution and warfare were the rule, not the exception. In Germany in 1524, for example, peasants spurred by the Reformation slaughtered scores of Roman Catholics, who retaliated with even greater atrocities, triggering the so-called Peasants' War in which an estimated 100,000 ultimately died. In Italy in 1569, Pope Pius V expelled all Jews from the Papal States. In France in 1572, as many as 10,000 Huguenots were slaughtered in celebration of St. Bartholomew's Day. In Poland over 50,000 Jews were massacred between 1648 and 1654.

Nor was the Spanish monarchy alone in attempting to force religious uniformity on its subjects. In the German states, ruling princes vied to impose either absolute Calvinism or absolute Lutheranism on their territories. In Sweden, there was a single state church; nonattenders were fined and religious education was mandatory. Catholic Bohemia expelled its entire Protestant nobility in 1627. In Hungary, there was coercive Catholicization. In England, where Catholics were frequently attacked, the Anglican Church was established by law, with criminal penalties for nonconformity.[15]

At the dawn of the seventeenth century, the population of France was roughly 16 million. Spain and Portugal combined could boast about 10 million. Taken together, the various principalities of Germany had a population of perhaps 20 million.[16] Smaller than all these was the Netherlands, with a population of no more than two million. Yet it would be the tiny Dutch Republic that, within a half century, would eclipse all the other powers of Europe.

SIX

THE DUTCH WORLD EMPIRE

Diamonds, Damask, and Every
"Mongrel Sect in Christendom"

So, Amsterdam has risen through the hand of God to the peak of prosperity and greatness. . . . The whole world stands amazed at its riches and from east and west, north and south they come to behold it.

—DUTCH AUTHOR, 1662

This Citty is nott divided in to parishes as with us, butt every one goes to what church hee pleases, there beeing only 8 or 9 publicke churches besides the English, French, Lutherans, Anabaptists, etts., and Jewish Sinagogues. . . . Organs they have in some of them, butt are nott played til the people depart, soe thatt itt seemes they serve to blowe them outt off church. . . . Few holidaies observed, Christmas, Easter, Whitesontide and Sondaies excepted; the latter butt badly kept. A Tolleration here off all sects [of] religion.

—ENGLISHMAN PETER MUNDY ON AMSTERDAM, 1640

The Dutch are famous for many things—clogs, windmills, tulips, Rembrandt, Vermeer—but these days it's often forgotten that the Dutch once presided over the world's preeminent maritime trading empire, the immediate predecessor to Britain's. It's often forgotten too that the Dutch were once the world's greatest producers of civet.

Civet is derived from civet cats, which are actually not cats at all but members of the mongoose family, native to Asia and Africa. In southern China, civet meat is a great delicacy—the "tiger" in the celebrated dragon, tiger, and phoenix soup. In 2004, civet cats were linked to the SARS outbreak and thousands were destroyed. In addition to its culinary importance, the civet cat also has a gland near its anus containing a musky, buttery substance. This secretion, called civet, has long been used to make some of the world's most expensive perfumes.

In the medieval era, civet was included in sweet-smelling pomanders thought to have the power to ward off disease. In the sixteenth century, it became a precious ingredient in high-end fragrances, coveted by the finest *parfumiers* of Paris. Before the advent of regular bathing and deodorants, fragrances strong enough to cover body odor were in great demand by the wealthy. Indeed, few things cost more per ounce than the highest-quality civet—in some cases, not even gold.

As a result, there was a thriving international trade in civet cats in the seventeenth century, and many tried to profit from it. England's Daniel Defoe, for example, earned a living by breeding civet cats before he wrote *Robinson Crusoe*. By the 1620s, however, the Dutch had cornered the civet trade.

Large merchant firms in Amsterdam sent Dutch ships to India, Java, and Guinea and brought back civet cats by the thousands. The civet cats were then raised in cages in Amsterdam, where they were fed milk and egg whites so that the civet they produced would be white, as opposed to its natural yellow or brownish color. Every several days, trained workers pinned down the live animals, squeezed open their perineal glands, and carefully scraped out the secretion. The civet was then quickly bottled—civet darkens and thickens when exposed to air—and exported along with certificates of purity to luxury markets throughout Europe.

Civet was just one commodity in Europe's "rich trades"—the

immensely lucrative traffic in luxury commodities—which the Dutch Republic dominated for much of the seventeenth century. The formula was straightforward. Dutch ships traveled to far-flung corners of the world, carrying back East Indies pepper and spices, sugar from Brazil and São Tomé, Turkish mohair, Castilian wool, and Indian cotton and raw diamonds. The Dutch either traded these riches throughout Europe or brought them back to Holland, where the raw materials were processed and reexported at enormous profit in the form of luxury tapestries, patterned silks, fine linens, and exquisitely cut gemstones. So spectacularly profitable was this global trade that the English, French, Germans, Venetians, and especially Spanish all vied to control it—or even just parts of it.[1]

A note on nomenclature, which in the case of the Netherlands can be quite confusing: The European country that today is officially named the Kingdom of the Netherlands is often called Holland, even by the Dutch themselves. Technically, however, Holland refers only to the Netherlands' two most economically and politically important provinces, North Holland and South Holland, which include the major cities of Amsterdam, Delft, Haarlem, The Hague, Leiden, and Rotterdam.

To complicate matters further, the Netherlands' borders and political configuration have changed significantly over time. In the Middle Ages, the territory roughly covering modern Belgium, Luxembourg, northwest France, and the Netherlands was known as the Low Countries. (Belgium and Luxembourg achieved independence in the 1830s.) The Reformation brought dramatic changes. For a time, southern Netherlands came under the authority of the Catholic Hapsburgs, while Protestant-dominated northern Netherlands became known as the United Provinces, and eventually the Republic of the United Provinces.[2]

In this chapter, I will use all these terms—the Low Countries, the Netherlands, the Dutch Republic, the United Provinces—depending on the historical context. Holland will generally refer only to the provinces of that name.

BEFORE THE RISE

Like the Great Mongol Empire, the Dutch Republic that shot to global prominence in the seventeenth century could not have had humbler beginnings. Before 1200, Holland and the other low-lying western regions of the Netherlands were practically—and in some cases, literally—under water. (The elevation of the Netherlands falls as one moves from east to west, toward the North Sea. The country's highest point is in the southeast. Even today, approximately 27 percent of the country, home to 60 percent of the population, is below sea level.) Lying in the swampy deltas of three rivers, this "sand and mud dump left over from the ice age" was barely populated, unfit for agriculture, and, because of constant flooding, often dangerous.

Starting in the thirteenth century, major areas of waterlogged Holland, including modern Amsterdam and Rotterdam, were reclaimed through the construction of ingenious dams, dikes, and drainage systems. Although the windmill was not invented in Holland—early versions existed in Persia in the ninth century—the Dutch perfected the technology, using wind power to pump water to safer areas. Even the English lampoonist Owen Felltham, who called the Dutch Republic a "universall quagmire" and "a green cheese in a pickle," conceded that the Dutch were "in some sort Gods, for they set bounds to the Ocean and allow it to come and go as they list."[3]

Nevertheless, as late as 1350, the Low Countries were an unremarkable spot on the broad European map, largely dependent on subsistence farming and collectively no larger than the state of Tennessee. Unlike in Spain or France, both of which were ruled by strong monarchies, government in the Low Countries was local and decentralized. In terms of religious tolerance, or rather the lack thereof, the Low Countries were also unexceptional. As throughout Europe, the bubonic plague in the Netherlands was blamed on many things—the unfavorable alignment of the planets, the sins of the world—but particularly on Jews:

> The Black Death was so devastating that it simply had to be
> a conspiracy against mankind. And who could be behind that

if not the Jews, who—as every Christian by then knew—were the enemies of the Church and . . . were seeking to destroy Christianity and rule the world in its stead? The Jews were the culprits: they had, it was reported, contaminated the wells with poison prepared from spiders, owls, lizards, basilisks, the blood of children, and the consecrated Host. The poison had been concocted in Toledo by rich Spanish Jews, and then been brought over in pouches and pieces of leather and thrown down the wells.[4]

Even after the plague passed, the few Jews left in the Low Countries were stigmatized and persecuted. As in England and France, Jews in the Netherlands were forced to wear identifying yellow patches (as opposed to the pointy red hats they were made to wear in Germany at around the same time). In 1439, a handsome Jewish man was accused of "turning the heads" of young girls. Known as "the Jew with the beautiful hair," he was imprisoned in a castle by the Duke of Rozendaal and eventually expelled from Arnhem. Starting in the fifteenth century, laws were passed restricting Jewish money-lending practices, effectively closing off the only source of livelihood available to Jews. Until the late sixteenth century, the Jewish population in the Low Countries remained negligible.[5]

CATHOLICS AGAINST PROTESTANTS: THE FORMATION OF THE DUTCH REPUBLIC

For most of the sixteenth century, the Low Countries were part of the Hapsburg Empire, which at the time stretched from Austria to Spain. How Spain came under Hapsburg control is worth a brief digression. Ferdinand and Isabella had five children, one of whom came to be known as Joanna the Mad. Joanna married Philip the Handsome, heir to both the Hapsburg and Burgundian territories, and gave birth to Charles V. After his grandfather Ferdinand of Aragon died in 1516, Charles became the first Hapsburg king of Spain. By 1519, as a result of his various royal bloodlines, Charles was ruler of Burgundy, archduke of Austria, and sovereign of the

Netherlands. The same year he was also crowned Holy Roman Emperor.

Charles, who was born in Ghent, was sympathetic to the Dutch. Under his rule, the Low Countries received unrestricted trading rights and came to control a majority of the world's trading volume. The advent of the Reformation, however, proved as divisive in the Netherlands as it was throughout Europe. Calvinism swept with intoxicating force across the Low Countries, pitting Protestants against Catholics in both the northern and southern provinces. This rift was exacerbated in 1556, when Charles abdicated his claims to the Netherlands and Spain in favor of his son Philip II.

Unlike his father, Philip was born and raised in Spain, spoke no Dutch, and openly disdained the Low Countries. He was also a far more zealous Catholic. Making it his holy mission to stop the expansion of the Reformation, Philip launched "one of the most dramatic, bloody, and confused episodes of early modern European history."[6]

Philip demanded absolute loyalty to the Roman Catholic Church and appointed Catholic, non-Dutch-speaking governors all over the Netherlands. In the 1560s, led by William the Silent of Orange, many of the northern provinces began agitating against the Spanish yoke. Philip responded by sending 10,000 troops, led by the Spanish Duke of Alva, to deal with the troublemakers. As one author describes him, the Duke of Alva was "unswerving, even fanatical, in his detestation of Protestant heresy. . . . Capable of great cruelty but always out of calculation, his outlook was a strange mixture of humanist cosmopolitanism and xenophobic bigotry. . . . His deeply suspicious attitude towards the Netherlands nobility and population was tinged with scarcely veiled contempt."[7]

Evidently in one of his less humanist moods, Alva, upon arriving in the Netherlands, promptly convened a tribunal—nicknamed "The Council of Blood"—and proceeded to execute one thousand Dutch, including many prominent citizens, while imprisoning and confiscating the property of many more. He also levied heavy new taxes. Starting in 1572, popular revolts erupted throughout the north Netherlands. Alva retaliated brutally, devastating Haarlem and massacring the townspeople of Mechelen, Naarden, and Zutphen. Aggravated by the arrival of the Dutch "Sea Beggars"—fiercely anti-Catholic, piratelike forces recently expelled from England's ports—violence stretched on for four years. What happened next was unexpected.[7]

In 1576, mutinous, starving Spanish troops—unpaid by the financially strained Philip II—left the rebellious north for the prosperous south, where they plundered Antwerp and slaughtered as many as seven thousand citizens. This incident became known as the Spanish Fury. Although the massacre occurred in the south, it had a far more lasting influence in the north, where it was captured in apocalyptic detail by contemporary poets and artists, becoming part of the Netherlands' national birth story. In one famous account by the Amsterdam poet Pieter Hooft, a bride is raped and murdered on her wedding day by a sadistic Spanish captain: "He stripped her, chains, clothing, underthings, everything from top to bottom taken from that pure body." Having abused her, the captain "hunted her, mother-naked, dripping with the blood of her innumerable wounds, through the city."

The Spanish Fury prompted the signing of the Pacification of Ghent, in which the northern and southern provinces of the Netherlands united to drive out the Spanish troops. But the Pacification was short-lived. In 1579, led by influential Catholic nobles, the southern provinces declared anew their loyalty to Philip II, Spain, and the Catholic Church. In response, the northern provinces proclaimed their autonomy and their right to religious freedom. Two years later, they enacted the Oath of Abjuration, a declaration of independence with an opening sentiment that found a striking echo in American history two hundred years later:

As 'tis apparent to all that a prince is constituted by God to be ruler of a people, to defend them from oppression and violence as the shepherd his sheep; and whereas God did not create the people slaves to their prince, to obey his commands, whether right or wrong, but rather the prince for the sake of the subjects. . . . [When a prince] does not behave thus, but, on the contrary, oppresses them, seeking opportunities to infringe their ancient customs and privileges, exacting from them slavish compliance, then he is no longer a prince, but a tyrant, and the subjects . . . may not only disallow his authority, but legally proceed to the choice of another prince for their defense. This is . . . what the law of nature dictates for the defense of liberty, which we ought to transmit to posterity, even at the hazard of our lives.

Thereafter, the seven northern provinces became the United Provinces of the Netherlands, while the ten southern provinces remained under the rule of Spain.[8]

Philip II, however, had by no means conceded defeat. On the contrary, he put a bounty of 25,000 gold coins on William the Silent's head and sent more troops to subdue the rebellious north. Recognizing Spain's superior military force, William responded by offering leadership of the new republic, limited by a host of constitutional safeguards, to the Duke of Anjou, the younger brother of the king of France. The duke accepted, but he fled after less than two years in the face of a mounting Spanish advance. In 1584, William the Silent was assassinated by a Spaniard named Balthazar Gérard. Gérard, however, never collected his reward. The Dutch were not above cruel and unusual punishment for assassins, and Gérard met a painful end involving the creative use of hot irons and boiling bacon fat.

Following William's death, the Dutch offered sovereignty over the Netherlands to the king of France himself. Preoccupied with civil war and reluctant to take on Spain, Henri III refused. The Dutch next offered themselves to England's Queen Elizabeth, who also eventually declined.[9]

MONGRELS AND SERPENTS: THE BIRTH OF
TOLERANCE IN THE DUTCH REPUBLIC

We are now at the year 1588. The United Provinces, incapable of their own self-defense, have tried unsuccessfully to give away their country to both France and England. The Dutch do not exactly seem world dominant. Yet by 1625, the Dutch Republic had become the "hegemonic power of the capitalist world-economy"— the "first truly global" empire.[10] What happened?

The tiny Dutch Republic became the world's economic hyperpower in the seventeenth century by turning itself into a haven for enterprising outcasts from the rest of Europe. To be sure, several other coincidental developments helped make this possible. War among Spain, England, and France, for example, kept those nations preoccupied, draining them financially and giving the Dutch a respite from Spanish aggression. But by far the most crucial factor underlying the Dutch surge to global primacy was an extraordinary economic explosion. It was here that the Dutch Republic's exceptional policies of religious tolerance proved indispensable.

Given the religious warfare, persecution, and zealotry all over seventeenth-century Europe, the tolerant policies of the Dutch Republic are all the more remarkable. Almost unique in Europe, the United Provinces had no established state church. Its founding charter, the 1579 Union of Utrecht, mandated, "Each person shall remain free in his religion and . . . no one shall be investigated or persecuted because of his religion." The state did not compel adherence to the Reformed Church, impose fines for nonconformity, or punish dissenters.

Of course, plenty of ministers preached orthodoxy from their pulpits, fulminating against the abomination of organ music in church, the persistence of "pagan" festivals and village fairs, and the scandalous rage "for curled long hair that swept the Republic in the 1640s." Moreover, the Dutch Reformed Church always occupied a privileged status. Nonmembers were officially barred from holding government positions, and other religions could not be professed "in public."

In practice, however, religious heterodoxy and lenience prevailed. Local parishes were permitted to choose how doctrinally pure they wanted to be, and most chose flexibility. Alongside the Calvinist majority, Catholics, Jews, Lutherans, Mennonites, and Remonstrants all were permitted to establish private, "inconspicuous" places of worship, to open seminaries, and to print their own sacred and scholarly books. In addition, many government officials were only nominal members of the Reformed Church and barely tried to conceal their true anti-orthodox inclinations.[11]

Thus, in 1616, when Jews in the rest of Christian Europe were being attacked and terrorized, Rabbi Izak Uziel wrote to a correspondent: "At present, [our] people live peaceably in Amsterdam. The inhabitants of this city, mindful of the increase in population, make laws and ordinances whereby the freedom of religions may be upheld. Each may follow his own belief but may not openly show that he is of a different faith from the inhabitants of the city." Although Jewish prayer sessions were initially held in private homes, by the 1620s several synagogues existed in Amsterdam. Indeed, as early as 1612, Amsterdam's city council "acted as if the Jews had the full right to practice their religion openly." In 1675, Amsterdam's splendid Sephardic synagogue was constructed. Inspired by the Temple of Solomon in Jerusalem and accommodating two thousand people, the synagogue, with its soaring columns, dark oak pews, and great brass chandeliers, was not exactly "inconspicuous." Around the same time, Ashkenazi Jews founded their own synagogue directly across the street, along with their own rabbinical authorities, dietary regulations, and Yiddish publishing houses.[12]

The Dutch Republic's extraordinary religious freedom became the talk of Europe. There were a few admirers, including one who wrote to Descartes in 1631, "[Is there another] country where you can enjoy such a perfect liberty . . . and where there has survived more of the innocence of our forefathers?" But most foreigners were appalled by what they saw as the Dutch Republic's religious debauchery. "Is there a mongrel sect in Christendom," demanded one English propagandist, "which does not croak and spawn and flourish in their Sooterkin bogs?" "Sometimes seven religions are found in one family," deplored another. Even those who benefited from asylum in the Dutch Republic expressed dismay at what the historian Simon Schama calls "the bargain basement of faiths" in which they found themselves—a "Den of several Serpents," as one Englishman put it, in which "you may be what Devil you will so long as you push not the State with your horns."[13]

There was a keenly calculating side to Dutch toleration. Many of the republic's leading political figures explicitly advocated religious freedom on the grounds that it would be economically advantageous. Pieter de la Court, for example, wrote in his *Interest of Holland* that "toleration was essential" to "stimulate the immigration so urgently needed to sustain the economy and population of Holland's cities." Insofar as Dutch tolerance was instrumentally motivated, it was enormously successful.

The Dutch Republic became a magnet for streams of religious refugees from all over Europe—Protestants from the south Netherlands, Huguenots from France, German Lutherans, Sephardic Jews from Spain and Portugal, Ashkenazi Jews from eastern Europe, and Quakers and Pilgrims from England. (The Pilgrims, a separatist branch of Puritans singled out for persecution in England, found a haven in Holland for twelve years before setting out on the *Mayflower* in 1620 for New England.) Many other immigrants came for purely economic reasons. Between roughly 1570 and 1670, while many European cities were stagnating, Amsterdam's population shot up from 30,000 to 200,000; Leiden's, from 15,000 to 72,000; Haarlem's, from 16,000 to 50,000; and Rotterdam's, from 7,000 to 45,000. Collectively, these immigrants formed the engine that propelled the Dutch Republic—for a brief half century—to global economic dominance in every economic sphere.[14]

THE "SPIRIT OF CAPITALISM": SPAIN'S LOSS AND HOLLAND'S GAIN

The Dutch economic explosion was fueled principally by Jews and, to an even greater extent, Protestants—both fleeing persecution from Hapsburg Spain. As these two groups built flourishing communities in Holland, they made the Dutch Republic the center of global trade, industry, and finance.

Take, for instance, the diamond trade. Before 1725, when diamonds were discovered in Brazil, virtually all of the world's raw diamonds came from India. Some of the most famous diamonds in history hail from India, including the legendary Hope, a rare blue diamond weighing 44.5 carats, the 280-carat Great Mogul (current whereabouts unknown), and the 100-plus-carat Kohinoor, now one of England's crown jewels. (In 2000, members of India's parliament demanded that the British government return the Kohinoor; for the moment, it is still embedded in the queen's crown in the Tower of London.) The early mining methods used in India were primitive. Poor laborers from the lowest castes, sometimes 60,000 at a site, dug shallow pits along riverbeds. The excavated gravel was then hand-sifted for diamonds.

The business of transforming these rough stones from India into the gorgeous, sparkling multifaceted gems that adorned the necks of Europe's aristocracy was dominated by Jews. As early as AD 1000 a network of Jewish merchants extending from Madras to Cairo to Venice had controlled the world's diamond trade. Moneylenders since antiquity (because they were barred from most other forms of livelihood), Jews had developed an expertise in appraising, cutting, and selling gems, which were often put up as collateral for loans. As a result, where the Jews settled, they brought the diamond business with them, together with an ever-expanding trading and financing network linking Europe and the Mediterranean to Asia, Africa, and the Americas.

When Spain expelled its Jews in 1492, many of them settled in Lisbon and later in Antwerp (at that time still under Hapsburg rule). Not coincidentally, both cities became booming hubs of international trade and finance. Lisbon became the entry point for almost every diamond destined for Europe, and Antwerp became the world's preeminent diamond-cutting center. By 1550, the port of Antwerp was so crowded that incoming merchant ships had to wait in long queues before unloading their cargo: The city had become the securities exchange for the entire Hapsburg Empire—indeed, the "supreme money market" for all Europe.[15]

But rising intolerance cost the Hapsburgs dearly. When the Inquisition hit Portugal in earnest in the 1540s, and as expulsion efforts mounted in Antwerp in the 1550s, Jews and *conversos* began fleeing to the more tolerant towns of Holland. These Iberian Jews and *conversos*, in contrast to the large numbers of impoverished and poorly educated Ashkenazi Jews flooding into the Netherlands to escape pogroms in Poland and Germany, were among the wealthiest merchants and financiers in the world. Elegant, erudite, and aristocratic—and many of them eventually ennobled—these Sephardic Jews poured capital into the Dutch Republic, infusing bank reserves, augmenting state funds, fueling Dutch colonialism, and playing a central role in the establishment of the famous Amsterdam Stock Exchange. By the mid-seventeenth century, Amsterdam had replaced Lisbon and Antwerp as the diamond center of Europe and the hub of the worldwide Jewish banking and trading network.

Jewish families also became prominent in lucrative industries such as tobacco spinning, sugar refining, silk weaving, chocolate making, and civet and diamond production. (It was common for Ashkenazi Jews to work as menial laborers for Sephardic employers. Poor Ashkenazi Jews, for example, were often seen outside Amsterdam scrounging up cheap meat to feed civet cats.) Many, including the Belmonte, Lopes Suasso, Nunes de Costa, and Pinto families, were also great philanthropists. They served as patrons for artists, poets, and musicians, established welfare programs, and funded both religious and secular scholarly academies. Concerts and operas were held at their magnificent homes, which were filled with artworks and rare books and manuscripts.[16]

The economic benefits brought by the Jews to the Dutch Republic hardly went unnoticed by the Spanish. Many advisors even urged the Spanish crown to reverse the Inquisition and to recruit *conversos* back to Spain. Diego de Cisneros, for example, warned in 1637 that Amsterdam's newly arrived Jews were making the republic too powerful:

[T]he Dutch rebels have raised their head and increased their power, the Jews assisting them in their wars, conquests, negotiations and other pretensions and becoming in the lands of Your Majesty, spies of the said rebels, penetrating the centres of trade, administration of the *armadas*, convoy and revenues of Your Majesty . . . sucking out the core of wealth (from Spain and Portugal).[17]

But important as Jews were to the Dutch economic boom, their overall numbers were small and their contributions paled by comparison to those of another group. In the late sixteenth century, a massive influx of Protestant merchants, skilled workers, and industrialists played an even greater role in bringing what Max Weber famously called "the spirit of capitalism" to the Netherlands.

———————

During the Middle Ages, the cities of Ghent and Bruges in the south Netherlands—with their long traditions of spinning, dyeing, and weaving—were flourishing producers of fine textiles. By 1500 nearby Antwerp was Europe's textile marketplace and a major industrial center. Although part of the Spanish Hapsburg Empire, Antwerp, Ghent, and Bruges were hotbeds of Calvinism, particularly among the working and merchant classes. As anti-Protestant persecution mounted under Philip II, these cities suffered a catastrophic exodus of Protestant skill and capital. Between 1560 and 1589, the population of Antwerp plunged from 85,000 to 42,000. Over roughly the same period, Ghent and Bruges each lost about half their inhabitants.

Most of these émigrés moved to the north Netherlands, typically settling in Amsterdam, Leiden, or Haarlem, where they could practice their religions freely. Many were highly skilled textile workers with sophisticated specialties. (Vermeer's father, for example, specialized in patterned satins, and Jacob van Ruisdael's father designed cartoons for tapestries.) These immigrants brought with them not just skill and experience but the most advanced techniques and technology for processing raw materials. By the 1590s,

most of Antwerp's wealthiest Protestant merchants and industrialists had also resettled in Holland, attracted by the Dutch Republic's new pools of skilled labor, exploding commercialism, and the
unrivaled economic and social opportunities open to individuals of
all religions.[18]

Almost overnight—and largely because of the infusion of immigrant skill—the Dutch Republic surged to dominance in an astonishing range of industries, from sugar refining to armament
manufacture to chemical production. Most crucially, Holland replaced Antwerp as Europe's leader in textile finishing and refining.
With talent and technology taken straight from Antwerp, "Haarlem became the centre where coarse linens from Germany were
bleached and finished. . . . Amsterdam dyed and dressed semi-
finished cloths imported 'in the white' from England. Leyden . . .
[was revitalized] by Southern Netherlands' immigrants to become
the largest manufacturing centre of the so-called 'New Draperies'
of seventeenth-century Europe."

Soon Holland had completely cornered Europe's "rich trades,"
which had formerly been dominated by the Hanseatic League (an
alliance of northern European trading guilds), the English, and in
earlier times the Venetians. Fleets of ships laden with fine linens,
velvets, camlets, satins, and damask sailed from Holland to the
great ports of Spain and Portugal. There, the Dutch sold their fine
textiles for Spanish silver, with which they bought raw materials
and luxury goods from the East Indies and the New World: pepper, sugar, spices, metals, coffee, tea, coral, cotton, silk, wool, and
mohair. With their supply of silver, their more efficient ships, and
their unmatched trading networks in the Baltics and northern Europe, the Dutch quickly became, in Daniel Defoe's words, "the
Carryers of the World, the middle Persons in Trade, the Factors
and Brokers of Europe."[19]

Indeed, the Dutch accumulated such sensational wealth from
the rich trades that in 1598 Spain placed an embargo on all Dutch
ships, barring them from Iberian ports, thus hoping to cut off
Dutch access to colonial products. This proved a fatal error. With
their fortunes threatened, and with more capital to invest than

ever, the elite merchants of Holland decided to bypass Spain and
Portugal completely and send their own ships directly to the East
Indies and the Americas. Thus was born the United East India
Company (Vereenigde Oostindische Compagnie) and later the
West India Company (Westindische Compagnie), and with them
the rise of the Dutch Republic as a world colonial power.[20]

EMPIRE: "GOLD IS YOUR GOD"

By 1601, there were eight private Dutch companies, with a total of
sixty-five ships, frantically vying with one another to buy up commodities in the East Indies. Initially reaping immense returns, the
Dutch merchants quickly found that competition among them was
driving up prices and threatening their profits. At the same time,
Dutch vessels were subject to raids by pirates, enemy warships, and
privateers. Moreover, unlike Spain and Portugal, the Dutch had no
collective, sovereign armed presence in Asia, Africa, or the New
World. In the East and West Indies, Spain and Portugal had conquered peoples and colonized lands, a convenient means of extracting raw materials for commerce. The Dutch merchants saw
these advantages and took a lesson from them.

In 1602, a collaboration of Dutch merchants, burghers, and
ministers established the East India Company, a joint-stock trading
monopoly armed with sovereign powers. The East India Company
could conduct diplomacy, sign treaties, form alliances, maintain
troops, install viceroys, and make war. All of its agents, whether
naval commanders or expatriate governors-general, had to swear
double oaths of alliance to the company and to the States General
of the United Provinces.

The composition of the founding investors of the East India
Company was striking. In the most important Amsterdam cham-
ber, there were more than a thousand initial investors, eighty-one
of whom provided about half the total capital. Of these eighty-one
"chief investors," roughly half were wealthy Protestant refugees
who had fled Spanish persecution, and roughly half were native
Hollanders. The former group, which contributed significantly

more capital, included famous Antwerp merchant-banking families such as the Bartolottis, Coymans, De Scots, and De Vogelaers. The native Hollanders, who were less wealthy (at least initially) but more politically influential, included Gerrit Bicker, son of a brewer, Reinier Pauw, son of a grain trader, and Gerrit Reynst, son of a soap boiler. All these men made immense fortunes in long-distance commerce. There were also three chief investors who were immigrants from Germany, including the magnate Jan Poppen, whose family by 1631 was the single wealthiest in all Amsterdam, followed by the Bartolotti and Coymans families. Although Holland's towns were typically ten to twenty percent Catholic, all the chief investors of the East India Company were Protestant.[21]

Nevertheless, Dutch overseas expansion was not driven by religious zeal. In contrast to the Spanish and Portuguese, very few Dutch missionaries went over to the East Indies or the Americas to "save heathens." Certainly there were some ardent Calvinists among the Dutch empire builders, including the God-fearing admiral Piet Heyn and the governor-general Jan Pieterszoon Coen. But men like Heyn and Coen complained constantly about the lack of religious piety among their fellow Dutch expatriates in Asia. One reverend grumbled, "Dutch sailors knew as little of the Bible as they did of the Koran." Dutch imperialism was fueled not by Calvinism but by profit seeking. As West African tribesmen said to Dutch traders in the early seventeenth century, "Gold is your god." Sweden's Charles X made the same point a few years later: When a Dutch envoy made a comment about freedom of religion, the king pulled a coin from his pocket and declared, *"Voilà votre religion!"*[22]

The early 1600s saw a burst of Dutch commercial and colonial expansion all over the globe. In 1605 the Dutch seized the Indonesian Spice Islands from the Portuguese. In 1610 the East India Company installed its first governor-general in Java, as well as trading posts on the neighboring islands of Ternate, Tidore, Amboina, and Banda. In 1619, the Dutch captured Jakarta and, renaming it Batavia, made it the company's new headquarters. Over the same period, the Dutch replaced the Portuguese as the dominant power on the West African coast, taking over the region's gold and ivory trade. Even more dramatically, between 1599 and 1605 the Dutch sent 768 vessels to the Caribbean and the shores of northern South America—formerly Spain's stranglehold—successfully procuring large quantities of salt, tobacco, hides, sugar, and silver bullion.

Meanwhile, back in Europe, the long Dutch struggle for independence from Spain (lasting from 1568 to 1648 and known as the Dutch Revolt or the Eighty Years' War) stretched on, with increasing victories for the Dutch. Fueled by the economic explosion, the Dutch adopted a series of military reforms soon copied all over Europe. Troops were paid regularly. More powerful weaponry was introduced and ammunition standardized. Battlefield training and techniques were revolutionized; soldiers, for example, were drilled to load and fire in synchronized fashion, allowing continuous volleys by successive lines of infantry. Dutch battlefield superiority grew so pronounced that in the Battle of Turnhout in 1597 an estimated 2,250 Spanish soldiers were killed, while the Dutch may have lost as few as four men—or, at the highest estimate, one hundred.

In 1607, Dutch warships crushed the Spanish in the Bay of Gibraltar, their own backyard. In 1609, Spain signed the Twelve Years Truce with "the Dutch rebels," allowing Dutch ships once again to enter the ports of Spain, Portugal, and Flanders and to ply international waters without fear of attack by Spanish warships or privateers. Dutch freight and shipping insurance charges immediately plunged. Dutch profits soared to new heights, and the republic's commercial ascendancy over the Baltic, Mediterranean, and northern European trade reached its zenith. When the truce expired, Spain did not renew its terms. In 1621, war resumed and Spain reimposed its embargo. The same year, the Dutch West Indies Company was officially created, and Dutch colonization in the New World took off.

By the 1630s, the Dutch had wrested from Portugal almost the entire sugar trade between Brazil and northern Europe. In 1634 the Dutch captured Curaçao from Spain and established a permanent base in the Caribbean. By 1648 the Dutch flag flew over Aruba,

Bonaire, half of St. Martin, and the other islands collectively known today as the Netherlands Antilles. Meanwhile, back in 1609, Henry Hudson, an Englishman hired and provisioned by the Dutch, had claimed much of New York State on behalf of his new employer. By the mid-seventeenth century, the Dutch, from bases in New Amsterdam (now Manhattan) and Fort Orange (now Albany), controlled North America's lucrative fur trade.[23]

Like the East India Company, the Dutch West India Company was founded in large part by immigrants who fled to the Dutch Republic because of its relative religious tolerance. Again, these included many wealthy Protestant refugees—indeed, the West India Company was far more belligerently Calvinist than its East India counterpart. On the other hand, whereas Jews played a relatively small role in the East India Company, they figured much more prominently in the activities of the West India Company.

With their fluency in both Dutch and the Iberian languages, as well as their long-standing expertise in trading sugar and other tropical raw materials, Holland's Sephardic Jews were particularly well suited to serve as Dutch colonists in the West Indies. By 1644, Dutch Jews represented approximately one-third of all the white civilians in Netherlands Brazil.

Dutch Jews also helped colonize Guyana, Barbados, Martinique, and Jamaica, as well as smaller islands like Nevis, Grenada, and Tobago. The largest and most important Jewish colony in the New World was Curaçao, followed by the five-hundred-person Sephardic community in Suriname, which by 1694 owned forty sugar plantations and nine thousand slaves.[24]

By the mid-seventeenth century, the Dutch Republic was "indisputably the greatest trading nation in the world, with commercial outposts and fortified 'factories' scattered from Archangel to Recife and from New Amsterdam to Nagasaki." Incalculable quantities of luxury goods flowed into and through Holland. On June 27, 1634, the following immense bounty was unloaded in the port of Amsterdam:

326,733½ Amsterdam pounds of Malacca pepper; 297,446 lb. of cloves; 292,623 lb. of saltpetre; 141,278 lb. of indigo;

483,082 lb. of sappan wood; 219,027 pieces of blue Ming ware; 52 further chests of Korean and Japanese porcelain; 75 large vases and pots containing preserved confections, much of it spiced ginger; 660 lb. of Japanese copper; 241 pieces of fine Japanese lacquer work; 3,989 rough diamonds of large carat; 93 boxes of pearls and rubies (misc. carats); 603 bales of dressed Persian silks and grosgreins; 1,155 lb. of raw Chinese silk; 199,800 lb. of unrefined Kandy [i.e., Ceylon] sugar.[25]

THE DUTCH GOLDEN AGE

The Dutch have long had a reputation for thrift. Owen Felltham accused the Dutch of being "frugal to the saving of an egg-shell." Even Sir William Temple, the English ambassador to The Hague in 1668–70 and generally an admirer of the United Provinces, expressed irritation that the Dutch had gotten so wealthy through "Parsimony":

For never any Countrey traded so much and consumed so little: They are the great Masters of the Indian Spices and of the Persian Silks; but wear plain Woollen, and feed upon their own Fish and Roots. Nay they sell the finest of their own Cloath to France, and buy coarse out of England for their own wear. In short, they furnish infinite Luxury, which they never practise, and traffique in Pleasures which they never taste.

While some in the republic may have worn "plain Woollen" and fed upon "Roots," others did not. As Simon Schama has shown in *The Embarrassment of Riches*, many Dutch, from blue bloods to artisans, had no problem reconciling the strictures of Calvinism with lives of superabundance—prodigious meals, extravagant festivals, and lavish consumerism.

Like the United States for much of its history, the Dutch Republic in its seventeenth-century golden age was known throughout Europe as a land of opportunity: a New Jerusalem flowing with milk and honey. There was also plenty of poverty and inequality: The thousands of immigrants who poured into the republic between 1500 and 1700 included not just financiers and magnates but also child vagrants, prostitutes, and penniless seamen from Norway and Sweden. Nevertheless, the Dutch Republic was the richest country in Europe by a long shot, with even its unskilled workers enjoying higher standards of living and better diets than most people in the world.[26]

Just as Americans today are the world's overeaters, so too the Dutch were famous for stuffing themselves. The seventeenth-century English naturalist John Ray was revolted by the sight of Dutch men and women, most of them "big-boned and gross-bodied," "almost always eating." And it wasn't just the rich who ate well. Aristocrats and commoners ate surprisingly similar breakfasts, typically including bread, butter, cheese, fish, pastries, buttermilk, and beer—the latter being "the most generally recommended" breakfast drink for both adults and children.

Midday and evening meals were hearty too. A bill from April 24, 1664, shows approximately twelve professors from Groningen ordering the following fairly standard supper: "a turkey, a jugged hare, a Westphalian ham, a bolt of mutton, veal on the spit, anchovies, bread, butter, mustard and cheese, lemons and twelve tankards of wine." In 1703, at most seven churchmen from Arnhem reportedly consumed, in one sitting, "fourteen pounds of beef, eight pounds of veal, six fowl, stuffed cabbages, apples, pears, bread, pretzels, assorted nuts, twenty bottles of red wine, twelve bottles of white wine and coffee." Even meals in the poorhouse usually included vegetable soup, meat stew, bread and butter, the occasional fowl, and fresh fruit and red wine for the sick.

The Dutch ate even more on special occasions. In addition to major holidays like Christmas, Martinmas, and Fat Tuesday (which required eating waffles, pancakes, sausages, and ham pies), the Dutch had feasts for births, baptisms, swaddlings, betrothals, funerals, school openings, lottery inaugurations, new apprenticeships, organ installations, ship arrivals, even "feasts of inversion," at which master and mistress exchanged roles with their servants. Guests at these feasts might be served as many as a hundred dishes. One deceased innkeeper, otherwise unmemorable, received what Simon Schama calls "a bumper send-off," with townspeople at his wake consuming

20 oxheads of French and Rhenish wine
70 half casks of ale
1,100 pounds of meat "roasted on the Koningsplein"
550 pounds of sirloin
28 breasts of veal
12 whole sheep
18 great venison in white pastry
200 pounds of "fricadelle" (mincemeat)
topped off as always with bread, butter, and cheese.

But food, even in gluttonous quantities, raised no serious religious difficulties. Bread, after all, had been broken at the Last Supper, and "[e]ven for the most excitable preacher, there was nothing *inherently* sinful about a waffle." The problem was that the Dutch were also notorious drinkers and smokers. "Men drink at the slightest excuse," deplored one pastor, "at the sound of a bell or the turning of a mill . . . the Devil himself has turned brewer." In 1613, there were said to be 518 alehouses in Amsterdam alone. Around the same time, it was estimated that 12,000 liters of beer were consumed daily in Haarlem, two-thirds of it at home. Meanwhile, tobacco smoking and even tobacco chewing were practically national addictions, among both sexes and at every level of society. "The smell of the Dutch Republic," writes Schama, "was the smell of tobacco." Foreign visitors found especially repulsive the tar-blackened teeth of Dutch women, and even locals liked to comment that "a Hollander without a pipe is a national impossibility."[27]

All this vice and excess caused deep distress among the sternest Calvinists. In 1655 in Amsterdam, a pious burgomaster pushed through a law prohibiting extravagant wedding feasts. At another point, the city of Delft banned gingerbread men. Clergymen from a number of towns tried to prohibit the consumption of alcohol on the Sabbath.

But in the end, such measures failed miserably. It was not just that they were unpopular. (An attempt to ban cookies on the feast of St. Nicholas triggered a furious revolt of eleven-year-olds.) The forces of capitalism also worked ruthlessly against them. Beer and tobacco were two of the Dutch Republic's most important commercial products. Roughly half the labor force of Gouda was employed in pipe making. Even the West India Company—famous for its hardline Calvinist core—made immense profits from its colonial tobacco trade. These economic interests easily triumphed over church-led suppression efforts. In Rotterdam, for example, a law banning Sunday drinking was immediately reversed by the town's powerful breweries. Neither was the church itself unconnected to the "vice" trades. It was perfectly common for local preachers to sneak a quick smoke between sermons, and Amersfoort's great tobacco magnate, Brant van Slichtenhorst, was himself a deacon of the Reformed Church.[28]

By the mid-seventeenth century, the Dutch Republic was famous throughout Europe for being excessively liberal—socially, morally, politically, and intellectually. Foreign visitors were constantly shocked by the disrespect shown to masters, husbands, and nobles by servants, wives, and commoners. The German Heinrich Benthem, visiting the republic in the 1690s, scoffed that Dutch servant girls dressed and acted so much like their mistresses that he could not tell them apart. He noted too that whereas German husbands walked to church together, with their wives behind them minding the children, it was just the opposite in Holland: "Here the hen crows and the cock merely cackles," he said. More generally, women in the Dutch Republic—young and old, of all classes—were famously independent, "free to come and go, unaccompanied and unchaperoned, to work, conduct business, and engage in conversation almost like men."

Worse still, there were no limits on who could get rich in the Dutch Republic—or so it seemed to European contemporaries used to a far more rigid social hierarchy. Upstart traders and sons of cheese makers lived in sumptuous palaces "with splendid marble and alabaster columns" and "floors inlaid with gold." They dressed luxuriously and bedecked their wives in Spanish taffeta, Brazilian emeralds, and East Indian sapphires. Even "base-born" shopkeepers and cobblers owned costly linens and wore velvet and damask. "Mr. Everyman thinks he is entitled to wear what he likes so long as he can pay for it," sputtered one indignant critic. "Can you bear it when you see that a tailor has a room or a parlour hung with gold leather or tapestry? Or here and there, a mercer or an artisan who decorates his house as if it was a gentleman's or a burgomaster's?"

The republic's religious tolerance and high wages attracted skilled and highly talented individuals from all over Europe, including Germans, French, English, Scots, and even Turks and Armenians. The Huguenots who arrived after France's 1685 Revocation of the Edict of Nantes were particularly successful in Holland's silk, dressmaking, hatmaking, wig-making, and watchmaking industries. Holland's major towns and universities became the most cosmopolitan in Europe. In 1700, an estimated one-third of the University of Leiden's students were British; thousands of Scottish and English scholars flocked to Groningen and Utrecht as well. By 1685, immigrants or descendants of immigrants formed a majority of Holland's population.[29]

Like Tang China in its golden age, the Dutch Republic in the seventeenth century saw a burst of extraordinary cultural, artistic, and intellectual creativity. The Dutch painters of this era—Rembrandt, Vermeer, Frans Hals, Jan Steen, Jacob van Ruisdael—are among the most famous artists of all time. Eschewing the sacred figures of traditional art, the Dutch Masters painted in a new, intensely realistic style, giving an unprecedented luminosity to domestic and middle-class subjects previously forbidden in great painting. (Rembrandt chose to live in Amsterdam's Jewish quarter.) Dutchmen of this period also flourished in other areas of cultural and intellectual achievement: The polymath and humanist Hugo de Groot, known today as Grotius, laid down the foundations of modern international law in the 1600s, while he was still in his twenties.

Finally, some of the most brilliant thinkers of the Enlightenment wrote or lived in Holland, attracted by the republic's intellectual liberty. Among these were René Descartes, Baruch Spinoza, and John Locke, "the three great luminaries of seventeenth-century thought." Descartes was a French Catholic squire who found tranquility in Holland and wrote his most famous work there. (He also wrote, of commerce-obsessed Amsterdam: "In this great town, where apart from myself there dwells no one who is not engaged in trade, everyone is so much out for his own advantage that I should be able to live my whole life here without ever meeting a mortal being.") Spinoza was a Jewish philosopher whose family came to the Netherlands in the 1620s; his radically modern ideas on reason and individualism eventually got him banished from his own Sephardic community. John Locke was an Englishman ejected by James II; his greatest writings—on government and toleration—were heavily influenced by his years of exile in Holland. Other great minds, for example the Italian Gregorio Leti and France's Pierre Bayle, settled in the Dutch Republic as well, and Holland became known as "a haven for philosophers."[30]

WAS THE DUTCH REPUBLIC A HYPERPOWER?

With its unsurpassed maritime and commercial supremacy, a fair case can be made that in its heyday, between roughly 1625 and 1675, the Dutch Republic was a world-dominant power. The obvious objection is that the Dutch army was not the largest in Europe—although it was one of the largest, best equipped, and most professional. Even during its seventeenth-century decline, Spain had more troops, and it is most doubtful that the Netherlands could have invaded and conquered the Hapsburg territories. Can it really be said then that the Dutch Republic was a hyperpower?

To focus on the size of its standing army is to misunderstand how the Dutch Republic triumphed over its rivals. The Dutch never sought to conquer the European continent. While Spain,

France, and England exhausted themselves in wars of aggression against one another, the Dutch Republic built a standing army sufficient to win independence from the Hapsburgs and to defend its borders—as it did in 1672 when, to the surprise of all Europe, it defeated a simultaneous English and French invasion. Far more important, like Venice of the early Middle Ages, the Dutch Empire was an ocean-borne empire, driven by a hunger for commercial expansion, not territorial expansion.[31]

By the seventeenth century, naval might had become the royal road to world dominance, and the Dutch Republic took control of the seas. The extent of Dutch maritime domination is astonishing. In 1639, in the Battle of Downs, Dutch warships humiliated Spain's once formidable navy, crushing a Spanish armada of nearly one hundred ships and twenty thousand troops, and "rais[ing] the naval reputation of Holland as high as it could well be carried." In 1667, the Dutch dealt the English perhaps the worst naval defeat in British history, adding insult to injury by towing away the *Royal Charles*, the flagship of the British navy. On the commercial side, Dutch maritime dominance was even more pronounced. According to one estimate, of the 20,000 ships involved in the world's carrying trade in the mid-seventeenth century, 15,000–16,000 were Dutch. By 1670, the Dutch owned more shipping tonnage than England, France, Portugal, Spain, and Prussia put together. At its peak, the Dutch navy was in size the rough equal of the French and English naval forces combined—all the more remarkable given that France was in population ten to twenty times larger than the Dutch Republic.[32]

The Dutch figured out before anyone else that there was a new way to achieve global dominance in the dawning modern age. Every previous hyperpower in history had begun by conquering its neighbors, expanding ever outward with the march of marauding armies, growing huge in population as it incorporated more and more peoples, and through strategic tolerance inducing these conquered peoples to contribute their strengths and talents to its imperium.

Dutch tolerance played a different role. Largely because of brutal religious persecution throughout Europe, the years 1492 to 1715 saw the greatest migration of skilled people in history.[33] As the United States would do two centuries later, the Dutch used tolerance to attract the talented and persecuted outcasts of Europe. This turned out to be the winning strategy, pulling some of the world's most economically dynamic groups—along with invaluable trade networks, cutting-edge industrial technology, and vast sums of capital—into tiny Holland, creating an economic boom that catapulted the Dutch Republic far beyond its continental rivals in wealth. The Dutch then used this wealth to globalize.

Technological advances and the rise of capitalism had vastly enlarged the parts of the globe now up for grabs and altered the objectives of power. Territorial expansion over neighboring countries had become much less important. Gold and silver in the far-away Americas, the pepper and spice trades of the Indies, Caribbean sugar, and other "rich trades"—in coffee, tea, cocoa, textiles, tobacco, jewelry, and other luxuries—from the Baltics to the Mediterranean to Africa were the new, exponentially more lucrative prizes. The Dutch would let future would-be conquerors—Napoleon and Hitler, for example—renew the misguided dream of subjugating all Europe, with the unthinkable destruction and self-destruction that dream has brought with it.

The new, modern strategy of world domination was not conquest as such but capitalism backed by military force. Although the Dutch had significant colonial holdings in Indonesia, the Caribbean, and elsewhere, much of the Dutch "empire" was essentially a network of trading outposts administered by the semiprivate West and East India companies, with warships protecting the companies' effective monopoly over the world's most lucrative trade routes. Given its clear "productive, commercial and financial superiority," as well as its technological preeminence and overwhelmingly dominant naval power, it is no wonder that Immanuel Wallerstein concludes that the seventeenth-century Dutch Republic attained the "rare condition" of global "hegemony."[34]

THE DUTCH "CONQUEST" OF ENGLAND

In 1688, a massive Dutch fleet invaded England, Dutch troops occupied London, and the stadtholder of the Netherlands, William III of Orange, became king of Britain, ruling jointly with his wife, Mary. Dutch supremacy might have seemed at its pinnacle, and Holland's commercial and military expansion unstoppable. In fact, William's ascendance to the throne marked the transfer of the mantle of world dominance from the Netherlands to Britain.[35]

The Glorious Revolution, or "Bloodless Revolution," of 1688 had been engineered in part by the British parliament. Ten years earlier, Holland's ambitious William had married his first cousin Mary Stuart, daughter of King James II and heir to the English throne. Unlike William and Mary, who were Protestant, James II was Catholic, making him highly unpopular with his English subjects.

Even with Parliament's acquiescence, William's bid to wrest the English throne from his uncle (and father-in-law) was a high-risk venture. Especially because James II was allied with France's Louis XIV, it was essential for William to mobilize and move troops across the channel quickly. The Dutch naval force that William landed in England in 1688—arriving in an armada of nearly five hundred vessels—was equipped and financed in significant part by a small group of Dutch Jews. After becoming king of England, William promptly brought over his Sephardic financiers to continue provisioning his forces, which now included the English army and navy as well. They would soon be followed by many of Holland's skilled textile workers, scientists, and even Dutch portrait artists, painters, and engravers. Thus began a massive outflow of capital, human and financial, from the Dutch Republic to England.[36]

As an ironic result, it was England that would overwhelmingly benefit from the amalgamation of Dutch and English power. Basically, the Dutch Republic exported its tolerance, its most enterprising financiers, and its entire "business model" to England, which then replaced the Dutch Republic as Europe's preeminent land of freedom and opportunity for immigrants and religious minorities.

Soon, England would also replace the Netherlands as the world's supreme maritime power, presiding over a global commercial and colonial empire of unprecedented magnitude. In doing so, England inherited a problem that the Dutch never solved.

Tolerance for the Dutch was principally an *internal* policy. The remarkable religious tolerance embraced by the Netherlands within its own borders never translated into ethnic or racial tolerance in its colonial outposts overseas. From Suriname to Java to South Africa, the Dutch treated their indigenous subjects as their racial and cultural inferiors, engaging in the familiar colonial practices of slavery, apartheid, and cultural destruction. There was thus a contradiction between Dutch tolerance at home and its colonial intolerance abroad—a contradiction that would become even more marked for the British.

To put it mildly, the Dutch never succeeded in turning Indonesians or Ceylonese into loyal subjects of a great Dutch empire. Indeed, the Dutch never pursued an empire of that kind. It fell to England to try to fit together the unlikely combination of Enlightenment principles, European ethnocentrism, and a Roman strategy of empire building, creating a world of British subjects who filled the ranks of Britain's armies, administered Britain's territories, emulated Britain's manners, and contributed more or less willingly to Britain's imperial fortunes.

SEVEN

TOLERANCE AND INTOLERANCE IN THE EAST

The Ottoman, Ming, and Mughal Empires

B efore turning to the Dutch Republic's successor, Great Britain, let us take a brief look outside the West. This chapter offers a snapshot of three non-Western societies— the Ottoman, Ming, and Mughal empires—that rose to impressive heights of power in the fifteenth to seventeenth centuries but never came close to achieving world dominance. In all three cases, the empire reached its pinnacle of power and prosperity during its most tolerant era. Conversely, intolerance in every case acted as a cancer, limiting the empire's success and precipitating its decline.

THE OTTOMAN EMPIRE

The astonishing meteoric rise of Islam beginning in the seventh century was accompanied almost from the beginning by inter-

Muslim fragmentation and warfare. Like Christianity, on which it was based, Islam could be at once remarkably ethnically and racially tolerant—open to anyone of any skin color or walk of life—and fundamentally intolerant when it came to religion. There was only one God and one Truth.

Throughout the Middle Ages, the Islamic world was occupied by intense internal schisms—including the split between Shiites and Sunnis, which would prove as bloody as the war between Catholics and Protestants, as well as rivaling dynasties, caliphates, and sects vying for control of the Muslim world. In 750 in Damascus, every member of the ruling Umayyad family except one prince was massacred by the rival Abbasids. Despite this internecine strife, powerful regional empires rose and fell in the Muslim world. Of these great Islamic empires, the largest and longest-lasting was the Ottoman.

Founded by the Turkish House of Osman, the Ottoman Empire survived from roughly 1300 to the First World War. At its peak, its territory stretched from the edge of Vienna to the Red Sea, from North Africa to the Balkans. One of the most striking features of the Ottoman Empire was its religious tolerance.

The empires of Islam, even while episodically slaughtering both Muslim and non-Muslim "heretics," had a long history of tolerance. Almost a thousand years before the Dutch Republic became the first European state to incorporate tolerance into its governing principles, conquering Muslim rulers of the eighth century famously permitted Christians and Jews to continue worshipping as they chose—as long as they recognized the supremacy of Islam. In part, this was shrewd policy, but it also reflected the Islamic principle of protection for the "Peoples of the Book"—that is, Christians and Jews, fellow monotheists whose writings were considered by Islam to contain elements of revelation. The Ottoman Turks built on this tradition, ruling with calculating tolerance over an extraordinarily racially and religiously diverse region.[1]

Interestingly, the Ottoman rulers were keenly aware that through their relative tolerance they were profiting at the direct expense of their intolerant Christian rivals. In particular, they saw

Sephardic Jews, with their extensive trade contacts in the Mediterranean, as potential revenue producers for the empire. In 1492, upon hearing of Spain's expulsion decree, Sultan Bayezid II issued proclamations of welcome to the exiles and ordered the governors throughout his empire "not to refuse entry to the Jews" but rather to given them a "gracious welcome." Those who did not do so were to be "put to death." Bayezid is said to have gloated that "[t]he Catholic monarch Ferdinand was wrongly considered wise, since he impoverished Spain and enriched Turkey by the expulsion of the Jews."[2]

The power and splendor of the Ottoman Empire reached its zenith under Suleyman the Magnificent, who ruled from 1520 to 1566, a period often referred to as the golden age of Ottoman history. A brilliant military commander who insisted on leading his armies in person, Suleyman conquered Hungary, Iraq, and North Africa, established Ottoman supremacy over the Mediterranean, and extended the borders of the empire to their farthest limit. Suleyman was also a legendary administrator. Described by the Venetian ambassador in 1525 as "the most just of all Emperors," Suleyman was famous the world over for his wisdom, fairness, and remarkable tolerance. (These attributes are usually not ascribed to Suleyman's father, Selim the Grim, who consolidated power by executing his brothers, six of his nephews, and three of his own sons.)

Suleyman continued the Ottoman policy of permitting Jews and Christians extensive freedom to worship their own religions and run their own communities. In exchange, non-Muslims paid special taxes, which, although an important source of imperial revenue, were based on ability to pay and not especially onerous. Under Suleyman, there were very few restrictions on where Jews and Christians could live and work, and at least in the cities, Muslims and non-Muslims casually intermingled on a daily basis. Jews and Christians participated in Muslim trade guilds and could even bring lawsuits against Muslims in Muslim courts.

Friendships across religious lines were possible; political and commercial alliances between families of different faiths were common. During religious holidays, Muslims and non-Muslims often made friendly gestures to each other. On Easter, for example, Christians might give red-dyed eggs to their Muslim neighbors, who later reciprocated by sharing meats prepared for the Muslim Feast of the Sacrifice. Perhaps most tellingly, Jews and Christians pursued whatever livelihoods they chose, and many flourished economically. Indeed, some of the wealthiest people in the Ottoman major cities were non-Muslims.[3]

Of course, even under the beneficent Suleyman the Ottoman Empire was a pre-Enlightenment power—no subjects had any political rights—and it would be misleading to suggest that Muslims, Jews, and Christians mutually respected one another. People of different faiths generally kept to their own communities, which frowned upon or even prohibited intermarriage. Because Jews, Christians, and Muslims used different calendars, "the demarcation of months and the very numbering of the years varied, with each community marking the passage of a shared time differently." More fundamentally, the Ottomans maintained a clear hierarchy based on religion, and it went without saying that Islam was supreme. No matter how wealthy or successful a Christian or Jew became, his social status was always below a Muslim, just as the social status of women was always below men.[4]

To underscore their social subordination, non-Muslims were officially subject to numerous, largely symbolic restrictions. Non-Muslims were in principle required to wear attire of designated colors, such as blue-dyed tunics or red shoes, and they could not wear green, the Prophet's color, or white turbans. In addition, at least on the books, Ottoman law prohibited Christians and Jews from carrying swords, riding horses or camels (they could ride only donkeys or mules), buying land, building new houses of worship (they could only repair existing ones), having a house taller than that of Muslim houses, and holding positions that exercised authority over Muslims.

In practice, however, most of these restrictions were ignored or laxly enforced. Many non-Muslims came to wield enormous power and influence. The career of Joseph Nasi provides a vivid example. Nasi was born in Portugal to a wealthy *converso* banking family with clients all over western Europe, including the monarchs of Spain and France. In 1554 Nasi left the Hapsburg lands for Istanbul, where he and his family reembraced Judaism, becoming leaders of the Ottoman Jewish community. Within a few years, the Nasi family was among the primary financiers of the Ottoman treasury, with extensive monopolies and commercial holdings throughout the empire and beyond.

By about 1570, Joseph Nasi—now one of the leading entrepreneurs in the country—had also become one of the most powerful individuals in the Ottoman court. A close advisor to the sultan, and a major influence in foreign affairs (in 1569, he helped persuade the Dutch to rise against Spain with the promise of Ottoman support), Nasi was rewarded with the governorship of Naxos and the Cyclades Archipelago, as well as the Italian title of duke. Nasi's story illustrates not only how high an "infidel" could rise in the Ottoman Empire, but also how loosely some of the official restrictions on non-Muslims were (at least in some cases) applied. It is most unlikely that Nasi rode only donkeys and mules to the imperial court or that his celebrated mansion near Istanbul was no taller than any Muslim houses. Moreover, as one of the most prominent imperial tax collectors, Nasi in practice, if not in the eyes of the law, must have exercised considerable authority over many Muslims.[5]

————————

Another major component of Ottoman tolerance was its embrace of Muslim converts. Notwithstanding extraordinary individuals such as Nasi, Ottoman society was generally characterized by a hierarchy, at the top of which was the *askeri*, or ruling class, open almost exclusively to Muslims. But almost anyone in the empire, of any ethnicity or social class, could become a Muslim and a member of the *askeri*. Moreover, converted Muslims were every bit as good as "natural-born" Muslims, with virtually no limits on their success. Thus Busbecq, the Hapsburg ambassador to the Ottoman Empire during Suleyman's reign, wrote admiringly:

It is by merit that men rise in the service, a system which in-
sures that posts should be assigned to the competent. . . . [The
Ottomans] do not believe that high qualities are either natural or hereditary . . . but that they are partly the gift of God,
and partly the result of good training, great industry, and . . .
zeal. . . . Honors, high posts and judgeships are the rewards of
great ability and good service. This is the reason that they are
successful in their undertakings.

The ability of enterprising Muslim converts to rise almost
without limit stood in marked contrast to the situation in Catholic
Spain, where Jews whose families had long converted to Christianity were frequently banned from holding high positions because of
their "impure blood" and for centuries risked being burned at the
stake.[6]

Ottoman strategic tolerance was, nonetheless, distinctly pre-
modern and certainly not rooted in the respect for human rights or
individual liberty familiar today, as attested by the fascinating Ottoman system for the recruitment and training of the special imperial guard known as the Janissaries. Every year, the Ottomans
collected as a "tax" a certain percentage of boys ages eight to
twenty from conquered Christian lands. Muslims were not eligible
as recruits, because it was thought that young Christians given the
chance to convert and rise in an alien land would be more zealous
and more loyal. Until the seventeenth century, the youths came
mainly from the Balkan peasantry, including Albanians, Bulgari-
ans, Croats, Serbians, and Greeks; later, boys were also drawn
from Russia and Ukraine.

Considered the sultan's property, the youths were completely
severed from their families, converted to Islam, and trained to be
either soldiers or administrators and officials in the Ottoman bureaucracy. Harsh restrictions were imposed. "Slaves of the state,"
all the recruits were bound to celibacy and lifetime service. The
most promising among them were handpicked and prepared for
entry to the *askeri*. At these elite schools, students became fluent in
Persian and Arabic, studied the Koran, and were groomed for mil-

itary leadership. The very brightest could rise all the way to the coveted imperial position of grand vizier, the sultan's chief minister and military advisor. All but one of Suleyman's nine grand viziers were former Christian slaves, from the humblest of backgrounds.

The recruits who did not make it into the *askeri* were assigned to the Janissaries, an elite infantry corps that formed the sultan's private guard. At the height of their effectiveness in the sixteenth century, when they were probably better trained than any troops in Europe, the Janissaries included roughly 20,000 men, none of them native Turks. The Janissaries enjoyed high living standards and, because they inherited the wealth of dead Janissaries, accumulated great collective wealth. Thus, while some Christian families saw the youth "tax" as the worst form of Ottoman oppression, others saw it as an avenue of upward mobility for their children, and a means of placing a family member in a position of status and authority otherwise unimaginable.[7]

———————

The Ottomans derived great benefits from their strategic tolerance. First, it bought them the cooperation, or at least the acquiescence, of conquered populations from Transylvania to Yemen to the Iranian plateau. As with every empire, there were sporadic rebellions, put down viciously by the Ottoman war machine. But by and large, the fundamental ethnic and racial tolerance of Islam proved a stunning strategic asset for the Ottomans. Large numbers of Christians converted to Islam shortly after being conquered. While some may have been touched by the Prophet's revelation, for most, conversion to Islam was pragmatic.

For the Ottomans, the "color-blind" embrace of conversion meant a swelling of the ranks of more or less cooperative Islamic subjects, a huge pool of available agricultural and military manpower, and at the top level, a core of genuinely talented individuals who had risen through the strikingly meritocratic Ottoman system. As the Janissaries and Suleyman's grand viziers illustrate, the Ottomans were able to deploy conversion to create specially loyal, elite servants of the sultan.

Among those who did not convert, the Ottoman Empire's relative religious tolerance worked to enormous advantage as well. Non-Muslims of all stripes—Christian Maronites, Jacobites, Egyptian Copts, Nestorian Christians, Greek Orthodox Christians, Armenian Orthodox Christians, and Greek and Iberian Jews, just to name a few groups—contributed immensely to the economic expansion and vitality of the empire. In particular, Jews who fled the Hapsburgs brought to Turkey invaluable trade and financial networks, which helped Ottoman cities like Istanbul, Cairo, Aleppo, and Salonika become major centers of international commerce.

European Jews also provided the Ottomans with scientific and medical knowledge, as well as new technologies for industry, arms, and munitions. The remarkable Jewish contribution to Ottoman success was attested to by Nicolas de Nicolay and Pierre Bellon de Mans, two well-known European travelers who visited the empire around 1550:

> [The Jews] have amongst them workmen of all artes and handicrafts moste excellent, and especially [the *conversos*] of late banished and driven out of Spaine and Portugale, who to the great detriment of Christianitie, have taught the Turks divers inventions, craftes and engines of warre, as to make artillerie, harquebuses, gunne powder, shot, and other munitions: they have also there set up printing, not before seen in those countries.

Many Greeks, Armenians, Lebanese Maronites, and other Christian groups were also extremely entrepreneurial, playing prominent roles in banking, shipbuilding, wool and tobacco production, and the luxury trades.[8]

———

In its heyday under Suleyman the Magnificent—with its spectacular territorial expansion, cultural blossoming, and prosperity—the Ottoman Empire looked as though it might become the first world-dominant Islamic power in history. It was not to be. Even at its peak, the Ottoman Empire was a regional power, surrounded on

all sides by well-matched rivals, from Safavid Persia to the Hapsburgs to the Muscovite Empire of Ivan the Terrible.

If Suleyman could have lived another hundred years, things
might have been otherwise. But Suleyman was succeeded by a
string of thirteen sultans ranging in talent from incompetence to
idiocy, and because of the extraordinarily hierarchical, indeed
despotic form of Ottoman government, a poor sultan was a catastrophe. Many factors conspired to weaken the empire beginning in
the second half of the 1500s, but the failure of Suleyman's successors to maintain his striking tolerance clearly played a role.[9]

Perhaps most significantly, the empire after Suleyman was unable to remain above the religious schism that has caused Islam's
most fanatic bloodletting from the seventh century to the present
day: the split between Sunnis and Shiites. Although the prevailing
Ottoman practices were always Sunni, Shiism had been generally
respected under Suleyman. After his death, however, the empire's
religious arteries began to harden. Officials sought to suppress
freedom of thought, including Shiite thought. The printing press
was banned. Shiite dissident movements emerged in Iraq and Persia, which were then crushed by fierce and overwhelming imperial
force, strengthening the hand of the Shiite kingdom of Safavid Persia and even leading the Safavids to ally themselves with European
powers against the Ottomans.[10]

At the same time, the welcoming embrace of foreigners and
non-Muslims that had characterized the empire in its golden age
also began to show strain. There had always been a strand of Islamic thought critical of merchants and commerce, particularly
commerce with non-Muslims. This aversion to trade may help explain why Jews and other non-Muslims came to dominate so much
of the empire's commercial activity. But the fact that most merchants, entrepreneurs, and financiers were "foreigners" created a
highly unstable situation. Whether due to resentment or genuine
theological scruple, merchants and traders in the late 1500s began
to be subject to increasing religious criticism and then to unpre-
dictable taxation and confiscation of property. Exporting goods
outside the empire was forbidden. Economic and technological in-

novation was suppressed, not only stifling trade but undercutting the Ottoman military, whose weapons and ships grew increasingly outdated.[11]

While non-Muslims still enjoyed better treatment and prospects under the Ottomans than non-Christians did in most of Europe in the late sixteenth century, fault lines began to appear and eventually to crack open. Throughout the empire, itinerant Jewish merchants and peddlers were attacked, robbed, and murdered. When a Jewish court physician died, the chief physician argued successfully for replacement by a Muslim because there were too many Jews already; over the next fifty years, the number of Jews among the court's physicians would decrease in number from forty-one to four. To be sure, Ottoman Jews still had more to fear from the empire's Christian opponents. In 1594, when Prince Michael "the Brave" of Wallachia rebelled against Ottoman rule, he immediately massacred every Jew (and Turk) in Bucharest to whom any Romanian owed money. But as internal strife worsened, Jews came under Ottoman attack as well. In the 1660s, the leader of a messianic Jewish movement, Shabbetai Tzevi, was forced to choose between death and conversion to Islam. (He chose conversion.) In 1688, in another war with the Austrians, Janissaries burned and plundered the Jewish quarter of Belgrade.[12]

As with every empire, the reasons for Ottoman decline are multiple and hotly debated. As the centuries wore on, there were military defeats and territorial losses. The western European powers achieved increasing economic and technological superiority, extending their reach to the Americas and Asia in the way the Ottomans never did. Proliferating internal revolts and the rise of nationalism played a critical, debilitating role. At the same time, the Ottomans' final collapse was a paroxysm of horrific intolerance. The eventual destruction of the empire in 1922 was preceded, and in many ways precipitated, by vicious ethnic and religious bigotry, sectarianism, and violence, particularly in the Balkans. Muslims attacked Muslims, Greek Orthodox Christians persecuted Greek Uniate Christians, and still others scapegoated and killed Jews. These ethnic horrors culminated in the Armenian genocide of World War I, in which an estimated 800,000 Armenian Ottoman subjects were slaughtered during and after their expulsion from the empire.[13]

MING DYNASTY CHINA

In the early fifteenth century, the Ming government sent the Muslim eunuch Admiral Zheng He, together with a fleet of three hundred giant "treasure ships" carrying more than 28,000 men, on seven spectacular ocean voyages through the Indian Ocean. At that time, the Ming dynasty had a much better shot at world dominance than any European power. Having inherited a united China from the Mongols, the Ming emperors ruled over more subjects than the Ottomans and the monarchs of Europe combined. Technologically, Ming China was far ahead of backward Europe, having already invented the printing press, gunpowder, and the magnetic compass. Fifteenth-century China outshone Europe in other respects too: At the Ming inauguration of their new capital, the Forbidden City, 26,000 guests were served a ten-course banquet on the finest porcelain; at the wedding feast of England's Henry V and Catherine of Valois, six hundred guests ate salted cod on "plates" consisting of stale bread.

As late as 1421, the Mings' massive naval might dwarfed that of any other power in the world. Altogether, the imperial fleet totaled more than 4,000 vessels, including not just the colossal nine-masted treasure ships, but 1,350 patrol ships, 400 warships, and 400 freighters just for carrying grain, water, and horses. A pertinent contrast is the "royal fleet" assembled by Henry V to conquer France; it consisted of four fishing boats, each capable of ferrying just a hundred men across the channel at a time. The Ming ships were teak leviathans, armed with enormous iron cannons, able to carry four hundred times more cargo than their largest European counterparts. Their rudders alone were often as long as the entirety of the *Niña*, Christopher Columbus's flagship.[14]

But Ming China declined to seek global dominance. After 1424, the Ming emperors took a pathological turn inward, breaking up their own navy and rejecting foreign trade and foreign ideas. By 1600, the Chinese had fallen far behind Europe technologically, militarily, and commercially.

———————

After driving out the Mongols in 1368, the early Ming rulers devoted their energies to domestic agricultural reform, ignoring the commercial world beyond China. Zhu Yuanzhang, the Ming founder, banned "foreign" hairstyles and clothing in his court, twice issuing orders that his subjects model their appearances after those in the seventh-century Tang dynasty. (It is ironic that Emperor Zhu saw the Tang dynasty as quintessentially "Chinese," given that it was founded by a prince who was probably half Turkic.) Born to a poor peasant family and enduring near-starvation conditions as a youth, Emperor Zhu believed that the government's primary duty was to protect farmers, on whom the state depended for all its wealth. He established an impressive agrarian tax system by registering China's entire immense population, and froze taxes at fourteenth-century levels. He also repeatedly banned overseas voyages by private merchants.

All this changed abruptly in 1403 with the ascension to the throne of Yongle, Emperor Zhu's son. Seizing power after a palace struggle with his nephew—whom his father had designated to be the next emperor—Yongle was conscious of being a usurper. To establish his legitimacy and grandeur, Yongle immediately embarked on a series of monumental projects. Partly to guard against the continuing Mongol threat in the north, Yongle ordered that China's capital be moved from Nanjing to Beijing, a task that required a massive repair of the Grand Canal, the construction of forty-seven new locks linking Hangzhou and Beijing, and the transport of 235,000 soldiers and their families. At the same time, Yongle was eager to project China's imperial power beyond its existing borders. He sent armies north to conquer Mongol territories and south to conquer what is now Vietnam (failing in both cases). It was also Yongle who commissioned Admiral Zheng He's extraordinary expeditions to explore the oceans, to exact tribute, and to demonstrate to the world the unsurpassed power and splendor of Ming China.

Zheng He was a Chinese Muslim whose father and grandfather had been to Mecca. Yongle probably appointed him admiral because of his familiarity with foreign customs, particularly in Islamic countries. Because the Tang dynasty had sent expeditions abroad centuries earlier, Zheng He navigated with surprisingly accurate maps—one was longer than twenty feet and included detailed sailing directions as well as the names of African coastal cities like Mombasa and Malindi (both in modern-day Kenya). The hulls of Zheng He's ships had separate watertight compartments, allowing repairs to be made while the ship was still sailing. These compartments also held fresh water and fish to feed the many travelers.[15]

Zheng He's treasure ships were the largest in the world, capable of carrying 2,500 tons, and exceeding European ships in size and staff by a factor of ten. Onboard Zheng He's ships were

> 868 civil officers, 26,800 soldiers, 93 commanders, two senior commanders, 140 "milleriorns" [captains of a thousand men], 403 centurions, a Senior Secretary of the Board of Revenue, a geomancer, a military instructor, two military judges, 180 medical officers and assistants, two orderlies, seven senior eunuch ambassadors, ten junior eunuchs and 53 eunuch chamberlains.

This was in addition to an unspecified number of translators, scribes, interpreters, navigators, mechanics, negotiators, sailors, and cooks. The number of doctors and herb specialists alone totaled 180—the size of Vasco da Gama's entire crew. Unlike Columbus's crew, which had dirty drinking water and ate flour baked with seawater, Zheng He's men had "an abundance of grain, fresh water, salt, soya sauce, tea, liquor, oil, candles, firewood and charcoal."[16]

Finally, the treasure ships also carried . . . treasure. Zheng He's ships brought back to the emperor the most valuable and exotic goods foreign rulers had to offer. But unlike the Mongols before them or the Portuguese after them, Zheng He's men did not plunder. Instead, they presented local rulers with symbolic gifts—colored silk, umbrellas, books, or calendars—in exchange for such rarities as "dragon saliva" (ambergris), prize horses, parrots, peacocks, sandalwood, gold, silver, "cat's eyes of extraordinary size, rubies and other precious stones, large branches of coral, amber and attar of roses" as well as strange "auspicious beasts" such as "camel-birds" (ostriches), giraffes, rhinoceroses, "gold-spotted leopards," zebras, and lions.[17]

Then in 1424 it ended, almost as abruptly as it had begun. Emperor Yongle died, and the Ming government suspended all further voyages. After reluctantly allowing Zheng He to make one final expedition in 1433, the imperial court banned the construction of all oceangoing vessels. The great treasure ships were put into "storage," eventually to rot away. Zheng He's sailors were reassigned to the Grand Canal, as tax collectors. Finally, an imperial edict prohibited the existence of any ship with more than two masts, and, astoundingly, the official records of Zheng He's expeditions were destroyed.

Many factors contributed to this "triumph of introversion." Officially, the Confucian mandarins who locked away the treasure ships asserted that the expeditions were too expensive, but historians generally agree that this was at least in part a pretext to wrest power away from their rivals, the palace eunuchs, who controlled the imperial navy. Like the first Ming emperor, the Confucian bureaucrats were also conservative, hostile to commerce, and resistant to any social change, including overseas expansion. Most important of all was the renewed threat from the Mongols, who had regrouped after Yongle's death and begun invading Chinese territory.

In 1449, Mongol forces dealt a disastrous defeat to Ming imperial troops at a site called Tumu, now a truck stop two hours north of Beijing. Humiliatingly, the Mongols captured the Ming emperor, taking him to Mongolia. Although the Mongols returned the kidnapped emperor to Beijing the following year, the Tumu defeat permanently shifted Ming foreign policy. From that point on, the Ming emperors grew progressively more xenophobic, resurrecting the ancient conception of China as the only civilized society, surrounded on all sides by dangerous barbarians who had nothing valuable to offer. Obsessed with the threat of Mongol invasion, the Ming emperors tried to seal themselves in, rebuilding the Great Wall and repeatedly banning foreign trade and any contact with foreign nations. By 1500, imperial subjects were prohibited not only from building seagoing ships but from leaving the country.

The Ming dynasty lasted until 1644, when ironically it was conquered not by the Mongols but by the Manchus, different "barbarians" from the northeast. Even after its mid-fifteenth-century turn inward, Ming China experienced periods of strong economic growth, fueled by its steadily increasing population and pockets of vigorous domestic commerce, particularly in the lower Yangtze valley and the southern regions of Fujian and Guangzhou.

But after the mid-fifteenth century, Ming China could not—and in many ways chose not to—compete on the world scene. Relative to the West, China declined technologically, forgetting many of its own inventions and never undergoing a scientific or industrial revolution of the kind that transformed Europe. At the same time, it allowed its once colossal navy to wither away, eschewing overseas expansionism and ceding domination of the world's oceans to the Europeans.[18]

THE MUGHAL EMPIRE: MUSLIM RULERS, HINDU SUBJECTS

Ayodhya is a small town in northern India and, according to Hindu mythology, the birthplace of Prince Rama, the seventh incarnation of Vishnu, the perfect man, and the embodiment of truth and morality. On December 6, 1992, a Hindu nationalist mob armed with hammers and pickaxes tore down a five-hundred-year-old mosque in Ayodhya, claiming that it desecrated Rama's birth spot. The destruction of the mosque, built during the reign of the first Mughal emperor, Babur, triggered an outbreak of fierce Muslim-Hindu fighting across India. More than a thousand were killed by rioting mobs. For their part, Hindu extremists justified their attacks on the "children of Babur" as revenge for centuries of oppression under Muslim rule.

The Mughal Empire, which immediately preceded the British Empire in India, was founded by a descendant of Genghis Khan. ("Mughal" is the Persian word for "Mongol.") At its peak, it ruled over the Indian subcontinent and parts of modern-day Afghanistan and Pakistan. Like the Ottoman sultans who ruled contemporaneously, the Mughal emperors were Muslims. Yet for two hundred years they ruled absolutely over more than one hundred million subjects, approximately 85 percent of whom were non-Muslims: principally Hindus, as well as Sikhs, Jains, and Christians.[19] Today, Hindu nationalists insist that the Mughals were brutal, intolerant oppressors of their non-Muslim subjects. Were they?

It is true that Babur, the founder of the Mughal Empire, rode to power on a wave of bloody zealotry. To defeat the great Hindu Rajput kings, whose troops outnumbered his by as many as ten to one, Babur inflamed the passions of his Muslim soldiers by calling his war against the Hindus a jihad, or holy war. To demonstrate his own commitment to Islam, Babur had his entire wine collection poured onto the ground and his wineglasses and flagons smashed before his men. This act of sacrifice is said to have infused his men with religious fervor and brought them victory at the decisive Battle of Khanua. To be sure, it probably helped that Babur's men had firearms while the Rajputs did not. In any event, after days of slaughter, the Rajputs fled the battlefield, leaving Babur triumphant over northern India.

But Babur ruled for just four years (1526–30) before he died. The empire he left his son Humayun was fragmented, hostile to Mughal rule, and plagued with open rebellion from all quarters. Indeed, Humayun lost control of the Mughal Empire for fifteen years, during which time Afghan rulers occupied the throne (and established a surprisingly efficient tax collection network). Eventually, after years of exile in Persia, Humayun reconquered the empire in 1555. Just seven months later, however, the unfortunate Humayun, rushing to prayer, tripped over his robe and fell down several flights of stairs to his death.[20]

It was only under Humayun's son Akbar, and his next several successors, that the Mughal dynasty consolidated its power to become one of the greatest empires of the time. Not coincidentally, Akbar and the other kings of the Mughal golden age were among the most religiously and ethnically tolerant rulers in the history of the pre-modern world. Indeed, without this turn to tolerance, it is highly unlikely that the Mughal Empire could have lasted as long as it did, or reached its dazzling heights of cultural grandeur. Conversely, the period of Mughal decline is associated with some of the most brutal episodes of ethnic and religious persecution in India's history.

———————

As a boy-emperor, Akbar was guided first by an ambitious guardian and then by a clique led by his foster mother, Maham Anga. As Akbar grew older, he increasingly chafed at attempts to curb his authority. In 1560, at the age of seventeen, he forced his guardian to resign and supposedly sent him on a pilgrimage to Mecca (the guardian was murdered en route). When Maham Anga's son killed one of Akbar's ministers, Akbar ordered his foster brother thrown repeatedly from the roof of the palace into the courtyard until he died. Before he was thirty, Akbar had clearly established his strength at the court.

But establishing his authority over the empire was a far more difficult feat. To prevent his kingdom from splintering, Akbar had to hold in check a formidable array of rivals. These included the recently deposed Afghans, Persian and central Asian noblemen, the Hindu Rajputs and Marathas, and the Muslim princes of Lodi.

Akbar's solution was one part shrewd diplomacy, one part multicultural copulation. Like Alexander the Great—but on a much greater scale because of the size of his harem—Akbar married into the families of his rivals. Perhaps his greatest success in this vein was his marriage to the eldest daughter of the Raja of Amber, one of the fiercely independent Hindu Rajput kings. The practice of a Hindu princess marrying a Muslim sultan was an uncommon but not unknown practice on the subcontinent. Akbar, however, went further. He allowed Princess Jodhabai to remain a Hindu and to worship at a Hindu shrine within his palace; occasionally Akbar himself participated in the rituals. This unusual tolerance encouraged other Rajput chiefs to negotiate entry into the imperial elite by offering their daughters as marriage partners for the emperor. By the time of Akbar's death he had more than three hundred wives, including Rajputs, Afghans, princesses from south Indian kingdoms, Turks, Persians and even two Christian women of Portuguese descent.

Marriage created alliances with the wives' male relatives, who could be called upon for support and assistance. Through such alliances, Akbar won the loyalty of thousands of Rajput warriors while preventing the rise of a Rajput insurrection. The Rajputs benefited as well. They became imperial generals and administrators; many grew influential enough to control their own fiefdoms. A few Rajput rulers resisted the Mughals—and paid a terrible price. The great Rajput fortresses of Chittor and Ranthambore crumbled before Mughal armies, often led by fellow Rajputs.

Akbar's patronage extended to men of all faiths. Though illiterate himself, he (like his distant relation Khubilai Khan) strove to fill his court with men of arts and learning. Among his courtiers the nine most illustrious were known as the *navratna*, or nine jewels of the Mughal crown. Four of these "nine jewels" were Hindu. They included Akbar's finance minister, his military commander, his counselor and court jester, Raja Birbal, whose witty exchanges with the emperor live on today in folktales, and the legendary Hindu singer-composer Tansen. It is said that when Tansen sang his ragas—a complex musical form with no equivalent in the West—day became night, and clouds burst into rain.

Akbar was fascinated by comparative theology. In 1575 he

constructed an immense hall to house debates on religion. Participants eventually included Muslim clerics, Hindu saints, Jain monks, Parsi priests, and even Jesuit missionaries from the Portuguese colony of Goa. In the tolerant atmosphere of the time, Sikhism, a syncretic religion combining elements of Hinduism and Islam, emerged in the region of Punjab. Folk culture also saw a merging of customs, ceremonies, and myths. The Bhakti and Sufi movements within Hinduism and Islam, respectively, each combined beliefs from both religions and called for the unity of God. (Even today, Hindus make pilgrimages to Muslim shrines at Ajmer and Fatehpur Sikri, while Muslims often pray to local Hindu deities, such as Sitlamata, the goddess of smallpox.) Indeed, in the Hindu songs and poetry of the period, Akbar, although Muslim, was often compared to the Hindu god Rama—the same Rama, ironically, in whose name Hindu nationalists tore down the mosque at Ayodhya in 1992.

Akbar believed in sharing his religious enlightenment with his fellow rulers. In a letter he dictated in 1582 to Philip II of Spain, he said:

> As most men are fettered by bonds of tradition, and by imitating the ways followed by their fathers, ancestors, relatives and acquaintances, everyone continues, without investigating the arguments and reasons, to follow the religion in which he was born and educated, thus excluding himself from the possibility of ascertaining the truth, which is the noblest aim of the human intellect. Therefore we associate at convenient seasons with learned men of all religions, thus deriving profit from their exquisite discourses and exalted aspirations.[21]

There is no record of a reply from King Philip, who, as we have seen, was busy extinguishing Protestant heresy and overseeing the "Council of Blood" in Holland.

To a surprising extent, Akbar did not favor Muslims. In war, he crushed resisting factions with the same brutality whether they subscribed to Hinduism or Islam. He attacked corruption among the Muslim clergy and initiated sweeping reforms equalizing land privileges for holy men of all persuasions. Along with Muslim festivals, he celebrated Diwali, the Hindu festival of lights. Defying orthodox Islamic law, he granted non-Muslims permission to repair their temples and to build new places of worship. He also decreed that Hindus who had been forced to convert to Islam could reconvert without being subject to the death penalty. Most dramatically, in 1579 Akbar abolished the *jiziya*, a mandatory tax levied exclusively on non-Muslims.

Akbar reigned for fifty years (1556–1605) and is known to this day as the Mughal Empire's most successful ruler. Many of his chief advisors were Persian, and the philosophy, painting, and literature of the period all reflect his deep appreciation of Persian culture. His greatest failure was his attempt to create a new "order of faith" called *Din-i-Ilahi*, supposedly incorporating elements of Islam, Hinduism, and Zoroastrianism. Akbar's objective, it seems, was not to displace existing creeds but rather to establish "a sort of universalist religion, literally religion of God rather than of Muhammad, Christ or Krishna" but demanding "unquestioning loyalty to the person of Akbar" himself. *Din-i-Ilahi* found few takers in the empire, or even within the emperor's own family. Its establishment outraged orthodox Muslim leaders, who regarded it as heresy and attempted a revolt. The imperial champion of universal tolerance crushed this revolt ruthlessly.[22]

———

The next two Mughal emperors generally continued Akbar's policies of religious tolerance. Akbar's eldest son and successor, Jahangir, was so religiously eclectic that the English ambassador remarked, "His religione is his owne invention." Like his father, Jahangir held public discussions on religion. He particularly enjoyed the sparring between Jesuit priests and Muslim clerics, often slapping his thighs in appreciation of a point scored. On one occasion he met with an eminent Hindu ascetic in his cave, and was profoundly moved. "Sublime words were spoken between us," Jahangir later wrote. "God almighty has granted him an unusual grace." Meanwhile, Jahangir's consumption of pork and wine, forbidden by Islam, seemed to grow during the holy month of Ramadan.

Jahangir was also deeply drawn to Christianity, although more for its ceremonial aspects than its doctrine. He attended Mass every Christmas Day and occasionally borrowed a Christian church to hold a banquet. While he never converted to Christianity—he believed that the idea that Christ was the son of God was as absurd as the Hindu belief in reincarnation—he permitted three of his grandsons to do so and held a grand public procession in Agra to celebrate their baptism. Jahangir not only allowed Jesuits to preach freely within the empire; he gave them a stipend of fifty rupees a month from the imperial treasury.

Jahangir's successor Shah Jahan ("Ruler of the World") is most famous for the breathtaking Taj Mahal, the mausoleum he erected for his beloved wife, Mumtaz Mahal. Built by 20,000 workers over a period of two decades, the white marble monument combines Persian and Indian architecture as well as synthesizing Hindu and Muslim motifs. Under Shah Jahan's rule, the word *Mughal* came to embody cultural grandeur. It helped that he was probably the richest man in the world at the time and that he had a penchant for extravagance. Sparing no expense—indeed to the point of fiscal irresponsibility—he ordered magnificent forts, palaces, and mosques constructed across the empire. For himself he commissioned the famous Peacock Throne, a gem-encrusted masterpiece wrought out of 2,500 pounds of pure gold, said to be the single costliest treasure made in the last thousand years.

Shah Jahan continued to allow non-Muslims within the empire to practice their religion, but he was more orthodox and less accommodating than his predecessors. Reversing his grandfather Akbar's policy, he prohibited non-Muslims from repairing or building new temples. He banned Muslims from converting to other religions while providing stipends to non-Muslims who converted to Islam. At the same time, Shah Jahan initiated a number of military forays into central Asia and Safavid Persia's territories. These expensive and largely unsuccessful attempts at expansion not only drained the imperial treasury; they nearly extinguished the previously robust flow of Persian immigrants into India.[23]

———————

In 1658, the Mughal Empire came into the hands of Aurangzeb Alamgir, the third son of Shah Jahan. Aurangzeb became emperor after killing his eldest brother, Dara—whose head he sent on a platter to their dying father. Dara had been an intellectually curious, open-minded scholar with a strong interest in Hinduism, Judaism, Sikhism, and Christianity as well as Islam. As Aurangzeb explained, "The fear of seeing the Muhammadan religion oppressed in India if my brother Dara ascended the throne" was what compelled him to seize power.

By all accounts—at least for a ruthless fratricidal killer—Aurangzeb was a deeply pious man. In stark contrast to some of his decadent predecessors, he lived a simple life, knitting prayer caps and copying the Koran, which he had memorized, over and over by hand.

Aurangzeb extended and accelerated the repression begun by Shah Jahan. Increasingly, the dictates of orthodox Islam shaped the imperial court. Aurangzeb prohibited the consumption of wine and opium and banned non-Muslim ceremonies. For the first time in a century neither the Hindu festival of Diwali nor the Persian spring festival of Nauroz was celebrated at court. To enforce his increasingly dogmatic ordinances, Aurangzeb appointed *muhtasibs*, or censors of public morals, all across the empire.

Reversing earlier policies of religious tolerance, Aurangzeb imposed Sharia (Islamic law) throughout the empire. He razed thousands of Hindu temples and shrines, including the great temple of Mathura. Land that had formerly been granted to Hindu institutions was redistributed to Muslim clerics. In 1679, Aurangzeb revived the *jiziya*, the punitive tax imposed on non-Muslims, provoking heated protests across the empire.

Aurangzeb's intolerance was an imperial catastrophe. To begin with, the persecution of Hindus was bad for business. When one of Aurangzeb's henchmen forcibly converted a Hindu clerk in

Surat, the heads of eight thousand Hindu trading families left the port city in anger, bringing commerce to an effective halt.

But far more destructively, Aurangzeb's Muslim zealotry tore the fragile religious and political unity of the Mughal Empire to pieces. His vicious campaign to eradicate Sikhism—including the destruction of temples and the execution of a revered Sikh holy man (on charges of converting Muslims)—earned the Mughals the hatred of tens of thousands in northern India and paved the way for Sikh militarism.

Meanwhile in the south, a number of Hindu Maratha clans banded together to fight Mughal supremacy. Their leader was Shivaji, a now legendary warrior viewed by many as the founder of guerrilla warfare in India. Shivaji successfully drove the Mughal armies out of Deccan (in the modern state of Maharashtra), becoming king of the Maratha confederacy in 1674. For the next two decades, Aurangzeb expended enormous resources trying to hold his ground against the Marathas, who, using their guerrilla tactics and familiarity with the terrain, bled the mighty Mughal army. Instead of strengthening his ties with the Hindu Rajputs—who might have remained his allies and who had formerly served as great empire builders for the Mughals—Aurangzeb sacked their temples and eventually turned them against him too.

Not only Hindus faced the might of Aurangzeb's Islamic orthodoxy. Shiite Muslims did too. A devout Sunni, Aurangzeb sent conquering armies to Bijapur and Golconda, where the ruling families had for centuries been Shiite.

Until his death in 1707, Aurangzeb kept the empire intact, ruthlessly deploying enormous marauding armies to crush enemies, stamp out heretics, and extend Mughal rule over Shiite and Hindu lands. When he died, the Mughal Empire was larger than it had ever been or ever would be again. But because of all his constant warring—external and internal—the empire was also bankrupt. More than that, the hatreds and divisions he sowed made India easy prey for the divide-and-conquer stratagems that the British would soon deploy to great success, turning India from a subcontinental Muslim empire to a jewel in the crown of the largest Western empire the world had ever seen.

Perhaps the devout Aurangzeb understood his own legacy. On his deathbed, he wrote to his son: "I came alone and I go as a stranger. I do not know who I am, nor what I have been doing. I have sinned terribly, and I do not know what punishment awaits me."[24]

EIGHT

THE BRITISH EMPIRE

"Rebel Buggers" and the "White Man's Burden"

Take a view of the *Royal Exchange* in *London,* a place more venerable than many courts of justice, where the representatives of all nations meet for the benefit of mankind. There the Jew, the Mahometan, and the Christian transact together as tho' they all profess'd the same religion, and give the name of Infidel to none but bankrupts. There the Presbyterian confides in the Anabaptist, and the Churchman depends on the Quaker's word. And all are satisfied.

—VOLTAIRE, 1733

A man should, whatever happens, keep to his own caste, race, and breed. Let the White go to the White and the Black to the Black.
—RUDYARD KIPLING, *Beyond the Pale,* 1888

Intolerance betrays want of faith in one's cause.
—MAHATMA GANDHI, 1921

When we left Britain two chapters ago, it was 1688 and William III of Orange, stadtholder of the Netherlands, had just become king of England. What kind of country did William and Mary take over? A country not very different from the rest of intolerant Christian Europe.

For most of the sixteenth and seventeenth centuries, what is now Great Britain was a pit of vicious religious and ethnic warfare. Protestants massacred Catholics, Catholics beheaded Protestants, Anglicans persecuted dissenters, and Englishmen slaughtered Irish, Scots, and Welsh, all of whom retaliated in kind. Indeed, the Britons of this period could almost be compared to the Mongols before the rise of Genghis Khan: exacting revenge on one another, caught in seemingly unending cycles of bloodshed and mutual destruction. In the words of one contemporary, Britons had inflicted on themselves more "killing and cutting throats . . . spoyling, and ruinating one another (under the fair pretences of Religion and Reformation) with more barbarous inhumanity and cruelty, than could have been committed here by . . . millions of Turkes, Tartars, or Cannibals."[1]

All this was to change dramatically, beginning with the reign of William and Mary. In 1689, the English parliament passed the Bill of Rights and the Act of Toleration, two revolutionary documents. Notwithstanding significant limitations—for example, the Act of Toleration protected only Protestant dissenters, not Catholics—these two decrees marked the beginning of a new era. Although there would be continuing bigotry and brutality, particularly toward Catholics, Britain would over the next two centuries earn the reputation of the most tolerant nation on earth.

Indeed, the rise of Great Britain vividly exemplifies the thesis of this book. Because of England's marked turn toward tolerance after 1689, three groups in particular—Jews, Huguenots, and, most important, Scots—were able to enter into British society with unprecedented freedom. Collectively, these three groups played an indispensable role in the financial and industrial revolutions that catapulted Great Britain to world dominance.

But once it achieved global dominance, Britain found itself in a profoundly schizophrenic position. At home, Britain had triumphantly embraced the values of pluralism and tolerance. At the same time, in India, Rhodesia, Jamaica, and almost all its overseas domains, British governors ruled as Occidental despots, who presumed white, Christian superiority and openly practiced ethnic and racial discrimination.

In other words, for the British, a funny thing happened on the way to world dominance—the Enlightenment. This may sound flip, but in fact Great Britain differs from every preceding world-dominant power in the following respect: It reached the pinnacle of global power after the threshold of modernity—with its fundamental ideas of liberty, equality, and democracy—had been irreversibly crossed. Britain during its Victorian heyday thus confronted a dilemma that never faced Genghis Khan or even the burghers of seventeenth-century Holland, who never imagined that the tolerance they practiced at home might require them to view the Javanese as their equals. How could Victorian Britain, a nation increasingly coming to see itself as the freest, most tolerant, most moral in the world, rule an empire of conquered subjects?

In the modern world, the meaning of tolerance has changed. The purely instrumental tolerance of the ancient empires, in which skilled groups or talented individuals were "harnessed" in the service of the empire like good horses or mules, cannot satisfy modern ideals of freedom, equality, and self-government. Thus the history of Britain raises an intriguing question. Is it possible for a world-dominant power to be genuinely tolerant in the modern, "enlightened" sense? Answering this question is especially important for today's global hyperpower—the United States of America—the only one to have been a former colony itself.

"THE PRODIGIOUS MULTITUDE OF EXCELLENT PEOPLE OF ALL KINDS": JEWS AND HUGUENOTS IN BRITAIN

After expelling its Jews in 1290, England had virtually no Jewish population for the next four centuries. In the early 1600s, James I was urged by Sir Thomas Shirley to invite the Jews back to England—or, if that was too objectionable, then at least to Ireland, which was filled with barbarians and miscreants anyway—in order to take advantage of their trading connections and commercial skills. Shirley's advice went largely unheeded. It was not until the second half of the seventeenth century, and particularly after the 1688 arrival of William of Orange, that a significant Jewish community in Britain began to take root again.

William had long had a strong, mutually advantageous relationship with Holland's Sephardic Jews. Among the Dutch Jews who followed William to England were members of the financially powerful Machado and Pereira families. Antonio (Moseh) Machado and Jacob Pereira were the chief provisioners for the Dutch Republic's military, supplying bread, grain, horses, and wagons to Dutch troops. In England, the newly arrived Dutch Jews continued to serve as William's military provisioners. The army contractor Solomon de Medina, one of Machado and Pereira's agents, proved so indispensable to William that the king dined at his home on Richmond Hill in 1699. The next year, Medina became the first openly practicing Jew to be knighted in England.[2]

But Britain's new Jews did not only supply armies. Far more important, they played a critical role in financing Great Britain's wars against its most formidable rival in the eighteenth century—France.

Between 1689 and 1763, and arguably for much longer, the rivalry between England and France was obsessive and constant. It extended, moreover, to seemingly every dimension of potential power: land wars, control of the seas, overseas colonies, the slave trade in Africa and the Americas. In many respects, France was in a better position than England to succeed the Dutch Republic as Europe's foremost power. In 1689, France's population was four times greater than that of England, and it had a much larger army, a comparable navy, and a chain of excellent ports and naval bases in the Atlantic and the Mediterranean. Moreover, in 1689, France's industrial production seemed, if anything, stronger than England's. How, then, did England prevail?[3]

In a nutshell, Britain triumphed over France because it had greater access to money. Throughout the seventeenth century, European monarchs were constantly scrambling for the resources needed to finance the skyrocketing costs of war. During this period, most of Europe's treasuries were empty. Armies marched into battle insufficiently provisioned, their soldiers hungry and unpaid. England's coffers were practically empty as late as 1603. (According to the Earl of Clarendon, it was "the popular axiom of Queen Elizabeth," who ruled from 1558 to 1603, "that as her greatest treasure was in the hearts of her people, so she had rather her money should be in their purses than in her Exchequer.") In this context, the "capacity to summon up large sums swiftly and transfer them secretly was crucial to the execution of sudden, bold initiatives of state." Jews were particularly well placed to do this: They were able to raise massive amounts of capital, relying on international family networks and drawing on funds from all over the world.

Jews played precisely this role for William III. Not only did Jewish loans finance the stadtholder-king himself, but it was Jewish loans to a nearly bankrupt Spain—provided, ironically, by Sephardic families who had fled the Inquisition just a few decades earlier—that allowed the anti-French alliance among England, the Netherlands, and Spain to turn the tide against Louis XIV.[4]

However, loans from a few wealthy individuals to desperate monarchs would soon become a thing of the past. (The individual loans, not the desperate monarchs.) In 1694, Parliament established the Bank of England, built on the modern system of privately financed public debt pioneered by the Dutch. Here too Britain's new Jewish community played an important, although less direct, role.

After they arrived in London around 1689, one of the first things that men such as Machado and Medina did was to establish a stock market like the one already flourishing in Holland. It was they who "helped to reproduce the intricate apparatus of speculation which had already been perfected at Amsterdam a hundred years before: settlement or 'contango' day, puts and calls, continuations, backwardation, and all the refinements of the modern stock exchange." More fundamentally, the London Exchange was the chief vehicle by which foreign capitalists—and eventually average British citizens—could invest in Britain's maritime expansion, its industrial and commercial explosion, or the long-term government bonds that funded Britain's wars.[5]

Once the Bank of England was created, Jews also served as brokers for the government's debt, specializing in placing government notes in smaller hands. Thus Samson Gideon, who first made his fortune speculating in government securities and joint-stock companies, became by the 1750s both the leading underwriter of government loans in Britain and the richest Jew in the country; when he died, he was worth £580,000, a staggering sum for the time. (In a familiar pattern, Gideon married a Protestant, raised his children as Christians, and wed his daughter to English nobility; although Gideon himself was refused a baronetcy, being still a Jew, his Eton-educated son and heir was granted that honor at the age of thirteen.) Similarly, the sons of Aaron Goldsmid, another immigrant magnate from Amsterdam, were among the Bank of England's most important brokers for short-term government securities such as three-month Exchequer bills. In the first decade of the nineteenth century, it was the Goldsmids who, by finding private investors for these bills, helped raise the hundreds of millions of pounds that gave Britain a crucial advantage in its war with France.

By introducing the stock exchange, developing new capital markets, and underwriting vast sums of public and private debt, Jews such as Medina, Gideon, and Goldsmid, along with the Montagus, Sterns, and members of the famous Rothschild family, helped turn London into the world's preeminent financial center. After 1815, "it was from London that the world's financial system was articulated, while Amsterdam had been relegated to a subordinate role."[6]

Lest the picture of Jews in Britain appear too rosy, it should be emphasized that immensely wealthy Jewish families were the exception, not the rule. There were roughly 200 such families by the 1830s, out of a total Jewish population in England of approximately 30,000. Before the 1800s, the majority of Jews in Britain— most of whom arrived from Germany, Poland, and central Europe, where Jews were routinely scapegoated and forced into ghettos—

were impoverished and poorly educated, typically eking out a living as peddlers and street hawkers. (The stereotype of the Jewish rag seller was still vivid enough in the 1870s that cartoonists routinely depicted Prime Minister Disraeli in that guise in order to highlight his Jewishness.) In addition, there was widespread anti-Semitic prejudice and discrimination. Jews remained barred, for example, from holding public office or attending ancient universities (such as Oxford or Cambridge, both of which required taking a Christian oath).[7]

Nevertheless, at least by comparison to the other countries of Europe, Great Britain after 1688 became a famously receptive haven for Jews. British Jews were generally not subjected to special taxes, as in other countries, and Parliament imposed virtually no restrictions on Jewish immigration, occupations, commerce, and residency. Jews born in Britain were considered British citizens, entitled to the same property rights as Christians. By 1860, Jews were officially allowed to attend Oxford and Cambridge, hold municipal office, and even run for Parliament. Between 1881 and 1914, as many as 150,000 additional Jews from eastern Europe arrived in Britain, although by then the United States had replaced Britain as the most popular destination.[8]

———————

Britain was a haven and land of opportunity for another enterprising religious minority. The Huguenots were French Protestants who, heavily influenced by John Calvin, fiercely opposed the hierarchy and rituals of the Catholic Church. The first Huguenot church was apparently established in a home in Paris around 1555. Thereafter, the movement spread quickly; at their peak, the Huguenots numbered between one and two million, as compared to roughly 16 million Catholics. They could be found on all rungs of society, including artisans and professionals as well as wealthy financiers and nobles. At one point, backed by the House of Bourbon, the Huguenots had their own fleet of warships and controlled dozens of fortified cities and towns throughout France.[9]

In the mid-seventeenth century, Louis XIV launched a campaign of brutal persecution of Protestants, culminating in the 1685 Revocation of the Edict of Nantes, which had granted a significant measure of religious liberty to them. Following the Revocation, Protestant pastors were hanged, churches destroyed, and property confiscated. Threatened with prison, execution, or the wheel of torture, many Huguenots converted to Catholicism, or pretended to do so. Others—perhaps 150,000 to 200,000—fled the country. Of these, approximately 50,000 sought refuge in the British Isles.

The Huguenot exodus was followed by a period of economic decline in France, but the causes of this decline are difficult to pinpoint. Some historians believe that the departure of the Huguenots was extremely important, adversely affecting France's steel, paper-making, shipping, and textile industries. Others point out that the majority of Huguenots remained in France, often practicing their religion in secret, and that factors such as bad harvests and Louis XIV's military overreaching contributed far more to France's economic problems.

There is no question, however, that England profited. Huguenot clock-makers helped turn London into one of the world's leading clock-making centers. The French town of Caudebec lost most of its master hatters to England, which, armed with new trade secrets for making fine, rain-resistant felt (the trick was mixing wool with rabbit fur), began producing its own "Caudebec" hats. Huguenots also brought with them skills in paper manufacturing, glassblowing, lace making, book printing, metalworking, and linen and silk production.[10]

The Huguenots flourished in England, assimilating and inter-marrying into English society over time. Some of the wealthiest Huguenot family names are now so Anglicized that they are no longer recognized as foreign. This is true, for example, of the Bernard, Janssen, Chamier, Pettit, and Olivier banking families. (Mistakes by English clerks often played a role too. The "English" names Ferry and Fash were originally Ferret and Fouache, respectively.) But as with the Jews, the most important contribution Huguenots made to Britain was in finance.

Between 1740 and 1763, England's national debt almost

tripled because of its wars with France, reaching roughly £121 million in 1763. A striking one-fifth of this sum came from the "Huguenot international," including both Huguenots who had settled in Britain and others—in Holland, Switzerland, and Germany—with whom they were closely connected. For obvious reasons, these exiled Huguenots preferred to bank in (and on) England rather than France. With their financial and rentier backgrounds in France, well-to-do Huguenots were apparently more willing to invest in English public funds than similarly situated Englishmen themselves, who were more likely to keep their money in land—or even "in a strong box in a house."

Despite the important role played by Anglo-Jews and Anglo-Huguenots, it would be absurd to suggest that they alone were responsible for Britain's ascendance to global dominance. Instead, as one historian puts it, their contributions were part of the "leaven" in Britain's rise.[11] Moreover, these contributions pale by comparison to the tremendous injection of economic and intellectual dynamism brought to England by another minority: the Scots.

EMPIRE BUILDERS FROM THE "SINK OF THE EARTH"

William Paterson was a "fast-talking Scot" born in a farmhouse in Dumfriesshire around 1658.[12] As a young man, he made a fortune traveling in the Americas and the West Indies—doing what it is not entirely clear. He has been variously described as a churchman, businessman, and buccaneer, and he was probably all of these things. He was also a financial visionary. In 1694, during a stint in London, Paterson developed the original proposal for the Bank of England and became, along with a number of London merchants, one of its founding directors. But whereas the bank, his brainchild, went on to become the linchpin of Britain's global ascendance, Paterson fell out with his fellow directors and eventually returned to Edinburgh.

At the time, Scotland's economy was traditional and largely rural. England's economy, by contrast, was booming through trade with its colonies and outposts all over the world and through injections of capital and entrepreneurialism supplied by new institutions like the Bank of England and the East India Company. Having founded the former, Paterson threw himself into outdoing the latter. In 1695 Paterson conceived the Darien scheme, which led to one of the most tragic chapters in Scottish history.

Paterson persuaded the Scottish parliament to establish a Scottish colony in Panama, on the isthmus of Darien. The new colony would serve as a trading center linking the Atlantic and Pacific oceans. Instead of having to sail all the way around the southern tip of South America, ships from Europe would simply unload their goods in Darien. The goods would then be transported to the other side of the narrow isthmus and reloaded onto different ships bound for Asia. As the middleman, the Scots would naturally charge a hefty commission on both sides. At the same time, Scotland would control "this door of the seas, and the key of the Universe."

The Darien scheme seemed so promising that it originally attracted investors not only from Scotland but from England and Holland as well. However, the English parliament, strongly lobbied by the East India Company, threatened legal action, even charging Paterson and his co-venturers with high misdemeanors, causing English and Dutch subscribers to withdraw. In response, thousands of outraged, patriotic Scots, high and low, rushed in to make up the shortfall. Aristocrats mortgaged their estates while commoners turned over their meager savings. In just two months, Paterson's company raised the entire amount needed to finance the venture—£400,000, nearly half the total money then circulating in Scotland. On July 18, 1698, five Scottish ships set sail for the New World, with Paterson and his family among the 1,200 passengers.

It would be hard to imagine a more disastrous outcome. The romantic Paterson had described Panama—although he had never been there—as a land of milk and honey, inhabited by friendly natives eager to trade. As a result, the colonists were utterly unprepared for what they found: a malarial morass, torrential rains, and soil in which their seeds would not grow. Instead of sufficient food, they had brought five thousand bibles, four thousand powdered wigs, and, for trading purposes, thousands more mirrors and combs (in which the Indians proved totally uninterested). Soon the settlers were down to a pound of moldy flour a week: "When boiled with a little water, without anything else," one wrote home, "big maggots and worms must be skimmed off the top." The same settler later reported: "Yet for all this short allowance we were every man . . . daily turned out to work by daylight, whether with the hatchet, wheelbarrow, pick-axe, shovel, fore-hammer. . . . My shoulders have been so wore with carrying burdens that the skin has come off them and grew full of boils. . . . Our bodies pined away and grew so macerated with such allowance that we were like so many skeletons."

Fever set in, along with alcoholism. The death rate rose to more than ten a day. The final blow was that the English refused to trade with the starving Scots, and Spain threatened to attack. In July 1699, just a year after sailing from Scotland, the colonists abandoned the settlement. Only one of the five ships made it home, with fewer than three hundred survivors. Paterson's own wife was among the dead.

The Darien fiasco effectively bankrupted Scotland. Paterson and his co-survivors were treated as pariahs. In 1707, a demoralized, famine-stricken Scotland signed the Act of Union with England, creating a new entity called Great Britain. The drive for unification was led by a number of ruined Scottish nobles who, according to many, had been bribed by London with a secret slush fund. In any event, the Scottish parliament dissolved itself, and the Scottish Privy Council relinquished its power over taxes, customs, and military and foreign affairs. In return, England paid off approximately £400,000 in Scottish debts, principally covering the Darien losses. For the many Scots who bitterly opposed unification, the Act of Union was "an entire surrender," a "devil's bargain," and the death of their nation.[13]

From the English point of view, the big question after 1707 was what to do with the Scots. Despite the Darien debacle, the Scots were famous for their ambition and commercial prowess. Many English were fearful of the Scots, whom they saw as shrewd, cunning, and aggressive. Highlander Scots were known for their bravery and belligerence. There were other, sometimes inconsistent stereotypes as well. "The principal part of the Scottish nobility are tyrants and the whole of the common people are slaves," declared one Scotophobe, while others made just the opposite point, railing against the dangerous radicalism of "Scotch rebel buggers." Through it all, the English maintained a firm belief in their superiority over their "poor and pushy" northern neighbors. As one grandee put it, Scotland was "the sink of the earth."

After the Act of Union, the English essentially had to decide whether to raise the Scots up or to keep them down: to try to incorporate, win the loyalty of, and utilize the Scots, or rather, as many in the north feared, to suppress them. The English chose the former path, and profited immeasurably from it.[14]

As the eighteenth and nineteenth centuries unfolded, British dominions expanded at an astounding rate. Indeed, between 1815 and 1865, the British Empire grew by 100,000 square miles on average every year. An empire of this unprecedented expanse required, first and foremost, manpower: soldiers, settlers, farmers, clerks, tradesmen, doctors, officers, governors. There were not nearly enough Englishmen willing or able to fill these positions. Oceans away, in lands filled with tropical disease and not always friendly natives, Britain's colonies did not necessarily appeal to the English, whose domestic economy was thriving.

The Scots, however, were differently situated. They were much poorer than the English. Many from the noble and gentry classes had been bankrupted by the Darien scheme. Scotland's relatively backward economy offered few prospects. Nor was it so easy for a Scot to advance in England, where the best jobs were likely to go to Englishmen. With everything to gain and little to lose, the Scots proved eager to seize the risks and rewards of empire building.

For the English, it was a match made in heaven. British statesmen made a conscious strategic decision to recruit the Scots into imperial service. After unification, and contrary to doomsayer predictions about "slavery to the English," the Scots experienced "an unprecedented freedom and mobility." To the dismay of many English, Prime Minister Henry Pelham declared in 1747 that "[e]very Scotch man who had zeal and abilities to serve the King should have the same admission with the administration as the subject of England had."

Instead of being the enemy, the "hardy" Scots were suddenly actively recruited for the British army—particularly Highlanders, who were now prized for their valor and obedience. By the mid-eighteenth century, roughly one-quarter of the British army's regimental officers were Scots. At the same time, Scots farmed barley in Lower Ontario and raised sheep in New South Wales. They dominated the lucrative American tobacco trade, sailed ships to the Niger, and sold opium in the Far East. In the 1780s, some 60 percent of the British merchants in Bengal were Scots. Many Scots rose to high positions, including James Murray, who became Britain's first governor of Canada in 1760, and James Dalhousie, who served as governor-general of India from 1848–56. "In British settlements from Canada to Ceylon, from Dunedin to Bombay," wrote one nineteenth-century English statesman, "for every Englishman that you meet who has worked himself up to wealth from small beginnings without external aid, you find ten Scotchmen." Indeed, Scots were so disproportionately represented in Britain's colonial exploits and outposts that some (Scottish) writers have suggested that the British Empire should more accurately be called the Scottish Empire.[15]

Scots not only provided manpower for the empire, but were also Britain's leading thinkers, writers, and inventors in the eighteenth and nineteenth centuries. The most famous philosopher of eighteenth-century Britain, David Hume, was Scottish. So was Adam Smith, often called the father of economics. Hume and Smith, along with less well known Scottish intellectuals such as William Robertson, Adam Ferguson, Francis Hutcheson, and Lord Kames, were products of Scotland's extraordinary universities, which, unlike Oxford or Cambridge, were relatively inexpensive and accessible to commoners. The Scots placed great value on education and erudition. By the end of the eighteenth century, Scotland boasted a higher literacy rate than any other country in the world, and even ordinary merchants could typically read Latin and Greek. The first edition of the *Encyclopedia Britannica* was published in Edinburgh. The historian Thomas Carlyle, the poet Robert Burns, and the writers James Boswell, Sir Walter Scott, and Robert Louis Stevenson were all Scottish.

Remarkably, Scots were also the driving force in Britain's industrial revolution. By the 1830s, Scotland was the world's leading producer of iron, and Scottish firms were Britain's preeminent shipwrights. Moreover, the most critical invention of the era—the Watt steam engine—was perfected by the Scotsman James Watt in partnership with the English industrialist Matthew Boulton. The world's first source of independent power—no longer did factories have to be built next to a waterfall or gushing river—Watt's steam engine revolutionized modern economic life. Watt's invention eventually gave rise to the faceless industrial city epitomized by Birmingham, Liverpool, and Manchester. The steam engine also spurred further Scottish innovations, including the integrated cotton mill, the steam hammer, the modern blast furnace, and standardized machine tools. Last but not least, it was a Scotsman, James Nasmyth of Edinburgh, who in 1839 invented that most beloved of modern instruments, the dentist's drill.[16]

THE FRUITS OF TOLERANCE

By the opening of the twentieth century, the British Empire covered more than twelve million square miles, or an astonishing 25 percent of the world's land surface. If one includes the oceans—over which Britain was supreme—the figure would be closer to 70 percent of the globe. As with the Dutch empire, the source of Britain's world dominance lay in its unrivaled naval, commercial, and financial power. With its titanic fleet of battleships, the Royal Navy was probably more powerful than the next three or four navies put together. Indeed, for eighty years after 1815, no other nation (or alliance of nations) came close to challenging Britain's control of the seas.

In 1860, "over one-third of the world's merchant marine flew under the British flag, and that share was steadily increasing." In addition, Britain became the world's banker, as well as the world's industrial and manufacturing giant. With just 2 percent of the world's population, mid-Victorian Britain had "a capacity in modern industries equal to 40–45 percent of the world's potential and 55–60 percent of that in Europe and was alone responsible for two-fifths of the world's manufacturing output."[17]

How much did Britain's tolerance after 1689 assist its rise to world dominance? This of course is impossible to know. Lest the obvious be overlooked, it should be noted that, if only by dint of England's far larger population, the majority of Britain's most important bankers, merchants, magnates, generals, and governors-general in the eighteenth and nineteenth centuries were English. Not only Scots were responsible for Britain's technological breakthroughs. It was the Englishman Jethro Tull, for example, who invented the seed drill, and other Englishmen who invented the fly shuttle, jenny, water frame, and spinning mule—all major factors in Britain's industrial revolution.

Nevertheless, the contributions of the Jews, Huguenots, and Scots—which would not have been possible without Britain's turn to tolerance—were not only disproportionate but pivotal. Take, for example, the Bank of England, "the most powerful financial institution in the world's most powerful country" and a chief reason Britain was able to triumph over France. A Scot conceived the bank, Huguenots funded it, and Jews brokered its biggest loans. (Other Dutch capitalists invested heavily in it too.) Likewise, Jews founded the London Stock Exchange, brought diamond and bullion trading to Britain, and almost single-handedly made London, as opposed to Amsterdam, the world's financial center.[18]

Without the steam engine and the iron-smelting hot blast furnace, both of which were Scottish inventions, Britain could not have built naval monsters like the HMS *Warrior*, described by Niall Ferguson as "the supreme expression of mid-Victorian might":

Steam-driven, "iron clad" in five inches of armour plate and fitted with the latest breech-loading, shell-firing guns, *Warrior* was the world's most powerful battleship, so powerful that no foreign vessel ever dared to exchange fire with her. And she was just one of around 240 ships, crewed by 40,000 sailors— making the Royal Navy the biggest in the world by far. And thanks to the unrivalled productivity of her shipyards, Britain owned roughly a third of the world's merchant tonnage. At no other time in history has one power so completely dominated the world's oceans.[19]

In sum, while impossible to quantify precisely, the benefits that Great Britain gained from harnessing the talents, capital, and ingenuity of non-English groups such as the Scots, Jews, and Huguenots were immense and far-reaching.

———————

Tolerance in nineteenth-century Great Britain transcended purely strategic calculation. To a surprising extent, the English embraced and practiced the Enlightenment ideal of tolerance: They espoused principles of universal equality and, to a remarkable degree, permitted members of different ethnic and religious groups to become full citizens of Great Britain with the same social and political rights as native Englishmen.

Indeed, the very idea of "Britain" overcame long-standing national and ethnic boundaries. Although a nation in its own right, Great Britain was created by incorporating at least three different peoples that could claim, and frequently did claim, national identities of their own: the English, Welsh, and Scots. Intermarriage among the nobility was one powerful indication that age-old barriers were coming down. In the second half of the eighteenth century, the number of marriages between the daughters of Scottish aristocrats and Englishmen more than doubled, creating a new landed "British" upper class. When the Scottish heiress Elizabeth, Countess of Sutherland, married the Englishman George Granville Leveson-Gower, the latter gained 800,000 acres of prime real estate in Scotland. Whereas before 1770 reference books about British nobility had almost always treated the English, Welsh, and Scottish peerage as distinct entities and kept them in separate volumes, between 1770 and 1830 most of the guides to the nobility published in Britain—and there were seventy-five such guides—treated the peerage of the United Kingdom as a single unit.

As the nineteenth century progressed, Scots and Welshmen rose to the highest positions in government. Jews became knights and barons. Most remarkably, Benjamin Disraeli became prime minister of Great Britain, first in 1868 and then again in 1874. Although his family had converted to the Anglican Church, Disraeli was known to be of Jewish background. By the First World War, the humorist John Hay Beith was able to write in his spoof *The Oppressed English*:

> Today a Scot is leading the British army in France, another is commanding the British grand fleet at sea, while a third directs the Imperial General Staff at home. The Lord Chancellor is a Scot; so are the Chancellor of the Exchequer and the Foreign Secretary. The Prime Minister is a Welshman. . . . Yet no one has ever brought in a bill to give home rule to England![20]

Meanwhile, stunning the world, Britain had by the 1830s abolished its slave trade while it was still extremely lucrative. Throughout the nineteenth century, the Royal Navy policed the world's oceans, crusading against other nations' slave trading from Africa to the Americas. Britain's abolitionist campaign gave it the moral high ground over not just its main rival, France, but also, even more satisfyingly, over its former colony the United States. At a cost of millions of pounds, and in precisely the same era that it achieved global dominance, Great Britain became known as the "most moral" power in the world. As the historian Linda Colley puts it, "Successful abolitionism became one of the vital underpinnings of British supremacy in the Victorian era, offering—as it seemed to do—irrefutable proof that British power was founded on religion, on freedom and on moral calibre, not just on a superior stock of armaments and capital."[21]

There was, however, a hitch. British identity from the beginning was forged on a bedrock of Protestantism, in opposition to Catholic Spain and France.[22] This core religious component of British identity planted a seed of intolerance that the empire never quite overcame. Indeed, British Protestantism created a fateful problem for the empire in the very heart of the United Kingdom: the problem of Catholic Ireland.

THE CATHOLIC PROBLEM AND THE LIMITS OF "BRITISH" TOLERANCE

The Irish never received the same treatment in Great Britain as did the Scots or the Welsh. The principal reason was religion. By 1700, the Scots, the Welsh, and the English were all predominantly Protestant, whereas the Irish remained stubbornly Catholic. Great Britain's loss of Ireland is in many ways a story of too little tolerance, too late.

It would be hard to overstate the persistence and intensity of mutual hatred between Catholics and Protestants in British history. Endless religious wars left a legacy of enmity and anger. Like witches in previous eras, Catholics in England were often scapegoated, physically assaulted, or plunged in water until near drowning. Even Locke, in his famous 1689 *Letter on Toleration*, excluded Catholics, whose opinions were "absolutely destructive of all governments except the Pope's." Catholicism was depicted as not only blasphemous but also primitive and superstitious. As one English newspaper put it in 1716: "A *Papist* is an Idolator, who worships Images, Pictures, Stocks and Stones, the Works of Mens Hands; calls upon the Virgin *Mary*, Saints and Angels to pray for them; adores Reliques," "eats his God by the cunning Trick of Transubstantiation," and "swears the *Pope* is infallible."[23]

At the same time, many in England suspected that Catholic "traitors" and "conspirators" were plotting to overthrow the Protestant monarchy. These fears were not entirely unfounded. In 1601, an invasion force of more than three thousand Spanish soldiers, invited by Ireland's Catholic chieftains, landed on the southern Irish coast (where they were defeated by the English on

Christmas Eve at the Battle of Kinsale). Repeatedly, Irish nobility allied themselves with Catholic Spain and France in attempts to oust their English overlords. Closer to home, in 1708, 1715, and 1745, European military forces landed in Scotland with the intention of marching on London and restoring the Catholic Stuarts to the throne.

Anti-Catholic riots were frequent all over eighteenth-century Britain, from Glasgow to Birmingham to Bath. The most horrific of these were the Gordon Riots of 1780. Initially demanding repeal of the Catholic Relief Act, which gave Catholics new rights of participation, an enraged London mob of 60,000 quickly turned violent. "The conflagration was horrible beyond description," reported one eyewitness. "Sleep and rest were things not thought of; the streets were swarming with people, and uproar, confusion, and terror reigned in every part." The Gordon Riots lasted a full week. In the end, at least a hundred Catholic churches and private homes were torched and looted. Nearly three hundred people were killed—many burned alive.[24]

Could Englishmen and Scots bring themselves to accept the Irish as fellow Britons? Could Protestant Britain extend religious freedom and political rights to the "ignorant," "indolent," and "despotic" papists? After the Gordon Riots, Britain took significant strides in that direction. In 1800 a new Act of Union incorporated Ireland into the United Kingdom. In 1829, the Catholic Emancipation Act granted Catholics the right to vote and to hold parliamentary office—although, like Jews, they were still excluded from the oldest universities and the highest offices. By 1831, there were some 580,000 Irish in England and Scotland, which represented approximately 5 percent of the labor force and a twelvefold increase since 1780. When the Houses of Parliament burned in 1834, one of the principal architects of the new Palace of Westminster, destined to be one of Great Britain's iconic symbols of imperial power, was a devout Roman Catholic.

Nevertheless, in Ireland, the on-the-ground reality for Catholics remained one of unrelenting subjugation and degradation. The Penal Laws of the seventeenth and eighteenth centuries had not only barred Catholics from public office, restricted their education, and denied them the vote, but effectively stripped them of their property. This, together with successive waves of "plantation"—the colonization of Ireland by government-sponsored Protestant settlers—had created a British ruling class throughout the country. By the time they were "emancipated" in 1829, the vast majority of Catholics lived in poverty, subsisting on potatoes and buttermilk and paying rent to a handful of English nobles who owned over 90 percent of Ireland's profitable land. Irish culture, and the Irish language in particular, was demeaned and increasingly marginalized. In the 1840s, Ireland was struck by a devastating potato blight. Although referred to as a "famine," the truth was that significant supplies of life-saving food continued to be produced. Unfortunately, Ireland's British landowners continued to ship this produce abroad at considerable profit, leaving a million (almost exclusively Catholic) Irish to die of starvation.

Thus, Ireland's Catholics were not overwhelmed by Britain's newfound "tolerance" in the nineteenth century. The Act of Union of 1801 was perceived—probably correctly—by most Irishmen not as an inclusive embrace but rather as a political ploy to abolish their parliament. Even the rights achieved in 1829 rang hollow to many Irish Catholics, who continued in reality to be subservient to and wholly dependent on their Protestant overlords. In Easter of 1916, while Britain was preoccupied with war, armed Catholic rebels rose up in Dublin, seizing buildings and declaring independence. The rebels were put down, but in the 1920s the British agreed to the creation of the Irish Free State (while retaining Northern Ireland as part of the United Kingdom), which in 1949 became the Republic of Ireland.[25]

From the Irish point of view, independence was an achievement long sought and hard won—a source of pride and (putting aside the Northern Ireland problem) a cause for celebration. From the empire's point of view, the loss of Ireland was politically devastating. The British loss of the American colonies was in many ways easier to accept. It was one thing for the British to have been unable in 1776 to maintain control over a large population of increasingly unruly frontier colonists three thousand miles away, separated from them by an ocean. It was quite another to lose a piece of the United Kingdom itself, hardly more than a stone's throw away from the rest of Great Britain.

To be sure, linguistic, cultural, national, and political cleavages always separated the British from the Irish. Yet none of this can explain Britain's loss of Ireland. The English made Britons out of conquered Welshmen. They made London a magnet for long-despised Jews. They embraced and assimilated 50,000 foreign-born, French-speaking Huguenots. They induced formerly scorned and feared Scots to become Britain's most aggressive and effective empire builders. In every one of these cases, the English overcame their prejudices, shrewdly winning the allegiance and profiting from the talents of all these groups.

The contrast with Ireland is stark and tragic. In a sense, Great Britain's loss of Ireland is a story of failed tolerance. Nineteenth-century Britain took real steps toward Catholic equality—although even to this day Catholics are barred from the British throne—but it was too little, too late. Over centuries of warfare and exploitation, British Protestants had reduced Irish Catholics to an impoverished underclass, debasing their culture and religion, expropriating their land, almost extinguishing their language, and, through at best callous indifference, contributing to the death and flight of millions. It is not surprising that the majority of Irish never came to see themselves as British.

Conceivably, things could have been different, although it takes a stretch of the imagination. Had the British treated the Irish with even the same strategic tolerance they had shown the Scots, Ireland today, with its booming economy, might still be part of the United Kingdom. But Britain did not, and probably could not, open itself to Irish Catholics in the same way.

Interestingly, a parallel story unfolded in Britain's nonwhite imperial possessions. As Protestantism became less central to nineteenth-century British identity, and as the empire expanded all over the globe, the British increasingly defined themselves as "white" and "civilized" in contrast to the colonial populations they conquered. This racial and ethnic arrogance created the same limits on British tolerance in its Asian and African dominions that anti-Catholic prejudice had in Ireland. Nowhere was this more apparent than in India, the "jewel of the empire."

ENLIGHTENMENT AND EMPIRE:
THE RISE AND FALL OF THE RAJ

In 1858, when Great Britain was near the zenith of its power, Queen Victoria issued a famous proclamation renouncing Britain's right and desire "to impose [its] convictions on any of [its] subjects" and promising "a perfect equality . . . between Europeans and Natives." The queen's rosy assurances were motivated by some not-so-rosy circumstances. Just the year before, mutinous Muslims and Hindus in northwest India slaughtered hundreds of British women and children. In revenge, British soldiers strapped Indians to cannons, blowing them to pieces, and indiscriminately hanged and shot thousands—perhaps tens of thousands—of others.

Queen Victoria's proclamation of "perfect equality" proved sadly empty. Britain continued to rule India absolutely, affording the queen's Indian subjects no political representation whatsoever. Not only in India but in all of its nonwhite domains, the British could not live up to the ideals of Enlightenment tolerance it professed. On the other hand, when it came to strategic tolerance—recruiting, rewarding, and utilizing individuals of diverse ethnicities and religions in the furtherance of empire—the British were masters.

As the English East India Company ascended in India, the Mughal Empire began its rapid decline, disintegrating from its own metastasizing intolerance. The directors of the East India Company saw the power vacuum opened up by the Mughal collapse— and they filled it. In essence, the company recapitulated the strategy of the Persian and Tang emperors. They identified the warrior classes among their subject populace—such as the Rajputs from the north, who had long-standing military traditions—and aggressively recruited them, using them to conquer and rule a territory and population far vaster than the British could otherwise have controlled. At its peak, the company's army numbered roughly 320,000 soldiers, of whom only 40,000 were European. By the mid-nineteenth century, the East India Company was the greatest power on the subcontinent, presiding over the largest civil service, wielding the largest army, and governing a population of approximately two hundred million. As the historian T. A. Heathcote put it, "The East India Company succeeded the Mughals as the next Indian empire."[26]

Unlike the ultraorthodox Mughal emperor Aurangzeb, the Company ruled with a tolerant hand—not out of idealism but expedience—following Wellington's principle that interfering with India's "ancient laws, customs and religion" was politically dangerous. Britain's Indian army included Muslims, Hindus, Christians, and Sikhs, as well as a number of Africans and Arabs. All were permitted to worship as they chose. British officers, acting under Company orders, joined in native religious ceremonies. Troops and cannons were made available for local festivals. Indeed, as successors to the kings and princes whom they had replaced, the Company's directors maintained Hindu temples and collected taxes for the benefit of religious pilgrims.[27]

The same precepts of calculated tolerance underlay the Company's commercial and governmental dealings in India. From the beginning, the Company profited enormously from alliances with indigenous entrepreneurial minorities, most of whom had previously worked in the service of the Mughal emperors. It was only through partnerships with these native capitalists—Jain moneylenders, Gujarati banking families, Hindu and Parsi merchants, *dubashes* in Madras, *banians* in Bengal—that the Company could penetrate India's interior. The Company's British merchants allowed their Indian counterparts to make great fortunes, in the process turning them into "uneasy collaborators in the creation of colonial India." At the same time, the Company employed more and more Indians as petty bureaucrats to administer its expanding territories. Here the strategy was a modern variation on Genghis

Khan's. The Company coopted and trained a pro-English cadre of Indian functionaries and elites who handled day-to-day administration under British supervision.[28]

Interestingly, the Company's men showed a similar openness to native "abilities" when it came to their sexual lives. During the period of Company governance in India (roughly between 1757 and 1858), marriage between British men and Indian women was common. And there was considerably more miscegenation than there was intermarriage. "I now commenced a regular course of f——ing with native women," wrote one Englishman, recalling his early days in India as a sixteen-year-old Company cadet. Another Company employee waxed more philosophical: "[T]hose who have lived with a native woman for any length of time never marry a European . . . so amusingly playful, so anxious to oblige and please [are they], that a person after being accustomed to their society shrinks from the idea of encountering the whims or yielding to the fancies of an Englishwoman."

The Company's promiscuity, both sexual and religious, outraged English evangelicals back in London. The evangelicals did not mince words about Christianity's superiority over the "abominable and degrading superstitions" prevailing in India. "Our religion is sublime, pure and beneficent," declared William Wilberforce to the House of Commons in 1813. "Theirs is mean, licentious and cruel." Wilberforce demanded that Parliament undo the barriers erected by the Company against Christian proselytizing in India. As time went on, the evangelical movement gained increasing influence over British imperial policy.

To deal with the problem of native mistresses, the Company was induced to start shipping young British women to India. The arrival of this "fishing fleet" became a signal event in nineteenth-century Calcutta's social calendar. At great parties thrown by Calcutta's leading British socialites, the hopeful bachelorettes would "sit up" for three nights in a row, while eligible soldiers and officers of all ages passed through. After a year, those who failed to land a husband were shipped back to England.

More fatefully, in 1829, the missionaries helped push through a ban on *sati*, the traditional Hindu practice of immolating widows upon their husband's funeral pyres. This ban represented the first explicit British interference with an important Indian religious practice and, as Company officials had feared, provoked broad resentment among the Hindu majority. In 1833 missionaries won the right to proselytize and set up schools in India without Company approval. In 1850, in direct violation of Hindu law, the British passed legislation allowing converts to Christianity to inherit property. In 1856, the British legalized second marriages by Hindu widows. Particularly obnoxious to India's Muslims were the missionaries' extension of education to women and their adoption and conversion of abandoned orphans.[29]

The evangelicals were not the only Britons interested in anglicizing and "civilizing" Indians. There were also the modernizers, such as the Scottish governor-general James Dalhousie, who brought railroads, the telegraph, and ingenious new inventions to India. Ironically, it was one of these inventions that set off the worst conflagration in the history of the Raj.

Introduced in 1857, the new muzzle-loading Enfield rifle was a technological triumph. Before using the rifle, a soldier had to bite off both ends of the new Enfield cartridges. Unfortunately, rumors—very possibly true—soon spread that the Enfield cartridges were greased with a mixture of pig and cow fat. For Indian soldiers (*sepoys*), touching their lips to these cartridges therefore risked defilement—pork being repugnant to Muslims and cows sacred to Hindus. Indeed, the Indians were convinced that the Enfield rifle was part of "an insidious missionary plot to defile them" and impose Christianity on India. On top of all this, the British had just forcibly annexed the rich province of Oudh, ignominiously deposing its king—an act of utmost hubris given that 75,000 *sepoys* in the army that invaded Oudh hailed from that very province.

Company after company of Indian soldiers refused to load the new Enfield rifles. In each case, the insubordinate *sepoys* were summarily discharged and stripped of their uniforms, weapons,

and pensions. On May 9, 1857, eighty-five men from the Third
Native Cavalry in Meerut were shackled and imprisoned for this
act of disobedience. The next day, while their British officers were
at church, the entire native brigade revolted, storming the prison
and freeing their comrades. In the words of one contemporary English private:

> There was a sudden rising . . . a rush to the horses, a swift
> saddling, a gallop to the gaol . . . a breaking open of the gates,
> and a setting free, not only of the mutineers who had been
> court-martialled, but also of more than a thousand cut-
> throats and scoundrels of every sort. Simultaneously, the na-
> tive infantry fell upon and massacred their British officers,
> and butchered the women and children in a way that you can-
> not describe.

The rampaging soldiers, joined by civilian mobs, then headed
for Delhi, "burning bungalows and murdering every European
man, woman and child they encountered." By the end of May,
what the British would call "the Mutiny" had spread across India.

There followed two years of mutual slaughter and savagery. At
Cawnpore, even after the British garrison surrendered, two hundred British women and children were killed, many hacked to
death. In return, the British unleashed a barbarous vengeance.
"Man-hunting" for mutineers became the "best sport," and soldiers whooped it up as they plunged the regulation twelve-inch
spike bayonet—renamed the Cawnpore Dinner because it went
"straight to the stomach"—into Indian captives. It was at Pe-
shawar that suspected rebels were tied to cannons and blown to
pieces; back in London, cartoons depicted severed Indian limbs flying amid clouds of smoke. At Delhi, the British "hanged all the villagers who had treated [the] fugitives badly until every tree was
covered with scoundrels hanging from every branch." At Cawnpore, Muslims were forced to eat pork and Hindus beef before
they were executed in front of jeering soldiers. Not only mutineers
but young boys, old men, and faithful domestic servants were shot

in cold blood. "I felt as if my heart was stone and my brain fire," a British lieutenant later recalled of a day when he had killed twelve and was desperate to kill more.[30]

————

The Mutiny provoked paroxysms of recrimination and self-questioning in England. The British, as had become unpleasantly clear, were not exactly universally adored by the millions of dark-skinned heathens living under British rule. So what exactly was Britain doing in places like India—or Jamaica, where in 1865 there was an almost equally vicious uprising of ungrateful freed black slaves?

Fierce debates ensued, but by the 1870s one thing was certain. Far from retreating, the English would embrace the idea of imperial Britain. The East India Company was abolished, and India was placed under direct crown rule. In 1876, Queen Victoria, amid great pomp and fanfare, was declared empress of India. In a famous speech, Disraeli challenged his countrymen to choose between "a comfortable England" and "a great country—an Imperial country" commanding "the respect of the world." The English chose the latter. More than ever, the empire became a defining source of national pride for Britons, working class and aristocracy alike.

But what kind of empire? Britain's two primary political parties had different answers, both riddled with inconsistency. The Conservatives, or Tories, glorified hierarchy. They romanticized the Roman and Mughal empires and allied themselves with India's native princes and feudal landowners (*zamindaars*). At the same time, they often explicitly avowed white racial superiority. For many late-nineteenth-century British Conservatives, immutable racial differences—which became the subject of voluminous pseudoscientific investigation—explained not only the inherent right of the British to rule over their darker Indian subjects but also the internal divisions within Indian society. Thus, H. H. Risley, ethnologist and India's census commissioner, developed a "nasal index," which simultaneously vindicated white supremacy and India's

caste system. If, he wrote, "we take a series of castes . . . and ar-
range them in order of the average nasal index, so that the caste
with the finest nose shall be at the top, and that with the coarsest
at the bottom of the list, it will be found that this order substan-
tially corresponds with the accepted order of social precedence."

On the other side were the Liberals, who at least in their rhetoric were more reluctant imperialists. Unlike the Conservatives,
the Liberals paid lip service to and in some cases genuinely sought
to implement the principle of universal human equality. For them,
British imperial rule was justified not because the Indians were
racially inferior but because, for reasons of history and culture
(and perhaps even climate), the Indians were backward, uncivilized, and unready for self-government. Like children, they were in
need of tutelage. As the famous philosopher and India hand John
Stuart Mill put it, self-government was not "suited" to all of Britain's subject peoples, some of whom ranked "in point of culture
and development . . . very little above the highest of beasts." The
good news was that progress was possible for all races, and with
help—primarily through education and law—Indians could one
day (in the far distant future) be just like Englishmen.

In the aftermath of the Mutiny there was at least one point on
which Liberals and Conservatives agreed. Britain's great mistake
had been "tampering with religion" and "introducing a system foreign to the habits and wishes of the people." Instead of trying to
Christianize India, Conservative statesmen like Disraeli joined
with Liberal leaders in proclaiming a new commitment to religious
tolerance and noninterference with local customs. (It was then that
Queen Victoria issued her famous promise not to "impose [British]
convictions" on any of Britain's subjects.) This commitment had
the ring of principle, but it also played conveniently into a divide-
and-conquer strategy. Nowhere was this clearer than in Britain's
post-Mutiny restructuring of the Indian army.[31]

The Indian army was deliberately reorganized to separate Indians of different regions, backgrounds, and castes into their own
companies or regiments. New uniforms were designed to highlight
the distinctions among the *sepoys'* divergent religious or regional

backgrounds. For example, Gurkhas, who tended to identify with the British more than other soldiers, were typically outfitted in Western-tailored rifle-green uniforms, while other *sepoys* were dressed in loose-fitting pantaloons. In many cases the British actually required their Indian soldiers to don distinctive traditional garb. As numerous historians have pointed out, British officers intentionally fostered a separate Sikh identity, requiring Sikh soldiers to carry their *kirpans*, or daggers, and to wear their traditional turbans. When Sikh *sepoys* did not have these accoutrements, the British supplied them; thousands of *kirpans* were manufactured in Sheffield and shipped overseas. In this way, the British were able not only to honor the diverse customs of their respective regions but also to rigidify and exploit India's internal divisions.

At the same time, British officers took new pains to accommodate native rituals. Hindus were permitted to make sacrifices to the goddess Kali on the eve of battle. Brahmin *sepoys* were allowed to conduct their lengthy food preparation rites, even at the expense of slowing down a regiment on the march. "Everything should be done to secure the contentment and loyalty of the Native Army by a scrupulous regard for their customs and their religion," urged Lord Roberts, the commander of the Indian army from 1885–93.

These British accommodations and manipulations were largely effective. "Colonel Sahib has made excellent arrangements and takes great trouble for us Musalmans," one Muslim soldier wrote during Ramadan. "His arrangements for our food during the fast are very good, and he has put us all together because during the fast it is not easy to live with Sikhs and Dogras. I cannot describe how good his arrangements are." Similarly, a Sikh soldier expressed his appreciation that, under British protocol, "animals intended for the food of Sikhs [were] slaughtered by a Sikh by a stroke of a sword on the back of the neck, and those intended for Musalmans, by a Musalman in the lawful way, namely by cutting the throat." A family member of another Sikh *sepoy*, upon learning that he had been allowed to celebrate the birthday of Guru Sri Nanak, wrote: "Thanks, a thousand thanks, to the Government under whose rule, not only we, but the members of every sect, are able to observe fittingly their holy days. May the Guru ever keep over our heads the shadow of this great King."[32]

At the same time, the British made a massive investment in education in India. By 1887, nearly 300,000 Indians were studying English; in 1907 the figure was over 500,000. This Anglo-educated elite, who would later play a central role in India's new nationalist movement, was at least initially deeply committed to the British Empire. Thus Dadabhai Naoroji, the "Grand Old Man" of Indian nationalism, published in 1871 a devastating critique of the Raj, but never argued for independence. On the contrary, he famously defended British rule, arguing that the colonial government was not living up to Britain's own principles of "fair play and justice," adding, "It is only in British hands that [India's] regeneration can be accomplished."

In the decades following the Mutiny, the British enlisted men like Naoroji to serve as lawyers, magistrates, and bureaucrats in the Indian Civil Service; indeed, British rule over India would have been impossible without this cadre of elite pro-British natives. Certainly without the allegiance of Indian *sepoys* and Indian bureaucrats a thousand British civil servants could never have governed a native population of hundreds of millions.

Most Indian bureaucrats occupied lower or at best midlevel positions. But a handful were permitted to rise to the highest levels, even in the mother country. In 1892, for example, Naoroji was elected to the British parliament by voters from Central Finsbury in London, the same constituency that would later elect Margaret Thatcher.[33]

———

British imperial policies during the ninety years of the Raj (1857–1947) were a contradictory, oscillating mixture of Liberalism and Conservatism. Neither camp could achieve dominance for long. First, the two political parties kept toppling each other in London. Moreover, even when Liberals were ascendant, their policies in India were repeatedly undermined by the nonofficial British community living there.

These Anglo-Indians—consisting mainly of hard-driving, often Scottish merchants, traders, railroad men, and tea and indigo planters—were notoriously racist. After the Mutiny, out of genuine fear as well as bigotry, the Anglo-Indians retreated into an essentially apartheid system in which whites lived in insular, militarily protected enclaves separated from the "Blacktowns," where the Indians lived. Most at home in their comfortable all-white social clubs—with names like "the Unceremonials" and "the Limited Liability Club"—these businessmen were not above beating their Indian workers for laziness or insolence. Between 1880 and 1900, no fewer than eighty-one recorded "accidental" shootings were recorded in which a sahib who had "bagged a coolie" went essentially unpunished.

The Anglo-Indians reacted with fury whenever Liberal administrations sought to dismantle the racial barriers that protected them. In 1883, a Liberal viceroy tried to pass the ill-fated Ilbert Bill, which would have allowed Indian judges to try white defendants. The Anglo-Indian response was a grotesque explosion of racist protests all across the country. "Are our wives," demanded one Anglo-Indian, "to be torn from our homes on false pretenses [to] be tried by men who do not respect women, and do not understand us, and in many cases hate us? . . . Fancy, I ask you Britishers, her being taken before a half-clad native, to be tried and perhaps convicted." "Verily the jackass kicketh at the lion," bellowed another orator to raucous applause. "Show him as you value your liberties; show him that the lion is not dead; he sleepeth, and in God's name, let him dread the awakening." Almost the entire white community in India swung against the government. Not long afterward, the Raj lurched back to Conservatism.[34]

But when Conservatives were in power, their policies met with the increasing and much more violent resistance of India's growing nationalist movement. When the patrician Lord Curzon became viceroy in 1898, he pitted himself squarely against the corps of anglicized Indian lawyers and civil servants that a previous generation of Liberals had worked so hard to cultivate. With Calcutta as their power base, members of this educated elite had in 1885 founded the Indian National Congress, a party that quickly became the most important voice of Indian political aspirations. Curzon spurned these so-called Bengali Babus, with their emergent (and English-taught) ideas of equality and nationhood. Viewing them as a threat to British rule, Curzon pointedly excluded them from the highest posts of the Indian Civil Service and took measure after measure to undermine the Congress Party. Curzon's most draconian step was the 1905 partition of Bengal into two new provinces, gerrymandered to make Bengali-speaking Hindus a minority in both.

Curzon's policies backfired. They fueled the rise of a revolutionary wing within the Indian National Congress, set off angry boycotts of British goods, and sparked a rash of bombings and assassination attempts. Curzon resigned in 1905, and the British eventually reinstated Liberal policies, which in turn did not last long.

In the end, Britain's loss of India was once again—as with Ireland—a case of too little tolerance, too late. In the case of India, however, Britain had actively squandered decades of goodwill built up within its subject populations. Led by men such as Naoroji, the Indian National Congress in its early years had been staunchly proBritish. Its founding members had a penchant for quoting Shakespeare and referred to the queen-empress as "Mother," cheering whenever her name was mentioned. Even the more extreme nationalist leaders, including the "terrorists," were overwhelmingly members of the British-educated, privileged Indian elite, men who had tried to pursue the career paths the British set out for them, only to find their advancement blocked by British racism.

As late as the eve of the First World War, many of India's leaders remained loyal to the crown. When Britain declared war on Germany in 1914, Gandhi told his followers: "We are, above all, British citizens of the Great British Empire. Fighting as the British are at present in a righteous cause for the good and glory of human dignity and civilisation . . . our duty is clear: to do our best to support the British, to fight with our life and property." Hundreds of thousands of Indian troops were dispatched to fight in theaters all over the world, and more than one million Indians in all served the empire abroad in some capacity. In return, Indian leaders, encouraged by ambiguous promises from London, believed that the war's end would bring India self-government similar to that enjoyed by Canada and Britain's other "white" dominions.[35]

Disillusion awaited. Instead of self-rule, India's post-armistice "reward" was a brutal crackdown and shocking repression.

Postwar India was tumultuous. A growing spirit of national awareness and pride pervaded the country, as did mounting anger at the diversion of India's wealth to Britain's imperial needs. The global economy, too, was changing. Protectionism surged around the world. In India, urbanization and unemployment set in even as new Indian-owned industries began to emerge. British-style education had been a double-edged sword; more and more Indians demanded the freedoms they had studied or seen firsthand overseas. Waves of protests, marches, strikes, and political agitation swept the Indian subcontinent, punctuated by bursts of violence.

For the Anglo-Indian community, all this change was profoundly threatening. Even as Whitehall continued to draft progressive Indian reform measures from afar, the British government in India enacted the repressive Rowlatt Acts, imposing curfews on natives and curtailing rights of protest, essentially extending martial law for three years after the war. In 1919, having banned public gatherings, Brigadier General R.E.H. Dyer ordered his men to open fire on some 10,000 unarmed peasants who had gathered inside a walled field in Amritsar in the Punjab, possibly to celebrate a Hindu festival. With no warning, Dyer's brigade fired 1,650 rounds of live ammunition into the helpless, trapped crowd. Hundreds of Indians were killed, and a thousand more were injured.

Although recalled by London for "an error of judgment," Dyer was unrepentant. Indeed, he initially received a hero's welcome back in England, where Conservatives gave him a jeweled sword bearing the motto "Saviour of the Punjab." Over the next few months, British soldiers inflicted ever more brutal punishment on the increasingly restless Punjabis—flogging them, forcing them to crawl on hands and knees—"in defense of the realm."

The Punjab atrocities were the last straw for India's once loy-
alist leaders. In 1919, Sir Rabindranath Tagore, Asia's first Nobel
laureate in literature, repudiated his knighthood in protest of the
slaughter. He explained: "The time has come when badges of hon-
our make our shame glaring in their incongruous context of humiliation, and I for my part, wish to stand, shorn, of all special
distinctions, by the side of those of my countrymen who, for their
so called insignificance, are liable to suffer degradation not fit for
human beings."

In 1920, Gandhi issued his revolutionary call for nonviolent
noncooperation with the British government. The Indian National
Congress followed Gandhi, finally abandoning decades of official
support for the Raj.

Public opinion in England swung against Dyer as well. Lord
Montagu, secretary of state for India, demanded of Dyer's defend-
ers in Parliament, "Are you going to keep your hold upon India by
terrorism, racial humiliation, and subordination?" Churchill called
the massacre "monstrous"—"without precedent or parallel in the
modern history of the British Empire"—and accused Dyer of destroying rather than saving British rule in India.[36]

In a desperate attempt to stave off independence, the British
government of India made one last-gasp effort to maintain power
through strategic tolerance. In the interwar period, official Britain
scrambled to "Indianize" the upper echelons of the Indian Civil
Service and the officer corps of the Indian army, both former bas-
tions of white authority. On the economic front, the new official
buzzwords were "industrialization" and "development." In the future, India would no longer just supply raw materials; it would become an economically impressive trading partner for Britain, with
mutual advantages for all—or so ran the party line. Most crucially,
the British government of India sought to enlist the cooperation of
India's increasingly powerful indigenous business community,
mainly Marwaris from Calcutta and Gujaratis from Ahmedabad
who after the war had come to control huge chunks of the Indian
economy.

These concessions hardly stemmed from altruism. On the contrary, the first concern of the Raj was to marginalize India's radical nationalists. As the historian Maria Misra puts it, the government of India "was determined to concede as much economic power to Indians as was compatible with maintaining the imperial interest."

Unfortunately for Britain, the Anglo business community on the ground in India went in the opposite direction, toward increasingly extreme intolerance. Rather than racially integrate their firms as the government of India encouraged, these Anglo-Indians refused to allow well-connected, capital-rich Indians like the Marwaris and Gujaratis onto their governing boards or to employ even highly qualified Indians for managerial positions. Whereas the East India Company in its most successful days had actively recruited and allied itself with entrepreneurial Indians, Anglo-Indians in the twentieth century stubbornly opposed collaboration with indigenous business interests. This strategy of aggressive intolerance proved spectacularly self-defeating. The Anglo-Indians' blatant racism intensified resentment among the Indian elite, who increasingly allied themselves with the mass nationalist movement and its calls for the nationalization or expulsion of British business interests.[37]

In 1946, civil war broke out among India's Muslims, Hindus, and Sikhs. India was now an albatross for the British. In 1947, London announced the partition of the subcontinent; thus were born the independent states of India and Pakistan. The following decades saw an exodus of British business, capital, and personnel.

It is of course impossible to know how history would have unfolded had the British behaved differently. Powerful forces like socialism, nationalism, and anticolonialism were gaining momentum in the early twentieth century. If not in 1947, India would certainly have achieved independence at some point. The days of European colonialism were numbered.

But perhaps India could have wrested itself from Britain in a way that was not so angry, so violent, so destructive of British interests. Throughout the ninety years of the British Raj, opportunity after opportunity to accept Indians as equals was squandered. After World War I, Indian business interests made repeated efforts to form interethnic alliances and partnerships with the old British firms, only to be snubbed. After independence, the new Indian government singled out these firms for attack, denouncing them as enemies of egalitarianism. Most of the Anglo-Indian firms eventually divested or shut down.

But it was not just British business that missed opportunities. The British government too, despite its belated push for Indianization and murky promises of "responsible government," fell grossly short. There was a glaring difference in the way the British treated its white and nonwhite colonial subjects. As late as 1922, Winston Churchill, then colonial secretary, disparaged the idea of "granting democratic institutions to backward races which had no capacity for self-government." In stark contrast, starting in the 1840s—at the same time that they were using *sepoys* in India as cannon fodder—the British voluntarily began granting its white subjects in Australia, Canada, and New Zealand the same rights and liberties won by the American colonies in the 1770s. According to the famous Durham Report of 1838, Britain's Canadian subjects were entitled to control their own destinies, free from rule by a distant authority. This principle was later applied to Britain's other white dominions. By the 1860s, all of Britain's white colonies had effectively been granted independence, with real power lying with the colonists' elected representatives. In Niall Ferguson's words:

> So there would be no Battle of Lexington in Auckland; no George Washington in Canberra; no declaration of independence in Ottawa. Indeed, it is hard not to feel, when one reads the Durham Report, that its subtext is one of regret. If only the American colonists had been given responsible government when they first asked for it in the 1770s—if only the British had lived up to their own rhetoric of liberty—there might never have been a War of Independence. Indeed, there might never have been a United States.[38]

We can go further. Had Great Britain in its Victorian heyday been able to overcome its racial and ethnic prejudices, had it been able to extend the same tolerance to its "dark-skinned" colonies that it extended to its white dominions, then the modern histories of not just India and Pakistan but Rhodesia, Kenya, Iraq, Egypt, Burma, and a long list of other imperial holdings might have played out very differently.

BRITAIN'S DECLINE, AND WHAT MIGHT HAVE BEEN

Like that of every world-dominant power before it, Great Britain's rise to global hegemony was fueled by—and almost certainly would not have occurred but for—a dramatic shift from destructive internal ethnic and religious infighting to policies of striking openness and tolerance, judged against the standards of the time. It is no coincidence that the period of Britain's uncontested global supremacy, usually dated to roughly 1858–1918, was also a time when Jews, Huguenots, and Scots were on the whole prospering and participating at virtually every level of British society, including Parliament and the prime ministership. Not only did the Jews and Scots in particular help Britain fund, conquer, and administer its colonial empire overseas; they contributed pivotally to Britain's industrial, financial, and naval supremacy.

Britain's decline did not stem from or even coincide with rising *domestic* intolerance. If anything, as the first half of the twentieth century unfolded, Britain at home displayed greater tolerance toward its ethnic and religious minorities, at least if immigration policies and the expansion of suffrage are any indication. While historians differ over whom to blame and what to emphasize, most agree that Britain's decline stemmed from some combination of the crippling costs of World Wars I and II; escalating government spending on the welfare state; a crushing foreign debt burden; the devaluation of the pound; the relative stagnation of British industry; and the increasing costs of maintaining control over far-flung colonies, especially ones rocked by anti-British hostility, nationalist insurgencies, and (sometimes British-fomented) ethnic or religious violence.

Nevertheless, in a larger sense Britain's collapse also stemmed from its failure of tolerance abroad. Paul Kennedy is surely right that by the mid-twentieth century Britain's position in its remaining colonies was militarily and economically untenable. As the Labour chancellor Hugh Dalton wrote in his diary in 1946: "When you are in a place where you are not wanted, and where you have not got the force to squash those who don't want you, the only thing to do is to come out." But the question is, how did Britain reach this position?

My point is emphatically *not* that, "alas, had only Britain been more tolerant it might still have colonies in Asia and Africa." But there were other, more visionary possibilities that went untapped. Even in 1931, when India's leaders were already committed to independence, Gandhi was asked, "How far would you cut India off from the Empire?" Gandhi replied, "From the Empire, entirely; from the British nation not at all, if I want India to gain and not to grieve." He added, "The British Empire is an Empire only because of India. The Emperorship must go and I should love to be an equal partner with Britain, sharing her joys and sorrows. But it must be a partnership on equal terms."[39]

What would have happened if in 1931 Britain had formed with India the "equal partnership" Gandhi sought? After all, Britain had done just that with its white ex-colonies, creating a British Commonwealth of Nations in which the United Kingdom, Canada, New Zealand, Ireland, and Australia all were recognized as "equal in status, in no way subordinate one to another." What would have happened if the Anglo-Indians, if only for instrumental reasons, had overcome their racism, integrated their firms, and merged them with Indian interests?

It is impossible to know. But if imperial Britain had made different choices at critical junctures in dealing with its nonwhite subjects, decolonization might have taken place on terms far more advantageous to both Britain and its former colonies. The commonwealth, for example, might not have developed into what it is today: a largely symbolic entity known principally for its athletic competitions and literary prizes. Embracing nearly a third of the world's citizens, spanning Asia, Africa, Europe, and the Americas, all linked by long-standing economic interrelationships, the commonwealth could conceivably have become a formidable trading bloc and political union—resembling the European Union, but with the advantage of a common language—with Britain at the hub.

Instead, having alienated its colonies and fomented intolerance within them, Great Britain fell from world-dominant empire to second-rate power while its former "nonwhite" colonial subjects descended into third world pathologies. Meanwhile, another power was rising—an immigrants' nation, pluralistic by necessity, built from its founding moment on principles of religious tolerance.

PART THREE

THE FUTURE OF WORLD DOMINANCE

NINE

THE AMERICAN HYPERPOWER

Tolerance and the Microchip

[I]t does me no injury for my neighbor to say there are twenty gods, or no god. It neither picks my pocket nor breaks my leg.

— THOMAS JEFFERSON, *Notes on the State of Virginia*,
1781–1785

[Whereas a computer] like the ENIAC today is equipped with 18,000 vacuum tubes and weighs 30 tons, computers in the future may have only 1000 vacuum tubes and perhaps weigh only 1½ tons.

— *Popular Mechanics*, MARCH 1949

In its heyday, the British Empire governed a quarter of the earth's surface and nearly a quarter of the world's people. The empire ruled by the grandsons of Genghis Khan was even larger in terms of territorial expanse. By contrast, the United States today governs a paltry 6.5 percent of the world's land surface and 5 percent of the world's population.[1] And yet America is today's hyperpower.

Is America an empire? Americans have debated whether the United States should strive for imperial power since the country's founding. That question continues to be debated today, even after the United States has achieved global preeminence. I will explore the question of what kind of power America is—and what it should strive to be—in Chapter 12. But before turning to the future, we should first examine the past.

Why has the United States been so extraordinarily successful economically and militarily? Its rich agricultural land certainly contributed, as did its bountiful raw materials, geographic separation from foreign threats, and its institutions, however imperfect, of private property, free markets, democracy, and the rule of law. But as with every preceding hyperpower, the real secret to America's strength lies in its human capital.

If relative tolerance is the key to world dominance, the United States has always had a huge advantage over the nations of Europe. Not only has America attracted immigrants; it is a nation of immigrants. The country's Founding Fathers were the sons and grandsons of immigrants, if not immigrants themselves. (Born on the Caribbean island of Nevis, Alexander Hamilton arrived in New York at the age of sixteen.) More than 95 percent of Americans today descend from someone who crossed an ocean to get here.

Of course, many who crossed the ocean did so in leg irons. For them, as for America's native peoples, the birth of the United States was a story not of tolerance but of ruthless oppression. The "nation of immigrants" was founded by—and for generations defined as a nation of—largely white Anglo-Saxon Protestants. As late as 1909, when Israel Zangwill, a Russian Jew, wrote his celebrated play *The Melting Pot*, he envisioned only "the races of Europe" in the crucible.[2]

Compared to all other contemporaneous powers, the United States has always been remarkably tolerant of religious diversity. In a truly revolutionary act, the United States in 1789 not only embraced religious freedom—as had countries like Britain and the Dutch Republic—but declared as a constitutional principle that there would be no national church. On the other hand, despite its generally open immigration policy, the United States for much of its history demonstrated extreme racial and ethnic intolerance toward certain groups, most notably Native Americans, African Americans, and other non-"whites." Notwithstanding repeated declarations that "all men are created equal," slavery, segregation, discrimination, and inequality of citizenship were long-standing American realities. It was only after World War II that the United States developed into one of the most ethnically and racially open societies in world history. Not coincidentally, this was also the period in which the United States achieved world dominance.

This chapter will trace the United States' transformation from ragtag colony to continental power to superpower and finally to hyperpower. This ascent was a direct product of America's continuing ability to attract, reward, and absorb the energy and ingenuity of vastly diverse groups. By accepting other countries' pariahs, and later by draining rival powers and developing nations of many of their best and brightest, the United States generated unprecedented economic dynamism and technological innovation, which in turn gave rise to the greatest accumulation of wealth and the most fearsome military the world has ever seen.

THE REVOLUTIONARY SEPARATION
OF CHURCH FROM STATE

The Puritans had their virtues. Epitomizing Max Weber's "Protestant work ethic," they were famous for their thrift and industry. They placed tremendous value on education. Puritans such as John Harvard founded America's earliest universities. Increase Mather, who served as president of Harvard from 1685 to 1701 and later helped found Yale, was able to read the Old Testament in ancient Hebrew, Greek, and Latin.

It's often forgotten, however, that the Puritans were not religiously tolerant. Having escaped persecution in Europe, the Puritans became persecutors in colonial America. Seeing themselves as God's chosen people—the carriers of the "true religion"—the Puritans denied religious liberty not only to Catholics and Jews but to Anglicans, Quakers, Baptists, and any other Protestants who did not conform precisely to their beliefs. According to Mather, "The *Toleration of all Religions* and Perswasions, is the way to have no Religion at all." Puritan fanaticism reached a fever pitch in the Salem witch trials of 1692, when more than one hundred men and women were jailed on charges of devil worship and witchcraft. Before the hysteria passed, nineteen "witches" were hanged at Gallows Hill in Salem Town, and two dogs executed as "accomplices."

Puritanism was only one of many denominations in early America. Between 1607 and 1732 the English "planted" thirteen colonies in North America. Because colonization was largely financed by private entrepreneurs, the religious character of the colonies varied, depending on the predilections of the financiers and the composition of the original settlers. Thus, while New England was largely Puritan Congregationalist, Pennsylvania was dominated by Quakers, New York had a significant Dutch Reformed populace, Maryland had a fair number of Catholics, and Virginia, Georgia, and the Carolinas were mostly Anglican. At the same time, Presbyterians and Baptists could also be found, along with tiny Jewish communities in some of the large cities.

Nevertheless, despite this geographical religious diversity, religious freedom in colonial America operated on the stingy principle of "if you don't like our religion, you're free to go somewhere else." As the Massachusetts pastor Nathaniel Ward put it, "[All non-Congregationalists] shall have free Liberty to keepe away from us, and such as will come to be gone as fast as they can, the sooner the better." With the exception of Rhode Islanders, colonial Americans had little compunction about establishing the majority's religion and denying basic rights to nonbelievers. By 1732, when the era of the founding of new English colonies came to an end, some 85 percent of Americans lived in towns or states with established churches. Typically, dissenters could not vote or hold public office. Sometimes they were run out of town. Any Quakers who happened to arrive in Anglican Virginia, for example, were immediately "imprisoned without baile" until they "with all speed" departed the colony, "not to returne again."[3]

But great changes were looming. Even while men like Nathaniel Ward were defending religious "purity" and "simplicity," America was undergoing a chaotic transformation. In the 1700s and 1800s, the population soared as immigrants from all over Europe flooded in, fueling a commercial explosion and bringing with them heterodox ideas and new religious denominations. Suddenly, alongside Congregationalists and Anglicans were German Pietists, Swedish Lutherans, French Huguenots, and Ulster Presbyterians.

Commerce was a powerful catalyst of religious toleration. Influential merchants championed religious freedom because exclusion was bad for business. After all, their agents, customers, suppliers, financiers, and trading partners included people of all faiths—even non-Christians. This was precisely the thinking of the English parliament when in 1740 it passed a general act enabling the naturalization of Jews in the American colonies. As Lord Chancellor Philip Hardwicke explained, "Even with respect to the Jews, the discouraging of them to go and settle in our American colonies would be a great loss, if not the ruin of, the trade of every one [of the colonies]."

Around the same time, a "consumer revolution" in religion—better known as the Great Awakening—swept the colonies. Led by charismatic men like George Whitefield, dozens of itinerant evangelical preachers began hawking their own new "brands" of gospel, ignoring parish lines and defying the orthodoxy of the established churches. Like today's "televangelists," these itinerants were mass-market entrepreneurs. They aggressively advertised their "product," offering messages of hope and stressing individual choice. Salvation, they taught, could be achieved only through personal experience, not church dogma. They self-promoted, overreported, and were wildly successful. Preaching from wherever they could draw a crowd—courthouse steps, street corners, public parks, even racecourses and taverns—they won over the souls of tens of thousands of colonists.

Traditional churchmen were dismayed. According to one Anglican minister from South Carolina, "Pennsylvania and New England send out a Sett of Rambling fellows yearly . . . among this Medley of Religions—True Genuine Christianity is not to be found. . . . If there is a Shilling to be got by a Wedding or Funeral, these Independent fellows will endeavor to pocket it." Virginia's Patrick Henry, also an Anglican minister, felt the same way: "[T]hese itinerants . . . screw up the People to the greatest heights of religious Phrenzy, and then leave them in that wild state, for perhaps ten or twelve months, till another Enthusiast comes among them, to repeat the same thing over again."

Then, in a flash, it was all over. By the close of the 1740s, the Great Awakening had largely petered out—but not before dramatically altering the colonial landscape. Many of the itinerants and their followers started their own congregations or joined minority sects like the Baptists; the ranks of dissenters exploded. Because the converts included not just "lower" and "middling" sorts but some prominent citizens, dissenters were no longer as stigmatized. Even strict Massachusetts became pluralistic. In 1747, one Bostonian reported that the churches in his city included three Episcopal congregations, ten "Independent[s]," "one French, upon the Genevan model, one of Anabaptists, and another of Quakers." The Puritan dream of a single, uniform established church had been extinguished.[4]

The itinerant evangelicals, who had insisted on individual religious choice, had some unlikely successors: the nation's Founding Fathers. While adopting Latin pen names such as *Publius* and *Fabius* in open emulation of the Roman Republic, the leaders of the American Revolution were above all men of the Enlightenment. Although not necessarily irreligious, George Washington, Thomas Jefferson, Benjamin Franklin, James Madison, and many others elevated reason over Scripture and were deeply critical of orthodoxy. As Thomas Jefferson put it, "Millions of innocent men, women, and children, since the introduction of Christianity, have been burnt, tortured, fined, imprisoned; yet we have not advanced one inch toward uniformity. What has been the effect of coercion? To make one half the world fools, and the other half hypocrites."[5]

Even before independence, the American revolutionaries had experienced the tangible benefits of tolerance. To have any chance against the British, the Americans had no choice but to field a religiously diverse army. As John Adams noted after the colonists' victory, those who fought included "Roman Catholicks, English Episcopalians, Scotch and American Presbyterians, Methodists, Moravians, Anabaptists, German Lutherans, German Calvinists, Universalists, Arians, Priestlyans, Socinians, Independents, Congregationalists, Horse Protestants and House Protestants, Deists and Atheists; and 'Protestants que ne croyent rien.' "

The Constitution adopted in 1789 by the Founding Fathers was truly radical. Going further than England's Toleration Acts, the representatives of the thirteen colonies deliberately refrained from making the Constitution a religious document or from establishing a single official church for the country. The only mention of religion in the original Constitution was a provision rejecting religious tests as a precondition for holding office.

The absence of religiosity in the Constitution produced outrage and charges of ungodliness and betrayal in many quarters. But the Founding Fathers—who were highly educated patricians, not necessarily representative of the general population—believed that free religious choice was the best way to avoid sectarian strife in a pluralistic society. Many of them, including Madison, were deeply influenced by the ideas of Adam Smith, who had written that, just as with unregulated markets in goods, "a great multitude of religious sects"—preferably at least two to three hundred—would lead to healthy competition among religious leaders and ultimately produce less fanaticism and more moderation.[6]

In 1791, the First Amendment was adopted, formally prohibiting Congress from establishing a national church and protecting the free exercise of religion. Eight years later, in amazing language for the time, the United States announced to the world in the Treaty of Tripoli, "The government of the United States of America is not in any sense founded on the Christian Religion. . . . it has in itself no character of enmity against the laws, religion or tranquility of Musselmen [Muslims]." Again, many colonists were aghast at the "rebellion against God" by public officials. Opponents of the Constitution predicted with horror that a papist, Jew, or Mahometan might become president.

The Founding Fathers were unflinching in their defense of a secular Constitution. George Washington, while believing that churches fostered moral character, proudly urged the rest of the world to follow the American model. "The citizens of the United States of America," he wrote, "have a right to applaud themselves for having given to mankind examples of an enlarged and liberal policy—a policy worthy of imitation. All possess alike liberty of conscience."

Perhaps most striking—and what sharply distinguishes America's first president from Cyrus the Great or even William of Orange—was Washington's view that religious liberty was a fundamental right, not just a favor granted by those in power. In his own words, "It is now no more that toleration is spoken of as if it were the indulgence of one class of people that another enjoyed the exercise of their inherent natural rights, for, happily, the Government of the United States, which gives to bigotry no sanction, to persecution no assistance, requires only that they who live under its protection should demean themselves as good citizens."[7]

Of course, even after 1791, many people in the United States did not actually enjoy full religious freedom in practice. For one thing, the First Amendment originally applied only to the federal government. A number of states, mainly in New England, continued to have established Protestant churches; some even had compulsory churchgoing requirements. In addition, most of the original American states limited voting rights and the right to hold public office to Christians. It would take a few decades before these last vestiges of established churches were eliminated.

But the bottom line is this: From its birth, the United States was founded on the Enlightenment principle of religious tolerance, which it inherited from Holland and Britain but then expanded and extended. By the end of the eighteenth century, no rival power on earth was more religiously tolerant than the United States.

Religious tolerance, however, is not to be confused with racial tolerance. With only a few arguable exceptions, all the Founding Fathers suffered from the blinding racism of their time. It probably never occurred to George Washington and Thomas Jefferson that freedom of religion might extend to their black slaves. As late as 1813, records show slaves on Southern plantations born with the traditional Muslim names "Fatima," "Saluma," and "Otteman," but renamed "Neptune," "Plato," and "Hamlet" by their owners. Under the "enlightened" United States Constitution, Native Americans and slaves had essentially no rights at all.[8]

For reasons that we may never fully understand, skin color and intolerance have often been closely related. We saw this in Great Britain's attitude toward its nonwhite colonies, and western Europe continues to confront the painful realities of racism today. In America's case, race-based discrimination has characterized the entire history of United States immigration and assimilation. The original colonists and the Founding Fathers of the United States were all of western or northern European descent. The more a new wave of immigrants looked and acted like them, the more they were likely to be tolerated.

Until the late nineteenth century, the vast majority of (voluntary) immigrants to the United States were what today we would consider "white." Of course, "white" was always a moving target. Consider, for example, the extraordinary statement on skin color made by Benjamin Franklin in his 1751 essay "Observations Concerning the Increase of Mankind":

> The Number of purely white People in the World is proportionally very small. All Africa is black or tawny. Asia chiefly tawny. America (exclusive of the new Comers) wholly so. And in Europe, the Spaniards, Italians, French, Russians, and Swedes, are generally of what we call a swarthy complexion; as are the Germans also, the Saxons only excepted who with the English make the principle [sic] Body of White People on the Face of the Earth. . . . Perhaps I am partial to the complexion of my Country . . . [yet] such partiality is natural to Mankind.

This was Franklin's view before America achieved independence, while he was still an ardent British patriot. (He himself deleted this passage before allowing the rest of the essay to be published in 1754.) But in the late 1760s, Franklin underwent a profound personal transformation. On a visit to London, he was disdained by the British elite and instead found company among Scots and Quakers. He was angered by descriptions of the American colonists in English newspapers as a "mixed rabble of Scotch, Irish and foreign vagabonds, descendants of convicts, ungrateful rebels, etc." When Franklin returned to Philadelphia, he was a changed man. Not only had he come to see the colonies as having a separate identity from the mother country, but he now favored an inclusive approach to American citizenship. By 1783, Franklin was one of the strongest champions of open immigration: "[E]very Man who comes . . . and takes up a piece of Land" added to the nation's strength.[9]

Franklin had come to believe that immigration would be the key to American success. The next two centuries would prove him right.

"CRAFTY" AMERICANS AND THE EARLY BATTLE FOR EUROPE'S SKILLED LABOR

"[N]ature has given a right to all men," Thomas Jefferson asserted in 1774, "[to leave] the country in which chance, not choice has placed them" and to seek out "new habitations." Characteristically, Jefferson's declaration of natural right coincided with America's self-interest. After the Revolution, America was starved for labor, particularly for skilled workers and artisans who possessed the latest manufacturing know-how so critical to economic success. Unsurprisingly, the nations of Europe did not agree with Jefferson. As Doron Ben-Atar has shown in his book *Trade Secrets*, Europe struggled mightily to prevent emigration of skilled workers to newly independent America. For their part, Americans did everything they could to attract Europeans with technological expertise.

Massachusetts towns placed ads in English newspapers offering free land and wood for any immigrants willing to build and operate a mill. Entrepreneurial New Yorkers recruited thirteen of Sheffield's "best" ironworkers by offering them a "cash award" for emigrating: two years' guaranteed salary and support payments for their family members who stayed back home. American recruiting agents scoured Europe in search of skilled laborers. In 1784, Connecticut's Wadsworth and Colt persuaded one hundred English textile workers to relocate to Hartford. The same year, a Baltimore entrepreneur brought back from Europe sixty-eight glassblowers from Germany and another fourteen from Holland.

The rivalry between the United States and Europe soon became cutthroat. Harsh laws were enacted in Europe prohibiting foreign recruitment. In 1788, for example, Thomas Philpot was imprisoned and fined five hundred pounds for inducing Irishmen to migrate to America. In England especially, anxiety mounted. An anti-emigration tract published in London in the 1790s avowed that "plenty of agents [were] hovering like birds of prey on the banks of the Thames, eager in their search for such artisans, mechanics, husbandmen, and labourers, as are inclinable to direct their course to America." In a similar pamphlet, William Smith, who would later serve as chief justice of Canada, warned that "crafty" Americans were enticing Englishmen to abandon their country. "Under the specious pretense of opening their ports by a commercial treaty" to English manufacturers, the Americans were actually trying to lure England's best artisans and industrial workers, making "Englishmen do what the whole House of Bourbon were never able to accomplish by the sword."

London responded by passing increasingly draconian laws prohibiting British and Irish artisans from migrating to the United States. By the early nineteenth century, no would-be emigrant could board a ship in Liverpool or other British port without a certificate signed by the "Churchwardens and Overseers" of his parish declaring that he "is not, nor hath ever been, a manufacturer or artificer in wool, iron, steel, brass, or any other metal, nor is he, or has he ever been, a watch-maker, or clock-maker, or any other manufacturer or artificer whatsoever." Penalties included loss of nationality and confiscation of property. If caught in the act, an illegal emigrant could be convicted of treason.

Such measures were not unique to England. Venice sequestered its glassblowers on the island of Murano, threatening potential emigrants with the death penalty. At one time or another in the eighteenth century every European country passed anti-emigration legislation (even while often sending spies to recruit skilled workers from rival powers). In Germany, emigrants were required to obtain—and pay dearly for—permission to leave. Tracts were published describing horrific poverty in America. One such account claimed that German immigrants to America had become so poor that they had to "give away their minor children," who would "never see or meet their fathers, mothers, brothers, or sisters again."[10]

But the tide of European immigration could not be stemmed. Determined Americans—both private entrepreneurs and government officials such as the secretary of the treasury Alexander Hamilton—found ways to counter anti-American propaganda abroad and to circumvent European restrictions. Letters from America to friends in the Old World spread the word:

> [Anyone], in any vocation, manual or mechanical, may by honest industry and ordinary prudence, acquire an independent provision for himself and family; so high are the wages of labour, averaging at least double the rate in England, and quadruple that in France; so comparatively scanty the population; so great the demand for all kinds of work; so vast the quantity, and so low the price of land; so light the taxes; so little burdensome the public expenditure and debt.

In the first half of the nineteenth century, more than 2.5 million "illegal emigrants"—illegal not in the sense of violating American immigration laws, which were virtually nonexistent, but of violating the laws of their *home* countries because they possessed prohibited skills—found their way to America from the Old

World. Most of America's cotton mills were managed by experienced English immigrants. As late as 1850, three-quarters of the skilled weavers and textile workers in Germantown, Pennsylvania, were new arrivals.

In large part because of immigrants, many of whom brought training and expertise acquired from years of working in Europe's factories, American industry exploded in the nineteenth century. One of the most critical contributors was Samuel Slater, often called the father of America's industrial revolution. As a teenager in England, Slater worked as an apprentice in a textile mill that used the innovative new spinning machines invented by Richard Arkwright. Quick and perceptive, Slater was soon promoted to overseer. But Slater could not resist the stories of America's bounty. By pretending to be a farmhand, Slater crossed the Atlantic, arriving in America without any technical drawings or equipment.

Reconstructing it by memory, Slater essentially transferred the world's most advanced textile technology from Britain to the United States. By the early nineteenth century, textile mills based on the Slater model were operating throughout America. Around the same time, Massachusetts' Francis Cabot Lowell, after several years of "touring" the factories of Glasgow and Manchester, invented a machine that allowed all stages of textile production— carding, spinning, weaving—to take place in a single factory. Within a few years, the world's first integrated cotton mill began operation in Waltham, Massachusetts. By the 1820s, America's manufacturing productivity had closed in on Britain's, and its textile technology was already in many ways more advanced.[11]

Many other immigrants further infused young America with vital technological secrets and know-how. Irénée Du Pont, an immigrant from France, brought gunpowder technology to the United States. He also founded E. I. Du Pont de Nemours & Company, today one of the largest chemical companies in the world. Joseph Priestley discovered oxygen and made major breakthroughs in electricity. (The inventor of carbonated water, Priestley has also been called the father of soda pop.) These and countless other "brain drains" from Europe helped transform nineteenth-century America from a technological backwater to one of the world's premier industrial powers.

American tolerance was essential to all this. Of course, the vast majority of these highly skilled and inventive immigrants were not fleeing religious or political persecution. They were seeking economic opportunity. But a vital part of what made the United States a land of opportunity was its relative openness and pluralism. The countries of Europe were not "nations of immigrants" in the way America was. For the most part, throughout the nineteenth (and even much of the twentieth) century, the ability of poor but enterprising Europeans to leave their homes and find success in another European country was burdened by a host of barriers, including historic religious enmity, cultural chauvinism, social rigidity, and linguistic differences. By comparison, America—with its religious pluralism, social fluidity, and polyglot communities—was remarkably open to talent and entrepreneurial drive from every European background. In America, relatively speaking, the sky was the limit.

Immigrants could and did ascend to the highest levels of early American society, politically and economically. Albert Gallatin, a brilliant financier from Switzerland, served as Jefferson's secretary of the treasury; it was Gallatin who arranged for the purchase of the Louisiana Territory and funded Lewis and Clark's explorations. John Jacob Astor, a German, started off in the New World selling musical instruments. Before long, he founded the American Fur Company and became the wealthiest man in pre–Civil War America. Marcus Goldman, a German Jew, began as a peddler in a horse-drawn cart. Soon he was buying and selling promissory notes. By 1906, Goldman Sachs & Co. had $5 million in capital. (The firm's market capitalization in June 2007 was around $100 billion.) In 1847, a penniless twelve-year-old Scot named Andrew Carnegie emigrated to Pittsburgh with his family. Fifty years later, having founded the company that would become U.S. Steel, he was the world's richest man.[12]

THE GREAT ATLANTIC MIGRATION AND THE
RISE OF AMERICA AS A REGIONAL POWER

European immigrants did not bring just know-how and entrepreneurialism to America. They also brought sheer manpower. Throughout the nineteenth century, America had an almost insatiable demand for labor to cultivate its land, build its railways, populate its interior, and expand its frontiers. As Abraham Lincoln put it in 1863, "There is still a great deficiency of laborers in every field of industry, especially in agriculture and in our mines, as well of iron and coal as of the precious metals."

Without the millions flooding in from Britain, Ireland, Germany, Scandinavia, and later Italy and eastern Europe, America's continental expansion would have been impossible. Irish immigrants built the Erie and Ohio canals (sometimes getting paid partly in whiskey), then went on to build railroads from Buffalo to Akron to Omaha to San Francisco. Scandinavian immigrants almost single-handedly settled the American Northwest, felling dense forests with the "Swedish fiddle" (a lumberjack's saw) and transporting timber to market by "Norwegian steam" (raw muscle power).[13]

Germans settled mainly in the North and West, but also in Texas, Louisiana, and Virginia. In the Civil War, more than 175,000 German immigrants fought for the Union, often under German officers and cheered on by their own German marching bands. Before and after the battle of Fort Sumter, German troops played a crucial role in keeping Missouri in Union hands. Without German and other immigrants, the United States could never have fielded the armies that seized California, Texas, and the American Southwest from Mexico, staved off France's advances in Central America, and defeated Spain in Cuba and the Philippines, allowing America to become the preeminent power of the Western Hemisphere by the end of the nineteenth century.

Neither could America have become one of the world's leading agricultural and industrial producers in the nineteenth century without a steady influx of immigrant labor. As nonimmigrant

Americans pushed westward, poorer newcomers from Europe populated urban centers and filled the ranks of unskilled labor. Irishmen made up half of the country's miners in the 1860s and 1870s. Buffalo's steel mills were worked largely by Poles, Rochester's textile mills by Italians, and the meatpacking houses of Cedar Rapids and Omaha overwhelmingly by Czechs. By 1910, when the United States led the world in heavy-industry manufacturing output, the majority of America's mass production workers were immigrants. In the country's twenty largest manufacturing and mining sectors, two-thirds of the men and about half the women were recent arrivals.

As late as 1920, immigration from Europe continued almost unrestricted. The total numbers were breathtaking. In 1900 alone some two million people crossed the Atlantic to find a new home in the United States. Between 1820 and 1914, more than thirty million people poured into the United States—the largest human migration in the history of the world.[14]

———

Americans did not always embrace the newcomers. On the contrary, the nineteenth century was punctuated by bursts of venomous popular xenophobia and "nativism." Anti-Catholic riots were especially intense in the 1830s and 1840s. In 1856, the so-called Know-Nothings formed a political party and ran a candidate for president on an anti-Catholic platform, specifically targeting German and Irish immigrants. Although their bid for the presidency failed, the Know-Nothings won dozens of victories in local elections, particularly in New England and the South.

But within a generation or two, the vast majority of European immigrants were brought into the fold of American society. They were allowed not only to worship according to their own religions but also to make their fortunes and rise to political power. By the 1860s, Roman Catholics represented the largest single religious grouping in the country and Know-Nothingism was defunct. The patriotism shown by hundreds of thousands of immigrants who fought for the Union in the Civil War—many of them just learning

English—went a long way toward dampening antiforeign sentiment. Indeed, during the Civil War Congress actively encouraged
immigration. The Homestead Law it enacted in 1862 granted "one
hundred sixty acres of government land to any settler, native or
foreign, who, declaring his intention of becoming a citizen, undertook to live on the land for five years and to make the necessary
improvements."[15]

Democracy and demographics worked in favor of immigrants
too. By the mid-nineteenth century, the "ethnic" vote had become
a force to be reckoned with, at least in cities with high immigrant
concentrations. Thus, despite some employers' "No Irish Need Apply" signs, through sheer voting power the Irish were able to gain
access to the highest levels of urban political machinery, controlling city hall and the police force alike in Boston, Chicago, and
New York.

The tolerance of the party bosses toward immigrants was
above all strategic. Boss Tweed of New York started off politically
as a nativist, yet eventually spent the rest of his career courting immigrants, if only because he had no choice. In exchange for votes,
he provided immigrants with jobs, loans, and services. Similarly,
John Powers became Chicago's most powerful boss between 1896
and 1921 by "taking care" of his Irish, German, Scandinavian,
Italian, Jewish, and Slavic constituencies. In addition to providing
employment and community facilities, Powers attended every variety of ethnic wedding, picnic, or parade. His skill at "working" funerals for political gain earned him the nickname "The Mourner."

The corruption practiced by the new machine bosses was staggering. Bribery, extortion, and vote buying were routine practices.
In New York City, Boss Tweed's Tammany Hall embezzled as
much as $200 million between 1865 and 1871 alone. In 1898, the
Chicago newspaper *L'Italia* quoted John Powers as saying, "I can
buy the Italian vote with a glass of beer and a compliment" and "It
is known that two years ago I bought the Italian vote for fifty cents
each; well this year I will buy it for twenty-five cents each." But
however sordid, the politics of the urban machine had positive aspects as well. In a pre–New Deal era, the ward bosses often pro-

vided desperately needed social services. More fundamentally, the symbiotic relationship between the bosses and immigrants served to integrate and lift previously excluded ethnic groups, particularly the Irish and Italians.[16]

————

The triumphal story of America's westward expansion was also of course a story of Native American contraction; the immigrants' gain was the natives' loss. As Americans marched west, they did not follow the formula of strategic tolerance and incorporation that the ancient Persians, Romans, or Mongols had pursued with their conquered peoples. Unfortunately for America's natives, the United States was in a unique position for an expanding, conquering power. It had another source of population growth, offering greater numbers and technologically superior skills. Americans, it seemed, had no use for a well-honed arrowhead. Such is the brutal reality of selective, strategic tolerance. Even as the United States welcomed the huddled masses of Europe, the indigenous tribes of America were decimated, cordoned off, and displaced.

Natives were not the only ones excluded from the benefits of America's strategic tolerance. Women could not vote and were almost totally excluded from positions of economic or political power (although the United States suffered no relative disadvantage, because women were similarly excluded elsewhere). In the Western states toward the end of the century, Chinese immigrants were subject to bigotry, discrimination, and physical attacks. Most glaringly, the United States did not abolish slavery until 1865, thirty years after Great Britain, and even after its postwar Reconstruction, the United States remained a deeply racist society.

Nevertheless, nineteenth-century American society had three crucial features that made it wide open to people of remarkably diverse backgrounds. Its religious pluralism was so freewheeling that it not only permitted newcomers to worship as they pleased but continually sparked brand-new faiths. (By the twentieth century, the United States boasted at least five "homegrown" religions with major followings: Christian Science, Mormonism, Seventh-Day

Adventism, Jehovah's Witnesses, and Pentecostalism.) Its democratic system of government was capable, both despite and because of its corruption, of giving newcomers some actual political influence, at least at the local level. And its rollicking free market sucked up labor, rewarded mechanical skill, and provided undreamt-of opportunities to the enterprising. Other nineteenth-century nations might offer bits or pieces of these three advantages; none had all three to the same extent as America.

Thus the United States became far and away the world's leading destination for newcomers. Between 1871 and 1911, some twenty million immigrants arrived in the United States. Over the same time frame, Argentina and Brazil together received six million immigrants, Australia and New Zealand 2.5 million, and Canada fewer than two million.[17]

THE TRANSFORMATION FROM REGIONAL
TO GLOBAL POWER

At the approach of the twentieth century, for all its explosive economic growth and territorial expansion, the United States was still only a regional power. Militarily, it was a pygmy compared to the great powers of Europe. Its navy in the 1880s ranked twelfth in the world by number of ships, outclassed even by Sweden. Its army was "insignificant compared with that of even a middle-sized European country like Serbia or Bulgaria." Although its armed forces were sufficient to defend its borders and maintain dominance in the Caribbean and the Americas, the United States in 1900 barely registered as a significant power on the global scene.[18]

Within just a few decades, all of this would change. World War I gave the United States its first taste of global power. The American intervention in 1917 shifted the balance in favor of the Allies and, according to President Woodrow Wilson, thrust on the United States the role of showing "the nations of the world how they shall walk in the paths of liberty."

But the United States was not yet ready to follow Wilson's vision. Instead of projecting its power outward, the United States took an "isolationist" turn, with the Senate refusing to ratify the treaty for the League of Nations that Wilson had poured his heart into creating.[19] At the same time, the nationalist passions inflamed by the war triggered a surge of xenophobia and nativism. In 1917, 1921, and 1924, Congress passed a series of immigration acts radically changing U.S. policy.

For the first time, these laws imposed numerical limits on immigration. More fundamentally, they created a national-origin quota system with an undeniable ethnic and racial bias.

The goal of the 1924 act, in the words of Congressman Albert Johnson, its principal author, was the achievement of a "homogeneous citizenry," putting an end to the "indiscriminate acceptance of all races." Johnson railed against the "dilution" of America's "cherished institutions" by "a stream of alien blood," specifically warning against "filthy, un-American" and "unassimilable" Jews. Accordingly, the number of immigrants allowed from a given country under the 1924 quotas was based on the number of natives from that country living in the United States in 1890. The result was a severe restriction on the admission of southern and eastern Europeans, not to mention an almost complete ban on Asians, Africans, and other nonwhites.

The Great Depression gave nativist politicians further opportunity to scapegoat the "hordes of penniless Europeans"—"mongrels" and "illiterates," many of them "dangerous radicals"—who were "lining up to come to America." President Hoover called for a tightening of immigration restrictions. Between 1931 and 1935, the United States experienced negative net immigration for the first time ever.

As World War II began, the first reaction of many Americans was to keep the United States out of the war—and to keep foreigners out of the United States. In 1939, in the wake of the Kristallnacht pogrom in Nazi Germany, a few members of Congress drafted a bill to admit 20,000 Jewish refugee children to the United States in excess of the normal German quota. Nativist organizations vehemently fought the bill, a majority of Americans opposed it, and it never came up for a vote in either house. Laura Delano,

President Roosevelt's cousin and the wife of the commissioner of immigration, famously warned that "20,000 charming children would all too soon grow into 20,000 ugly adults."

The negative immigration rates of the 1930s proved short-lived and completely exceptional in U.S. history. Ironically, the anti-immigration attitudes of the interwar years may have been a boon to the tens of millions of newcomers who had already arrived. The massive influx of Europe's "poorest and least fortunate"—almost a million Italians, Poles, Russians, Finns, Jews, Germans, Czechs, and Hungarians annually between 1900 and 1914—had created enormous social strains in America.[20] The relatively closed-door interwar years provided a respite, allowing these immigrant communities to be absorbed and assimilated. This was a lucky thing, because so many of the sons of these new Americans would be called on to fight and die in the war that relaunched America, this time irrevocably, onto the world stage.

———

If World War I left the great European powers considerably weakened, World War II dealt the decisive blow. The world that emerged in 1945 was no longer Europe-centered. When the carnage and rubble were cleared, the United States stood as a world superpower, with the shattered nations of Europe dependent on its might and wealth.

Horrific in so many ways, the war triggered an unprecedented economic boom in the United States. Shaking off the Great Depression, U.S. industry between 1940 and 1944 exploded, expanding at a higher rate than ever before or since. By the war's end, the United States was the world's greatest exporter of goods and accounted for more than half of the world's total manufacturing output. It had gold reserves of $20 billion (roughly two-thirds of the world's total) and boasted a higher standard of living and per capita productivity than any other country. Under the Marshall Plan, the United States provided Europe with $13 billion, helping to get the ravaged economies of West Germany, Italy, and France back on their feet.

At the same time, the United States became the preeminent military power of the Western world. By the war's end, America had mobilized an astonishing 12.5 million service personnel. Its naval forces, with 1,200 warships and a devastating submarine fleet, had replaced the British Royal Navy as the world's most powerful. Its bombers commanded the air, with a thousand long-range B-29s that had obliterated Japanese cities. Most fatefully, the United States alone had the atomic bomb, which had turned Nagasaki and Hiroshima into infernos unlike anything the world had ever seen.

Tolerance played a critical role in every dimension of the United States' rise to superpower status. Again, the sheer manpower advantage possessed by the United States resulted directly from the country's open immigration policies before 1920. In 1816, America's population was just 8.5 million, compared to Russia's 51.2 million. By 1950, the United States' population was more than 150 million, while Russia's was around 109 million. Even more crucially, immigrants were also directly responsible for the revolutionary technological breakthroughs that catapulted the United States to military preeminence.[21]

In 1930s Europe, Nazi intolerance caused the loss of incalculable scientific talent. The list of brilliant physicists and mathematicians who fled Hitler is astounding, including Edward Teller, known as the "father of the hydrogen bomb"; the aeronautical genius Theodore von Karman; John von Neumann, a child prodigy and the cocreator of game theory; Lise Meitner, after whom Element 109, meitnerium, is named; Leo Szilard, conceiver of the nuclear chain reaction; Enrico Fermi, builder of the first experimental nuclear reactor; the Nobel Prize–winning physicists Hans Bethe and Eugene Wigner; Niels Bohr; and of course Albert Einstein. With the exception of Meitner and Bohr, every one of these scientists emigrated to the United States.

The immigration to the United States of these refugee scientists, most of whom were Jewish, represented the single greatest "influx of ability of which there is any record." Up until the 1930s, Germany and Hungary were home to some of the world's leading physicists. Practically overnight, their departure turned America into "the world's dominant force in pure science." Einstein, whose property was confiscated by the Nazis in 1933, explained that he would "only live in a land where there reigns political freedom, tolerance and equality of all citizens before the law."[22]

Jews were hardly equal citizens in the United States in 1945. Formal quotas and informal social discrimination kept Jews largely out of the top universities and highest government posts until at least the 1960s. But *relative* tolerance is what matters, and by comparison to the other options, the United States was for Einstein and so many of his fellow brilliant scientists a new Jerusalem. It was their work that led to the development of the atomic and hydrogen bombs, giving America the world's first nuclear weapons. Perhaps never in world history has an infusion of immigrant talent so immediately translated into a scientific advance and military advantage of such planet-altering magnitude.

Within a few years, however, the United States was no longer the world's sole atomic power. To the east of Europe had risen another colossus, the Soviet Union, whose rivalry with the United States would be the defining geopolitical reality of the ensuing decades.

Interestingly, as the Cold War began, it was not at all clear which of the two superpowers was the more tolerant. While the United States certainly offered more religious freedom, its commitment to ideological openness was undermined by the McCarthy witch hunts of the 1950s. Moreover, in some parts of the country, racial apartheid was practiced under the name of Jim Crow. By contrast, the U.S.S.R. did not respect religious or ideological freedom but proudly proclaimed its racial and ethnic universalism.

The territory taken over by the Bolsheviks in 1917 included a complex array of ethnic, national, and tribal minorities. In their rise to power, the Bolsheviks harnessed the discontent of Russia's ethnic minorities, promising them "equality" and "the genuine right to self-determination." The first all-Union Census of 1927 identified 172 separate "nationalities" in the Soviet Union, although (through various political and ethnographic manipulations) by 1939 this number had been whittled down to just 57. At least in principle, Soviet "nationalities" policy was supposed to promote non-Russian cultures and languages, to give "all the nations" within the Union considerable autonomy, and to allow the best and brightest non-Russians to participate and rise in the Soviet system. On the international front, the U.S.S.R. invited delegates from Cuba, China, and African nations to Moscow in order to strengthen ties within the Communist bloc. At the same time, Soviet propaganda reported constantly on American blacks' "semi-slave" status and the "frequency of terroristic acts against negroes," including "the bestial mobbing of four negroes by a band of 20–25 whites" in Monroe, Georgia, in 1946.[23]

There is no doubt that racism caused the United States considerable international embarrassment. In one notorious case, when Haiti's secretary of agriculture arrived in Biloxi, Mississippi, in 1947 for a conference, the hotel (not expecting the secretary to be black) refused for "reasons of color" to let him stay with the other conference attendees. After the incident, an outraged editorial in a Haitian newspaper wrote, "The Negro of Haiti understands that the word democracy in the United States has no meaning."

In part, the U.S. government's postwar receptivity to civil rights reform reflected American interests in bolstering the country's international stature. In a 1948 *New York Times Magazine* article, Robert E. Cushman, a member of President Truman's Committee on Civil Rights, argued: "[T]he nation finds itself the most powerful spokesman for the democratic way of life, as opposed to the principles of a totalitarian state. It is unpleasant to have the Russians publicize our continuing lynchings, our Jim Crow statutes and customs, our anti-Semitic discriminations and our witch-hunts; but is it undeserved?" Cushman concluded, "[Americans] are becoming aware that we do not practice the civil liberty we preach; and this realization is a wholesome thing."[24]

As the twentieth century unfolded, the oppressiveness of the Soviet regime became increasingly manifest, and its claims of equality increasingly bankrupt. Corruption, patronage, and ossification spread throughout the Soviet Union. Even its supposed ethnic tolerance proved hollow. Russian hegemony and chauvinism vis-à-vis non-Russian peoples—not to mention occasional brutal military interventions—generated intense resentment throughout central Asia, the Baltic Republics, and Eastern Europe. Meanwhile, as the U.S.S.R. grew ever more closed and stagnant, the United States went in a very different direction.

America's civil rights revolution in many ways began with the 1954 landmark case of *Brown v. Board of Education*. In *Brown*, the Supreme Court struck down race-based school segregation, rejecting the doctrine of "separate but equal" in public education. In the early 1960s, President John F. Kennedy put his presidency squarely behind the cause of civil rights, passionately arguing in a nationwide television address:

> We preach freedom around the world, and we mean it, and we cherish our freedom here at home, but are we to say to the world, and much more importantly, to each other that this is a land of the free except for the Negroes; that we have no second-class citizens except Negroes; that we have no class or [caste] system, no ghettoes, no master race except with respect to Negroes?[25]

Kennedy also summoned to Washington the leaders of America's most prestigious universities and implored them to diversify their student bodies, telling the group, "I want you to make a difference. . . . Until you do, who will?"

President Kennedy was assassinated in 1963. A year after his death, Congress passed the 1964 Civil Rights Act, which enacted sweeping voting reforms, required employers to provide equal employment opportunities, and made it illegal to discriminate on the basis of race in public places such as hotels, restaurants, and theaters. Around the same time, Yale University president Kingman Brewster embarked on unprecedented institutional reforms, with Harvard shortly following suit. Brewster hired R. Inslee ("Inky") Clark to be Yale's new admissions director, with the mandate of building a more pluralistic student body. Brewster and Clark eliminated geographical factors for admission—which had been a way to limit Jewish students—and reduced preferences for alumni legacies and prep school students. The result was a spike in the percentage of Jewish students in the freshman class, from 16 percent in 1965 to about 30 percent in 1966. Clark's first class contained 58 percent public school students, more financial aid applicants than non-financial aid applicants, more minorities of every kind— and the highest SAT scores in Yale's history.

Clark's new admission policies came under direct fire from members of the Yale Corporation and alumni contributors. Summoned before the Yale Corporation in 1966 to discuss the changes, Clark explained that in a changing country, leaders might come from nontraditional places, including in the future minorities, women, Jews, and public school graduates. A Yale Corporation member retorted, "You're talking about Jews and public school graduates as leaders. Look around you at this table. These are America's leaders. There are no Jews here. There are no public school graduates here."

But Brewster and Clark, as well as their counterparts at other institutions, persisted. The number of black and other minority students accepted to Ivy League schools rose dramatically during the sixties. In 1960, the "Big Three" had collectively just 15 African American freshmen; in 1970, there were 284 (83 at Yale, 103 at Princeton, and 98 at Harvard). Overall, between 1970 and 1980, the number of African American college graduates increased by 91 percent.[26]

The changing face of U.S. higher education was part of a much more radical transformation of American society. The sixties and their aftermath did not end the primacy of white Anglo-Protestant men in the corporate world or in Washington, but women, blacks, and other minorities made impressive inroads in American business, politics, and culture. At the same time, new immigration policies dramatically changed the demographics of American society.

The 1965 Immigration Act abolished the racially and ethnically discriminatory national-origin quota system instituted in the

1920s. Immigration rates exploded, from roughly 70,000 a year during the quota years to about 400,000 a year by the early 1970s, 600,000 a year by the early 1980s, and over 1 million in 1989. Between 1990 and 2000, approximately 9 million immigrants arrived in the United States, more than in any other decade except the heyday of Ellis Island at the turn of the century. The sources of immigration changed as well. Whereas before 1965 the vast majority of immigrants to the United States hailed from Europe, after 1965 they came overwhelmingly from Asia and Latin America. The rise in legal migration was accompanied by an increase in illegal entries. In 1960, foreign-born residents of the United States were distributed principally as follows:

Italy	1,257,000
Germany	990,000
Canada	953,000
United Kingdom	833,000
Poland	748,000

In 2000, the distribution was as follows:

Mexico	7,841,000
China	1,391,000
Philippines	1,222,000
India	1,007,000
Cuba	952,000[27]

AMERICAN WORLD DOMINANCE

In January 1991, during the First Gulf War, viewers around the world watched, rapt, as the world's most powerful bombs and smartest missiles, fired from history's first stealth aircraft and guided by the world's most sophisticated satellite navigation system, took out target after target—bunkers, bridges, air defense towers, Scud missile launchers—with laser precision. For the next five weeks, U.S. Apaches, Pave Lows, Hornets, and Nighthawks pounded enemy territory, inflicting maximum destruction with a staggeringly low American fatality rate. Then, it was over: "the most awesome and well-coordinated mass raid in the history of air power." If there was any doubt before, the breathtaking precision of Operation Desert Storm made it crystal clear: The U.S. military was light-years ahead of any other military force on the planet.[28]

It was not only in military might that the United States had achieved a stunning global preeminence. In the 1980s, the productive capacity that America *added* to what it already possessed exceeded the *entire* productive capacity of West Germany—Europe's largest economy. After a relatively mild recession in 1990–91, the U.S. economy exploded yet again, reaping massive gains from the microprocessing revolution and yielding "the greatest period of wealth creation in the history of the world." While only a decade before, doubters had wondered whether U.S. business could remain competitive with Japan and a uniting Europe, by the 1990s America's economy had opened up a staggering lead over all other nations of the world. At the opening of the twenty-first century, America's gross domestic product, calculated in current dollars, represented an astonishing one-third of total world output, twice the size of Japan's and China's economies combined, and more than three times Great Britain's share of gross world output at its imperial height.

America was the country that benefited most from globalization. In the words of George Soros, an immigrant who had built a multibillion-dollar fortune in the United States from scratch, "The trend of globalization is that surplus capital is moving from the periphery countries to the center, which is the United States." Throughout the 1990s, American corporations like Wal-Mart, Nike, McDonald's, ExxonMobil, Coca-Cola, and Disney continued to dominate the world economy, despite anti-American sentiments. The dollar was the world's dominant currency, English the dominant language, and America's the most emulated culture. As the twentieth century came to a close, with Russia in chaos, Europe stagnant, and Japan mired in recession, the United States of America had no real competition—militarily, economically, even culturally. The world had a new hyperpower.[29]

There were many reasons behind the United States' sudden vault to world dominance, the most spectacular being the collapse of the former Soviet Union. Had the U.S.S.R. not imploded, we might still live in a bipolar world today. On the other hand, all the same factors that had steadily brought the United States to superpower status also underlay its achievement of world dominance.

It is well known that the United States won the race for the atomic bomb because of the contributions of Albert Einstein and other refugee physicists. Less well known is the similar role that immigrant scientists played in America's stunning triumph in the "information technology" race, which has transformed the world in the last quarter century. The boom America enjoyed during the 1980s and 1990s was directly fueled by two revolutionary developments, one technological and one financial: the discovery of the microchip and the creation of venture capitalism. The former gave birth to the computer age, and the latter to Silicon Valley, which in turn allowed new "information technology" to be exploited at lightning speed. The origins of these two developments are closely connected, and, once again, both were the fruit of American openness to immigrant talent and enterprise.

———————

Eugene Kleiner arrived in the United States in 1941 at the age of eighteen, having fled Vienna just before the Nazi takeover. Although lacking a high school diploma, Kleiner later graduated from Brooklyn Polytechnic with an engineering degree. In the early 1950s, Kleiner was recruited to California by the controversial physicist William Shockley, who, a few years earlier at Bell Labs, had participated in an unexpected invention. Using a bent paper clip, strips of foil, and a small piece of semiconducting material, Shockley's team produced a tiny device that, to their astonishment, amplified electric current. They called the device a transistor.

Shockley left Bell Labs to start his own company with the idea of developing a multiple-transistor semiconductor. Shockley insisted on using germanium as the semiconducting material. Kleiner and others on the team believed silicon would be superior, but the difficult and increasingly paranoid Shockley brooked no disagree-

ment. Soon, Kleiner and seven colleagues broke away, scraping together $3,500 of their own money to pursue their silicon-based re-
search. But even in the 1950s, $3,500 was woefully inadequate,
and it was virtually impossible to secure investment funding to
back an untried scientific idea in its germinal stages. Nevertheless,
after writing a now famous letter to a New York stockbroker,
Kleiner managed to get his group funded. As a result, Kleiner and
his colleagues became the officers of their own company, Fairchild
Semiconductor.

Shockley won the 1956 Nobel Prize for his role in discovering
the transistor. He also went on to gain considerable attention as a
professor at Stanford, particularly for his racist eugenic beliefs. (He
often publicly warned that "intellectually inferior" blacks were
procreating at a dangerously high rate.) But his company, Shockley Semiconductor, was a commercial failure.

By contrast, Kleiner and his colleagues succeeded in producing
the world's first commercially practical integrated circuit—out of
silicon. Within a short time, Fairchild Semiconductor grew from
twelve employees to 12,000, with revenues of $130 million a year.
Santa Clara Valley, previously known mainly for its plums and
walnuts, would never be the same again.

Now wealthy, Kleiner decided to try something new. No doubt
reflecting on his own difficulties starting Fairchild Semiconductor,
Kleiner had the idea of creating an investment fund for break-
through scientific innovations. Although venture capital is a familiar concept today, it was not in the early 1970s. Virtually unique
in its time, the investment firm that Kleiner cofounded—which
eventually became the now legendary Kleiner, Perkins, Caufield &
Byers adopted the strategy of aggressively searching out and bet-
ting big on untried technology while allowing (indeed encouraging) the inventors to retain a large ownership stake in the new
companies. The formula succeeded: The companies that Kleiner,
Perkins helped launch include AOL, Genentech, Compaq, Lotus
Development, Netscape, Quantum, Sun Microsystems, Amazon
.com, and Google.

Kleiner, who died in 2003, is often credited with both "starting

Silicon Valley" and "virtually inventing venture capital." The Kleiner, Perkins business model transformed American finance, fueling an explosion of venture capitalism in the last quarter of the twentieth century. It is no coincidence that the rise of venture capitalism owed so much to a refugee from Nazi Europe or that it played so large a role in America's world leadership in the computer age. Venture capitalism was nothing less than a late-twentieth-century incarnation of strategic tolerance. Just as in Rome or the Great Mongol Empire, America's global dominance has depended on its ability to bring in and mobilize the world's cutting-edge talents and intellectual capital. In the 1980s and 1990s, American venture capitalism was phenomenally successful in doing just that, offering enormous inducements to young scientists, inventors, and entrepreneurs of all backgrounds, rich or poor, white or minority, native or immigrant, to pursue their ideas in America.

———

Andrew Grove, born András Gróf in Budapest, Hungary, was one of those entrepreneurs. In 1956, the twenty-year-old Grove and his family fled the turmoil of the Hungarian Revolution, arriving in New York City onboard a rusty ship the following year. Like Kleiner, Grove did not attend a fancy school. He graduated at the top of his class from the City College of New York, waiting tables to cover tuition. Hating the cold Northeast winters, Grove then made his way to the University of California, Berkeley, where he received his Ph.D. in chemical engineering in 1963.

For Grove, America was truly a land of tolerance and opportunity. As a boy in Hungary, he successfully hid from the Nazis with his family, only to be humiliated after the war by a childhood friend who told Grove that his father had forbidden him from playing with Jews. Later, when Hungary became a puppet state of the U.S.S.R. and the Soviet tanks rolled in, Grove's prospects seemed only bleaker.

Sunny California could not have been more different. After Berkeley, Grove got a job at Fairchild Semiconductor, the firm Eugene Kleiner had cofounded. There, Grove impressed everyone with not just his energy and brilliance but his extraordinary attention to detail. In 1968, when Robert Noyce and Gordon Moore, two of Fairchild's other original founders, left the company to strike out on their own, they invited Grove to be their director of operations. The decision was a surprise to many: Grove's thick Hungarian accent and impaired hearing did not make him the likeliest of choices. But Noyce and Moore had only one employment criterion: they wanted the best talent available.

Noyce was one of the inventors of the integrated circuit. Moore was arguably the best pure engineer at Fairchild. Their plan in founding a new company was to turn the multiple-transistor integrated circuit into a memory device. In 1968, computer memory storage was still being handled through magnetic-core technology. Noyce and Moore believed they could pack more transistors onto their silicon chips and turn them into memory devices smaller, cheaper, and more powerful than magnetic-core memory. In short, Noyce and Moore set out to build what the world would soon call microprocessors, also known as microchips. They called their new company Integrated Electronics—later shortened to Intel.

Interestingly, the man who came to be widely regarded as the driving force behind Intel was neither Noyce nor Moore but Andy Grove. Before Intel could mass-produce its microprocessors, there were a thousand problems to overcome—technical, administrative, strategic, and commercial. It was Grove, more than anyone else, who solved these problems. Described in company pamphlets as one of Intel's three cofounders, Grove became Intel's president in 1979 and its CEO in 1987. When *Time* magazine named Grove as its 1997 Man of the Year, it described him as "the person most responsible" for the microchip and hence the Digital Revolution, which, in *Time*'s words, transformed the end of the twentieth century "the way the Industrial Revolution transformed the end of the [previous] one."

Under Grove's stewardship, Intel by the late 1990s was worth $115 billion, more than IBM. It produced almost 90 percent of the world's PC microprocessors—churning out a quadrillion transistors every month, with seven million of them etched onto silicon microchips smaller than a dime. Among the foreign giants that Intel towered over in the 1990s were Samsung, Toshiba, Hitachi, Fujitsu, NEC, and Siemens. Today, despite fierce competition and sporadic crises, Intel remains the world's largest producer of microprocessors.[30]

―――――

Like the printing press and the steam engine in their eras, the microchip was the core invention of the computer age. It underlay all the new software and hardware that would give us CDs, DVDs, VCRs, iPods, iTunes, TiVo, digital cameras, cell phones, BlackBerries, and other products that would forever change the way human beings live, think, and communicate. It drove the explosion of a new Internet-connected global economy and what Thomas Friedman has called the "new talent era."

Grove was just one of a sea of immigrant venture-capital success stories that flooded America with wealth and catapulted the country to undisputed global economic and technological preeminence in the last decades of the twentieth century. Of the thousands of engineering and technology companies started in Silicon Valley between 1995 and 2005, an amazing 52.4 percent had at least one key founder who was an immigrant. Sun Microsystems cofounder Vinod Khosla and Hotmail cofounder Sabeer Bhatia emigrated from India. Tim Berners-Lee, creator of the World Wide Web, came to America from Britain. In 1998, a young Russian student named Sergey Brin took a leave of absence from Stanford's computer science Ph.D. program to found a small Internet search company with his fellow graduate student Larry Page. Today that company—Google—employs more than ten thousand people and has a market capitalization of more than $136 billion.

Of course, the thousands of nerds, geeks, and visionaries that created Silicon Valley included plenty of third-, fifth-, and seventh-generation Americans. Fred Terman, Stanford University's influential engineering dean in the 1950s, was not an immigrant; neither was Bill Hewlett, Dave Packard, Robert Noyce, Gordon Moore, Bill Gates, or Steve Jobs. Nor were the gigantic fortunes made in the 1980s and 1990s limited to immigrants. On the contrary, the unprecedented explosion in wealth displayed once again the unique ability of the American economy to reward enterprise and talent from any background, whether homegrown or imported. Of the four hundred richest Americans in 2000, an extraordinary two-thirds had built their fortunes from nothing.[31]

America's technological and economic dominance has trans-lated directly into military supremacy. Today, the United States has ten *Nimitz*-class, nuclear-powered supercarriers, each one capable of carrying more than seventy fighter jets. No other country has a single aircraft carrier remotely comparable to these behemoths. The United States has a fleet of stealth aircraft, undetectable by radar, armed with one-ton radar-guided bombs. No other country has any. The United States also has by far the world's largest, most ad-vanced arsenal of "smart" bombs, cruise missiles, unmanned high-altitude "drones," satellite surveillance systems, armored tanks equipped with night vision and laser range-finders, and nuclear-powered attack submarines—none of which would have been pos-sible without the new microprocessor technology.[32]

In short, the United States' rise to world dominance depended heavily on its winning the high-tech race. Then, on September 11, 2001, technology was turned on the United States.

TEN

THE RISE AND FALL OF
THE AXIS POWERS

Nazi Germany and Imperial Japan

We have now canvassed all of history's hyperpowers, observing that every one of them owed its rise to world dominance in critical part to tolerance. What we have not examined are the forces of *in*tolerance. This chapter does so, examining both the deadly power of mobilized intolerance and its inherent limits.

No society based on racial purity, ethnic cleansing, or religious zealotry has ever become world dominant. In the middle of the twentieth century, however, two brutally intolerant regimes—Nazi Germany and imperial Japan—achieved enormous power and, together, threatened to take over the world. The meteoric rise and stunning defeat of the Axis Powers illustrate both the frightening potency of extreme intolerance and the ultimate inability of societies based on such intolerance to attain world dominance.

NAZI GERMANY: THE DREAM OF
ARYAN WORLD DOMINANCE

At 3:15 p.m. on June 21, 1940, Adolf Hitler and his top commanders descended on the forest of Compiègne, fifty miles north of Paris, to preside over the surrender of the French. Hitler had personally chosen this hallowed forest—hunting grounds for the French monarchy for a millennium and the site of Joan of Arc's capture—for its more recent historical pedigree. It was here in November 1918 that Germany surrendered to France, ending World War I. As a pleasant June sun beat down, Hitler emerged from his Mercedes. His face, according to one eyewitness's account, was "grave, solemn, yet brimming with revenge. There was also in it, as in his springy step, a note of the triumphant conqueror, the defier of the world." The führer insisted on dictating the terms of the armistice in the same railway car where Germany had surrendered twenty-two years earlier. After a day of fruitless attempts to soften the treaty's harsh terms, Marshal Henri Philippe Pétain, the French hero of the battle of Verdun, succumbed categorically to the Nazi demands.[1]

The reversal of fortune at Compiègne marked the zenith for Hitler and Nazi Germany. Rising from the rubble and disgrace of World War I, Germany had not only miraculously rearmed and reindustrialized in less than a decade but had gone on to conquer most of continental Europe in only nine months. By the time France capitulated, the Nazis already controlled Austria, Belgium, Czechoslovakia, Denmark, Norway, and the Netherlands and were poised to invade Britain. A year earlier, the seemingly invincible Wehrmacht had unleashed on Poland its blitzkrieg, "a monstrous mechanized juggernaut such as the earth had never seen." Just seven years after Hitler's rise to power in 1933, the Nazi promise of a "Thousand-Year Reich" no longer seemed so implausible.

Five years later, it was all over. Hitler was dead, and Germany lay in ruins. In its climb to power, Hitler's regime brought state-sponsored intolerance to a new level, instituting "a reign of terror over the conquered peoples which, in its calculated butchery of human life and the human spirit, outdid all the savage oppressions of the previous ages."[2] More than just a by-product of Nazi domination, brutal intolerance had been critical to the Nazis' ability to amass power in the aftermath of World War I. Nazi ideology— with its potent mixture of militant nationalism, ethnic chauvinism, and religious hatred—was fantastically successful in generating loyalty and sacrifice from Germany's humiliated population. But Hitler and his party's unflagging devotion to bloody race purification ultimately proved a grotesque cancer within the regime and helped seal its eventual obliteration.

THE POWER OF HATE

World War I left Germany a bloodied and beaten nation. Nearly two million of its young men perished in the war, and almost as many were crippled for life. Among the general population, millions of working- and middle-class Germans suddenly found themselves unemployed and destitute. Adding to the trauma of defeat was the Treaty of Versailles. Imposed in 1919, the treaty forced Germany to admit that it was solely responsible for having caused the war. As punishment, Germany was saddled with staggering war reparations, stripped of its colonial holdings, and forced to forfeit cherished national territory to France and to the hated Poles. Germany's proud and once formidable armed forces were to be reduced to a volunteer force of 100,000 men, among other stinging restrictions. Not everyone thought that the treaty's crushing terms were wise. John Maynard Keynes, advisor to the British delegation, ominously predicted that the peace contained the seeds of the next war.[3]

It was from this crucible of ignominy, suffering, and suppressed rage that Adolf Hitler and the Nazis emerged. Spewing a combination of Aryan supremacy, conspiracy theories about Jewish-Communist plots, and calls for extermination of racial inferiors, Hitler promised a return to the primordial German past and with it the rise of an all-powerful expansionist German state under his leadership. Hitler and his supporters lashed out at Jews, Communists, Slavs, homosexuals, and anyone else not sufficiently "German," blaming them for the country's runaway inflation, massive unemployment, and diminished international standing. Hitler's bombastic rhetoric of racial supremacy proved to be a popular draw at Nazi speeches. One repeated charge was that minorities had "stabbed Germany in the back," a claim the Nazis used to explain how Germany could have lost the Great War despite never having fallen victim to a ground invasion.

In the 1920s and early 1930s, few German politicians thought the Nazis posed any serious threat of taking power. But by building a coalition that encompassed big business, the military, and above all the middle class, the Nazis grew from a group of back-alley brawlers to a broad-based movement that succeeded in winning 43 percent of the German vote in 1932, paving the way for Hitler to become Germany's next chancellor in 1933.[4]

It is almost trivializing to call the Nazi regime "intolerant." Racial hatred pervaded every aspect of Nazi policy, from health to agriculture to defense. Precisely because its principal commitment was to German nationalism, the Nazi Party had little need for an economic policy. (Once heard at a Nazi gathering: "We don't want higher bread prices! We don't want lower bread prices! We don't want unchanged bread prices! We want National Socialist bread prices!") The historians Roderick Stackelberg and Sally Winkle have summarized the singular focus of Nazi policy: "Hitler had no vision of domestic social reform other than the elimination of Jews and all forms of diversity and dissent from German society, the creation of an authoritarian system based on race, and the preparation of the populace for war."

While Jews were the primary targets of Nazi fanaticism, they were hardly alone. Gypsies, Poles, gays, the disabled, the sick, and various other groups were also singled out for removal to concentration camps, forced labor, and arbitrary execution. At Nazism's core was a belief in the unquestionable supremacy of Aryans—the "master race"—and their proper role as rulers of the earth.[5]

THE COSTS OF INTOLERANCE

The Nazis' persecution of Jews and other groups enriched the party and financed the German war machine—but only for a fleeting historical moment. First, Jewish banks and businesses were expropriated by the state. Then, as Jews were rounded up and sent to ghettos or concentration camps, their valuables—pocket watches, gold necklaces, earrings, brooches, bracelets, and diamond rings—were confiscated. Jewish homes, cars, art collections, and "great wads of banknotes" were seized. Finally, special SS squads were charged with pulling gold fillings from the mouths of Jews sent to the gas chambers—sometimes even before the victims were killed. These fillings were melted down and, along with the rest of the bounty, deposited in a secret Reichsbank account under the cover name "Max Heiliger."[6]

Quickly, however, the Nazis' commitment to the extinction of "inferior" peoples came to cost the regime in crucial ways. To begin with, untold resources, time, and even talent were required to implement the deaths of those who could not be tolerated in the "New Order." A vast bureaucracy had to be organized to locate, count, and classify Jews according to minutely defined blood-percentage categories. Indeed, with increasing frequency, the requirements of Nazi ethnic cleansing conflicted with urgent war needs.

For example, entire SS units were dedicated to guarding prisoners at Nazi concentration camps. Precious materials like marble, sandstone, and polished nickel were ghoulishly lavished on the construction of crematoria and gas chambers. Trains were devoted to shuttling Jews to their deaths even as the Germans were scrambling to move troops. In the winter of 1942, with German soldiers surrounded at the pivotal battle of Stalingrad, Heinrich Himmler, commander of the SS, personally intervened to divert desperately needed trains in order to kill more Jews. Himmler pleaded to the head of railroads: "I know very well how taxing the situation is for the railroads and what demands are constantly made of you. Just the same, I must make this request of you: Help me get more trains." Even in their darkest hour, the Nazis chose racial hatred over military success.[7]

Moreover, by murdering millions of conquered subjects and hundreds of thousands of German citizens, the Nazis deprived themselves of incalculable manpower and human capital. As already mentioned, Germany lost an array of brilliant scientists, including Albert Einstein, Theodore von Karman, Eugene Wigner, Leo Szilard, Hans Bethe, Edward Teller, and Lise Meitner, many of whom went on to play an integral role in the construction of the world's first atomic bomb, which the United States used to win the war. Who knows how many other great minds were lost?

Everything in Nazi Germany was filtered through the lens of German racial superiority. Almost comically, the Nazi scientist Bruno Thuring attacked Albert Einstein's theory of relativity for its contradiction of the "Nordic's instinctual understanding of the meaning of energy." Nazi rejection of "Jewish" science also led Germany to fall behind in the development of radar, a technology that proved pivotal to the Allies' success in the Battle of Britain. Meanwhile, the Nazis' confidence in their own scientific supremacy blinded them to the possibility that the Allies might have cracked their codes—another decisive mistake.[8]

"EXPELLED OR EXTERMINATED, NOT ASSIMILATED"

When German troops first entered the western frontiers of the Soviet Union, they were often hailed as liberators, especially by Ukrainians and the Baltic peoples, who had long been terrorized by Soviet domination. Even in Russia, some high-ranking German officials felt that "if Hitler played his cards shrewdly, treating the population with consideration and promising relief from Bolshevik practices . . . the Russian people could be won over."

Nowhere was this truer than in Ukraine, where Nazi ideology was popular and many longed for independence from the Soviet Union. But instead of enlisting Ukrainian brigades to fight against the Soviets, the German army was followed directly by SS death squads charged with subjugating, enslaving, and killing the local population. In addition to almost wiping out Ukraine's Jewish population, the Nazis slaughtered an estimated five million non-Jewish Ukrainians.[9]

Unlike Genghis Khan, Hitler was not interested in enlisting the superior talents of conquered nations. Unlike the Romans, Hitler was not interested in incorporating their populations. Instead, he was interested in incorporating their land. For Hitler, international relations was "fundamentally a struggle for space" in which "the stronger won, took the space, proliferated on that space, and then fought for additional space." This struggle for German "living space," or Lebensraum, became the core of Nazi foreign policy. In *Mein Kampf* and numerous speeches, Hitler broadcast his intention to achieve Lebensraum through "conquest of additional land areas whose native population would be expelled or exterminated, not assimilated." According to Hitler, world peace would come about only "when one power, the racially best one, has attained complete and uncontested supremacy."

It did not take long for Hitler to demonstrate that Lebensraum was not just rhetoric. For the Nazis, the "living space" Germany needed was located primarily in Poland, Ukraine, and Russia. Hitler saw the Slavs as a race "incapable of organizing a state or developing a culture." Accordingly, Nazi policy called for the German army to eliminate or enslave the Bolshevik "subhumans." The "great cities of the East, Moscow, Leningrad and Warsaw," were to be "permanently erased," and the "culture of the Russians and Poles and other Slavs" was to be "stamped out."[10]

These policies did not curry much favor among the populations the Nazis conquered, to put it mildly. Indeed, some high-ranking German officials acknowledged that the Nazis' hard-line anti-Slavism represented a strategic miscalculation of enormous proportions. For example, the reich minister for the east, Alfred Rosenberg—even though he was a notorious Aryan nationalist—wrote in 1942 that "[a] better gift could not come to Germany" in the war than the support of the disaffected populations of the Soviet Union. Rosenberg and others argued, almost certainly correctly, that many Soviet subjects would willingly fight "on the

German side for the prize of national autonomy and independence from the Soviet Union." The Poles in particular, with their pervasive anti-Semitism, were natural German allies. But Hitler remained committed to "extermination, not assimilation," viewing the Poles as "an Eastern European species of cockroach" who "had no right to live," except perhaps as slaves for their German masters.[11]

The genocidal brutality of the Nazi occupiers, coupled with their publicly declared goal of obtaining more "living space" for Germany, only succeeded in mobilizing the Soviet populations against the Nazis with a determination that Stalinist leaders could never have managed on their own. Even as the Soviet Union suffered more than twenty million wartime deaths, the Red Army fought on. Had Hitler pursued a shrewder strategy of tolerance and assimilation in the east, it is frightful to imagine the success the Nazi empire might have had.

Even in Western Europe, there were prospects for collaboration that the Nazis squandered through their rapacious intolerance and savagery. After the Nazis successfully bypassed the Maginot Line and defeated the French, for example, France's leaders initially proved willing enough to cooperate. In fact, the French resistance was at first very small in scale, confined mostly to left-wing intellectuals, socialists, and later, Communists. But the German policy of forced labor for French adult males and the wanton killing of civilians in towns like Oradour-sur-Glane fueled the resistance and ultimately facilitated the Allied invasion of Normandy that turned the tide of the war.

Hitler was no Cyrus the Great. He could never have prostrated himself before the conquered Babylonians in order to win their loyalty. Nazi ideology viewed conquered peoples as *untermenschen*—subhumans—to be swept away to make room for their racial masters. The historian Klaus Fischer captured the essence of the Nazi dilemma, writing, "No matter how much skill and competence was brought" to Hitler's task of "the ruthless subjugation of conquered people, and the physical extermination of racially inferior breeds," the "bestial mission was bound to arouse the world into determined opposition."[12]

IMPERIAL JAPAN: CONQUEST BY THE
MOST "VIRTUOUS" OF PEOPLES

Germany was not the only Axis power with visions of global domination. On August 1, 1940, Foreign Minister Matsuoka Yosuke publicly unveiled Japan's scheme for territorial expansion. The so-called Greater East Asia Co-Prosperity Sphere—to be conquered by the Imperial Army and united under the benevolent rule of the Japanese emperor—was to grow in four stages.

The core of the sphere was to include Korea, Manchuria, the south of China, and Taiwan—all of which would be under Japanese control within two years. Second, Japan would take over the rest of China, as well as former European colonies such as the Dutch East Indies (now Indonesia), French Indochina (including modern Vietnam, Cambodia, and Laos), Burma, Thailand, Malaysia, Australia, and New Zealand. Third, Japan would extend its reach into eastern Soviet territory, the Philippines, and India. Finally, central Asia and parts of the Middle East, including Iran, Iraq, and Turkey, would all be brought under Japanese control.

As the "master race" (*shūjin minzoku*), the Japanese believed that they had a moral right and duty to exercise leadership within the Co-Prosperity Sphere. "Asia," moreover, was defined remarkably broadly. Japanese wartime cartographers showed both Europe and Africa as part of the Asian continent, and Japanese officials described America as Asia's "eastern wing." In Emperor Hirohito's words, the Co-Prosperity Sphere would "enable all nations and races to assume their proper place in the world"—with Japan, of course, on top.[13]

By 1945, this lofty plan, like Japan itself, was a smoldering ruin. Intolerance was simultaneously the basis of these dreams of Japanese world domination and the catalyst for imperial Japan's destruction.

JAPAN'S STRANGELY CONTRADICTORY
CONCEPT OF "RACE"

During the early twentieth century, Japanese writers combined Western ideas of race, Confucian philosophy, and Shinto notions of moral and spiritual purity to produce a uniquely Japanese world-view. Japan modernized during a period when social Darwinism and so-called scientific racism were in vogue in the West. Western scientists and social scientists had purported to offer "empirical evidence" demonstrating the biological inferiority of Asians, along with blacks and other "colored" peoples. At the same time, gunboat diplomacy, coercive treaties, and superior Western economic development seemed to confirm Asia's (and Japan's) inferiority. In response, Japanese nationalist thinkers developed an elaborate mythic history that reversed Japan's inferior status by emphasizing the divine origin of the imperial line and the "purity" and superior moral virtue of the Japanese (or *Yamato*) people.

As a rationale for conquest, mastery, and exploitation, the story the Japanese told themselves was perfect. As Nakajima Chikuhei, a major industrialist and political leader, declared in 1940: "There are superior and inferior races in the world, and it is the sacred duty of the leading race to lead and enlighten the inferior ones."[14]

At the same time, Japan's self-serving myths were suffused with ironies and contradictions. To begin with, the Japanese depicted themselves as not only the "purest" of peoples, but physically white. Fair skin had been highly esteemed in Japan since at least the eighth century. A light complexion was associated with personal beauty and high social status (hence the white painted faces of geisha or Noh actors). But by the twentieth century, the Japanese obsession with whiteness had been intensified by a deep inferiority complex vis-à-vis the West. Woodblock prints from the first Sino-Japanese war portrayed the Japanese as not only white-skinned and tall but clad in Western clothes. By contrast, the Chinese were shown as yellow-skinned, stocky, and dressed in Oriental garb.[15]

Especially with respect to their colonial subjects in the South Pacific, Japanese racism almost perfectly echoed European colonial racism. Official Japanese reports referred to Micronesian islanders as "lazy, uncivilized, inferior people" who could never escape their "lewd customs, barbarity . . . and debauchery." According to a Japanese scholar in the 1950s: "Because their life is extremely simple and primitive . . . their thought is also childish. They do not possess any desire or spirit of self-improvement. Their pleasures are eating, dancing, and satisfying their sexual desires." As a result, these "tropical peoples" urgently needed Japanese direction.[16]

With respect to the Chinese and Koreans, however, the Japanese had to tell a more complicated story. After all, many Chinese and Koreans were physically indistinguishable from the Japanese, and the countries shared many cultural traditions. As the newspaper editor and Japanese member of parliament Arakawa Gorō wrote of the Koreans in 1906:

> There is nothing especially different about them. They all look just like the Japanese, of the same Oriental race, with the same coloring and physique, and the same black hair. . . . Considering that the appearance and build of the Koreans and Japanese are generally the same, that the structure and grammar of their language are exactly the same, and that their ancient customs resemble each other's, you might think that the Japanese and the Koreans are the same type of human being.

Gorō went on, however, to clarify that these superficial similarities were deceiving:

> If you look closely [at the Koreans], they appear to be a bit vacant, their mouths open and their eyes dull, somehow lacking. . . . In the lines of their mouths and faces you can discern a certain looseness, and when it comes to sanitation or sickness they are loose in the extreme. Indeed, to put it in the worst terms, one could even say that they are closer to beasts than to human beings.[17]

Every Japanese virtue was contrasted with a Korean vice. The Japanese were pure and clean; Koreans were "polluted" and "filthy." Japanese were selfless; Koreans were selfish. Japanese were orderly and modern; Koreans were "barbarous" and "disorderly." The complex tasks of modern life were thought to be completely beyond Koreans; they lacked the mental capacity even to work as railway station employees because they were "hopeless at adding up how many tickets they had punched." "Like most barbarians (*yabanjin*), they cannot understand precise arithmetic." Worse still, they were prone to lying, "gambling, swindling, stealing, and adultery."

On the other hand, although lazy by nature, the Koreans had "an absurd degree of endurance" and thus were perfect beasts of burden. As Gorō explained, "The Koreans have great strength for carrying things; indeed, they carry things heavier than a Japanese horse could. I hear that it is not unusual for a Korean to carry a load weighing sixty or seventy *kanme* [490–570 pounds]. If you encourage them and put them to work under supervision, they are quite useful."

The solution, then, was clear: The Koreans needed Japanese leadership.[18]

As with their Nazi allies, the theme of purification—racial, moral, and spiritual—was a constant theme in wartime Japan, finding expression in religion, popular culture, and (quite literally) the color of everyday life. In 1942, a patriotic song called "Divine Soldiers of the Sky" exalted parachuting troops who descended on their enemies like "pure white roses" from heaven. White, the color of Shinto priestly robes, had long been the color of Japanese purification rituals. But red, representing "brightness," was Japanese as well. A famous article entitled "Establishing a Japanese Racial Worldview," which appeared in 1942 in one of Japan's most popular magazines, explained that red was the color of blood and life:

> The conception of purity associated with Shinto has been thought of hitherto as something pure white. . . . The experi-

ence of the day the war broke out, however, has shown the error of such thinking; and this error is indeed apparent to those who have actually engaged in the rite of purification (*misogi*). The color of purification is faint red, tinged with the pinkness of blood; it is the color of life itself. It is this very warmth of life which has made the cherry blossom the symbol of the Yamato spirit.

But it was not enough that the Japanese were themselves "pure-blooded" if the world they inhabited was not. In order to attain a "higher state of perfection and purity," the Japanese were called upon to help purify the whole Asian continent and reform its polluted, beastlike, demonic inhabitants. As an influential group of Kyoto Imperial University professors explained, war was a "creative and constructive" means of advancing the ongoing historical process of "purification of sins." Giving up one's life in battle, moreover, was the purest accomplishment of all. As the historian John Dower writes, "The 'sacrifices' of war were portrayed as truly sacerdotal, a bath of blood becoming the supreme form of spiritual cleansing."[19]

But what of the "inferior Asian peoples" who were to be "purified"?

THE JAPANESE OCCUPATION OF GREATER
EAST ASIA: A DIVINE MISSION

By December 7, 1941, when the bombs fell on Pearl Harbor, Japan had emerged as a major world power with a formidable military and expansive imperial ambitions that were rapidly being realized. A year later, Japan had taken over Indonesia, Malaysia, Singapore, Thailand, parts of Burma and China, the Philippines, and many South Pacific islands; it already controlled Korea, Manchuria, and Taiwan. Throughout this "Co-Prosperity" zone—with one exception to be discussed in a moment—Japan's policies were quintessentially intolerant.

Like the Nazis, the Japanese had no interest in winning the

hearts and minds of conquered populations. Instead, imperial Japan's goal was to extract local resources, exploit native manpower for the most menial and dangerous jobs, and eventually to use conquered territory as living space for the overcrowded Japanese.[20]

In Korea, for example, forced labor was practiced on a massive scale. As many as one million Korean youths were conscripted into hard labor in construction and coal mining and sent far from their homes, even to Japan. Thousands of young Korean females who were promised "administrative positions" were turned into "comfort women" for Japanese troops. The local population was heavily taxed, even as the Japanese took for themselves the bulk of the nation's chief food supply, rice, leaving the Koreans to subsist on barley and millet. Widespread starvation soon set in. At the same time, the Korean language was banned in public schools, Korean surnames were replaced with Japanese ones, and Shinto worship was made mandatory. The Japanese also attempted to eliminate the Korean tradition of wearing white clothes. When their efforts failed, Japanese officials resorted to spattering ink or paint on Koreans dressed in white.[21]

Things were even worse in Indonesia. The Japanese did not even attempt to "civilize" the native Javanese or Sulawesi. Rather, the Japanese saw Indonesia merely as a pool of resources to be sucked dry. In particular, the Japanese looked hungrily on Indonesia's vast reserves of desperately needed petroleum, timber, and labor.

Ironically, when the Japanese first arrived in Indonesia in 1942, many Indonesians had a relatively positive view of their new overlords. After all, the Japanese had evicted the detested Dutch, Indonesia's colonial master for more than three hundred years. Many of Indonesia's nationalist leaders, including Sukarno, who would later become president, welcomed the Japanese as liberators and bought into Japan's rhetoric of a Pan-Asian unity triumphing over the West. These pro-Japanese sentiments were reflected in slogans like "Japan the Protector of Asia" and "Japan the Light of Asia," which became popular with Indonesian pro-independence parties at the time. But as with the Germans in Ukraine, the blatant, extreme intolerance of the Japanese quickly turned the Indonesian population bitterly against their new "masters."[22]

During their occupation of Indonesia from 1942 to 1945, the Japanese displayed a cruelty and racial arrogance exceeding even that of the Dutch. Public slapping and caning of locals were routine. Devout Muslims were required to acknowledge the Japanese emperor's divinity, in direct violation of their faith. Forced labor was gargantuan in scale and unimaginably harsh; estimates vary, but several millions were probably taken from their homes and put to work in backbreaking conditions that resulted in hundreds of thousands of deaths. Deforestation was so extreme that entire villages became floodplains. The commandeering of agricultural lands caused millions to starve. Cloth became so scarce that thousands could not leave their homes because they had nothing to wear. Throughout the occupation, torture—by bayonet, electric shock, forced ingestion of water, or dislocation of knee sockets—was common.

Japan's greatest strategic disaster may have been in Singapore, a British colony since 1819. Before the Japanese arrived in 1942, Singapore was a booming center of international trade. Singapore's prosperity and British rule both came to an abrupt halt in 1942, when the island fell to the Japanese in a bloody battle that resulted in the largest surrender of British-led troops in history. (Some 138,000 British, Australian, and Indian soldiers were taken as prisoners of war.) Japan's objective was to turn Singapore into the economic capital of Japan-controlled Southeast Asia. This plan failed badly.

As soon as they occupied the island, the Japanese military banned Singapore's largely Chinese population from engaging in economic activity without state-issued licenses. Monopolies were granted to large Japanese corporations like Mitsubishi and Mitsui, while Chinese retail and smaller manufacturing interests were handed out to Japanese "concession hunters," many of whom lacked the skills or the commercial networks to run Singapore's economy. Hyperinflation, price gouging, corruption, and severe food shortages wracked the economy.

At the same time, the Japanese took brutal measures to root

out Chinese resisters. In what came to be known as the Sook Ching Massacre, Japanese military forces went from house to house in February and March 1942, rounding up all Chinese residents deemed potentially "anti-Japanese," including many women, children, and elderly. After being imprisoned under horrific conditions and violently interrogated, some of the captives were released. Others, however, were not. Up to 25,000 were herded into trucks, driven to remote sites, and bayoneted or machine-gunned to death. Instead of becoming the hub of the Japanese Co-Prosperity Sphere, Singapore had by 1945 descended into a welter of disease, malnutrition, and brutal oppression.

The story was painfully similar in other Southeast Asian countries. As with Nazi Germany, it is a grotesque understatement to say that the Japanese did not allow occupied populations to participate, rise, and prosper. Symbolic of the Japanese occupation was the "railroad of death," a railway line the Japanese constructed from Burma to Thailand (then known as Siam) in the 1940s. To build the railroad, the Japanese conscripted men from all over Asia to labor under slavery-like conditions; an estimated 60,000 people died. In the Philippines, Carlos Romulo, an editor who had escaped from Bataan in 1942, offered the following account on his return to Manila in 1945:

> These were my neighbors and my friends whose tortured bodies I saw pushed into heaps on the Manila streets, their hands tied behind their backs, and bayonet stabs running through and through. This girl who looked up at me wordlessly, her young breasts crisscrossed with bayonet strokes, had been in school with my son. I saw the bodies of priests, women, children, and babies that had been bayoneted for sport.[23]

The response to such atrocities in the occupied territories was a loathing of the Japanese so intense that it persists in many parts of Asia even to the present day. While there were of course collaborators in each of the occupied countries, there was also widespread resistance, sabotage, and rebellion. In Korea, demonstrations and popular uprisings demanded independence from the Japanese. In the Philippines, Indonesia, and elsewhere, underground movements fought Japanese forces with guerrilla warfare.[24]

It is impossible to prove that Japan's brutal intolerance undermined its own imperial ambitions. It could be argued that the Japanese would have been hated and resisted as foreign occupiers no matter what their policies had been. There is, however, one occupied territory where the Japanese pursued policies of strategic tolerance rather than intolerance, and this one exceptional case provides surprisingly strong evidence that Japanese rule over the conquered peoples of Asia could have been much more effective.

———————

The island of Formosa, today called Taiwan, fell under Japanese control in 1895 after Japan's victory against China in the first Sino-Japanese War. At that time, Japan was still riding the crest of Meiji modernization and industrialization and had not yet fallen under the sway of its ultranationalist military camp, which would later rise to power in the 1930s. Formosa, Japan's first official colony, not only was of great strategic interest because of its proximity to China; it also represented an opportunity to showcase Japan's emergence on the global scene as a modernizing imperialist force. For whatever reason, Japan's occupation of Formosa differed strikingly from the policies it pursued in places like Burma, Indonesia, and Korea during World War II.

To begin with, in the first decades after taking over Formosa, the Japanese did not actively suppress the local culture. Whereas later the Japanese would ban Koreans from speaking and teaching in their own language, they permitted Formosans to speak their native Chinese dialect, taught Taiwanese children both Chinese and Japanese in Japanese-funded schools, and trained their colonial officers to speak Chinese as well. In 1922, Japanese authorities integrated the island's elite primary schools, allowing children of the Taiwanese gentry to study side by side with the children of Japanese colonials.[25]

One of the most important Formosan institutions that the Jap-

284   THE FUTURE OF WORLD DOMINANCE

anese left in place was the Chinese *pao-chia* system of local governance, under which groupings of approximately one hundred households were made collectively responsible for wrongful acts committed by individual members. By making use of the *pao-chia* system and allowing influential Formosan families to maintain their positions of leadership, the Japanese gained the loyalty of local elites. To the same end, Japanese colonial authorities granted business privileges to prominent Formosans, occasionally bestowing on them the rank of "gentleman" (*shinsho*). At the same time, the Japanese poured money into Formosan infrastructure and agriculture. They modernized Formosa's banking system; built roads, railroads, and hospitals; and vastly improved communications, sanitation, irrigation, and farming productivity. Crop yields increased so much that even after massive exportation of rice to Japan, Formosans ate relatively well compared to Chinese on the mainland.

There was certainly Japanese repression in Formosa, even before World War II. It is estimated that the Japanese military killed as many as 12,000 Formosan resisters during the initial period of Japanese rule. Yet to a surprising extent Japanese colonial authorities won over the local population. Eighty thousand Formosans served voluntarily in the Japanese army in World War II. Even today, many Taiwanese have an affinity for Japanese culture. Some who are old enough to remember the occupation still speak Japanese on occasion and remember the colonizers as people who brought order, modernity, and the rule of law. Had the Japanese pursued similar policies elsewhere in the "Co-Prosperity Sphere," their bid for imperial hegemony might have been far more successful.[26]

The potency of intolerance is undeniable. There may be no force on earth so galvanizing, so identity-creating, so war-enabling as racist nationalism—unless perhaps it is religious fundamentalism of the jihadist variety. Yet fortunately for the world, the same elements that make these ideologies so ferociously mobilizing also set the limits on their reach.

It is astonishing in retrospect that the Germans failed to take advantage of the tens of millions of Russians, Poles, Ukrainians, and others who might well have become their enthusiastic supporters and soldiers. It is similarly surprising that the Japanese, who had seen in Taiwan how effective strategic tolerance could be in an occupied territory, chose nevertheless to brutalize and slaughter conquered populations elsewhere, guaranteeing the fiercest possible resistance to their rule. But it was the very same ideology that supercharged their rise to power—the same nationalist racial pathology, the same thirst for blood and ethnic cleansing—that prevented both Nazi Germany and imperial Japan from pursuing policies that might have better served their bid for world domination. Needless to say, ideologies of racial supremacy and ethnic cleansing are not particularly good at generating the loyalty of, or recruiting valuable human capital from, the peoples who are to be cleansed.

Only tolerance can achieve that result. As we return to the twenty-first century in the next chapter, we will see that the three most discussed challengers to U.S. hegemony today—including China and the European Union—are learning this lesson. Can any of these societies gain sufficient wealth and power to bring America's unipolar world dominance to an end?

ELEVEN

THE CHALLENGERS

China, the European Union, and India

in the Twenty-first Century

We've had a couple hundred bad years, but now we're back.
— Shanghai resident

[The United States] can bribe, bully, or impose its will almost anywhere in the world, but when its back is turned, its potency wanes. The strength of the EU, conversely, is broad and deep: once sucked into its sphere of influence, countries are changed forever.

— Mark Leonard, *Why Europe Will Run the Twenty-first Century*

If international public opinion polls are correct, the majority of world citizenry would prefer to see the end of American world dominance and the restoration of a more balanced constellation of global power.[1] This chapter considers the three most frequently mentioned challengers to U.S. dominance: China, the European Union, and India. Interestingly, each of these powers has already been pursuing its own distinctive version of strategic tolerance. Although their models of tolerance are very different from that of the United States—and, in China's case, at first glance barely recognizable as tolerance at all—they go a surprisingly long way toward explaining the enormous successes of these rising powers.

CHINA ASCENDANT

In the January 22, 2007, issue of *Time* magazine, the journalist Michael Elliott concluded his cover story on "the world's next great power" as follows: "[I]n this century, the relative power of the U.S. is going to decline, and that of China is going to rise. That cake was baked long ago." Elliott also reported on a 2006 survey conducted in China, in which 87 percent of the Chinese respondents felt that China "should take a greater role in world affairs" and more than 50 percent "believed China's global influence would match that of the U.S. within a decade." According to Kenneth Lieberthal, senior director at the National Security Council's Asia desk under President Bill Clinton, "The Chinese wouldn't put it this way themselves. But in their hearts I think they believe that the 21st century is China's century."[2]

Can China become the world's next hyperpower? Any way you look at it, China's economic transformation over the last quarter century has been breathtaking. In 1978, China's per capita income was $230, among the world's lowest, and its growth was stagnant. In terms of development, China was comparable to Indonesia and Tanzania. For the last thirty years, however, China's economy has been expanding at the phenomenal rate of 9.5 percent annually, and today no other country is shaking up the global economy like China.

In 2003, China overtook the United States as the most popular destination for foreign direct investment. No longer is China dominant merely in labor-intensive sectors like toy, shoe, and clothing manufacturing. Today, China is the number-one producer of cell phones, television sets, and DVD players. Significantly, China is now moving into the manufacture of computer chips, automobiles, jet engines, and military weaponry—sectors typically dominated by advanced economies. It is also the number-one *consumer* of cell phones and consumer electronics and will probably be the number-one consumer of automobiles in the not-distant future. By 2030, according to some experts, China's economy will be three times larger than that of the United States.[3]

What's more, on the international trade front, China is already giving the current hyperpower a run for its money. While the United States continues to battle increasing global hostility, China has quietly connected with nearly all of the world's major countries, both developed and developing, often using debt forgiveness and foreign aid to boost its public image and leverage deals. In the process, China has locked up long-term contracts for billions of tons of Chilean copper, Australian coal, Brazilian iron, and the other raw materials it desperately needs to feed its exploding economic machine.

In an ironic twist, China has done particularly well by taking advantage of the West's refusal to deal with "rogue states." In the Middle East and Africa, for example, China has openly refused to condition trade on compliance with international human rights treaties, as have the European Union and the United States, giving China greater access to valuable resources in countries like Angola, Burma, Congo, and Iran. While many protest the U.S. government's inadequate peacekeeping and humanitarian response in Darfur, China has happily established itself as the largest investor in Sudan's massive oil fields. Meanwhile, adding insult to injury, a recent Pew Foundation global survey found that a majority of citizens in Canada, France, Germany, the Netherlands, Russia, Spain, and the United Kingdom now view China more favorably than they do the United States.[4]

Yet none of this makes the case for Chinese world dominance. If the thesis of this book is correct, America is a hyperpower today above all because it has out-tolerated the rest of the world. More than anything else, the United States' ability to draw in and exploit the world's most valuable human capital has been responsible for its unstoppable ascent to economic, military, and technological preeminence. If this is true, and if history is any guide, China can overtake the United States as the world's next hyperpower only if it outdoes the United States at strategic tolerance. Can an authoritarian, rogue-state-friendly China possibly do so?

At first glance, the answer would seem to be no. With only occasional exceptions, China has a long history of xenophobia and ethnocentrism, and for the last fifty years has been notorious for crushing political and religious dissent. Moreover, China—officially described as 92 percent ethnically homogeneous, 94 percent atheist, and with a net negative migration rate—is essentially the opposite of a pluralistic immigrant society.

But things are more complicated. China's tremendous potential today stems precisely from the fact that it is a spectacular success story of strategic tolerance. Let me explain.

––––––––––

For most Westerners, even those trying to be open-minded, China's population today probably seems relatively ethnically un-diverse. On any given square block in New York City there can be found Cuban Americans, Korean Americans, Scots-Irish Americans, Italian Americans, and African Americans hailing from different ethnic and racial backgrounds. By contrast, China sports more than a billion people, almost all of whom have black hair (although hair dye is becoming increasingly popular), claim a common ancestry, and consider themselves Chinese.

But what Westerners and Chinese alike tend not to realize is that the very idea of "Chinese-ness" reflects a triumph of strategic tolerance. Indeed, over its three-thousand-year history, China has essentially accomplished exactly what the European Union is trying to do today—it has brought and kept together in a single political unit a huge number of individuals from vastly different cultural, geographical, and linguistic backgrounds.[5] Chinese civilization in fact grew out of a great intermixing of diverse cultures.

The nation today known as China was "a land long peopled by plural groups" with "extreme linguistic heterogeneity" and stark differences in dress, customs, rituals, and religions. In particular, there has long been a deep divide between the peoples of north and south China, with the Yellow River serving as a rough boundary line.[6] Even today, people in southern provinces like Guangdong or my home province, Fujian, speak among themselves Chinese dialects unintelligible to most northern Chinese (or for that matter each other). Chinese from the north tend to eat wheat-based products like the steamed bread called *mantou*, whereas Chinese from the south tend to eat rice and rice-based products. Moreover, many Chinese (myself included) purport to be able to tell whether someone is from the north or south of China based simply on their physical appearance.

China was built through a process of conquest and merging of diverse groups. As with the Romans, peoples from the Sichuan basin to the Taiwan Strait found they could not resist the Chinese cultural, political, and military package. Just as the toga and Latin spread from Scotland to Egypt, so too Chinese culture—with its notions of ethnic superiority, Confucian-Taoist strands, the imperial examination system, and the supreme Son of Heaven ruling over all—was embraced by hundreds of millions between the Gobi Desert and the South China Sea. Like the Spaniards and Libyans who turned into Romans in the second century, previously distinct ethnic groups such as the Min, Yue, and Wu peoples all became Han Chinese.

In overcoming not just north-south, but coastal-inland, rural-urban, and provincial divides, China has succeeded in integrating its peoples beyond the European Union's wildest dreams. A single language—at first only written and now, under the People's Republic, spoken as well—unites nearly all of China's population. Much more fundamentally, a sense of belonging to the Chinese people—of being "Han"—is embraced by at least 92 percent of the population as their primary national and ethnic identity. Western experts on ethnic studies have long insisted that the Cantonese, Shanghainese, Hunanese, and so forth, given their considerable differences in speech, customs, and even physical appearance, are and ought to consider themselves different ethnicities. But they don't. On the contrary, for all their differences and mutual snobberies, these groups, along with the Sichuanese, Tianjinese, Anhuinese, and many others, all think of themselves first and foremost as Chinese—as *Zhongguo ren*, literally "people of the Middle Kingdom."[7]

This then is the often overlooked story of China's historical internal tolerance. For good reason, what makes the headlines in Western newspapers tends to be the intolerance and repression directed at political dissidents, religious sects such as the Falun Gong, and ethnic minorities like the Tibetans. But the flip side of this intolerance has been the staggering success of Chinese ethnonationalism as an instrument of strategic tolerance—a success already achieved hundreds of years ago and now simply taken for granted. Today, while the European Union struggles to hold together 450 million people, China commands the loyalty and ethnic identification of nearly 1.3 billion people, a fifth of the world's population.

So is it possible that unlike every hyperpower in world history, China does not need the talents of immigrants and outsiders? With 1.3 billion people, there is a lot of talent waiting to be mobilized. Moreover, it should not be forgotten that Chinese communities all over the world are famously entrepreneurial, outperforming indigenous majorities throughout Southeast Asia and often disproportionately successful in Western countries.[8] Could it be that in the race for world power China already has all the human capital it needs?

It's possible—but highly unlikely. To begin with, China's own pool of human capital remains sorely undereducated. Although China's education level is much more advanced than that of other developing countries—for example, China's literacy rate for women is 87 percent as compared to India's 45 percent—it is not close to Western standards. Only about half of China's population attends high school, compared to at least 90 percent in the United States. Moreover, China's education system is widely criticized for its tendency to teach rote learning rather than innovative thinking, placing "undue emphasis on speed and memorization of obscure facts" and failing to "produce the kind of students who are able to apply their knowledge in rapidly changing situations in a modern economy." "Students cram and recite," complained an education ministry official in 2005. "They remember, but they don't understand."[9]

Meanwhile, at the highest levels of education, China is still reeling from the Cultural Revolution, when forty years ago the country's most gifted and accomplished scientists, researchers, and academics were sent to the countryside to work as field hands—not only a colossal human tragedy and waste of talent but a crippling setback for China's scientific and technological sectors. As of 2000, China had only about 460 scientists and engineers involved in research and development for every 1 million people, whereas in the United States the ratio is roughly ten times higher.[10]

To upgrade its "humanware," as one Chinese official puts it, the Chinese government is devoting massive resources to improving education, with a special emphasis on originality and innovation. Today, some 25 percent of China's student population attend "experimental" primary and secondary schools, designed to encourage debate, "scientific exploration," and "flexible thinking." And in a bizarre alliance, the Disney Corporation recently teamed up with the Communist Youth League to hold workshops aimed at "raising creativity"—with the additional benefit of familiarizing the Chinese market with Disney characters.

At the same time, China has been sending growing numbers of promising young scientists and scholars to study abroad. Known as *haigui*, or "overseas returnees," these students were to bring back valuable know-how and to serve as the vanguard of China's technological revolution. (The Chinese word for "turtle" is also pronounced *haigui*—a source of wordplay among Chinese and a frequent mistranslation in English.) Instead of doing so, however, the great majority of these students chose to remain abroad after obtaining their degrees. From 1986 to 1998, for example, some 85 percent of Chinese students graduating from American universities said they planned to stay in the United States.[11]

But this trend may be changing dramatically. In the last five years, as China's standard of living continues to rise, increasing numbers of foreign-educated Chinese are returning to the People's Republic.[12] These prize engineers and scientists are often lured back to China with Western-style perks: luxury cars, state-of-the-art condos, and internationally competitive salaries. Many, moreover, are moved by patriotism. The possibility of China's becoming a world superpower fills them with pride and motivation—once again, Chinese ethnonationalism at work.

Nevertheless, although China's economy has opened considerably, there remains a strong popular perception that hard work and intelligence will not produce commensurate rewards. Shanghai may have a new crop of Prada-wearing real estate moguls, but because corruption in China remains rife, connections continue to be of critical importance. As long as this continues to be the case, China's best and brightest may not want to stay in (or return to) the country. They will try to go where their talents can translate more directly into success.

But even if China makes great strides in harnessing the energies and talents of its vast population, it is still exceedingly unlikely that this would put China at the cutting edge of the human talent frontier. Why? Because the Western nations have a massive head start. And more fundamentally, because at any given point in time the world's most brilliant, most inventive, most skilled, and most enterprising will never all be found in one locale or among one ethnicity. This, of course, is the thesis of this book: To achieve not regional but *world* dominance, a society must attract, command the loyalty of, and motivate the *world's* most valuable human capital.

Can China do this?

———

There is now a surprising number of Americans and other Westerners working as bartenders and fitness instructors in Shanghai. But attracting relatively unskilled foreigners probably isn't going to be China's ticket to world dominance. More beneficial to China are the significant numbers of Western expatriates who now work for multinational corporations in China. In addition to bringing skills, training local Chinese workers, and consuming luxury goods, these Western expatriates often invest millions of dollars in Chinese property.

It is worth emphasizing just how dramatically the face of China has changed in the last quarter century. Even after formally "open-ing up" to the world in 1978, Chinese leaders remained deeply sus-picious of the West. Foreigners arrived in a tiny trickle and were viewed as oddities, even in the major cities. According to corporate expats who arrived in Shanghai in the early 1990s, they felt "very James Bond-ish" in a land where few spoke English, "money was flowing really, really stupidly," and "anything seemed possible."[13]

Around 1995, China began much more aggressively accepting and even recruiting foreigners, explicitly trying to harness the skills and technological know-how of Japanese, French, and Dutch man-agers, German archaeologists, Lebanese industrialists, Swiss archi-tects, General Electric, Motorola, and the Getty Foundation, to name just a few. Today, China is more cosmopolitan than it has been since the Tang dynasty. Shanghai and Beijing have long ceased to be "hardship posts" for Western expats, who now live in tony Westernized complexes called "Soho" and "Chelsea" and drink lattes at Starbucks and mojitos (or Chivas and green tea) at trendy bars alongside wealthy young Chinese professionals. For better or worse, hummus, bagels, fresh mozzarella, and any number of for-eign consumer products are now readily available in Beijing. In ad-dition to the traditional McDonald's and KFC in China, one doesn't have to go far in Shanghai before stumbling on a Taco Bell, a Subway, or even a Mr. Softee truck.[14]

Nevertheless, the reality remains that foreign expats are . . . foreign expats. American Google software engineers and Boeing scientists living in China are not Chinese citizens. Neither are the Japanese technicians who work at Mitsubishi China or the Ger-man executives who work at Siemens China.

Could they be, if they wanted to?

This brings us to the fascinating puzzle of contemporary Chi-nese identity. In researching this book over the last five years, I posed different versions of just this question to numerous people from the People's Republic.

"Could an ethnic Malay or Filipino ever be Han Chinese?" The answer was always a resounding no.

"Could a member of one of China's fifty-five ethnic minorities ever become Han Chinese?" When I was visiting Sichuan a few years ago, I asked this of a young man from the minority Yi community. To my surprise, he replied, "Oh yes. My parents are both Yi. But unlike them I don't speak the Yi language, so I'm not really Yi anymore. Also, I married a Han Chinese woman. So I am really Han Chinese now, and certainly my son is Han." To my further surprise, I found that his attitude was confirmed by many others, both Han and non-Han.

Finally, I framed the question in terms of citizenship. "Could a Westerner who speaks fluent Chinese, loves Chinese culture, and wants to move permanently to the PRC ever become a Chinese citizen?" I asked this of numerous Chinese officials, Chinese lawyers, and Chinese visiting legal scholars. In a country like the United States, this kind of question would have an easily ascertainable answer. But the Chinese I asked all hemmed and hawed, looking baffled. Many pointed out that most foreigners do not *want* Chinese citizenship (which is probably true). In the end, no one was able to answer the question squarely, although more than one person said, "A foreigner? I don't think so."*

These uncertainties and confusions reflect a millennia-old struggle over the meaning of Chinese identity—a struggle that if anything grew more intense in the twentieth century. During the tumultuous period leading up to the 1911 revolution that overthrew three thousand years of imperial dynastic rule, Sun Yat-sen and other revolutionary leaders championed an explicitly ethnic—indeed racial—concept of the Chinese nation. They saw China as "more than a national state: it was a race-nation that should be ruled by the Han Chinese." The "Chinese nation" thus included anyone of Han Chinese blood, whether he or she lived in San Francisco or Malaysia. This racial concept of China was extremely powerful in uniting the Chinese against their "alien" Manchu Qing rulers—descendants of the Jurchen steppe people—who although

---

*The relevant statute, the Nationality Law of the People's Republic of China (1980), provides that foreign nationals may acquire Chinese nationality "upon approval of their application" but provides no right or entitlement to that status (Article 8).

they had lived in China for centuries, were always perceived and resented as foreigners.[15]

After the Communist victory in 1949, this ethnic concept of Chinese nationality became problematic for the government in its dealings with China's millions of ethnic minorities who, although representing just a tiny fraction of the population, occupy roughly 60 percent of China's territory, including strategically important border areas such as Tibet, Mongolia, and Xinjiang. For purposes of maintaining control over China's vast territory, the government found it expedient to adopt a geographical concept of Chinese nationality. Today, the official line is that China is a multiethnic nation that happens to be 92 percent Han Chinese but also includes fifty-five ethnic minorities, all of whom are Chinese nationals.*

But like other nations, China cannot escape its history. Lucian Pye once wrote, "China is not just another nation-state in the family of nations"; rather, China is "a civilization pretending to be a state."[16] It is a civilization, moreover, rooted in notions of ethnic identity and superiority. For three thousand years, the Chinese have understood themselves as sharing a common ancestry, an ancestry not shared by Tibetans or Uighurs, and certainly not by any Westerners.

With respect to the twenty-first century, the bottom line is that China is still the farthest cry from an immigrant society. The Western and Japanese expats working in foreign enclaves in Chinese cities today are not immigrants. They are not en route to becoming Chinese citizens; neither is the government seeking to make them citizens. Although there are more foreigners working in China today than there have been for a long time, the government is not trying to integrate them into Chinese society or encouraging them to view themselves as Chinese. In part, this is why China is not even close to being a magnet pulling in the best scientists, engineers, thinkers, and innovators from the West—or anywhere else.

---

*For the single English word "Chinese" there are many Chinese terms (*Zhongguo ren, Zhonghua minzu, hanren, huayi, tangren, huaren, huaqiao,* etc.), each with a slightly different, often fluid connotation, such as "the Chinese people," "Chinese nationals," "the Chinese race," "the Han people," "descendants of Chinese," "the Tang people," etc.

Chinese leaders, of course, fully realize this. China doesn't especially want to be an immigrant society. But it has found two other ways to bring in international skills, technology, and know-how. First, again playing the "ethnic card," China has appealed with astounding success to the pride and loyalty—not to mention self-interest—of "overseas Chinese": some fifty-five million people of Chinese descent living in more than 160 countries.* In many ways, the overseas Chinese are an extraordinary pool. They collectively control some $2 trillion in assets, and generate an estimated annual economic output of $600 billion, roughly the current GDP of Australia.[17] In addition, they include many highly educated individuals, among them Nobel Prize winners.

Other countries, for example Israel and India, have also successfully made use of their "diaspora" populations. But the size and resources of China's diaspora are unparalleled. From its initial opening in 1978, the central government shrewdly targeted this pool, offering special investment incentives and tax preferences to foreign investors of Chinese descent. At the same time, many local governments bestowed "honorary titles" on overseas Chinese who were particularly generous and "loyal" to their "motherland" and "ancestral home villages."[18]

These strategies paid off. In the 1980s and 1990s, overseas Chinese poured more than $190 billion into China, accounting for more than half of the foreign direct investment that helped catapult China from third world backwater to "Rising Dragon." (In the booming southern provinces of Fujian and Guangdong, as much as 80 percent of foreign investment has come from overseas Chinese.) Moreover, overseas Chinese are transferring not only wealth to China, but knowledge. For example, Shing-Tung Yau, a professor at Harvard and winner of the Fields Medal (the highest international honor in mathematics), has recently joined forces with China's government and a Hong Kong real estate mogul in an effort to build a new generation of world-class Chinese scientists.[19]

---

*By "overseas Chinese" I am loosely referring to citizens of the People's Republic living abroad; the Chinese in Hong Kong, Macao, and Taiwan; and foreign citizens of Chinese descent.

At the same time, China has found ways to acquire Western know-how from non-Chinese corporate behemoths. For example, dangling the prize of access to China's immense domestic market, the Chinese government conditioned a $900 million turbine-engine deal with General Electric on the latter's agreement to share technology. General Electric is hardly alone. According to a *Wall Street Journal* article titled "China's Price for Market Entry: Give Us Your Technology, Too":

> [T]o gain easier access to markets in China, Motorola Inc. has poured more than $300 million into 19 technology-research centers in the country. A Microsoft Corp. center in Beijing now employs more than 200 researchers. Siemens AG says it has spent more than $200 million since 1998 working with a Chinese academic institution to develop a mobile-phone technology that the government wants to be the country's standard.

Many other foreign corporations, including Japan's Kawasaki and France's Alstom SA, have agreed to similar technology transfers in exchange for market access.[20]

In the end, however, these strategies are highly imperfect substitutes for bringing in the world's best talent and know-how. The preferences granted to overseas Chinese in the 1980s and 1990s opened the door to the large-scale corruption mentioned above. For every Shiing-Shen Chern—the brilliant UC Berkeley mathematician who dedicated much of his later life to promoting the study of math and science in China—there are dozens of Chinese businessmen from Hong Kong and Southeast Asia who have made millions in China through bribery and other backdoor techniques. Because of the visibility of powerful overseas Chinese tycoons like Indonesia's James Riady, there is a widespread perception that "personal connections" (*guanxi*) are everything—that commercial success in China depends on who has the most "old friends" and who can offer local officials the biggest gifts and the most sumptuous banquets. Thus, while the Chinese government may have hoped that overseas Chinese—being "all in the family"—would make loyal and dependable investors, ironically their prominence in China has fueled local resentment and contributed to the sense that there is no level playing field in China.

Meanwhile, China's approach to getting Western technology has clear limits as well. Western firms compelled to share know-how with China (in exchange for market access) have predictably avoided revealing their most cutting-edge technologies. According to GE chairman Jeffrey Immelt, China's engineers remain at least "two generations" behind in turbine engine manufacturing, despite GE's technology-sharing agreement with them. Or as one Chinese official pointedly put it: "The foreigners are now agreeing to tell us how and where to dig a hole, but we still do not know why to dig a hole there."[21]

———————

China's ascent to superpower status is practically a foregone conclusion. True, China faces a daunting list of internal challenges, including staggering pollution, corruption, regional wealth disparities, and soulless mass consumerism. Nevertheless, in terms of building on its present successes, China seems to be doing everything right. Keeping an eye on the long term, it is pouring massive sums into infrastructure, research and development, and education at all levels. Few today doubt that China will become one of the great powers of the world within a short time.

But if my thesis is correct, China will not become a hyperpower. Today, more than ever, global dominance depends on the ability to attract and retain the world's top scientific, technological, and creative talent, and China—a quintessential nonimmigrant, ethnically based nation—is not in a position to do so. This is hardly a calamity for China, which may not want the burdens or the global resentment that world dominance entails. Indeed, China's official foreign policy emphasizes "noninterference." Being a "mere" superpower may suit China just fine.

In a world in which China is a superpower, could America remain a hyperpower? In principle, it's possible. If America continued to be the destination for the world's best and brightest—including even China's best and brightest—the United States could conceivably retain its technological, military, and economic edge over all rivals. More likely, however, a Chinese superpower would dictate a return to at least a bipolar world order. If China becomes the economic colossus many predict, its sheer wealth will command enormous power in the modern world, with many countries (including possibly the United States) dependent on its trade and investment capital. At the same time, China's defense spending has been mounting rapidly over the last decade, and it is by no means impossible that by the middle of the twenty-first century China's military could rival (if not surpass) that of the United States.

THE EUROPEAN UNION: A "POST-IMPERIAL SUPERPOWER"

As the clock struck midnight and the champagne glasses clinked on May 1, 2004, the European Union officially welcomed ten new member states, increasing its membership from fifteen to twenty-five. "Fireworks exploded and church bells rang out" across a Europe with borders now stretching across three time zones, from Poland to Ireland, from Finland to Malta. A Europe divided by decades of Cold War and centuries of internecine conflict came together—warmly, and for the first time in history, peacefully.

The occasion was particularly poignant for the people of the eight nations who had spent fifty years behind the iron curtain. The Polish Solidarity leader, Lech Walesa, called the moment the fulfillment of his "dreams and lifetime's work," while the Hungarian prime minister Peter Medgyessy "set a giant hourglass in motion to symbolise the beginning of a new era." Meanwhile, in the former Soviet republic of Lithuania, the government urged its citizens to light lamps and candles to make their country "the brightest spot in Europe." Founded largely as a bulwark against the westward expansion of Communism, the community that is now the EU not only outlasted its rivals but lived to take them in.[22]

The moment's triumph was not limited to formerly Eastern Bloc EU members. The inclusion of ten new countries also marked a stunning victory over a much deeper history of division, rivalry, and bloodshed. For centuries, leading European philosophers and statesmen—among them Victor Hugo, Jean-Jacques Rousseau, Immanuel Kant, and Winston Churchill—had recognized that unity held the best hope for European peace, prosperity, and power. In the mid-fifteenth century, Bohemia's King George proposed a federation arrangement strikingly similar to the EU's current structure, albeit to guard against the external threat of Turkish invasion, not to address internal division. But these nascent visions of a pan-European union could not overcome the fierce nationalism, enmity, and religious division that had grown increasingly entrenched in the bloody millennium following the fall of Rome. Over and over, culminating in World War II, ferocious nationalist ambition had torn Europe apart, killing and maiming millions.[23]

Yet, astonishingly, what began as a modest economic agreement over coal and steel production between postwar France and Germany has, in just two generations, forged a European unity unprecedented since the height of the Roman Empire. Today the EU numbers twenty-seven nations—Bulgaria and Romania joined in January 2007—sharing a common body of law covering nearly half a billion people. The EU has been called "the largest single market in the developed world," and its gross domestic product of roughly $13 trillion is comparable to that of the United States.[24] In population the EU has an edge—by 150 million. With two nuclear powers (Britain and France) and more troops under arms than the United States, the EU is at least on paper a potential military giant as well. And the EU has not finished expanding. Under the EU's rules for enlargement, candidate countries may join provided that they meet certain economic and political criteria, including the observance of human rights and fundamental freedoms. Countries currently under consideration include Albania, Croatia, Serbia, and, most controversially, Turkey. In theory, the EU could someday extend to Africa and the Middle East and even incorporate Russia.

———

The EU's territorial expansion—not through military conquest but through a process of qualification and accession—represents an astonishing new form of strategic tolerance. In the past, with a coveted package of freedoms and economic incentives, countries such as the Dutch Republic or the United States made themselves magnets for *individuals*. With a new package of freedoms and economic incentives, the EU has made itself a magnet for *nations*.

In this sense, the EU is comparable to Rome. In its golden age, Rome too attracted entire peoples into its orbit. But Rome always had its legions, which could threaten to achieve by sword the incorporation of peoples who did not willingly submit. The EU has become a magnet for nations without force or even the threat of force. As the British author Mark Leonard puts it, the EU is a "post-imperial superpower," increasing its dominion "not by threatening to invade other countries" but rather by dangling economic carrots. Rather than imposing democracy and the rule of law on other countries, the EU gives countries incentives to transform themselves. Rather than taking over governments, the EU, which has only a skeletal bureaucracy, works through national parliaments and local councils. Precisely because it is *anti*-empire, Leonard suggests, the EU eventually "will change the way the world works."[25]

As part of its anti-imperial challenge to U.S. hegemony, the EU is seeking to establish itself as the world's true beacon of freedom, equality, and Enlightenment values. Even before 9/11, many Europeans saw their own societies—with their generally much more generous welfare systems and social services—as superior to that of the United States, offering more genuine tolerance and opportunity despite the rhetoric of the American Dream. In a 2000 survey, for example, the French public was asked, "As far as you're concerned, what kind of a country is the United States?" Forty-five percent answered "A nation of great social inequality," and 33 percent said "A racist nation." Only 24 percent answered "A nation where anyone can get rich," and just 15 percent replied "A nation that welcomes immigrants."[26]

Since the U.S.-led invasion of Iraq, European criticism of the United States has grown only more intense. In a 2003 article that appeared in newspapers throughout Europe, the eminent German and French philosophers Jürgen Habermas and Jacques Derrida assert a European identity defined acerbically in opposition to the United States, highlighting Europe's softer approach to capitalism, its rejection of the death penalty, and perhaps most critically its "moral sensibility, informed by the memory of the totalitarian regimes of the twentieth century and the Holocaust." America's "unilateralism"—its perceived willingness to violate international law and to undermine the United Nations—is widely criticized in Europe, where from Ireland to Poland the maze of EU treaties and charters today offers the most progressive stance on human rights and nondiscrimination the world has ever known.[27]

There is, of course, a strategic dimension to all this. To reap the economic rewards of integration, the European states had to overcome their historical enmities, suppress their own nationalist tendencies (for example, relinquishing their national currencies), tolerate one another's religions, and ensure that workers and products from the various states would not be discriminated against in other states. In other words, if the EU's stirring devotion to international human rights and "Unity in Diversity" (the EU's motto, published in twenty different languages) reflects a new European moral sensibility, it also reflects a shrewd calculation of free market self-interest.

———

Although most Europeans would undoubtedly say that they oppose global bullies and would prefer a world with no hyperpower, it is nevertheless true that a primary goal behind the EU is to create a political entity large and strong enough to rival the United States. Because the EU's formula for amassing power is essentially one of strategic tolerance, one critical question becomes how well the EU's model of tolerance can compete with that of the United States.

At first glance, it might seem that the EU has already outdone the United States on the tolerance front. Not only has the EU become a magnet for nations (a kind of strategic tolerance for which there is no current U.S. parallel), but it has also adopted a set of individual rights at least as tolerant as those famously set forth in the U.S. Constitution.

But the reality is more complex. Throughout the 1970s, 1980s, and 1990s, while the United States was draining brainpower from all over the world and vaulting to the forefront of the computer revolution, Europe could not remotely keep up. By the late 1990s, countries such as Germany and Great Britain had serious shortages of skilled information technology (IT) workers, and it looked increasingly like Europe was missing the high-tech boat. Even today, the powerhouse Western European states are still scrambling to attract highly skilled foreign professionals, engineers, and IT technicians while a stream of such international talent continues to flow into the United States. Why so, if Europe is so tolerant?

The answer is that the EU's tolerance has been primarily directed inward, not outward—a strategy for uniting Europe, not for attracting third world immigrants into Europe or for turning the European states into multiethnic immigrant societies like the United States. When the EU's Charter of Fundamental Rights speaks of "free movement of persons," it is not guaranteeing the freedom of Africans to move to Norway. On the contrary, during the very decades when the European Union was coming into being, the general attitude toward immigration throughout most of Europe was quite hostile.

In the last quarter of the twentieth century, Great Britain, France, and Germany at various points declared themselves "zero immigration" countries.[28] From the 1970s until about 2000, the non-European populations of the European states consisted principally of migrant or "guest workers" (often from former colonies) and their families, refugees claiming asylum, and illegal aliens drawn by relatively generous welfare and social service programs. More problematically, the European nations did little to promote the cultural or political assimilation of the poor migrant communities that sprang up in and around major cities.

Today, leading European countries such as France, Germany, and the Netherlands are still experiencing chronic shortages of skilled labor even while unemployment fuels frustration and alienation in their poor migrant communities. Despite recent immigration reforms openly aimed at attracting high-tech workers from countries such as India, Korea, or China, the EU nations continue to lose out to more popular destinations, in particular, the traditional "immigrant nations" of Australia, Canada, and the United States.[29]

The German experience is telling. In order to create its own Silicon Valley, the government created in the late 1990s a new German green card specifically directed at attracting foreign IT professionals, particularly from countries such as India. Germany hoped to lure at least 20,000 highly qualified migrants a year. But unlike its American counterpart, which is a relatively sure path to naturalization, the German green card offered no possibility of citizenship. As Fareed Zakaria writes, "Germany was asking bright young professionals to leave their country, culture, and families; move thousands of miles away; learn a new language; and work in a strange land—but without any prospect of ever being part of their new home." The program was a dismal failure, and subsequent efforts to lure high-tech workers have not yet produced major results. At the end of 2006, Germany had 22,000 unfilled engineering positions, 30 percent more than the previous year.[30]

In this important respect—the competition for the world's best and brightest—the EU's strategy of making itself a magnet for *nations* has come up short in comparison to the U.S. strategy of making itself a magnet for *individuals*. Yet throughout the EU, anti-immigration sentiment seems to be rising. Why is this, especially given the EU's manifest commitment to Enlightenment values of equality, human rights, and nondiscrimination?

———

It is impossible to understand the current immigration debate in Europe without talking about Islam. Muslims are the fastest-growing segment of Europe's population. Some analysts predict that in fifteen years the EU will be 20 percent Muslim. In France, Muslims may already represent 10 percent (or perhaps even more) of the population, outnumbering all non-Catholic groups put together, including Protestants and Jews. In major Dutch cities such as Amsterdam and Rotterdam, Muslims are expected to become a *majority* of the population within a decade. (For purposes of comparison, Muslims represent only 1–2 percent of the U.S. population.) Yet this substantial and growing minority just happens to be a population that European tolerance—despite its asserted universalism—may have the most difficulty tolerating.[31]

For Europe, this problem goes deeper than the French ban on head scarves in public schools. Many in Eastern Europe still regard Christianity as central to Europe's heritage. In 2003, Poland's president, Aleksander Kwasniewski, attacked the "Godless tone" of the EU constitution, declaring it shameful that the constitution made no references "to the Christian values which are so important to the development of Europe." At the same time, more secular Western Europeans increasingly see Islam as a potential threat to Europe's modern Enlightenment identity. The late Italian journalist Oriana Fallaci railed against "Muslim invaders," engaged in a "Reverse Crusade" to conquer and profane Europe. And in the words of a Danish member of parliament, "It is . . . naive to think you can integrate Muslims into the Danish society. . . . [Islam] is not only a religion but a fascist political ideology mixed with a religious fanaticism of the Middle Ages, an insult against the human rights and all other conditions necessary for creating a developed society." Undoubtedly, one of the reasons for the broad popular resistance to Turkey's accession to the EU is Turkey's 68 million–strong Muslim population. Thus, with Islam, European tolerance—in terms of both territorial expansion and openness to immigration—has hit a potential wall.[32]

Meanwhile, within Europe, the relatively poor Muslim communities are at the center of an intensifying ethnic, religious, and racial conflict. Nearly no EU country has escaped these problems. Denmark's experience is illustrative. A largely homogeneous society and "once the epitome of Scandinavian liberalism," Denmark in the late twentieth century confronted what was by its standards a sizable Islamic community, representing about 3 percent of the population. Hailing largely from Turkey, Morocco, Iraq, and Somalia, Denmark's Muslims are disproportionately poor and unemployed.

In the 2001 election, the extreme right-wing Danish People's Party (DPP) captured 12 percent of the vote, making it the third-largest political party in Denmark's parliament. The DPP's "party program" declares that "Denmark is not an immigrant country and has never been so. Therefore, we will not accept a transformation to a multiethnic society. Denmark belongs to the Danes." According to the DPP's program, "To make Denmark multiethnic would mean that reactionary cultures, hostile to evolution, would break down our so-far stable, homogeneous society." Meanwhile, the Liberal Party, which actually won the 2001 elections, also took an anti-immigration stance, although less virulent than the DPP's. Particularly successful were pro-law-and-order campaign ads showing young Muslim immigrants convicted of rape and their head scarf–wearing relatives screaming at the press. The leader of the Liberal Party, Anders Fogh Rasmussen, focused his campaign on immigration reform, promising to protect Denmark's cradle-to-grave welfare system from exploitation by outsiders. "Denmark must not be the social security office for the rest of the world," he declared.[33]

Part of what makes Islam so difficult for the EU to tolerate is the resistance to assimilation and the violence endorsed by Islamic extremists. The problem of "tolerating intolerance" is one that all Western nations now face. In Europe's case, however, the problem is compounded by the "ghettoization" of its Muslim communities: the fact that from Scandinavia to Spain, despite starkly different approaches to minorities, Europe's Muslims tend overwhelmingly to live in isolated enclaves, separated physically, culturally, and psychologically from their European compatriots.

These enclaves—typically slumlike, crime-filled, frustration-ridden housing projects on the outskirts of major cities such as Marseilles or Amsterdam—are not only poor vehicles for assimilation into the larger society. They are breeding grounds for militant Islam, as witnessed by the popularity of bin Laden posters in teenage bedrooms in French Muslim apartments and the terrorist cells recently uncovered in Madrid, Hamburg, Frankfurt, Milan, and London.[34]

Europe's difficulties with its immigrant, and especially Muslim, communities do not seem to be abating. On the contrary, the headlines of violence and unrest have grown more ominous, from the 2004 Madrid train bombings; to the murder of Dutch filmmaker and critic of Islam Theo van Gogh; to the 2005 race riots in France; to the "cartoon jihad" that began in Denmark and quickly spread throughout Europe and the Middle East; to the London Tube bombings that left fifty-two dead; to the foiled 2006 plot by British Pakistani Muslims to detonate liquid explosives on multiple airliners over the Atlantic. Ironically, while Americans presumably remain the primary object of extremist Islamic hatred, the consensus is now that the United States has a done a better job than Europe integrating its Muslim communities, thereby staving off, at least so far, the problem of "homegrown" Islamic terrorism.

––––––––––

The EU's "Muslim problem" profoundly shapes and complicates current European attitudes toward not only immigration but the eventual size and nature of the Union itself. While in theory the enlargement of the EU has no inherent geographical limits, there are important real-world constraints on the EU's expansion. Turkey's accession negotiations have slowed down considerably, with France and Austria insisting that Turkey's "special" circumstances require new procedures—specifically, popular referenda—before accession can be permitted. And certainly the EU has no present plans for trying to incorporate, say, India, with its immense and overwhelmingly poor, non-Christian population.

These practical limits on the EU's expansion, together with the resistance to immigration prevalent in many EU nations, leave Europe in one respect at a significant disadvantage relative to the United States. Despite its phenomenal successes, the EU has not found a way to attract and exploit the most valuable human capital from all over the world. It remains, by comparison to the United States, less open and less appealing to the enterprising, tech-savvy young talent from India, Pakistan, Russia, Israel, Taiwan, China, and elsewhere who are looking to leave their home countries and capitalize on their skills.

On the other hand, there are signs on the horizon that the United States cannot take its advantage for granted. For example, perhaps because of 9/11 and the plethora of new European scholarships and free tuition packages, Europe today attracts almost twice as many foreign students as does the United States. Nevertheless, the United States remains by far the world's leading single-country destination for foreign students, particularly attractive to students from China, India, and elsewhere in Asia.[35]

On a more personal level, I asked a Yale Law student of Indian descent, who spent the summer of 2006 in India, to conduct a series of interviews for me. The interviewees included small-business owners, students, bank employees, technology consultants, and other upwardly mobile Indians in Mumbai, Bangalore, and New Delhi. They were questioned about their perceptions of relative economic opportunity around the world. One question was whether the United States, the EU, or Canada offered better prospects for Indian immigrants. Here is a representative sampling of their responses:

Europe is less attractive than the U.S. for Indians. Except for England, the countries are not welcoming. The culture just does not match with ours, and we cannot speak their languages.

Europe offers fewer opportunities. People are crazy for the U.S. The U.S. has much more opportunity; it is easier to survive because of the system—it is a full-fledged democracy. The language makes it easier. And people in Europe are more racist.

Canada is big and half of it is covered in snow. . . . The U.S. obviously offers more opportunities. But there are a few industries in Canada that I think do well globally, like steel.

Still, even for that I wouldn't want to work there. They have very little vegetarian food.

Canada is still considered and referred to as a subnation and only in relation with the U.S. It has still to develop an identity of its own.

Europe will offer more opportunities in time, but not yet. The EU is taking a much more proactive approach in investing and in establishing and promoting trade and commerce. But there are language barriers.

Europe is a very very costly state. Therefore the opportunities are not often looked to by Indian people. Also India and the U.S. have better financial and cultural ties.

[Europeans] are much more racist against Indians. And the language and the climate are a problem. London is nice, but for work people should go to the U.S.

These responses are obviously not a scientific study, just the impressions of a tiny handful, but they do confirm what a larger body of evidence suggests. At least for now, the United States is still perceived as the place where motivated immigrants can most easily rise, where hard work is most likely to cash out. This is why America continues to draw even *European* brain power rather than vice versa; as of 2004, there were roughly 400,000 European science and technology graduates employed in the United States and very few comparable Americans working in Europe.[36] Of course, from the European perspective, the EU's relatively restrictive immigration policies may not be a bad thing. Like China, the European states have never claimed the goal of turning themselves into multiethnic immigrant societies. Similarly, most Europeans probably favor the slowdown of the EU's expansion. As a postimperial superpower, the EU has no interest in incorporating Russia or the countries of Asia and Africa simply for the sake of enlargement. But if one of the EU's goals is to restore a multipolar world order, these limits may prevent its attainment of that goal. For so long as the EU permits America to remain the destination for the world's most valuable human capital, Europe may be ceding to the United States the global technological and economic edge that has made America a hyperpower.

THE UNDERDOG: INDIA

During the 2006 World Economic Forum in Davos, Switzerland, the Confederation of Indian Industry chose the logo "India Everywhere." And in Davos, India *was* everywhere. India's slogan leapt from buses and billboards, Indian delegates handed out free iPods with Bollywood's latest hits, and members of the Indian government known to economists as India's "Dream Team" lauded their country's prospects with potential investors. During the final social extravaganza, the chairman of the forum, Klaus Schwab, donned an Indian turban and shawl while discussing Indian investment opportunities against the backdrop of an electric-blue Taj Mahal. "No country," *Newsweek* announced in its coverage of Davos, "has [so] captured the imagination of the conference and dominated the conversation as India in 2006."

India's success at the World Economic Forum has added to the growing talk of India as the next potential world superpower. With an annual crop of 400,000 graduates in technology and engineering, a large English-speaking professional base, and an economy booming with an average of 7 percent growth for the past four years running, India, according to many pundits, politicians, and investors, has become the power to watch in the twenty-first century.[37]

India's economic star began rising in the early 1990s, when finance minister Manmohan Singh slashed government spending and devalued the rupee to prevent the country from defaulting on its international debt. In exchange, Singh, a Cambridge-educated economist, received several billion dollars from the World Bank and the International Monetary Fund. Singh then moved aggressively to eliminate bureaucratic restrictions hampering foreign investment. These moves to liberalize India's economy led to high inflation and an increase in unemployment in the short term. However, within five years, the Indian economy had grown more than it had in the previous forty years. A decade later, *Foreign Affairs* declared India to be "a roaring capitalist success story."[38]

India's success in siphoning off capital and jobs from more developed countries has already begun to rankle Americans. In the 2004 U.S. presidential race, the outsourcing of business and employment to India emerged as a hot-button political issue. Since that time, India has only gotten better at attracting U.S. investment: Today, more than half of the Fortune 500 companies outsource IT work to India. Multinationals such as Intel, IBM, Dell, Motorola, Yahoo!, and AOL all have major operations in India. On average, forty international companies set up business in an Indian city every month. President Bush noted the rise of India and China as new competitors in his 2006 State of the Union address, and in March 2006 he became the fifth U.S. president to pay a state visit to India.[39]

President Bush's March 2006 visit to India highlighted not only the country's economic strength but also its military power. With approximately two million people in its regular and paramilitary forces, India has one of the largest armies in the world. In 1998, India burst into the ranks of nuclear powers by conducting five nuclear tests, but was promptly slapped with economic sanctions by President Clinton. By contrast, President Bush legitimized India's nuclear program by brokering an agreement in which the United States would sell nuclear fuel and reactor components to India (in exchange for India's opening its civilian facilities to international inspections).

Meanwhile, India continues to make world economic headlines. In July 2006, Lakshmi Mittal, the world's fifth-richest man, took over the European steel giant Arcelor. India's leading business newspaper euphorically proclaimed it "The Global Indian Takeover."[40]

Could India become a world-dominant power? I'll begin by

making the best case for India within the terms of my thesis. I'll then address some of the major challenges facing the country.

————————

What is genuinely remarkable about India is not its recent economic upturn, however impressive. Comparatively, India's share of the global economy is still quite small. With 17 percent of the world's population, India accounts for just 2 percent of global GDP and 1 percent of world trade. China's economy is more than twice as large as India's, and in 2005, China received about ten times as much foreign direct investment. In 2006 India's GDP per capita was $3,400 compared to China's $6,300 and Japan's $30,700. More generally, the growth that India has experienced, while significant, fails to place India's standard of living anywhere near that of the major world powers. Some 80 percent of Indians live on about two dollars per day. The United Nations Human Development Index, which assesses countries by factors such as health, income, and literacy, ranks India at 127 out of 177 countries.[41]

Rather, what is singular about India is that it is the world's largest democracy, despite an extraordinary degree of ethnic and religious diversity exceeding even that of the United States. Since its birth as a republic, India has juggled a dizzying array of discrete microcultures, religions, languages, castes, sects, and ethnic and tribal groups. India is home to sixteen official languages, more than twenty-two languages that are spoken by at least one million people, and more than a thousand dialects. India's 2004 national elections featured 230 parties. Although the vast majority of Indians are Hindu (over 827 million), the practice of Hinduism varies widely; indeed, there are thousands of different Hindu castes and subcastes throughout the country. India is also home to 150 million Muslims, the second-largest Muslim population in the world after Indonesia. In addition, Sikhs, Christians, Buddhists, Parsis, and Jains all represent significant minorities in India.[42]

The fact that India exists at all—especially as a democracy—is a triumph of tolerance. Both Mahatma Gandhi and Jawaharlal

Nehru, two of modern India's founding fathers, were leading voices of tolerance in the twentieth century, passionately opposing fundamentalism of any kind. Under their leadership, India from independence strove to balance its religious diversity through pluralistic laws that provide different regulations for members of different religions. India's "personal law," for example, permits polygamy among Muslims but requires monogamy among Hindus. In the last fifty years, India has also made great strides in overcoming the extreme intolerance long directed at so-called untouchables and other "backward" classes.

As the thesis of this book would predict, India's success in holding together and harnessing the talents of an extraordinarily diverse population has paid off handsomely. Indeed, the Nobel Prize–winning economist Amartya Sen has argued that the secret to India's greatness over the centuries lies precisely in its remarkable "heterogeneity" and "openness." For Sen, India's greatest rulers were the emperors Ashoka and Akbar—the former a Buddhist and the latter a Muslim, but both champions of secular tolerance. Almost 2,200 years ago, Ashoka wrote, "For he who does reverence to his own sect while disparaging the sects of others . . . in reality inflicts, by such conduct, the severest of injury on his own sect." Thus, tolerance and pluralism had roots in India, Sen argues, long before the European Enlightenment.[43]

Nevertheless, the state of tolerance in India today is not as happy as this history might suggest. In 1998, the Hindu nationalist Bharatiya Janata Party (BJP) swept into power, calling for the establishment of India as a Hindu state. Frequently referring to Muslims as "invaders" and "outsiders," BJP politicians promised to destroy mosques across the country and replace them with Hindu temples. In states where the BJP won electoral majorities, it used its new power to restrict Hindu-Muslim marriages, suppress Christian missionaries, and rewrite history textbooks to reflect the view of India as a Hindu state.

In 2002, India saw its worst outbreak of religious violence in recent decades. More than two thousand Muslims were massacred in cold blood in the northern state of Gujarat. The violence was sparked by an attack by Muslim militants on a train containing Hindu pilgrims from Ayodhah, where, more than a decade earlier, saffron-robed Hindus had destroyed a venerated mosque and looted and burned the surrounding area in a surge of anti-Muslim riots. The Muslim attack on the train killed at least fifty-eight people.

In retaliation, Hindu civilians and police engaged in a four-day killing spree, looting shops, burning homes, and gang-raping Muslim girls and women. The violence against Muslim women was particularly grotesque, with rioters cutting off breasts and, in some cases, ripping fetuses out of pregnant women's bellies before killing the women. The violence was at least partly state-sponsored; police officers and the National Volunteer Corps led the raids. It was also carefully organized. Rioters identified Muslim homes using computer printouts listing Muslim families and addresses, and they coordinated their attacks through the use of cell phones. Afterward, the BJP government denied that the attacks had occurred, and designated many of the dead as "missing" despite the uncovering of mass graves. The violence had repercussions across the region, resulting in the displacement of more than 100,000 Muslims into refugee camps.[44]

Although the BJP was defeated in the 2004 national elections, Hindu nationalism remains a potent force in Indian politics. Tensions between Hindus and Muslims, along with the specter of religious violence, continue to simmer. In 2004, India was the site of 44 percent of the deadlist terrorist attacks around the world. In a 2006 survey, 17 percent of Indian university students cited Hitler as a model for the leader of India.[45] Thus, despite the inclusive ideals championed by Gandhi and Nehru, whether India is in fact today—or will remain in the future—one of the world's most tolerant societies is an open question.

Moreover, even if India avoids further sectarian strife and remains a stable, multiethnic democracy, it is still hardly a magnet for the world's most enterprising success-seekers. On the contrary, for many Indians who compare their situation with those of their more prosperous counterparts overseas, the old adage continues to ring true: Indians can succeed everywhere in the world except India itself. Despite India's recent economic strength, Indians continue to emigrate at high rates. In 2004, nearly 70,000 Indians emigrated to the United States, composing the second-largest group of new legal immigrants to the United States. Many of these Indians never return permanently to their home country, and they invest in India at a far lower rate than, for instance, their Chinese diaspora counterparts. For the Indians who "cast their vote with their feet" by expatriating, India has far to go before it can match the opportunities that countries such as the United States or the United Kingdom offer for the ambitious and talented.

There is certainly reason to be optimistic in India. India has a large base of educated graduates ready to take on the next wave of economic growth. Whereas the EU's population is aging, half of India's population is under twenty-five years old. In contrast to China, the growth of which has been powered largely by manufacturing, India's most booming sectors are software, information technology, media, advertising, and Bollywood—areas that all rely heavily on creativity and individual talent.[46] As a result, there are possibilities of upward mobility in contemporary India that were unimaginable a couple of decades ago: Today, members of the so-called untouchable caste are managers in prominent technology firms. And for the first time in history, small numbers of noncolonizing middle-class Westerners are moving to India for better jobs than their own countries can offer. Even so, India would have to overcome many intractable problems—pervasive rural poverty, disease-filled urban slums, entrenched corruption, and egregious maternal mortality rates, just to name a few—before significant streams of the world's best and brightest would even think of moving to India.

In sum, India has made tremendous strides. Some of its achievements since independence, such as its progress in dismantling a centuries-old caste system and its success in maintaining a diverse democracy that is the world's largest, are historically unprecedented. These achievements probably explain why India has become a kind of darling to so many commentators on globalization. Perhaps, as some experts have suggested, India's "bottom up" model of development will prove superior in the long run to China's "top down" strategy.[47]

Nevertheless, talk of India's becoming a superpower, let alone a hyperpower, is probably premature. Indeed, India itself does not seem interested in displacing or disrupting U.S. global dominance. On the contrary, as one of the countries in the world most favorably inclined toward the United States—a 2005 poll showed that 71 percent of Indians had a positive view of America[48]—India seems far more interested in becoming partners with the United States in the global economic system.

———————

No hyperpower lasts forever. U.S. world dominance too will come to an end; the only question is how long it will last—if it hasn't passed its zenith already. Even if none of them ever replaces America as a hyperpower, sooner or later China, the European Union, India, or perhaps Russia, Japan, or some other unforeseen rival will, individually or through an alliance, become strong enough to re-create a bipolar or multipolar world order.

Yet asking how long America can remain a hyperpower assumes that world dominance is something the United States ought to try to maintain. The next and final chapter will address this question. Should America seek to preserve its hegemony? Would an American empire be in the best interest of the world—or of the United States itself?

TWELVE

THE DAY OF EMPIRE

Lessons of History

> And the end of all our exploring
> Will be to arrive where we started
> And know the place for the first time.
> —T. S. Eliot, *Little Gidding*

In the suddenly unipolar world that emerged in the last decade of the twentieth century, the only remaining superpower seemed without serious rival or foe. For many, the hard geopolitical choices had melted away. Free markets and democracy, working hand in hand, would transform the world into a community of modernized, productive, peace-loving nations. In the process, ethnic hatred, religious zealotry, and other noxious aspects of underdevelopment would be swept away. It was the "end of history," Golden Arches instead of war.[1] When it came to U.S. military might, the most controversial issues were whether the United States should intervene abroad for purely humanitarian reasons (as in Kosovo or Rwanda) and what America should do with its "peace dividend," the billions of dollars the United States would no longer be spending on its military.

In a way, this optimism was a testament to the great goodwill the United States had built up in the world over the twentieth century, notwithstanding Vietnam or its chronic Latin American misadventures. Here was a society with unthinkable destructive capacity, facing no countervailing power. Yet it seemed to go without saying that the United States would not use its unrivaled force for territorial expansion or other aggressive imperialist ends.

Today, not even twenty years after the fall of the Berlin Wall, this bubble of optimism has burst. Although America remains the world's hyperpower, its goodwill abroad has been all but squandered. Inside the United States, confidence is down and a sense of precariousness pervades, whether the fear is of terrorists, immigrants, or economic downturn. The attacks of 9/11 and the rise of an intensely interventionist U.S. policy changed the whole landscape.

AN AMERICAN EMPIRE?

A year after the 9/11 attacks, in September 2002, the White House issued a new National Security Strategy (NSS), which began as follows: "Today, the United States enjoys a position of unparalleled military strength and great economic and political influence. . . . [T]he United States will use this moment of opportunity to extend the benefits of freedom across the globe. We will actively work to bring the hope of democracy, development, free markets, and free trade to every corner of the world." So far, the NSS sounded like something the Clinton administration could have issued. As President Clinton declared in 1996: "Because we remain the world's indispensable nation, we must act and we must lead."[2]

But the NSS went further. It also declared that to forestall further terrorist attacks, "the United States, will, if necessary, act preemptively." "We must be prepared to stop rogue states and their terrorist clients before they are able to threaten or use weapons of mass destruction against the United States and our allies." Finally, the NSS formally announced the United States' determination to maintain a unipolar world order: "It is time to reaffirm the essential role of American military strength. We must build and maintain our forces beyond challenge. . . . Our forces will be strong enough to dissuade potential adversaries from pursuing a military build-up in hopes of surpassing, or equaling, the power of the United States."[3]

These sentiments were echoed in various quarters throughout the United States and elsewhere in the period following September 11. Well-known neoconservatives such as Paul Wolfowitz, Richard Perle, and Elliott Abrams—all of whom were influential figures in the Bush administration's decision to go to war in Iraq—argued for an aggressive use of American military might to overturn authoritarian rogue governments, replacing them with democratic regimes, which, it was claimed, would be pro-market, pro-American, pro-peace, and pro-liberty.

Influential liberals also favored the invasion of Iraq. The *New York Times* columnist Thomas Friedman argued that the Iraq war, if "mounted in the right way for the right reasons," could stabilize the Middle East, producing "a decent government in the heart of the Arab-Muslim world." Christopher Hitchens, a longtime contributor to *The Nation,* supported the use of U.S. military force to uproot "fascism with an Islamic face."[4] The question was no longer whether America would use military force abroad but how it would do so—how unilaterally, how preemptively, how unimpeded by other nations' sovereignty or international law.

Talk of an American empire was suddenly on the table, with a swell of voices—both in and outside the United States—increasingly in favor. A month after 9/11, in his much-quoted essay entitled "The Case for American Empire," the former *Wall Street Journal* editor and security expert Max Boot argued that "[t]he most realistic response to terrorism is for the United States unambiguously to embrace its imperial role." Deepak Lal's 2004 book *In Praise of Empires* warned of dire global consequences "[i]f the U.S. public does not recognize the imperial burden that history has thrust upon it, or is unwilling to bear it." Around the same time, in *Colossus,* the British historian Niall Ferguson called on the United States to get over its "imperial denial" and take on the civilizing and modernizing burden that Great Britain had carried in past centuries.[5]

The argument for an American empire—including the vigorous use of U.S. military force to replace dictatorships with free-market and democratic institutions—was perfectly understandable. After World War II, America had deployed its unrivaled military to occupy and democratize Germany and Japan while taking measures to prevent those countries from ever posing a military threat to the United States again. Those postwar exercises in nation building proved enormously successful. Given the horrendous threats of terrorism, why shouldn't post-9/11 America take advantage of its military preeminence to disarm and democratize rogue states in the Middle East? Indeed, why *wouldn't* the United States follow Rome and use its world-dominant power to modernize, civilize, and pacify its enemies?

The almost instantaneous 2003 collapse of Saddam Hussein's regime in Iraq seemed to give further strength to those advocating the aggressive use of American military might for regime change and nation building. But three years later, with American military power looking less and less effective in Iraq, the previously widespread support for the war in the United States had eroded severely. Many who had originally supported the war, both liberals and conservatives, asserted that they had done so solely because of an exaggerated threat of weapons of mass destruction.[6] Perle, long described as one of the architects of the Iraq war, publicly recanted his support for it. President George W. Bush's approval ratings among Americans fell to 31 percent, and in November 2006 the Republican Party lost both houses of Congress. A CBS News poll a month later found that 62 percent of Americans thought it had been "a mistake" to send U.S. troops to Iraq.[7]

What calls for an American empire missed was something crucial: history. There are lessons in the rise and fall of hyperpowers past—lessons reflecting both the similarities and differences between the United States and the world-dominant powers that preceded it. Over the centuries, there has been a slow but relentless transformation in what it means—and what it takes—to be a hyperpower. Reduced to its simplest terms, this transformation has been a shift from conquest to commerce, from invasion to immigration, from autocracy to democracy. At the same time, notwithstanding this transformation, there is one fundamental challenge that all hyperpowers necessarily confront—the problem that I have called "glue." Because of the changed nature of world dominance today, the United States confronts this ancient problem in a modern form. It is this combination of old and new that holds the key to understanding the prospects of American power in the twenty-first century.

THE EVOLUTION OF HYPERPOWERS

American world dominance is the result of a long process of evolution in the history of hyperpowers. In ancient times, military power and economic power were linked in a very direct way. The more a society conquered, the wealthier it got, whether by taxing, looting, annexing, or exacting tribute. The Achaemenid kings pulled in the "most valuable possessions" and "productions" of every subjugated kingdom, "whether the fruits of the earth, or animals bred there, or manufactures of their own arts."[8] The Romans gained millions of pounds of silver and gold by conquering Dacia alone. The Mongols, who themselves had no industry or technology, became a hyperpower by conquering the territory and absorbing the wealth of the world's then most advanced civilizations—Persia, China, and the Arab lands.

If the key to wealth was military might, then the key to military might was strategic tolerance. It was through tolerance that pre-modern hyperpowers amassed the most powerful armies, both by successfully enlisting hundreds of thousands of conquered foot soldiers and by recruiting the most skilled warriors and commanders of all backgrounds. Greek mercenaries formed the cream of the Achaemenid military. The Roman legions were filled with Libyans, Syrians, Caledonians, Gauls, and Spaniards. Tang China extended its rule to Afghanistan, Samarkand, and Tashkent only by securing the loyalty of the "barbarian" horsemen from the steppe. The Mongols could not have overcome the great walled cities of central Asia and Europe if they had not drawn into their nomadic ranks the Chinese engineers who built their massive siege engines.

With the dawn of the modern age, economic dominance continued to require military dominance, but the parameters began to change. Naval power became increasingly important. Starting around the fourteenth and fifteenth centuries, technological advances vastly enlarged the reach of the largest, strongest societies. Gold and silver in the faraway Americas, the pepper and spice trades of the Indies, Caribbean sugar, and other so-called rich trades—in coffee, tea, cocoa, textiles, tobacco, jewelry, and other luxuries—from the Baltics to the Mediterranean to Africa became the new, dazzlingly lucrative prizes. Suddenly, the key to wealth and world dominance lay in control over the world's navigable waters, as the Dutch and British were to prove.

But as the levers of global wealth shifted from land to sea, and from conquest to commerce, the link between military and economic power began to shift as well. Invasion, occupation, and annexation were no longer essential prerequisites for a hyperpower seeking to reap the riches of faraway lands. Conquest and rule were expensive, and control over trade could be far more efficient.

This was a lesson the Romans had begun to learn the hard way a millennium earlier. The conquest of Dacia (AD 101–106) was in fact the last time that the Roman treasury would reap large profits from the plunder of foreign lands. Yet Rome, "[a] society persistently primed for war, most of whose adult males could expect to see active military duty," continued to field its massive legions on missions of conquest and expansion long after the material costs of warfare had far outstripped its benefits.[9]

With the Dutch Republic, the balance between trade and conquest shifted decisively in favor of the former. To an unprecedented degree, the Dutch strategy for global preeminence dispensed with the whole enterprise of conquest and territorial expansion. In the Americas, Africa, and Southeast Asia (with a few exceptions like Java and Ceylon), most of the Dutch "empire" consisted of mere trading outposts, with native peoples and inland cities left largely to their own devices.[10] These outposts were protected by the Netherlands' extraordinary navy, which also did its best to keep out competitor merchants from other European countries, securing the republic its fantastically lucrative commercial monopolies.

For the Dutch, strategic tolerance was just as essential to world dominance as it had been for the ancient hyperpowers, but Dutch tolerance began to assume a radically new and modern form. Tolerance for the ancients essentially meant tolerating conquered peoples: leaving intact their customs and languages, co-opting their elites, and recruiting their best craftsmen and warriors. By contrast, Dutch tolerance turned the Netherlands itself into a magnet, not for conquered peoples but for persecuted religious minorities from all over Europe. Amsterdam in the seventeenth century became the most cosmopolitan city in the world—"a veritable melting pot," in which "Flemings, Walloons, Germans, Portuguese and German Jews, and French Huguenots" all became "true Dutchmen."[11] As a direct result of its immigrants' contributions, the Dutch Republic became the center of world trade, industry, and finance.

For a brief moment in history, the Dutch Republic pointed the way to a new kind of world dominance in which military conquest and colonization could play a much diminished role. But the next hyperpower on the world stage—Great Britain—was as much a successor to Rome as it was to the Netherlands. Like Holland, England became famous for its tolerance at home and thereby attracted immigrants fleeing religious persecution in neighboring countries. But unlike the Dutch, Great Britain took up Rome's civilizing and expansionist mission. The British sought to rule and to legislate over all the immense territories they conquered; Victoria was not only queen of England but empress of India. At the same time, the British rediscovered the ancient formula for imperial expansion, amassing through strategic tolerance enormous armies filled with hundreds of thousands of soldiers native to India and other conquered lands.

It fell to the United States to follow the path the Dutch had charted. Like the Netherlands in the seventeenth century, America's tolerance turned it into a magnet for refugees and others seeking better opportunities. Although the United States certainly has had its imperialist moments, and although its westward expansion was based in part on military conquest, the true key to America's success has always been its ability to attract and reward talented, motivated, and enterprising individuals of all backgrounds. From the beginning, immigration has been the fuel of American wealth and innovation, providing the United States with a continuing human-capital edge that has proven equally decisive in the industrial, atomic, and computer ages. In an important sense, then, the United States is a hyperpower on the Dutch model, but taken to entirely different orders of magnitude. The Dutch Republic was receptive to immigrants; the United States is a nation of immigrants—and thus the first nation of immigrants to rise to hyperpower status. Moreover, like the Dutch but far more so, America built its world dominance not through conquest but commerce.

Historically, while the British were "planting the Union Jack on one territory after another," America for most of the nineteenth century "contented itself with carving out . . . [an] 'empire of the seas'—an informal empire based on trade and influence."[12] In 1942, the historian Rupert Emerson observed, "With the exception of the brief period of imperialist activity at the time of the Spanish-American war, the American people have shown a deep repugnance to both the conquest of distant lands and the assumption of rule over alien peoples."[13]

Even today, as John Steele Gordon writes, "[i]f the world is becoming rapidly Americanized as once it became Romanized, the reason lies not in our weapons, but in the fact that others want what we have and are willing, often eager, to adopt our ways in order to have them too." English is today's dominant global language not because of the threat of U.S. stealth bombers but because of the prospect of U.S. dollars. Notwithstanding the United States' terrifying nuclear arsenal, "[t]he ultimate power of the United States"—like that of the Dutch Republic in the seventeenth century—lies "not in its military," "but in its wealth."[14]

The United States thus represents a kind of culmination in the evolution of hyperpowers. In antiquity, the only way to become the richest society on earth was through military conquest. Today, the links between economic and military power, while still important, are far more attenuated; not even the most hawkish supporter of U.S. militarism calls for the annexation of foreign territories. Commerce and innovation—not plunder and expropriation—have proven to be the greatest engines of wealth creation. At the same time, the face of strategic tolerance has changed, with immigration replacing conquest as the most effective way for a society to incorporate the world's best and brightest.

The good news, then, is the emerging possibility of a much less militaristic form of global dominance in the modern world, which the United States—as the world's economic and technological leader rather than its military overlord—could exemplify in the decades to come. There is, however, a catch. Precisely because of this transformation in what it means to be a hyperpower, the United States today is ill equipped to deal with the one crucial challenge that has confronted every hyperpower in history—and will necessarily confront every hyperpower to come.

THE DEMOCRATIC HYPERPOWER AND THE ANCIENT PROBLEM OF "GLUE"

The United States is not only the first nation of immigrants to become a hyperpower. It is also the first mature universal-suffrage democracy to do so. This is not a coincidence. For all its imperfections, democracy in America has been, in addition to a source of strength and liberty, part of its tremendous appeal to outsiders. Like its relatively open free market system, which has allowed untold numbers to rise economically, the United States' democratic system of government is part of its distinctively modern brand of strategic tolerance, in principle providing Americans of any background, creed, or skin color—and regardless of when they or their families became citizens—an equal opportunity to participate and rise in politics. As such, democracy is part of the formula that has made America the hyperpower it is.

But democracy also imposes limits on America, as compared to hyperpowers of the past. Those calling for an American empire often compare the United States to Rome. This comparison is apt in many ways. Not only was Rome the military and economic giant of its time, but it was astonishingly "multicultural," tolerant both ethnically and religiously up to the highest levels of power. At the same time, alone among the ancient empires, Rome offered a cultural package that was extraordinarily appealing to people throughout its dominions—at least if they weren't slaves. Similarly, the United States today offers a cultural package—blue jeans and baseball, hip-hop and Hollywood, fast food and Frappuccino Light—that is maddeningly attractive to millions if not billions around the world.

But Rome, as we have seen, had an advantage: It could make those it conquered and dominated part of the Roman Empire. Subjugated peoples from Scotland to Spain to West Africa all became subjects of the greatest power on earth. Even more significantly, Rome turned large numbers of conquered men, both elites and common soldiers, into Roman citizens, clothed with the high status and privileges that such citizenship entailed.

The United States can do no such thing. Precisely because it is a democracy, the United States does not try or want to make foreign populations its subjects—and certainly not its citizens. When Americans imagine bringing U.S. institutions and democracy to the Middle East, they are not envisioning the people of Baghdad and Falluja voting in the next U.S. presidential election. Even when the United States invades and occupies other countries, the goal today is never annexation but, at least ostensibly, an eventual military withdrawal, leaving behind a constitutional (and hopefully pro-American) democracy.

During the Cold War, America's support of democratic movements around the world—particularly in the 1980s—was part of a general strategy to counter Soviet influence. This strategy included spreading economic liberalism along with democratic institutions. At that time, resentment of the American superpower was relatively mild, mainly because it represented a clear alternative to the much-more-repressive Soviet system. The collapse of the Soviet Union—the leading obstacle to the spread of free market democracy—could have made the rest of the world more receptive to American leadership.

Instead, the ironic result of the United States' "democratic world dominance" has been rampant, raging anti-Americanism. Today, America faces billions of people around the world, most of them poor, who know that the American dollar is the world's dominant currency, that English is the world's dominant language, that American corporations are the most powerful and visible in the world, and that American brands are the most pervasive and coveted. In the eyes of billions, America is the antithesis of what they are. They are poor, exploited, and powerless, often even over the destiny of their own families. America, in their eyes, is rich, healthy, glamorous, confident, and exploitative—at least if Hollywood, our multinationals, our advertisements, and our leaders are any indication. America is also "almighty" and "able to control the world," whether through our military power, our "puppets" the International Monetary Fund and World Bank, or our formidable economic leverage. In short, large numbers of people all over the world feel dominated by—but no connection or allegiance to— the United States.

This, then, is America's dilemma. Inside its borders, the United States has over time proven uniquely successful in creating an ethnically and religiously neutral political identity capable of uniting as Americans individuals of all backgrounds from every corner of the world. But America does not exert power only over Americans. Outside its borders, there is no political glue binding the United States to the billions of people who live under its shadow.

————

The problem facing the United States is as old as empire itself. The first hyperpower in history, Achaemenid Persia, never solved it. As the Achaemenid Empire expanded, it came to include increasingly diverse peoples, which remained distinct communities under their Persian rulers. The Achaemenid Empire had no overarching political identity; only military might held it together. Indeed, the tolerance that allowed the Achaemenids to assemble their mighty war machine also encouraged their different subject peoples to preserve their own languages, identities, and political affiliations. Less than a century after its founding, the empire was riven by fragmentation and separatist rebellions. When a stronger, more charismatic military leader, Alexander of Macedon, began sweeping through the region, elites throughout the Achaemenid Empire simply switched their allegiances. They were not traitors, because they had never been patriots.

A similar fate befell the Mongols. Through strategic tolerance, Genghis Khan succeeded in creating a single people out of the warring tribes of the Mongolian steppe. Thus Genghis Khan accomplished what Cyrus the Great never did, establishing a new political identity for his people. But this identity—the Great Mongol Nation or "People of the Felt Walls"—extended no farther than the nomadic steppe. Beyond the steppe, the fearful and disdainful populations the Mongols subdued never acquired any affiliation with the empire that swallowed them up. On the contrary, like Khubilai Khan, who embraced Chinese culture and established a Chinese dynasty, or the Mongols of central Asia who embraced Islam, the Mongol khans and courts in foreign lands increasingly assumed the identities of their more civilized subjects. Its armies were the mightiest in the world, but with no common identity to bind together its culturally dissimilar components, the Mongol world empire quickly splintered into four large kingdoms before breaking up altogether.

China's Tang Empire offers another example. In some ways, the story of the Tang is the mirror image of the Mongols'. The conquering Tang emperors were the "civilized" ones; their genius lay in subduing, winning over, and ultimately harnessing the fierce militarism of the "barbarians" beyond China's walls.

What is most remarkable about the great emperors of the early Tang was their attempt to establish a universal empire in which Chinese and barbarians were at least nominally equal. But the political affiliation the Tang emperors offered their non-Chinese subjects was too weak to hold together the disparate groups—Tibetans, Sogdians, and Turks; Muslims, Zoroastrians, and Nestorians—whom the

Tang sought to govern. As with Achaemenid Persia, the tolerance of the Tang rulers eventually worked against them. Because they did not try to impose a "Han" Chinese identity on their non-Chinese subjects, they left intact large subcommunities with distinct cultural, ethnic, and religious bonds. As the Tang Empire reached its zenith, insurrections by non-Chinese peoples spread in all the frontier areas. Tang military commanders of foreign descent increasingly turned on their Chinese overlords.

Of all of history's hyperpowers, Rome came closest to solving the problem of creating a common identity capable of generating loyalty among its far-flung subjects (which goes a long way toward explaining the spectacular longevity of the empire). Through its appealing cultural package and its extension of citizenship to Greeks, Gauls, Britons, and Spaniards alike, Rome managed to "Romanize" vastly different peoples living continents apart. A millennium and a half later, Great Britain was surprisingly successful in this respect too. As late as the 1890s, members of the Indian National Congress cheered whenever Empress Victoria's name was mentioned. Hundreds of thousands of Indian soldiers fought for the British in World War II, and even men like Gandhi and Nehru, the eventual leaders of India's independence movement, were deeply loyal to the crown in their early days, seeing themselves as "above all, British citizens of the Great British Empire."[15]

But democratization inside Great Britain and out caught up to the empire by the late nineteenth and early twentieth centuries. As they struggled with extending the suffrage within the British Isles, the British had no mechanism for, or interest in, making voting citizens out of 250 million Indians, or for that matter any of the empire's other nonwhite colonial subjects. In the end, this limit on British tolerance, together with the increasing costs of imperial rule and the rising demand for self-determination after World War II, tore the empire apart.

In the twenty-first century, the right of all nations to govern themselves, while not always realized, is almost universally recognized. As an ironic result, America's relationship to the peoples it dominates is more analogous to that of Achaemenid Persia than that of Rome or Great Britain. Under Persian hegemony 2,500 years ago, "a Greek felt that he was a Greek and spoke Greek," and "an Egyptian felt that he was an Egyptian and spoke Egyptian."[16] And so it is today under the hegemony of the world's first democratic hyperpower.

The great mistake made by those championing an American empire lies in assuming that the global spread of free markets, democracy, and American products, brands, and consumer culture would somehow "Americanize" other nations, creating common values and even a desire for American leadership. This assumption was as naive as the belief that liberated Iraqis were going to greet American troops with sweets and flowers. Wearing a Yankees baseball cap and drinking Coca-Cola does not turn a Palestinian into an American.

It's one thing for a rising power to make itself a haven for the persecuted and to hold out its institutions of tolerance as an example to be emulated throughout the world. It's an entirely different thing for a global hegemon to take on the task of spreading those institutions to—or imposing them on—the rest of the world without extending American citizenship to foreign populations or in some other way creating a common political identity with them. To the dismay of many well-intentioned Americans, the United States' recent attempts to export Western tolerance, including free markets and democracy, has provoked the resentment and in some cases violent wrath of millions who see it as imperialism and a threat to their way of life.

Anti-Americanism is of course most intense in the Islamic Middle East, where Uncle Sam is often portrayed as blood-spattered and shark-toothed, feasting on the flesh of Muslims. The Saudi princess Reem al-Faisal, granddaughter of the late King Faisal, recently delivered a particularly scathing attack: "How dare America look the rest of the world in the face. . . . It is time for the American nation to acknowledge its crimes and apologize and ask forgiveness from the many people it has harmed. . . . The U.S. should leave Iraq after apologizing for over a million dead after an unlawful embargo and a colonial war which at best is a farce and at worst a crime." In Latin America, even pro-market elites such as Oscar Arias Sanchez, a Nobel Prize winner and former president of Costa Rica, protest that America "wants to tell the world what to do. You are like the Romans of the new millennium."[17] Resentment and distrust of the United States extend beyond the developing world. In 2005, a Pew poll of fifteen major countries outside the United States found that a majority of respondents (both collectively and in each country surveyed) would favor "another country challenging America's global military supremacy."[18] According to a 2007 BBC survey, 51 percent of respondents all over the world believed that the United States had a "negative influence on the world," giving America a less favorable ranking than North Korea, Russia, or Venezuela.[19]

Yet people around the world are not lining up to immigrate to North Korea, Russia, or Venezuela. The truth, particularly in poorer parts of the world, is that attitudes toward the United States are deeply schizophrenic—a perverse blend of admiration and envy on one hand and seething hatred and contempt on the other. For millions of Bolivians, Nigerians, Moroccans, and Indonesians around the world, America is arrogant, greedy, preachy, and hypocritical—but also where they would go if only they could. A student in Beijing summarized this attitude nicely. A few weeks after joining other students in a stone-throwing protest in front of the U.S. embassy, he returned to apply for a U.S. visa. Interviewed by *U.S. News & World Report,* he explained that he was hoping to attend graduate school in America. "If I could have good opportunities in the U.S.," he said, "I wouldn't mind U.S. hegemony too much."[20]

———————

Could a democratic hyperpower such as the United States enter into a political union with the people all over the world whom it dominates? Realistically, it is difficult to see how. To do so, the United States would have to give up either its national identity, its sovereignty, or its hyperpower status.

In theory, for example, America could offer every nation in the world an opportunity to become another state in the United States. Possibly, some nations might accept. But if, say, 234 million Indonesians and 190 million Brazilians were to become American citizens, the United States would be a very different country. In any case, this option is politically inconceivable.

Theoretically, the United States might also throw itself behind a new democratic world government ruled by international institutions under international law. In this scenario, there would still be a hyperpower, but it would not be the United States; it would be the world government to which the United States had ceded authority. Many idealists support a world order of this kind, but at present—especially given the problems plaguing the United Nations and other global institutions—such a scenario is completely unrealistic.

Indeed, if anything, after 9/11 the United States moved in the opposite direction. In the last several years, it refused to join the International Criminal Court; walked away from the Kyoto Protocol on climate change; and invaded Iraq without UN authorization or the support of traditional NATO allies such as France, Germany, and Canada. None of these actions has improved America's status in the world. Unilateralism is especially problematic for a democratic hyperpower. No one ever expected Alexander the Great or Genghis Khan to give weaker nations a say in world affairs. But a democratic hyperpower is supposed to recognize the principle that everyone in the world has a right to participate and prosper in global society. Unfortunately for the United States, it is decidedly not the rest of the world's impression that America respects this principle.

THE LAST HEGEMON

Where does this leave the United States? All the factors so far discussed—the lessons of the old and the face of the new—point in one direction: against an American empire.

As the first nation of immigrants and the first mature democracy to become a hyperpower, the United States confronts a far more limited set of choices than the Romans or even the British. To begin with, it is by no means clear that an American empire would pass democratic muster at home. The effort to sustain the Iraq war, particularly after the exposure of prisoner abuse at Abu Ghraib and the continuing violence in Iraq, quickly exhausted U.S. popular support. Unless there is a stunning turnaround in Iraq, it is unlikely that the American electorate would support continuing aggressively interventionist military policies designed to effectuate regime change and democratization. In this way, Americans are very different from the Victorian British, who took great pride in their imperial role. Perhaps because of their country's own anti-colonial history, most Americans do not wish to see themselves as imperialists—even "enlightened" ones.

At the same time, as a democratic hyperpower, the United States is fundamentally limited in what it can offer to, and take from, foreign populations. Although America has the power to invade foreign countries and topple their governments, as a practical matter it cannot simply seize local resources—Iraqi oil, for example—or annex their territory. The United States can (and does) offer ballot boxes, model constitutions, troop training, weapons, and billions of dollars in loans and aid. But it cannot (and does not want to) turn these foreign populations into Americans. Yet without some kind of "glue," America has no means of overcoming the hostile, disintegrative forces that quickly tore apart Achaemenid Persia, the Great Mongol Empire, Tang China, and every other hyperpower in history that was unable to forge a common political identity that bound the central power with the peoples it dominated.

Moreover, democracy rests ultimately on legitimacy and consent. An "enlightened" or "liberal" empire may be an impossible feat, precisely because it requires an element of coercion inconsistent with democratic ideals. In June 2003, for example, L. Paul Bremer III, the head of the American military occupation in Iraq, unilaterally canceled local elections, even though the Iraqis were eager and ready to vote. Mr. Bremer based his decision on the grounds that conditions in Najaf were not yet appropriate for elections. A senior official in his office elaborated: "The most organized political groups in many areas are rejectionists, extremists, and remnants of the Ba'athists. . . . They have an advantage over the other groups." Not surprisingly, the barring of elections in Najaf, as well as later postponements of elections elsewhere in the country, produced tremendous anger at America throughout Iraq. This anti-Americanism—not to mention the continuing bombings and beheadings—in turn fueled a wave of hostility within the United States against the "ungrateful" Iraqis and "hopeless" Middle Easterners generally.

It is hard to imagine how an American empire could possibly flourish or even serve United States interests. In today's world, an aggressively militaristic hyperpower incurs massive costs—whether measured in terms of money spent, lives lost, legitimacy squandered, or hatred provoked—without any of the benefits that accrued to empires of the past. The face of an American empire is present-day Iraq: hundreds of thousands of U.S. troops caught far from home in the middle of a sectarian war, disliked and targeted on all sides, with no obvious upside or even concrete objective in sight.

To be clear, this is not an argument for America to embrace pacifism or isolationism. The battle against terrorism may require strong military measures, and the United States could, if it chooses, deploy its armed forces on limited humanitarian missions to prevent ethnic cleansing or other crimes against humanity. The argument rather is against empire building—the use of America's world-dominant military abroad to achieve regime change and remake other nations by imposing American-style institutions. At the same time, trumpeting the United States' intention to maintain its global hegemony at any cost, including through military means, has only hurt our standing among other nations.

Instead, the United States would be better off following the formula that served it so well for more than two hundred years. America pulled away from all its rivals by turning itself into a magnet for the world's most energetic and enterprising; by creating a society in which individuals of all ethnicities and backgrounds have an opportunity to rise; by rewarding talent and ingenuity no matter what its source; and finally, with a few notorious exceptions, by shrewdly avoiding unnecessary, self-destructive military entanglements and expansionist adventures overseas. The United States would be far truer to its own history and principles striving to be an exemplar for the world—a "city on a hill"—rather than arrogating to itself the Sisyphean task of remaking societies around the world in its own image.

But America in the twenty-first century cannot think of itself only as a city on the hill. Having achieved world dominance, America—like every hyperpower that preceded it—is acutely dependent on the cooperation, the contributions, and the goodwill or at least the acquiescence of the foreign populations it dominates. If anything, America is more dependent on the goodwill of foreign populations than the hyperpowers of the past because the global economy is now so extensively interconnected (billions around the world today are America's consumers, suppliers, investors, and laborers), the right of other countries to govern themselves is so well established (so that even a hyperpower cannot impose its will by direct rule), and weapons of mass destruction can now be transported in a backpack.

Thus the crucial question for the years and decades to come will be whether America can address what I've called the problem of "glue." Given that America cannot generally extend citizenship to foreign populations, are there other mechanisms through which the United States can, without losing its sovereignty, create a sense of shared purpose or even a kind of common identity with the billions of people around the world it dominates, giving others more of a stake in America's success and leadership?

This challenge underlies and has implications for some of the most contentious issues in American politics today. I will briefly discuss three of these issues below.

Immigration. Perhaps the most obvious place to start is U.S. immigration policy. Despite its legacy as a nation of immigrants, America today harbors deep anxieties about the porousness of its borders. These anxieties are driven by both the threat of terrorism and a wider backlash against the influx of immigrants from Latin America. In his provocative book *Who Are We?*, Samuel Huntington argues that continued immigration, particularly from Mexico, endangers America's unity as well as its core identity as "a deeply religious and primarily Christian country" rooted in "Anglo-Protestant" values. Many, including recent presidential candidates and television hosts, have followed Huntington's lead. CNN's highly popular Lou Dobbs, for example, has warned against the "army of invaders" from Mexico, stealing America's jobs, infecting the country with leprosy, and plotting to reannex the American Southwest.[21]

It goes without saying that the United States has a right and a need to restrict immigration. No sensible immigration policy would open the floodgates to unlimited foreigners or sacrifice national security. Nevertheless, the recent fear-mongering groundswell to shut down America's borders is triply wrongheaded.

First, if the history of hyperpowers has shown anything, it is the danger of xenophobic backlash. Time and again, past world-dominant powers have fallen precisely when their core groups turned intolerant, reasserting their "true" or "pure" identity and adopting exclusionary policies toward "unassimilable" groups. From this point of view, attempts to demonize immigrants or to attribute America's success to "Anglo-Protestant" virtues is not only misleading (neither the atomic bomb nor Silicon Valley was particularly "Anglo-Protestant" in origin) but dangerous.

Second, a relatively open immigration policy is one of the most effective mechanisms available for creating goodwill and close ties between the United States and non-Americans. It signals America's receptivity to individuals of all backgrounds. It grants almost a million foreigners annually a right to participate directly in American society, with full citizenship the potential reward for their contributions. It allows many millions more to think of America as a home to their relatives and as a place where they themselves might someday live. Even those "left behind" can benefit tangibly from open American immigration policies. In 2005, foreign-born workers in America sent nearly $40 billion back home; the most popular day of the year for these remittances was Mother's Day.[22]

Programs that bring younger foreigners to the United States only temporarily, like the F-visa program for students, can also foster important connections. They offer a glimpse of American society up close and, in many cases, a lifelong identification with an American institution. Above all, they immerse foreign students in American norms and values, which some will carry home with them. Contrary to much thinking after 9/11, such programs can be an effective way to keep Middle Eastern and South Asian students from the radicalism of campuses often dominated by Islamist organizations. To the extent that America seeks to win over the next generation of foreign elites, these opportunities cannot be overlooked.

Third, and most important, like every world-dominant power before it, the United States is a hyperpower today because it has surpassed all its rivals in pulling in and motivating the world's most valuable human capital. Turning its back on immigration would destroy the very underpinnings of its prosperity and preeminence at a time when, in the words of Google vice president Laszlo Bock, "we are in a fierce worldwide competion for top talent unlike ever before." The destructive effects of anti-immigration policies might be felt far sooner than Americans realize. Microsoft founder Bill Gates recently testified before a U.S. Senate committee that the United States' post-9/11 immigration measures are "driving away the world's best and brightest precisely when we need them most."

Bock similarly testified before a House subcommittee that tight visa caps are seriously damaging "the ability of U.S. companies to innovate and create the next generation of must-have products and services. . . . Each and every day we find ourselves unable to pursue highly qualified candidates because there are not enough H-1B visas." Bock added, "Simply put, if U.S. employers are unable to hire those who are graduating from our universities, foreign competitors will. The U.S. scientific, engineering, and tech communities cannot hope to maintain their present position of international leadership if they are unable to hire and retain highly educated foreign talent."[23]

What should America's immigration policy look like in the twenty-first century? Borrowing a page from its own early history and from all the pre-modern hyperpowers, the United States today should pursue a much more aggressive, incentive-based strategy for identifying and attracting immigrants with high-value skills, training, and know-how. At the same time, America should not follow the lead of Germany and other European states in making the recruitment of high-tech workers the sole platform of its immigration policy. Rather, the United States should leave an avenue available to immigrants of all classes and education levels, holding open a significant number of immigration slots in a first-come-first-served or lottery-like system.

Countless immigrants in the past—including some of the most successful, such as Andrew Carnegie and Eugene Kleiner—have demonstrated the potential contributions of those who came to this country "in rags," possessing only the drive and ingenuity that allowed them to reach these shores in the first place. Many today believe that they can tell which immigrant groups are the most desirable, the most likely to contribute to American prosperity, the most intelligent and hardworking. But it should be remembered that some of the most successful minorities in the United States today—for example, Chinese and Jewish Americans—were described as unintelligent and unassimilable a hundred years ago.

Multinationals and Outsourcing. When U.S. companies "go international," establishing headquarters, plants, telemarketing operations, or research and development facilities abroad, Americans are often filled with unease. The patriotism of these "multinationals" is sometimes questioned, and they are accused of "outsourcing" American jobs in their callous pursuit of profit.

Undoubtedly, U.S. corporations globalize for reasons of profit, not patriotism. Ironically, however, the emergence of the multinational U.S. corporation and even the growth of outsourcing may do more good for America than is commonly recognized.

The usual defense of "outsourcing" is purely economic. Taking advantage of cheaper foreign labor, it is said, will allow our corporations to save American consumers money and increase American shareholders' returns. (Against this, opponents object that corporations are not paying the costs suffered by Americans who lose their livelihoods.) But the multinational operations of U.S. corporations can produce important noneconomic benefits for America as well.

The most successful hyperpowers of the past invariably found ways to co-opt and enlist the services of local elites, providing these elites with a stake in the hyperpower's success and a sense of identification with its institutions. This "glue" was essential to their strength and longevity. America, as we have seen, does not have a foreign legion or civil service that it can staff with native-born populations. It does, however, have Google India and Microsoft Ukraine, which can serve as twenty-first-century analogs. If America cannot give foreigners prestigious governmental or military positions—as Rome and, to some extent, Great Britain did—it can give them prestigious and lucrative positions in its corporations.

Not every outsourced job will produce the "glue" that America needs; it is much debated whether low-wage garment workers at American-owned factories in Guatemala feel on the whole stronger or weaker ties to the United States as a result of their employment. But for those foreigners who obtain well-paid jobs in American-owned enterprises, and especially for those who become managers and executives, U.S. multinationals can unquestionably provide people outside the country's borders with a sense of gain from America's prosperity, a real stake in America's continued growth, and an affiliation with America's institutions. It is no coincidence (although other factors of course contribute as well) that India, one of the chief beneficiaries of U.S. outsourcing, is also one of the few countries in which popular attitudes toward America have remained strongly positive.

Unilateralism and Multilateralism. The Iraq war has left Americans profoundly uncertain about their role in world affairs. On one hand, the "go it alone" attitude of the early Bush administration has been deeply discredited, based as it seems to have been on painfully overconfident premises about America's ability to achieve geopolitical objectives through sheer military might. On the other hand, the war has caused some Americans to feel that the United States would be best served by hardening its borders, erecting fences, and in general getting out of the geopolitical business.

Like it or not, as a world-dominant power, America no longer has the luxury of isolationism. Nor can America rely on commerce as its sole source of global solidarity; multinationals like General Electric and Google, however enlightened, cannot be the only institutions representing America on the world stage. As this book has argued, the United States should avoid the self-destructive perils of empire building, but America can and should take an aggressive leadership role in those genuinely global problems that can be solved, if at all, only by collaboration among nations.

Environmental degradation is a prominent example of just such a problem. No matter what pollution regulations are enacted in the United States, if other countries destroy the ozone layer, America will suffer the effects along with everyone else. In other words, protecting the environment presents a classic collective-action problem. Every country needs the cooperation of others in order to achieve results. Many hazards have a similarly international face today. With the mobility of goods and persons at unprecedented levels, infectious diseases like avian flu cannot be dealt with by any one country acting alone. Famine and genocide in faraway countries can have spill-over effects, with tens or hundreds of thousands of refugees fleeing across borders. And terrorism, of course, has taken on worldwide dimensions, too.

In all these areas, the United States must look for ways to foster multilateral, coordinated campaigns with other nations. This does not necessarily mean working within the confines of the existing international legal and political framework, which is centered on the United Nations. The UN may be useful, but the United States might also pursue bilateral or multilateral agreements with like-minded countries outside the UN framework, or even create brand new international institutions.

Americans should regard this new multilateralism not as a surrender, but as an opportunity. By acknowledging how it contributes to the existence of these global problems, by recognizing how much it stands to gain from their solution, and by assuming a leadership role in international efforts to deal with them, the United States can advance its own interests while also creating the solidarity it needs with other nations—the sense of affiliation and common purpose that a democratic hyperpower cannot do without.

In 1997, at the age of ninety-three, my mother's father became a U.S. citizen. There was no need for him to do so. He was already a permanent resident, having lived in the United States for forty years. Nevertheless, although feeble and practically deaf, my grandfather had insisted on taking the U.S. citizenship test. At the celebration dinner, I asked him why getting citizenship was so important to him. He replied, in his heavily accented English, "Because America has given me so much." This amazed me. His time in the United States had been spent working incredibly hard at a struggling Asian grocery store and then delivering newspapers until he was ninety (he was a great favorite in the neighborhood because he never missed a day). My grandfather then added, "This is the greatest country! Everyone wants to be American!"

My parents remember the same admiration of Americans when they were living in the Philippines in the 1950s and 1960s—it was part of what made them so eager to immigrate—and I remember it while traveling in China and Europe with my parents in the 1970s and 1980s. Today while traveling in other countries with my own family, I wish that my two daughters could hear the same views of America that always made me so proud. Sadly, they don't.

What will the twenty-first century bring? America's chief rivals face many obstacles of their own, but, simply by virtue of their growing strength (whether individually or through alliances), the United States may well cease to be world dominant in the near future. A return to superpower status is not necessarily a bad result for the United States. Being a hyperpower, after all, is a historical anomaly and brings costs as well as benefits.

On the other hand, the United States remains today in many ways a paragon of strategic tolerance. If America can rediscover the path that has been the secret to its success since its founding and avoid the temptations of empire building, it could remain the world's hyperpower in the decades to come—not a hyperpower of coercion and military force, but a hyperpower of opportunity, dynamism, and moral force.

ACKNOWLEDGMENTS

My parents, Leon and Diana Chua, were the inspiration for this book; I would like to thank them as well as my sisters, Michelle, Katrin, and Cynthia, for their unflagging support over the years. Nor could this book have been written without the help and guidance of my husband, Jed Rubenfeld, who for the last fifteen years has read every word I've written; I am the fortunate beneficiary of his generosity and genius. I am also deeply grateful to my editor, Adam Bellow, and my colleagues Jack Balkin, Daniel Markovits, James Whitman, and especially Bruce Ackerman, all of whom provided brilliant criticisms and suggestions at crucial stages. Their contributions have made this a far better work; any remaining errors are of course mine alone. YiLing Chen-Josephson and Russell Pittman both read the manuscript in its entirety and offered incisive comments; they have my sincere gratitude. I would also like to thank Walter Austerer, Ian Ayres, R. J. Contant, Henry Hansmann, Tony Kronman, Susan Rose-Ackerman, Marina Santilli, Jordan Smoller, and Sylvia Smoller for their encouragement and critical interventions.

This book reflects the invaluable help of numerous research assistants. In particular, I would like to thank Jonathan Baum, Max Helveston, Eleni Martsoukou, Hari O'Connell, Patrick Toomey, Julie Wilensky, and Julie Xu, each of whom devoted dozens, in some cases hundreds, of hours to this book. Aditi Banerjee, Wei-Tseng Chen, Nusrat Choudhury, Stephen Clowney, Neha Gohil,

Seth Green, Jean Han, Vijay Jayaraman, Eunice Lee, Stephen Lilley, Brian Netter, Marc Silverman, Elizabeth Stauderman, Ting Wang, and Marcia Yablon were remarkable students in a seminar I taught in Spring of 2004; I am very grateful for the insights they provided during this book's formative stages. The following former students also provided critical assistance on particular chapters: Patricia Adura-Miranda, Werner Ahlers, Zack Alcyone, Chris Bebenek, Michael Bretholtz, Nishka Chandrasoma, Jinhua Cheng, Dennis Clare, Elbridge Colby, Jose Coleman, Rohit De, Hugh Eastwood, Kenneth Ebie, Yunlong Gao, James Grimmelman, Josh Hafetz, Ethel Higonnet, Mimi Hunter, Eisha Jain, Shruti Ravikumar Jayaraman, Svilen Karaivanov, Lara Kayayan, Abha Khanna, Aaron Klink, Nancy Liao, Katherine Lin, Sarah Lipton-Lubet, Anna Manasco, Elliott Mogul, Alex Parsons, Intisar Rabb, Jeremy Robbins, Nick Robinson, Brian Rodkey, Erin Roeder, Saleela Salahuddin, Jeff Sandberg, Martin Schmidt, Tim Schnabel, Vance Serchuk, Shahrzad Shafaghiha, Jingxia Shi, Fredo Silva, Bart Szewczyk, Krishanti Vignarajah, Clarence Webster, Carine Williams, Shenyi Wu, and Justin Zaremby.

In addition, I would like to express my gratitude to Dean Harold Koh of the Yale Law School for his support and friendship; Gene Coakley and Theresa Cullen for their amazing library assistance going far above and beyond the call of duty; my assistant, Patricia Spiegelhalter, for her unsurpassed efficiency; and my exceptional agents, Glen Hartley and Lynn Chu.

The preface to this book is adapted from an essay entitled "Asian Immigration," which originally appeared in David Halberstam, ed., *Defining a Nation: Our America and the Sources of Its Strength* (Washington, D.C.: National Geographic, 2003).

Last, apologies, love, and thanks to my daughters, Sophia and Louisa, genuinely the pride and joy of my life.

NOTES

INTRODUCTION

1. "To Paris, U.S. Looks Like a 'Hyperpower,' " *International Herald Tribune*, Feb. 5, 1999; "France Presses for a Power Independent of the U.S.," *New York Times*, Nov. 7, 1999.
2. Niall Ferguson, *Colossus: The Price of America's Empire* (New York: Penguin, 2004), pp. 301–2.
3. See, for example, Noam Chomsky, *Hegemony or Survival: America's Quest for Global Dominance* (New York: Henry Holt and Company, 2003); Patrice Higonnet, *Attendant Cruelties: Nation and Nationalism in American History* (New York: Other Press, 2007).
4. The literature on empires is truly massive. For a tiny sample from just the last several years, see J. H. Elliott, *Empires of the Atlantic World: Britain and Spain in America, 1492–1830* (New Haven: Yale University Press, 2006); Niall Ferguson, *Empire: How Britain Made the Modern World* (London: Allen Lane, 2003); John Steele Gordon, *An Empire of Wealth: The Epic History of American Economic Power* (New York: Harper Perennial, 2004); Valerie Hansen, *The Open Empire: A History of China to 1600* (New York: W. W. Norton, 2000); Michael Hardt and Antonio Negri, *Empire* (Cambridge, Mass.: Harvard University Press, 2001); Dominic Lieven, *Empire: The Russian Empire and Its Rivals* (New Haven: Yale Nota Bene, 2002); Anthony Pagden, *Peoples and Empires* (London: Weidenfeld & Nicolson, 2001); and Colin Wells, *The Roman Empire* (Cambridge, Mass.: Harvard University Press, 2004).
5. Thucydides, *History of the Peloponnesian War*, E. V. Riev, ed., Rex Warner, trans. (New York: Penguin Classics, 1954); see also Victor Davis Hanson, *A War Like No Other: How the Athenians and Spartans Fought the Peloponnesian War* (New York: Random House, 2005); Bernard Grofman, "Lessons of Athenian Democracy: Editor's Introduction," *PS: Political Science and Politics*, vol. 26 (Sept. 1993), pp. 471–74.
6. Edward Gibbon, *The History of the Decline and Fall of the Roman Empire*, vol. 3 (1776; edited and abridged by Hans-Friedrich Mueller, New York:

Modern Library, 2003), pp. 982–83; see also David P. Jordan, *Gibbon and His Roman Empire* (Urbana: University of Illinois Press, 1971), pp. 221–23.

7. Paul Kennedy, *The Rise and Fall of the Great Powers: Economic Change and Military Conflict from 1500 to 2000* (New York: Vintage Books, 1989); Jared Diamond, *Collapse: How Societies Choose to Fail or Succeed* (New York: Penguin, 2005).

8. Post–9/11 writings on the possibility of an American empire include Andrew J. Bacevich, *American Empire: The Realities and Consequences of U.S. Diplomacy* (New York: Penguin, 2004); Ferguson, *Colossus: The Price of America's Empire*, pp. 3, 301–2; Deepak Lal, *In Praise of Empires: Globalization and Order* (New York: Palgrave Macmillan, 2004), p. 215; and Michael Walzer, "Is There an American Empire?" *Dissent* (Fall 2003).

9. Population and territory estimates for both the Aztec and Roman empires vary significantly. For support for the figures I cite, see Richard E. W. Adams, *Prehistoric Mesoamerica* (Boston: Little Brown and Company, 1977), p. 36; Michael E. Smith, *The Aztecs*, 2nd ed. (Malden, Mass.: Blackwell Publishing, 2003), pp. 57–59; Dirk R. Van Tuerenhout, *The Aztecs: New Perspectives* (Santa Barbara: ABC Clio, 2005), pp. 146–48; and Keith Hopkins, "Conquerors and Slaves: The Impact of Conquering an Empire on the Political Economy of Italy," in Craige B. Champion, ed., *Roman Imperialism: Readings and Sources* (Malden, Mass.: Blackwell Publishing, 2004), p. 108.

10. There is a large, multidisciplinary academic literature on the history of tolerance. For a sampling of different perspectives, see Peter Garnsey, "Religious Toleration in Classical Antiquity," in W. J. Sheils, ed., *Persecution and Toleration* (Great Britain: Blackwell, 1984); John Christian Laursen and Cary J. Nederman, eds., *Beyond the Persecuting Society: Religious Toleration Before the Enlightenment* (Philadelphia: University of Pennsylvania Press, 1998); W. K. Jordan, *The Development of Religious Toleration in England*, vol. 1 (London: George Allen & Unwin Ltd., 1932); Wendy Brown, *Regulating Aversion: Tolerance in the Age of Identity and Empire* (Princeton: Princeton University Press, 2006); and Henry Kamen, *The Rise of Toleration* (London: Weidenfeld & Nicolson, 1967). For two excellent collections of essays, on which I relied heavily, see Ole Peter Grell and Roy Porter, eds., *Toleration in Enlightenment Europe* (Cambridge: Cambridge University Press, 2000) and Ruth Whelan and Carol Baxter, eds., *Toleration and Religious Identity: The Edict of Nantes and Its Implications in France, Britain and Ireland* (Dublin: Four Courts Press, 2003).

11. See J.P.V.D. Balsdon, *Romans and Aliens* (London: Gerald Duckworth & Co., 1979), pp. 2, 59–60, 214–15; A. N. Sherwin-White, *Racial Prejudice in Imperial Rome* (Cambridge: Cambridge University Press, 1967), pp. 57–58.

12. See generally Linda Colley, *Britons: Forging the Nation, 1707–1837* (New Haven: Yale University Press, 1992); Colin Haydon, *Anti-Catholicism in Eighteenth-Century England c. 1714–80: A Political and Social Study* (Manchester: Manchester University Press, 1993).

13. Thomas L. Friedman, *The Lexus and the Olive Tree* (New York: Anchor Books, 2000), pp. ix, xvi, 12; see also Francis Fukuyama, *The End of History and the Last Man* (New York: Avon Books, Inc., 1992).

14. See Office of the President, "The National Security Strategy of the United States of America" (Sept. 2002), available at www.whitehouse.gov/nsc/nss

NOTES347

.pdf.; Ferguson, *Colossus*, pp. 3, 301–2; Max Boot, "The Case for American Empire," *Weekly Standard*, Oct. 15, 2001, pp. 28–29; Michael Ignatieff, "The Burden," *New York Times Magazine*, Jan. 5, 2003, p. 22; Paul Johnson, "The Answer to Terrorism? Colonialism," *Wall Street Journal*, Oct. 9, 2001.

15. Ignatieff, "The Burden," p. 22.

16. Thomas Friedman, "Liberal Hawks Reconsider the Iraq War: Four Reasons to Invade Iraq," Slate.com, Jan. 12, 2004; Ignatieff, "The Burden," p. 22.

17. Samuel P. Huntington, *Who Are We? The Challenges to America's National Identity* (New York: Simon & Schuster, 2004), pp. 19–20, 69, 338.

18. Pagden, *Peoples and Empires*, p. 40 (quoting Machiavelli).

19. Immanuel Wallerstein, *Mercantilism and the Consolidation of the European World-Economy, 1600–1750*, vol. 2 of *The Modern World-System* (San Diego: Academic Press, 1980), pp. 38–39.

20. Ferguson, *Empire: How Britain Made the Modern World*, p. 242 (quoting a Victorian-era postage stamp).

PART ONE: THE TOLERANCE OF BARBARIANS

ONE: THE FIRST HEGEMON: THE GREAT PERSIAN EMPIRE FROM CYRUS TO ALEXANDER

Epigraphs: The quote from A. T. Olmstead is from his classic book *History of the Persian Empire* (Chicago: University of Chicago Press, 1948), p. 1. My source for Alexander the Great's quote is Peter Green, *Alexander of Macedon, 356–323 BC: A Historical Biography* (Berkeley and Los Angeles: University of California Press, 1991).

1. Beverly Moon, *An Encyclopedia of Archetypal Symbolism* (Boston: Shambhala, 1991), p. 32; Mehdi Khansari et al., *The Persian Garden: Echoes of Paradise* (Washington, D.C.: Mage Publishers, 1998), pp. 29–32.

2. Pierre Briant, *From Cyrus to Alexander: A History of the Persian Empire*, Peter T. Daniels, trans. (Winona Lake, Ind.: Eisenbrauns, 2002), pp. 175, 201–2, 297–98, 346, 404. Territorial estimates for the Achaemenid Empire vary greatly, ranging from one million to three million square miles. My estimate is from Peter Turchin, Jonathan M. Adams, and Thomas D. Hall, "East-West Orientation of Historical Empires and Modern States," *Journal of World-Systems Research*, vol. 12 (Dec. 2006), pp. 216–29 (2.1 million square miles).

3. Briant, *From Cyrus to Alexander*, pp. 81, 88–89, 168–69, 429–30; Richard N. Frye, *The Heritage of Persia* (London: Weidenfeld & Nicolson, 1962), p. 126; Olmstead, *History of the Persian Empire*, pp. 56, 176–77, 238–47.

4. See Jean-Noël Biraben, "The Rising Numbers of Humankind," *Population & Societies*, no. 394 (French National Institute of Demographic Studies [INED]) (Oct. 2003), pp. 1–4.

5. Olmstead, *History of the Persian Empire*, pp. 16–17.

6. Frye, *The Heritage of Persia*, pp. 2–3, 43–47; Josef Wiesehöfer, *Ancient Persia: From 550 BC to 650 AD* (London: I. B. Tauris Publishers, 1996), p. xi.

7. Briant, *From Cyrus to Alexander*, pp. 18–19; Frye, *The Heritage of Persia*, p. 45; Wiesehöfer, *Ancient Persia*, pp. xi–xii.

8. Briant, *From Cyrus to Alexander*, pp. 5–7; Olmstead, *History of the Persian Empire*, p. 51 (quoting from the Cyrus cylinder).

9. Briant, *From Cyrus to Alexander*, pp. 5–7, 286–93, 1007–8; Wiesehöfer, *Ancient Persia*, pp. 79–88.

10. Briant, *From Cyrus to Alexander*, pp. 15–16; Frye, *The Heritage of Persia*, pp. 78–80.

11. Briant, *From Cyrus to Alexander*, pp. 15–18, 36–37, 40–44; Frye, *The Heritage of Persia*, pp. 78–81; Olmstead, *History of the Persian Empire*, pp. 34–41, 50–51, 59.

12. Briant, *From Cyrus to Alexander*, pp. 71–72, 81; Frye, *The Heritage of Persia*, p. 127; Wiesehöfer, *Ancient Persia*, pp. 7, 57. On satrapies, and the historical debates surrounding them, see Olmstead, *History of the Persian Empire*, p. 59; Wiesehöfer, pp. 59–62.

13. Frye, *The Heritage of Persia*, p. 82; H.W.F. Saggs, *The Might That Was Assyria* (London: Sidgewick & Jackson, 1984), pp. 114–15.

14. Briant, *From Cyrus to Alexander*, pp. 40–44; Frye, *The Heritage of Persia*, p. 81; Olmstead, *History of the Persian Empire*, pp. 52–53; Wiesehöfer, *Ancient Persia*, pp. 44–45.

15. Wiesehöfer, *Ancient Persia*, pp. 43–44.

16. Briant, *From Cyrus to Alexander*, p. 226.

17. Isa. 45:1–3; Ezra 6:2–5.

18. Briant, *From Cyrus to Alexander*, pp. 41, 46–47, 79; Wiesehöfer, *Ancient Persia*, pp. 49–51.

19. Wiesehöfer, *Ancient Persia*, pp. 49–55.

20. Briant, *From Cyrus to Alexander*, p. 55; Olmstead, *History of the Persian Empire*, pp. 87, 92, 129.

21. Briant, *From Cyrus to Alexander*, pp. 57–61; Frye, *The Heritage of Persia*, p. 88; Olmstead, *History of the Persian Empire*, pp. 88–95.

22. Regarding Cambyses' conquests and the creation of the Persian navy, see Briant, *From Cyrus to Alexander*, pp. 51–54, 62. On Cambyses' death, see Briant, p. 61; Olmstead, *History of the Persian Empire*, pp. 92–93.

23. As with many of the Achaemenid kings, there is some dispute about the exact year that Darius acceded to the throne. Most scholars, however, agree that it was between 522 and 520 BC. Briant, *From Cyrus to Alexander*, pp. 139–43, 159–61; Olmstead, *History of the Persian Empire*, pp. 107–8; Wiesehöfer, *Ancient Persia*, p. 15. On the Scythians, see William Montgomery McGovern, *The Early Empires of Central Asia: A Study of the Scythians and the Huns and the Part They Played in World History* (Chapel Hill: University of North Carolina Press, 1939), pp. 36, 47, 49, 56.

24. Briant, *From Cyrus to Alexander*, pp. 165–79, 369–71; J. M. Cook, *The Persian Empire* (London: J. M. Dent & Sons, 1983), pp. 69–70; Frye, *The Heritage of Persia*, p. 116; Wiesehöfer, *Ancient Persia*, pp. 63–65, 76–77.

25. Briant, *From Cyrus to Alexander*, pp. 390–94; Cook, *The Persian Empire*, p. 70.

26. Briant, *From Cyrus to Alexander*, pp. 170–71, 177–78, 507–10; Cook, *The Persian Empire*, pp. 68–69; Wiesehöfer, *Ancient Persia*, pp. 19, 29.

27. Briant, *From Cyrus to Alexander*, p. 77; Cook, *The Persian Empire*, pp. 147–48; Frye, *The Heritage of Persia*, p. 117; Wiesehöfer, *Ancient Persia*, pp. xi, 59, 99. On the debates about the religion of the Achaemenids, see Briant, pp. 93–94; Wiesehöfer, pp. 94–100.

28. Briant, *From Cyrus to Alexander*, pp. 510–11; Olmstead, *History of the Persian Empire*, p. 222.
29. Briant, *From Cyrus to Alexander*, pp. 168, 172; Frye, *The Heritage of Persia*, pp. 100–101, 126.
30. Briant, *From Cyrus to Alexander*, pp. 81, 363; Frye, *The Heritage of Persia*, p. 126.
31. Frye, *The Heritage of Persia*, pp. 108–9. On the close relationship between the Medes and the Persians, see Cook, *The Persian Empire*, pp. 42–43.
32. Frye, *The Heritage of Persia*, pp. 108–9; Olmstead, *History of the Persian Empire*, pp. 238, 247 (quoting Herodotus).
33. Frye, *The Heritage of Persia*, pp. 108–9; Olmstead, *History of the Persian Empire*, pp. 239, 242.
34. Briant, *From Cyrus to Alexander*, pp. 384–87; Frye, *The Heritage of Persia*, pp. 111–12; Olmstead, *History of the Persian Empire*, pp. 243–44.
35. Briant, *From Cyrus to Alexander*, pp. 792–800; Frye, *The Heritage of Persia*, pp. 109–12.
36. Briant, *From Cyrus to Alexander*, pp. 77, 82, 122–23, 180–83; Frye, *The Heritage of Persia*, pp. 107–8. On the migratory habits of the Achaemenids, see Briant, pp. 186–89.
37. Briant, *From Cyrus to Alexander*, pp. 200–201, 289–91.
38. Ibid., pp. 13–14, 200–201, 286–94, 331.
39. Ibid., p. 171.
40. Percy Sykes, *A History of Persia* (London: MacMillan and Co., 1930), p. 169.
41. Briant, *From Cyrus to Alexander*, pp. 543–47, 551, 567–68; Frye, *The Heritage of Persia*, p. 123; Wiesehöfer, *Ancient Persia*, pp. 42–43, 46–47, 52.
42. Briant, *From Cyrus to Alexander*, pp. 543, 549, 554, 567; Wiesehöfer, *Ancient Persia*, pp. 46, 54–55.
43. Briant, *From Cyrus to Alexander*, pp. 687, 769.
44. Ibid., pp. 852–53, 868–69; Guy MacLean Rogers, *Alexander: The Ambiguity of Greatness* (New York: Random House, 2004), pp. 125–27. For vivid accounts of Alexander's military tactics and brilliance on the battlefield, see generally Green, *Alexander of Macedon*; J.F.C. Fuller, *The Generalship of Alexander the Great* (London: Eyre & Spottiswoode, 1958), pp. 285–305. The quote about Alexander's military prowess is from Green, p. xv.
45. Briant, *From Cyrus to Alexander*, pp. 868–69.
46. My description of young Alexander is taken from Green, *Alexander of Macedon*, pp. 54–55. On young Alexander and Aristotle, see Green, pp. 53–54, 58–61; Waldemar Heckel and J. C. Yardley, *Alexander the Great: Historical Texts in Translation* (Malden, Mass.: Blackwell, 2004), pp. 35–39; Rogers, *Alexander: The Ambiguity of Greatness*, pp. 4–5, 8–9.
47. Green, *Alexander of Macedon*, pp. 59–60; Rogers, *Alexander: The Ambiguity of Greatness*, pp. v, xviii, 88–89.
48. My account of Alexander's approach and attitude toward conquered Babylon and Egypt draws heavily on Green, *Alexander of Macedon*, pp. 269–70, 303; see also Rogers, *Alexander: The Ambiguity of Greatness*, pp. 89, 98, 120.
49. Green, *Alexander of Macedon*, pp. 369–70, 446–48; Rogers, *Alexander: The Ambiguity of Greatness*, pp. 171–73, 251–52. Modern scholars began to debate the extent to which Alexander sought a fusion of races after the publi-

cation of W. W. Tarn's 1948 biography, in which Tarn argued that Alexander
had a "unity of mankind" policy. See W. W. Tarn, *Alexander the Great*
(Cambridge: Cambridge University Press, 1948), excerpted in Ian Worthington, ed., *Alexander the Great: A Reader* (London: Routledge, 2003), pp.
198–207. For a strong critique of this view, see A. B. Bosworth, "Alexander
and the Iranians," *Journal of Hellenic Studies*, vol. 100 (1980), pp. 1–21, excerpted in Worthington, pp. 208–35.

50. Green, *Alexander of Macedon*, pp. 453–56, 487–88; Rogers, *Alexander: The
Ambiguity of Greatness*, pp. 213–14, 221–26, 251, 256, 259–61.

51. Green, *Alexander of Macedon*, pp. 473–75; Rogers, *Alexander: The Ambiguity of Greatness*, pp. xvii, 87, 265, 273; Worthington, *Alexander the
Great*, p. 198.

TWO: TOLERANCE IN ROME'S HIGH EMPIRE: GLADIATORS, TOGAS, AND IMPERIAL "GLUE"

Epigraphs: The quote from Claudian can be found in Clifford Ando, *Impe-
rial Ideology and Provincial Loyalty in the Roman Empire* (Berkeley and Los
Angeles: University of California Press, 2000), p. 65. The quote from
Claudius is reproduced in A. N. Sherwin-White, *Racial Prejudice in Imperial
Rome* (Cambridge: Cambridge University Press, 1967), p. 60.

1. "For all its material impressiveness and occasional grossness, the core of the
explanation of the Roman achievement was an idea, the idea of Rome itself,
the values it embodied and imposed, the notion of what was one day to be
called *romanitas*." J. M. Roberts, *The New History of the World* (Oxford:
Oxford University Press, 2003), p. 227.

2. See Anthony Pagden, *Peoples and Empires* (London: Weidenfeld & Nicolson, 2001), pp. 42, 45; and Keith Hopkins, "Conquerors and Slaves: The Impact of Conquering an Empire on the Political Economy of Italy," in Craige
B. Champion, ed., *Roman Imperialism: Readings and Sources* (Malden,
Mass.: Blackwell Publishing, 2004), p. 108. My opening paragraph also
draws on Fergus Millar, ed., *The Roman Empire and Its Neighbours* (New
York: Delacorte Press, 1967), p. 9.

3. See Pagden, *Peoples and Empires*, p. 42; Chris Scarre, *The Penguin Historical Atlas of Rome* (London: Penguin, 1995), pp. 82–83.

4. See Pagden, *Peoples and Empires*, pp. 35–37, 41. The quote from Theodor
Mommsen can be found in Colin Wells, *The Roman Empire* (Cambridge,
Mass.: Harvard University Press, 2004), p. 1.

5. For a detailed discussion of Rome's provincial system and its administration,
see Peter Garnsey and Richard Saller, *The Roman Empire: Economy, Society,
and Culture* (Berkeley and Los Angeles: University of California Press, 1987),
pp. 20–40. On the native backgrounds of the emperors Trajan, Hadrian, Antoninus Pius, Marcus Aurelius, and Septimius Severus, as well as the diversity of Roman elites more generally, see Michael Grant, *The History of Rome*
(London: Faber and Faber, 1979), pp. 236, 238–39; Peter Heather, *The Fall
of the Roman Empire* (London: Macmillan, 2005), p. 44; Christopher S.
Mackay, *Ancient Rome: A Military and Political History* (Cambridge: Cambridge University Press, 2004), pp. 229, 231–35; Pagden, *Peoples and Empires*, pp. 41–42 (quoting Cicero); Wells, *The Roman Empire*, pp. 152
(quoting Tacitus), 170–71; Pierre Grimal, *L'Empire Roman* (Paris: Editions

des Fallois, 1993), p. 133; Géza Alföldy, *Das Imperium Romanum—ein Vorbild für das vereinte Europa?* (Basel, Switzerland: Schwabe & Co. AG Verlag, 1999), pp. 29–30; Basil Kremmydas and Sophocles Marcianos, *The Ancient World–Hellenistic Times–Rome* (Athens: Gnosis Editions, 1985), p. 200. The quote in the section heading beginning "The single native land" is from Pliny and cited in Ando, *Imperial Ideology and Provincial Loyalty in the Roman Empire*, p. 65.

6. See Champion, *Roman Imperialism*, p. 263 (quoting Claudius); Edward Gibbon, *The History of the Decline and Fall of the Roman Empire*, vol. 1 (1776; reprint, London: Allen Lane 1994), p. 64; Millar, *The Roman Empire and Its Neighbours*, p. 149; Pagden, *Peoples and Empires*, p. 40 (quoting Wilson).

7. Garnsey and Saller, *The Roman Empire*, pp. 110–25, 178; Andrew Lintott, *Imperium Romanum: Politics and Administration* (London: Routledge, 1993), pp. 14–15; Roberts, *The New History of the World*, pp. 248–49. My discussion of Roman slavery draws heavily on J.P.V.D. Balsdon, *Romans and Aliens* (London: Gerald Duckworth & Co., 1979), pp. 77–81. On the gore of the gladiator games, see Daniel P. Mannix, *The History of Torture* (Gloucestershire, U.K.: Sutton Publishing, 2003), p. 30.

8. Champion, *Roman Imperialism*, p. 209 (citing Livy and Cicero); Grant, *The History of Rome*, pp. 38, 45, 49–50, 54–55; Roberts, *The New History of the World*, p. 227.

9. Grant, *The History of Rome*, p. 101; Roberts, *The New History of the World*, pp. 234–36; M. Rostovtzett, *Rome*, J. D. Duff, trans. (New York: Oxford University Press, 1960), pp. 41, 76.

10. On Rome's shift from indirect to direct provincial rule and its conquests of Europe, Asia Minor, and the Middle East, see Grant, *The History of Rome*, p. 121; Lintott, *Imperium Romanum*, pp. 9–11, 13–14; Edward Luttwak, *The Grand Strategy of the Roman Empire: From the First Century A.D. to the Third* (Baltimore: Johns Hopkins University Press, 1976), pp. 9–12, 19–25, 49–50, 57, 60–61; Mackay, *Ancient Rome*, pp. 81–84; Roberts, *The New History of the World*, pp. 248–49; Rostovtzett, *Rome*, pp. 76–77. On "government without bureaucracy," see Garnsey and Saller, *The Roman Empire*, p. 20.

11. In his magnum opus, Edward Gibbon characterizes the golden age as the reign of five emperors from AD 96–180: Marcus Cocceius Nerva (AD 96–98), Trajan (AD 98–117), Hadrian (AD 117–38), Antoninus Pius (AD 138–61), and Marcus Aurelius (AD 161–80). Gibbon, *The History of the Decline and Fall of the Roman Empire*, vol. 1, p. 31. Other historians include Marcus Aurelius's successor, Commodus (AD 180–92), as well as Vespasian (AD 70–79), Titus (AD 79–81), and Domitian (AD 81–96). See, for example, Alan K. Bowman, Peter Garnsey, and Dominic Rathbone, eds., *The Cambridge Ancient History*, 2nd ed., vol. 11 (Cambridge: Cambridge University Press, 2000), front page.

12. On Trajan and Hadrian generally, see Anthony R. Birley, *Hadrian: The Restless Emperor* (London: Routledge, 1997); Grant, *The History of Rome*, pp. 236–39; Millar, *The Roman Empire and Its Neighbours*, pp. 42–43; Wells, *The Roman Empire*, pp. 174, 184, 202–7, 285. Specifically on the Jewish rebellion, see Birley, pp. 2, 268–76; Mackay, *Ancient Rome*, pp. 229–31; Roberts, *The New History of the World*, p. 271.

13. My discussion of Antoninus Pius and Marcus Aurelius draws on Anthony R.

Birley, *Marcus Aurelius*, rev. ed. (New York: Routledge, 2000), pp. 37–38, 58–59; Mackay, *Ancient Rome*, pp. 230–35; Roberts, *The New History of the World*, p. 271; Ando Schiavone, *The End of the Past: Ancient Rome and the Modern West* (Cambridge, Mass.: Harvard University Press, 2002), pp. 21–22; Wells, *The Roman Empire*, pp. 213–29.

14. On Rome as a free-trade zone and "global economy," see Garnsey and Saller, *The Roman Empire*, p. 20; Rostovtzeff, *Rome*, pp. 248, 257–63; Alföldy, *Das Imperium Romanum—ein Vorbild für das vereinte Europa?*, p. 33. The quote from Aristides is reproduced in Schiavone, *The End of the Past*, p. 7. There are a number of fascinating scholarly articles exploring the relationship between the Roman and Han Chinese empires. See, for example, H. H. Dubs, "A Roman City in Ancient China," *Greece & Rome*, 2nd ser., vol. 4, no. 2 (Oct. 1957), pp. 139–48, and J. Thorley, "The Silk Trade Between China and the Roman Empire at Its Height, *Circa* AD 90–130," *Greece & Rome*, 2nd ser., vol. 18, no. 1 (Apr. 1971), pp. 71–80.

15. See Montesquieu, *Considerations on the Causes of the Greatness of the Romans and Their Decline*, David Lowenthal, trans. (New York: The Free Press, 1965), pp. 36–37; Rostovtzeff, *Rome*, p. 263; Wells, *The Roman Empire*, pp. 224–26.

16. My discussion of Roman stereotypes draws heavily on two sources: Balsdon, *Romans and Aliens*, pp. 1–2, 59–70, 214–19; and Sherwin-White, *Racial Prejudice in Imperial Rome*, pp. 57–58.

17. See Gibbon, *The History of the Decline and Fall of the Roman Empire*, vol. 1, p. 103.

18. Gibbon, *The History of the Decline and Fall of the Roman Empire*, vol. 1, p. 70; see Garnsey and Saller, *The Roman Empire*, p. 15; Heather, *The Fall of the Roman Empire*, pp. 37, 44.

19. Garnsey and Saller, *The Roman Empire*, pp. 178, 186; Mackay, *Ancient Rome*, p. 258; Montesquieu, *Considerations on the Causes of the Greatness of the Romans and Their Decline*, p. 24; Roberts, *The New History of the World*, pp. 236–40, 250–51.

20. On the empire's linguistic diversity, see Garnsey and Saller, *The Roman Empire*, pp. 186, 189–92; Millar, *The Roman Empire and Its Neighbours*, p. 153; Wells, *The Roman Empire*, pp. 134–35.

21. Garnsey and Saller, *The Roman Empire*, pp. 35, 110–12, 115; Roberts, *The New History of the World*, pp. 249–50; Mackay, *Ancient Rome*, p. 257; Schiavone, *The End of the Past*, p. 6 (citing Aristides); Wells, *The Roman Empire*, pp. 6, 126–29, 142; *Holy Bible*, C. I. Scofield, ed. (New York: Oxford University Press, 1967), Acts 16:35–40, 22:22–29.

22. Balsdon, *Romans and Aliens*, pp. 85–86, 91, 93–95; Garnsey and Saller, *The Roman Empire*, pp. 116–17, 178; Mackay, *Ancient Rome*, p. 257; Millar, *The Roman Empire and Its Neighbours*, p. 196; Roberts, *The New History of the World*, pp. 249–50; Wells, *The Roman Empire*, pp. 9, 116–17, 127–29; G. Woolf, "Becoming Roman: The Origins of Provincial Civilization in Gaul," in *Roman Imperialism*, pp. 231–42. The quote from Aristides is reproduced in Ando, *Imperial Ideology and Provincial Loyalty in the Roman Empire*, p. 58.

23. Sherwin-White, *Racial Prejudice in Imperial Rome*, pp. 3–5, 7, 58–60.

24. See Balsdon, *Romans and Aliens*, p. 82 (quoting Claudius); R. MacMullen,

"Romanization in the Time of Augustus," in *Roman Imperialism*, pp. 215, 223–24.

25. Gibbon, *The History of the Decline and Fall of the Roman Empire*, vol. 1, p. 56.

26. Garnsey and Saller, *The Roman Empire*, pp. 168, 170–73; Grant, *The History of Rome*, pp. 37, 43; Roberts, *The New History of the World*, pp. 254–56.

27. Garnsey and Saller, *The Roman Empire*, pp. 168–73, 202; Millar, *The Roman Empire and Its Neighbours*, pp. 153–54.

28. Champion, *Roman Imperialism*, pp. 272–75; Garnsey and Saller, *The Roman Empire*, pp. 169–70, 173, 202–3; Mackay, *Ancient Rome*, pp. 227–28, 230; Roberts, *The New History of the World*, pp. 263–65, 271. On Julius Caesar and the Jews, see Antony Kamm, *Julius Caesar: A Life* (London: Routledge, 2006), pp. 120–21, 151.

29. Garnsey and Saller, *The Roman Empire*, pp. 174–75; Gibbon, *History of the Decline and Fall of the Roman Empire*, vol. 1, pp. 526, 550; Roberts, *The New History of the World*, pp. 270–72; Wells, *The Roman Empire*, p. 241.

30. On theories of the Roman Empire's decline, see generally Grant, *The History of Rome*, pp. 332–51; Heather, *The Fall of the Roman Empire*, pp. 49–142; Roberts, *The New History of the World*, pp. 276–83; Wells, *The Roman Empire*, pp. 219–21.

31. Pagden, *Peoples and Empires*, p. 46; see also Garnsey and Saller, *The Roman Empire*, p. 178; Grant, *The History of Rome*, p. 324; Mackay, *Ancient Rome*, p. 257; Roberts, *The New History of the World*, pp. 276, 289, 292.

32. Garnsey and Saller, *The Roman Empire*, pp. 174–75; Naphtali Lewis and Meyer Reinhold, *Roman Civilization, Selected Readings*, 3rd ed., vol. 2 (New York: Columbia University Press, 1990), pp. 583–84; Millar, *The Roman Empire and Its Neighbours*, p. 209; Roberts, *The New History of the World*, pp. 271–73; Wells, *The Roman Empire*, p. 243.

33. Edward Gibbon, *The History of the Decline and Fall of the Roman Empire*, vol. 3 (1776; edited and abridged by Hans-Friedrich Mueller, New York: Modern Library, 2003), pp. 982–83; see Grant, *The History of Rome*, pp. 304–5, 308. Gibbon's view of the role Christianity played in Rome's decline has been much debated. For just one helpful analysis, see David P. Jordan, *Gibbon and His Roman Empire* (Urbana: University of Illinois Press, 1971), chap. 7.

34. Averil Cameron, *The Later Roman Empire* (London: Fontana Press, 1993), pp. 52, 56–59, 69, 71–72; Edward Gibbon, *The History of the Decline and Fall of the Roman Empire*, vol. 4 (annotated by Dean Milman and M. Guizot, London: John Murray, Albemarle Street, 1862), pp. 179–80; Grant, *The History of Rome*, pp. 308, 311–12, 348; Lewis and Reinhold, *Roman Civilization*, p. 584; Millar, *The Roman Empire and Its Neighbours*, pp. 240–41, 246–48; Montesquieu, *Considérations sur les Causes de la Grandeur des Romains et de Leur Décadence* (Paris: GF Flammarion, 1968), p. 162; Roberts, *The New History of the World*, pp. 287, 294–97.

35. Gibbon, *The History of the Decline and Fall of the Roman Empire*, vol. 1, pp. 1046–51; Grant, *The History of Rome*, pp. 324, 343; Heather, *The Fall of the Roman Empire*, pp. 186, 211–12, 215; Roberts, *The New History of the World*, pp. 291–93, 294.

36. Grant, *The History of Rome*, pp. 324–26, 343–45, 352–56; Heather, *The Fall of the Roman Empire*, pp. 211–12, 215–28; Roberts, *The New History of the World*, pp. 292–94, 301–11.

THREE: CHINA'S GOLDEN AGE: THE MIXED-BLOODED TANG DYNASTY

1. See generally Arthur F. Wright and Denis Twitchett, *Perspectives on the T'ang* (New Haven: Yale University Press, 1973), pp. 1–2, 29, 37–43.

2. Jacques Gernet, *A History of Chinese Civilization*, J. R. Forster, trans. (Cambridge: Cambridge University Press, 1989), pp. 73–100, 680–84; Charles O. Hucker, *China's Imperial Past* (Palo Alto: Stanford University Press, 1975), pp. 37–40; see generally Wing-Tsit Chan, ed. and trans., *A Source Book in Chinese Philosophy* (Princeton: Princeton University Press, 1963).

3. Hucker, *China's Imperial Past*, pp. 21, 43–45; Conrad Schirokauer, *A Brief History of Chinese and Japanese Civilizations*, 2nd ed. (New York: Harcourt Brace & Co., 1989), pp. 51, 53.

4. Yihong Pan, *Son of Heaven and Heavenly Qaghan: Sui-Tang China and Its Neighbors* (Bellingham, Wash.: Western Washington University, 1997), pp. 18–24; Edwin G. Pulleyblank, "The An Lu-shan Rebellion and the Origins of Chronic Militarism in Late T'ang China," in *Essays on Tang and Pre-Tang China* (Hampshire, U.K.: Ashgate, Aldershot, 2001), pp. 33, 36–37; Denis Sinor, ed., *The Cambridge History of Inner Asia* (Cambridge: Cambridge University Press, 1990), pp. 4–5.

5. Hucker, *China's Imperial Past*, pp. 135–36, 141; Pan, *Son of Heaven and Heavenly Qaghan*, pp. 3–4, 169, 231–35.

6. Edmund Capon, *Tang China: Vision and Splendour of a Golden Age* (London: Macdonald & Co., 1989), pp. 52–53; Valerie Hansen, *The Open Empire: A History of China to 1600* (New York: W. W. Norton, 2000), pp. 153–57.

7. Hansen, *The Open Empire*, pp. 175–84; Hucker, *China's Imperial Past*, p. 140; Pan, *Son of Heaven and Heavenly Qaghan*, p. 31.

8. Hucker, *China's Imperial Past*, p. 140.

9. Pan, *Son of Heaven and Heavenly Qaghan*, p. 181–82 (citation omitted); Pulleyblank, "The An Lu-shan Rebellion," p. 38.

10. Pan, *Son of Heaven and Heavenly Qaghan*, p. 182 (citation omitted); Pulleyblank, "The An Lu-shan Rebellion," p. 38.

11. Edward Schafer, *The Golden Peaches of Samarkand: A Study of T'ang Exotics* (Berkeley and Los Angeles: University of California Press, 1963), pp. 1, 28–29, 43–57, 81–86, 91, 134–39, 144–62, 176–84.

12. Capon, *Tang China*, pp. 39, 59, 74–75; C. P. Fitzgerald, *China: A Short Cultural History* (New York: Frederick A. Praeger, 1954), pp. 287–88, 336–37; Pan, *Son of Heaven and Heavenly Qaghan*, pp. 37, 215.

13. Tansen Sen, *Buddhism, Diplomacy, and Trade: The Realignment of Sino-Indian Relations, 600–1400* (Honolulu: Association for Asian Studies and University of Hawai'i Press, 2003), pp. 46–49.

14. Capon, *Tang China*, pp. 61–63; Hansen, *The Open Empire*, p. 205.

15. Capon, *Tang China*, pp. 59, 62–63; Fitzgerald, *China: A Short Cultural History*, p. 336.

16. Capon, *Tang China*, pp. 26–27; Gernet, *A History of Chinese Civilization*,

pp. 244–45; Schirokauer, *A Brief History of Chinese and Japanese Civilizations*, p. 104.

17. Capon, *Tang China*, pp. 32–33; Fitzgerald, *China: A Short Cultural History*, pp. 297–98; Gernet, *A History of Chinese Civilization*, pp. 256–57; Hansen, *The Open Empire*, pp. 199–202; Hucker, *China's Imperial Past*, p. 142.

18. Hansen, *The Open Empire*, pp. 199–202; Sen, *Buddhism, Diplomacy, and Trade*, pp. 56, 87–97.

19. Capon, *Tang China*, pp. 27, 32–33; Gernet, *A History of Chinese Civilization*, p. 257; Hansen, *The Open Empire*, pp. 206–7; Wright and Twitchett, *Perspectives on the T'ang*, pp. 47–49, 64.

20. Hansen, *The Open Empire*, pp. 200, 202.

21. Fitzgerald, *China: A Short Cultural History*, p. 325; Hansen, *The Open Empire*, pp. 191, 206, 208.

22. Wright and Twitchett, *Perspectives on the Tang*, p. 1.

23. Fitzgerald, *China: A Short Cultural History*, pp. 330–31. On the protection the Tang court offered Uighur Manichaean priests, see Colin MacKerras, "Uygur-Tang Relations, 744–840," *Central Asian Survey*, vol. 19, no. 2 (2000), pp. 223, 224, 226–27.

24. Fitzgerald, *China: A Short Cultural History*, p. 329; G. R. Hawting, *The First Dynasty of Islam: The Umayyad Caliphate AD 661–750*, 2nd ed. (London: Routledge, 2000), pp. 2–3; William H. McNeill, *The Rise of the West: A History of the Human Community* (Chicago: University of Chicago Press, 1963), p. 418; Bat Ye'or, *The Dhimmi: Jews and Christians Under Islam*, trans. David Maisel, Paul Fenton, and David Littman (Rutherford, N.J.: Fairleigh Dickinson University Press, 1985), pp. 48, 60, 182–83.

25. Enno Franzius, *History of the Byzantine Empire: Mother of Nations* (New York: Funk & Wagnalls, 1967), pp. 99–100; Edward Gibbon, *The Decline and Fall of the Roman Empire*, vol. 2 (New York: Modern Library, 1932), p. 873; Constance Head, *Justinian II of Byzantium* (Madison: University of Wisconsin Press, 1972), pp. 63, 68, 100; Cyril Mango, *Byzantium: The Empire of New Rome* (London: Weidenfeld & Nicolson, 1980), p. 91; McNeill, *The Rise of the West*, p. 418.

26. Fitzgerald, *China: A Short Cultural History*, pp. 327–30 (most brackets in original).

27. J. K. Fairbank and S. Y. Teng, "On the Ch'ing Tributary System," *Harvard Journal of Asiatic Studies*, vol. 10, no. 2 (June 1941), pp. 135, 182, 187, 190 (portions omitted).

28. J. C. Russell, *The Fontana Economic History of Europe: Population in Europe: 500–1500*, vol. 1 (London: Fontana Books, 1969), pp. 19–21; J. C. Russell, "Late Ancient and Medieval Population," *Transactions of the American Philosophical Society*, vol. 48, part 3 (1958), p. 148 table 152; Hansen, *The Open Empire*, p. 191; Hugh Kennedy, *The Armies of the Caliphs: Military and Society in the Early Islamic State* (New York: Routledge, 2001), pp. 18–20; Howard Wechsler, "T'ai-tsung (Reign 626–49) the Consolidator," in Denis Twitchett, ed., *The Cambridge History of China*, vol. 3, *Sui and T'ang China 589–906*, part 1 (Cambridge: Cambridge University Press, 1979), p. 207; Charles Issawi, "The Area and Population of the Arab Empire: An Essay in Speculation," in *The Islamic Middle East 700–1900*, A. L. Udovitch, ed. (Princeton: Darwin Press, 1981), pp. 381, 388.

29. Fitzgerald, *China: A Short Cultural History*, pp. 299–300; Hansen, *The Open Empire*, pp. 222–23; Pan, *Son of Heaven and Heavenly Qaghan*, pp. 151–56.

30. Fitzgerald, *China: A Short Cultural History*, p. 300; Gernet, *A History of Chinese Civilization*, pp. 259–60, 266; Hansen, *The Open Empire*, p. 223; Pan, *Son of Heaven and Heavenly Qaghan*, pp. 152–55.

31. Gernet, *A History of Chinese Civilization*, pp. 260–61; Hansen, *The Open Empire*, pp. 221, 223–24, 227; Pulleyblank, "The An Lu-shan Rebellion," p. 37.

32. Capon, *Tang China*, p. 33; Gernet, *A History of Chinese Civilization*, pp. 259–62; Hansen, *The Open Empire*, pp. 227–28; Hucker, *China's Imperial Past*, pp. 144, 146; Pan, *Son of Heaven and Heavenly Qaghan*, pp. 152–56.

33. Gernet, *A History of Chinese Civilization*, pp. 267, 291–93; Pan, *Son of Heaven and Heavenly Qaghan*, p. 161; Pulleyblank, "The An Lu-shan Rebellion," p. 40.

34. Fitzgerald, *China: A Short Cultural History*, p. 338; Gernet, *A History of Chinese Civilization*, pp. 294–95; Pan, *Son of Heaven and Heavenly Qaghan*, p. 165.

35. Gernet, *A History of Chinese Civilization*, pp. 294–95; Hansen, *The Open Empire*, pp. 241–42.

36. Fitzgerald, *China: A Short Cultural History*, pp. 302–7; Gernet, *A History of Chinese Civilization*, pp. 268–73; Hansen, *The Open Empire*, pp. 243–44; Hucker, *China's Imperial Past*, pp. 146–47.

FOUR: THE GREAT MONGOL EMPIRE: COSMOPOLITAN BARBARIANS

Epigraphs: Both quotes can be found in Jack Weatherford, *Genghis Khan and the Making of the Modern World* (New York: Crown Publishers, 2004), pp. 79, 160.

This chapter draws heavily on the following secondary sources: Walther Heissig, *A Lost Civilization: The Mongols Rediscovered*, D.J.S. Thomson, trans. (London: Thames and Hudson, 1966); Harold Lamb, *Genghis Khan: The Emperor of All Men* (New York: Robert M. McBride & Co., 1927); David Morgan, *The Mongols* (Oxford: Basil Blackwell, 1990); J. J. Saunders, *The History of the Mongol Conquests* (London: Routledge & Kegan Paul, 1971); Bertold Spuler, *The Muslim World: A Historical Survey*, F.R.C. Bagley, trans., part 2, *The Mongol Period* (Leiden: E. J. Brill, 1969); and especially Weatherford, *Genghis Khan and the Making of the Modern World*. These modern histories in turn rely on various Chinese, Persian, and European primary materials, as well as, most critically, an extraordinary Mongol work known as *The Secret History of the Mongols*, believed to be written contemporaneously with the Mongols' rise to world dominance. Neither the author of *The Secret History* nor its exact date of compilation is known. In addition, the original document, most likely written in an adapted Uighur script (the Mongols had no alphabet of their own), has never been found. The version of *The Secret History* that has come down to us is a Chinese character transcription, probably dating from the fourteenth century, which was discovered in Beijing in the nineteenth century. See Morgan, *The Mongols*, pp. 5–11; Weatherford, *Genghis Khan*, pp. xxvii–xxxv.

In researching the Mongols, I came across a surprising number of factual discrepancies, no doubt reflecting the linguistic and interpretative difficulties involved in the study of Mongol history. (Even Genghis Khan's exact year of birth is reported differently by different authors.) In these instances, I usually relied on those sources based on the most recent scholarship, research, and archaeological evidence: The collapse of communism in the former Soviet Union opened up many exciting research opportunities for Mongol scholars and historians and cultural anthropologists from around the world.

1. Weatherford, *Genghis Khan and the Making of the Modern World*, p. xviii.

2. Lamb, *Genghis Khan*, p. 13; Morgan, *The Mongols*, pp. 58–59; Weatherford, *Genghis Khan and the Making of the Modern World*, pp. xviii, xxii, xxxiii, 9–27, 134, 169, 198.

3. The authority for Genghis Khan's infamous quotation was a medieval chronicler from Asia Minor whose people had been conquered by Genghis Khan; many historians have questioned whether the quotation is authentic. The particular translation I use is from Lamb, *Genghis Khan*, p. 107; see also Heissig, *A Lost Civilization*, pp. 9–10. On the gruesome cruelty of the Mongols, quite possibly exaggerated by unsympathetic historians, see Lamb, p. 134; Weatherford, *Genghis Khan and the Making of the Modern World*, pp. 93–94, 113, 164.

4. Lamb, *Genghis Khan*, p. 18; Weatherford, *Genghis Khan and the Making of the Modern World*, p. 162.

5. Ala-ad-Din Ata-Malik Juvaini, *The History of the World-Conqueror*, John Andrew Boyle, trans., vol. 1 (Cambridge Mass.: Harvard University Press, 1958), p. 21; Weatherford, *Genghis Khan and the Making of the Modern World*, pp. 14, 27–28.

6. Thomas J. Barfield, *The Perilous Frontier: Nomadic Empires and China* (Cambridge, Mass.: Basil Blackwell, 1989), pp. 187–89; Heissig, *A Lost Civilization*, pp. 44–45; Weatherford, *Genghis Khan and the Making of the Modern World*, pp. xix, 13, 25, 50–53.

7. Heissig, *A Lost Civilization*, p. 44; Juvaini, *The History of the World-Conqueror*, p. 35; Lamb, *Genghis Khan*, pp. 35–37; Weatherford, *Genghis Khan and the Making of the Modern World*, pp. 25–29. Even before Temujin was born, his father had, at a critical point, helped Ong Khan consolidate his power. The two men then formed a so-called *anda* bond, in which each pledged to aid the other in times of distress. See Paul Kahn, *The Secret History of the Mongols: The Origin of Chingis Khan* (San Francisco: North Point Press, 1984), p. xxiv.

8. Lamb, *Genghis Khan*, pp. 55–56; Weatherford, *Genghis Khan and the Making of the Modern World*, pp. 30–35, 42–54.

9. Weatherford, *Genghis Khan and the Making of the Modern World*, pp. 28, 52–53.

10. Barfield, *The Perilous Frontier*, pp. 191, 193; Lamb, *Genghis Khan*, pp. 45–46; Weatherford, *Genghis Khan and the Making of the Modern World*, pp. 40, 52, 67, 152–54.

11. Barfield, *The Perilous Frontier*, pp. 190–91; Lamb, *Genghis Khan*, pp. 57–59; Weatherford, *Genghis Khan and the Making of the Modern World*, pp. 32, 55–58.

12. Barfield, *The Perilous Frontier*, p. 191; Weatherford, *Genghis Khan and the Making of the Modern World*, pp. 54, 58–59, 61–62, 64–65.

13. Lamb, *Genghis Khan*, pp. 201–4; Weatherford, *Genghis Khan and the Making of the Modern World*, pp. 67–71. In addition to conquering much of the Eastern Hemisphere, Genghis Khan is usually credited with introducing the *Yassa Gengizcani*, or Great Laws of Genghis Khan. It is not known whether these laws were actually codified during Genghis Khan's lifetime. No complete version of the *Yassa* from Genghis Khan's time has ever been found, although the Persian chronicler Juvaini gave a lengthy description of Genghis Khan's rules and regulations thirty years after Genghis Khan's death. For an erudite discussion of the origins and widespread influence of the *Yassa*, as well as the scholarly debate surrounding it, see Robert D. McChesney, "The Legacy of Chinggis Khan in Law and Politics," lecture delivered to the Indo-Mongolian Society at New York University, Mar. 28, 1997.

14. Heissig, *A Lost Civilization*, pp. 36–39; Weatherford, *Genghis Khan and the Making of the Modern World*, pp. 70–71.

15. Lamb, *Genghis Khan*, pp. 77–80.

16. Barfield, *The Perilous Frontier*, p. 199; Heissig, *A Lost Civilization*, p. 46; Lamb, *Genghis Khan*, pp. 83–84; Weatherford, *Genghis Khan and the Making of the Modern World*, pp. 82–85.

17. Lamb, *Genghis Khan*, pp. 85–87, 121; Weatherford, *Genghis Khan and the Making of the Modern World*, pp. 84, 86–87.

18. Weatherford, *Genghis Khan and the Making of the Modern World*, pp. 92–94.

19. Lamb, *Genghis Khan*, pp. 91–92; Weatherford, *Genghis Khan and the Making of the Modern World*, pp. 96–97.

20. Heissig, *A Lost Civilization*, pp. 9, 46–47; Weatherford, *Genghis Khan and the Making of the Modern World*, pp. 96–99.

21. Lamb, *Genghis Khan*, pp. 13, 91–92, 101, 104–7, 119, 190–91; Weatherford, *Genghis Khan and the Making of the Modern World*, pp. 97–105.

22. I quote Jack Weatherford's translation of Genghis Khan's message. Weatherford, *Genghis Khan and the Making of the Modern World*, pp. 105–7; see also Lamb, *Genghis Khan*, pp. 109–11, 113–15.

23. Lamb, *Genghis Khan*, pp. 119–21; Weatherford, *Genghis Khan and the Making of the Modern World*, pp. 4–5, 7–8.

24. Barfield, *The Perilous Frontier*, pp. 201–2; Heissig, *A Lost Civilization*, p. 10; Lamb, *Genghis Khan*, pp. 115, 135, 138–39; Weatherford, *Genghis Khan and the Making of the Modern World*, pp. 5–7, 108–9, 113–14, 117–18.

25. Weatherford, *Genghis Khan and the Making of the Modern World*, pp. 4–6, 9, 110–13.

26. Kahn, *The Secret History of the Mongols*, p. xxvi; Lamb, *Genghis Khan*, pp. 143–44, 175–76; Weatherford, *Genghis Khan and the Making of the Modern World*, pp. xx–xxi, 128, 130–31.

27. Lamb, *Genghis Khan*, pp. 188–89; Weatherford, *Genghis Khan and the Making of the Modern World*, pp. 119–25, 130.

28. Lamb, *Genghis Khan*, pp. 144, 181, 231; Weatherford, *Genghis Khan and the Making of the Modern World*, pp. 133–43.

29. Weatherford, *Genghis Khan and the Making of the Modern World*, pp. 144–50.

30. Ibid., pp. 152, 155–59.

31. Morgan, *The Mongols*, pp. 151, 153; Saunders, *The History of the Mongol Conquests*, pp. 104–10; Spuler, *The Muslim World*, pp. 19–20; Weatherford,

Genghis Khan and the Making of the Modern World, pp. 166–67, 177, 180–81.

32. Thomas T. Allsen, *Mongol Imperialism: The Policies of the Grand Qan Möngke in China, Russia, and the Islamic Lands, 1251–1259* (Berkeley and Los Angeles: University of California Press, 1987), pp. 3, 7; Morgan, *The Mongols*, pp. 153–54; Saunders, *The History of the Mongol Conquests*, pp. 110–11; Weatherford, *Genghis Khan and the Making of the Modern World*, pp. 178–84.

33. Saunders, *The History of the Mongol Conquests*, pp. 111–13; Spuler, *The Muslim World*, pp. 19–20; Weatherford, *Genghis Khan and the Making of the Modern World*, pp. 183–84.

34. Weatherford, *Genghis Khan and the Making of the Modern World*, pp. 171–73.

35. Enno Franzius, *History of the Byzantine Empire: Mother of Nations* (New York: Funk & Wagnalls, 1967), pp. 349, 353; Weatherford, *Genghis Khan and the Making of the Modern World*, pp. 173–74.

36. Saunders, *The History of the Mongol Conquests*, pp. 68, 103–4, 114–15; Spuler, *The Muslim World*, pp. 17, 20; Weatherford, *Genghis Khan and the Making of the Modern World*, pp. 6, 33, 82–84, 169–70, 185, 188.

37. Morgan, *The Mongols*, pp. 117–20; Saunders, *The History of the Mongol Conquests*, pp. 116, 119–21; Weatherford, *Genghis Khan and the Making of the Modern World*, pp. 185–91.

38. Valerie Hansen, *The Open Empire: A History of China to 1600* (New York: W. W. Norton, 2000), p. 347; Morgan, *The Mongols*, p. 120; Saunders, *The History of the Mongol Conquests*, pp. 121–22; Weatherford, *Genghis Khan and the Making of the Modern World*, pp. 195, 208–9.

39. Hansen, *The Open Empire*, pp. 344, 352, 366; Heissig, *A Lost Civilization*, p. 51; Lamb, *Genghis Khan*, p. 193; Morgan, *The Mongols*, pp. 119, 120–23, 127–28, 163; Saunders, *The History of the Mongol Conquests*, pp. 121–27; Spuler, *The Muslim World*, pp. 32–33; Weatherford, *Genghis Khan and the Making of the Modern World*, pp. 195–97, 203–7.

40. Hansen, *The Open Empire*, p. 352; Morgan, *The Mongols*, pp. 123–24, 128–30; Saunders, *The History of the Mongol Conquests*, pp. 124–26; Weatherford, *Genghis Khan and the Making of the Modern World*, pp. 198–200, 203.

41. Morgan, *The Mongols*, pp. 128–30; Saunders, *The History of the Mongol Conquests*, pp. 124–25; Weatherford, *Genghis Khan and the Making of the Modern World*, pp. 223–24.

42. Morgan, *The Mongols*, pp. 120, 131–32; Weatherford, *Genghis Khan and the Making of the Modern World*, pp. 200–1, 206.

43. Morgan, *The Mongols*, pp. 103–6; Weatherford, *Genghis Khan and the Making of the Modern World*, pp. xxiii, 220–21, 224, 228–34.

44. Saunders, *The History of the Mongol Conquests*, pp. 123, 127; Weatherford, *Genghis Khan and the Making of the Modern World*, pp. 195, 205–6, 209, 223, 230–31, 234.

45. Morgan, *The Mongols*, pp. 133–34, 157–60; Saunders, *The History of the Mongol Conquests*, pp. 116–17, 134–36, 140–41, 146, 156–60; Weatherford, *Genghis Khan and the Making of the Modern World*, pp. 243–48, 250, 252–53.

46. Morgan, *The Mongols*, pp. 132–35; Saunders, *The History of the Mongol*

360 NOTES

Conquests, pp. 152–54; Weatherford, *Genghis Khan and the Making of the Modern World*, pp. 243, 248–51.

PART TWO: THE ENLIGHTENING OF TOLERANCE

FIVE: THE "PURIFICATION" OF MEDIEVAL SPAIN: INQUISITION, EXPULSION, AND THE PRICE OF INTOLERANCE

Epigraph: The 1492 expulsion decree is translated by Henry Kamen and reproduced in his chapter "The Expulsion: Purpose and Consequence," in Elie Kedourie, ed., *Spain and the Jews: The Sephardi Experience 1492 and After* (London: Thames and Hudson, 1992), pp. 80–81.

1. See J. H. Elliott, *Imperial Spain, 1469–1716* (New York: St. Martin's Press, 1964), pp. 5–7, 9.

2. Elie Kedourie, "Introduction," in *Spain and the Jews*, p. 8, David Nirenberg, *Communities of Violence: Persecution of Minorities in the Middle Ages* (Princeton: Princeton University Press, 1996), pp. 19, 21–23, 133.

3. Angus MacKay, "The Jews in Spain During the Middle Ages," in *Spain and the Jews*, pp. 33–34, 46–50; Kamen, "The Expulsion," pp. 79–80; Nirenberg, *Communities of Violence*, pp. 130, 132–33, 140. On Spain's "premodern" brand of toleration, see Henry Kamen, "Inquisition, Toleration and Liberty in Eighteenth-Century Spain," in Ole Peter Grell and Roy Porter, eds., *Toleration in Enlightenment Europe* (Cambridge: Cambridge University Press, 2000), pp. 250–52.

4. Nirenberg, *Communities of Violence*, pp. 23, 25–26, 38–39.

5. Elliott, *Imperial Spain, 1469–1716*, pp. 9, 95; Kedourie, *Spain and the Jews*, pp. 8, 10, 33–35, 49, 61, 68–69; Nirenberg, *Communities of Violence*, pp. 27–29.

6. MacKay, "The Jews in Spain During the Middle Ages," pp. 35–36, 48; Jonathan Israel, "The Sephardim in the Netherlands," in *Spain and the Jews*, pp. 189–90; Nirenberg, *Communities of Violence*, pp. 174–75.

7. Henry Kamen, *Spain's Road to Empire: The Making of a World Power, 1492–1763* (London: Allen Lane, 2002), pp. 22, 181; Kamen, "The Expulsion," pp. 75, 82, 85; Haim Beinart, "The Conversos and Their Fate," in *Spain and the Jews*, pp. 106, 108, 114, 142.

8. Elliott, *Imperial Spain, 1469–1716*, pp. 1, 15, 19–23; Julius Klein, *The Mesta: A Study in Spanish Economic History, 1273–1836* (Cambridge Mass.: Harvard University Press, 1920), p. 38; Immanuel Wallerstein, *Capitalist Agriculture and the Origins of the European World-Economy in the Sixteenth Century*, vol. 1 of *The Modern World-System* (San Diego: Academic Press, 1980), pp. 192–93 and 193n.136 (citations omitted); John Elliott, "The Decline of Spain," *Past & Present* (Nov. 1961), pp. 52, 54–55, 69–70; Ruth Pike, "The Genoese in Seville and the Opening of the New World," *The Journal of Economic History*, vol. 22, no. 3 (1962), pp. 355, 357, 359.

9. Kamen, *Spain's Road to Empire*, pp. 69–70, 88–89; John Lynch, "Spain After the Expulsion," in *Spain and the Jews*, pp. 147–48, 151; Wallerstein, *Capitalist Agriculture and the Origins of the European World-Economy*, pp. 183, 185, 195.

10. Kamen, "The Expulsion," p. 84; Lynch, "Spain After the Expulsion," pp. 140, 144–45, 148–53; Wallerstein, *Capitalist Agriculture and the Origins of the European World-Economy*, pp. 194–96.

11. Kedourie, *Spain and the Jews*, pp. 16, 149–52; James MacDonald, *A Free Nation Deep in Debt* (New York: Farrar, Straus & Giroux, 2003), pp. 133–35; Wallerstein, *Capitalist Agriculture and the Origins of the European World-Economy*, pp. 186–87, 195, 204–5. On the expulsion of the Jesuits, see Bernard Moses, *Spain's Declining Power in South America, 1730–1806* (Berkeley: University of California Press, 1919), pp. 104–7.

12. Max Boot, *War Made New: Technology, Warfare, and the Course of History, 1500 to Today* (New York: Gotham Books, 2006), pp. 30–45; MacDonald, *A Free Nation Deep in Debt*, pp. 132–34; Wallerstein, *Capitalist Agriculture and the Origins of the European World-Economy*, pp. 192–97.

13. The nineteenth-century Spanish writer was Marcelino Menéndez Pelayo, who is quoted in Lynch, "Spain After the Expulsion," pp. 159–60.

14. Kamen, "The Expulsion," pp. 75, 84; Lynch, "Spain After the Expulsion," p. 145.

15. Lynch, "Spain After the Expulsion," p. 140. On the general intolerance of seventeenth-century Europe, see Wiebe Bergsma, "Church, State, and People," in Karel Davids and Jan Lucassen, eds., *A Miracle Mirrored: The Dutch Republic in European Perspective* (Cambridge: Cambridge University Press, 1995), pp. 204–13.

16. Wallerstein, *Capitalist Agriculture and the Origins of the European World-Economy*, pp. 197–98.

SIX: THE DUTCH WORLD EMPIRE: DIAMONDS, DAMASK, AND EVERY "MONGREL SECT IN CHRISTENDOM"

Epigraphs: The Dutch author was Melchior Fokkens, quoted in Simon Schama's wonderful book *The Embarrassment of Riches: An Interpretation of Dutch Culture in the Golden Age* (New York: Alfred A. Knopf, 1987), p. 300. The quote from Peter Mundy can be found in Richard Carnac Temple, ed., *The Travels of Peter Mundy in Europe and Asia, 1608–1667*, vol. 4 (London: Cambridge University Press, 1925), p. 68.

1. On civet cats and the civet trade, see Jonathan I. Israel, *Empires and Entrepots: The Dutch, the Spanish Monarchy and the Jews, 1585–1713* (London: Hambledon Press, 1990), pp. 357, 427, 435–36; William Jackson, "The Story of Civet," *Pharmaceutical Journal*, vol. 271 (Dec. 2003), pp. 859–61; Brendan Koerner, "What Does Civet Cat Taste Like?," *Slate*, Jan. 6, 2004, at slate.msn.com/id/2093538/.

2. I. Schöffer, "Introduction," in J.C.H. Blom, R. G. Fuks-Mansfeld, and I. Schöffer, eds., *The History of the Jews in the Netherlands*, Arnold J. Pomerans and Erica Pomerans, trans. (Oxford: Littman Library of Jewish Civilization, 2002), pp. 9–10; Mark T. Hooker, *The History of Holland* (Westport, Conn.: Greenwood Press, 1999), pp. 3, 14, 87–90.

3. Schama, *The Embarrassment of Riches*, p. 44. On the watery, inauspicious origins of the Netherlands before its dramatic rise, see Jonathan I. Israel, *The Dutch Republic: Its Rise, Greatness, and Fall, 1477–1806* (Oxford: Clarendon Press, 1995), pp. 9–10; Hooker, *The History of Holland*, pp. 7–8. The

"sand and mud dump" description is from Joh. Van Veen, *Dredge, Drain, Reclaim* (The Hague: Martinus Nijhoff, 1948), p. 11.

4. B.M.J. Speet, "The Middle Ages," in *The History of the Jews in the Netherlands*, p. 18; Israel, *Empires and Entrepots*, p. x; J. L. van Zanden, *The Rise and Decline of Holland's Economy* (Manchester: Manchester University Press, 1993), p. 19.

5. Speet, "The Middle Ages," pp. 21, 26–29.

6. See Thomas Colley Grattan, *Holland: The History of the Netherlands* (New York: Peter Fenelon Collier, 1899), pp. 84–94; Hooker, *The History of Holland*, pp. 77–79; Israel, *The Dutch Republic*, pp. 27–28, 34–35; Immanuel Wallerstein, *Capitalist Agriculture and the Origins of the European World-Economy in the Sixteenth Century*, vol. 1 of *The Modern World-System* (San Diego: Academic Press, 1980), pp. 180–81. On the rise of Calvinism, the early Dutch Reformation, and growing conflict under Philip I, see Grattan, pp. 96–98; Israel, chaps. 5 and 6, especially pp. 101–5, 129, 141–47, 193–94; Charles Wilson, *The Dutch Republic and the Civilisation of the Seventeenth Century* (New York: McGraw-Hill, 1968), pp. 8–9.

7. The quote is from Israel, *The Dutch Republic*, pp. 155–56; see also pp. 140–54, 157, 160–61, 164, 167, 169, 177–80; Hooker, *The History of Holland*, pp. 83–87; P.J.A.N. Rietbergen and G.H.J. Seegers, *A Short History of the Netherlands* (Amersfoort, Netherlands: Bekking Publishers Amersfoort, 1992), pp. 67–76.

8. Hooker, *The History of Holland*, pp. 83–87; Israel, *The Dutch Republic*, pp. 184–86, 198–99, 202, 209, 213–14; Rietbergen and Seegers, *A Short History of the Netherlands*, pp. 67–76. The Hooft quote is from Schama, *The Embarrassment of Riches*, p. 86. The text of the Oath of Abjuration can be found at Oliver J. Thatcher, ed., *The Library of Original Sources*, vol. 5 (Milwaukee: University Research Extension Co., 1907), p. 190.

9. Hooker, *The History of Holland*, pp. 88–89; Israel, *The Dutch Republic*, pp. 208–10, 212–13, 218–30; Rietbergen and Seegers, *A Short History of the Netherlands*, p. 76.

10. Israel, *Empires and Entrepots*, p. ix; Immanuel Wallerstein, *Mercantilism and the Consolidation of the European World-Economy, 1600–1750*, vol. 2 of *The Modern World-System* (San Diego: Academic Press, 1980), p. 38.

11. Wiebe Bergsma, "Church, State, and People," in Karel Davids and Jan Lucassen, eds., *A Miracle Mirrored: The Dutch Republic in European Perspective* (Cambridge: Cambridge University Press, 1995), pp. 196–97, 202–4, 217, 223; Israel, *The Dutch Republic*, pp. 392, 637–76; Schama, *The Embarrassment of Riches*, pp. 61–62.

12. Schama, *The Embarrassment of Riches*, pp. 587–89, 594; Daniel M. Swetschinski, "From the Middle Ages to the Golden Age, 1516–1621," and Yosef Kaplan, "The Jews in the Republic Until About 1750: Religious, Cultural, and Social Life," both in *The History of the Jews in the Netherlands*, pp. 68–71, 117, 126–27, 137–40, 142–44.

13. Schama, *The Embarrassment of Riches*, pp. 266–67; see also Israel, *The Dutch Republic*, pp. 639–40. The quotes from Balzac and Mundy can be found in Bergsma, "Church, State, and People," pp. 196, 203.

14. Israel, *The Dutch Republic*, pp. 308, 319–20, 328, 374–75, 621, 657–58, 786, 910; Van Zanden, *The Rise and Decline of Holland's Economy*, pp.

23–26, 35–36, 44–48, 52–53, 62; Wallerstein, *Mercantilism and the Consolidation of the European World-Economy*, pp. 45, 64, 67. On the English Pilgrims, see Russell Shorto, *The Island at the Center of the World* (New York: Doubleday, 2004), p. 26.

15. On the history of diamonds, see Harry Emanuel, *Diamonds and Precious Stones*, 2nd ed. (London: John Camden Hotten, 1867), pp. 53–55, 79–80, 84; Edward Jay Epstein, *The Rise and Fall of Diamonds* (New York: Simon & Schuster, 1982), pp. 76–77, 103–4; Godehard Lenzen, *The History of Diamond Production and the Diamond Trade* (London: Barrie and Jenkins), pp. 32–34; Gedalia Yogev, *Diamonds and Coral: Anglo-Dutch Jews and Eighteenth-Century Trade* (Leicester: Leicester University Press, 1978), pp. 154–55. On Antwerp in the sixteenth century, see Grattan, *Holland*, p. 94; Wallerstein, *Capitalist Agriculture and the Origins of the European World-Economy*, pp. 175–76.

16. Israel, *Empires and Entrepots*, pp. 417–18, 422, 425–28, 432–35, 444–46; Kaplan, "The Jews in the Republic Until About 1750," pp. 146–49.

17. See Israel, *Empires and Entrepots*, pp. 356, 417–22, 426, 433–34.

18. C. R. Boxer, *The Dutch Seaborne Empire, 1600–1800* (New York: Alfred A. Knopf, 1965), pp. xx–xxi, 2–3; Israel, *The Dutch Republic*, pp. 22–23, 104, 116, 146–47, 193–94, 308–9, 311, 344–45, 349–50, 413; Wilson, *The Dutch Republic*, pp. 8–9.

19. Karel Davids, "Shifts of Technological Leadership in Early Modern Europe," in *A Miracle Mirrored*, chap. 11; Israel, *The Dutch Republic*, pp. 16, 18, 116–17, 316, 348–50; Van Zanden, *The Rise and Decline of Holland's Economy*, pp. 30–36; Wallerstein, *Mercantilism and the Consolidation of the European World-Economy*, pp. 39–42, 46 (quoting Daniel Defoe); Wilson, *The Dutch Republic*, pp. 30–31.

20. Israel, *The Dutch Republic*, pp. 311–13, 316–18, 320–21, 326, 345–46, 350; Wallerstein, *Mercantilism and the Consolidation of the European World-Economy*, pp. 50–55.

21. Israel, *The Dutch Republic*, pp. 319–24, 344–48, 380–82; Wallerstein, *Mercantilism and the Consolidation of the European World-Economy*, pp. 48–51.

22. Boxer, *The Dutch Seaborne Empire, 1600–1800*, pp. 114–15.

23. Grattan, *Holland*, pp. 215–16; Israel, *The Dutch Republic*, pp. 244–45, 262–71, 322–27, 399–405, 934; Israel, *Empires and Entrepots*, pp. 199–204; Shorto, *The Island at the Center of the World*, pp. 24–33; Wallerstein, *Mercantilism and the Consolidation of the European World-Economy*, pp. 64–65 & 65n.169.

24. Boxer, *The Dutch Seaborne Empire, 1600–1800*, p. xxi; Israel, *The Dutch Republic*, pp. 326, 934–40; Israel, *Empires and Entrepots*, pp. 419, 424–25, 430–33, 437–40, 443–44; Wallerstein, *Mercantilism and the Consolidation of the European World-Economy*, pp. 50–51.

25. Boxer, *The Dutch Seaborne Empire, 1600–1800*, p. 27. The list of unloaded luxury goods is from Schama, *The Embarrassment of Riches*, pp. 346–47.

26. In this section I draw heavily on chaps. 3 and 5 of Simon Schama's *The Embarrassment of Riches*, especially pp. 295–304. On the Dutch Republic's relatively high standard of living, see pp. 322–23 of Schama's book and Israel, *The Dutch Republic*, pp. 351–53, 622–24, 630–33. William Temple's quote

on Dutch parsimony can be found at Peter Spufford, "Access to Credit and Capital in the Commercial Centers of Europe," in *A Miracle Mirrored*, p. 316.

27. Schama, *The Embarrassment of Riches*, pp. 150–52, 174–75, 182–85, 189, 191, 196, 198, 200.

28. Ibid., pp. 182–85, 191–92, 194–95, 197.

29. Israel, *The Dutch Republic*, pp. 627–30, 677; Van Zanden, *The Rise and Decline of Holland's Economy*, pp. 50–52, 62–63; Wallerstein, *Mercantilism and the Consolidation of the European World-Economy*, pp. 45, 64–67; Wilson, *The Dutch Republic*, p. 165–67.

30. Wilson, *The Dutch Republic*, pp. 60–64, 118–24, 165–77. The quote from Descartes is from Boxer, *The Dutch Seaborne Empire, 1600–1800*, p. 184.

31. Boxer, *The Dutch Seaborne Empire, 1600–1800*, pp. xx–xxi; Israel, *The Dutch Republic*, pp. 267–71, 796–97, 812–14, 825; Wallerstein, *Mercantilism and the Consolidation of the European World-Economy*, pp. 64–65 & 65n.169, 70; Jonathan Scott, "What the Dutch Taught Us: The Late Emergence of the Modern British State," *Times Literary Supplement*, Mar. 16, 2001, p. 6.

32. Grattan, *Holland*, pp. 81–85; Israel, *The Dutch Republic*, pp. 537, 773; Alfred Thayer Mahan, *The Influence of Sea Power Upon History, 1660–1783* (New York: Sagamore Press, 1957), pp. 58–59, 81–82, 84–85; Wallerstein, *Mercantilism and the Consolidation of the European World-Economy*, p. 46 & 46n.60 (citation omitted); Wilson, *The Dutch Republic*, p. 40.

33. Davids, "Shifts of Technological Leadership in Early Modern Europe," p. 341.

34. See M.A.M. Franken, "The General Tendencies and Structural Aspects of the Foreign Policy and Diplomacy of the Dutch Republic in the Latter Half of the 17th Century," *Acta Historiae Neerlandica*, vol. 3 (1968), pp. 4–5; Wallerstein, *Mercantilism and the Consolidation of the European World-Economy*, pp. 37–39, 64nn.166, 168, and 169.

35. Israel, *The Dutch Republic*, pp. 9, 802, 850–52.

36. On the Glorious Revolution and the role played by Dutch Sephardic Jews, see Israel, *The Dutch Republic*, pp. 819, 841, 849–53; Israel, *Empires and Entrepots*, pp. 444–45; Jonathan I. Israel, *European Jewry in the Age of Mercantilism, 1550–1750*, 2nd ed. (Oxford: Clarendon Press, 1989), pp. 127–30. Regarding the transfer of human and financial capital from Holland to Britain after 1688, see Spufford, "Access to Credit and Capital in the Commercial Centers of Europe," pp. 328–29, and Karel Davids and Jan Lucassen, "Conclusion," in *A Miracle Mirrored*, p. 450.

SEVEN: TOLERANCE AND INTOLERANCE IN THE EAST: THE OTTOMAN, MING, AND MUGHAL EMPIRES

1. C. E. Bosworth, "The Concept of *Dhimma* in Early Islam," in Benjamin Braude and Bernard Lewis, eds., *Christians and Jews in the Ottoman Empire: The Functioning of a Plural Society*, vol. 1 (New York: Holmes & Meier Publishers, 1982), pp. 41, 49–50; Avigdor Levy, "Introduction," in Avigdor Levy, ed., *The Jews of the Ottoman Empire* (Princeton: Darwin Press, 1994), pp. 15–16; Bruce Masters, *Christians and Jews in the Ottoman Arab World:*

The Roots of Sectarianism (Cambridge: Cambridge University Press, 2001), pp. 18–26; María Rosa Menocal, *The Ornament of the World: How Muslims, Jews, and Christians Created a Culture of Tolerance in Medieval Spain* (Boston: Little, Brown and Co., 2002), pp. 5–31.

2. Levy, "Introduction," pp. 10–12, 24–25; Aron Rodrigue, "The Sephardim in the Ottoman Empire," in Elie Kedourie, ed., *Spain and the Jews: The Sephardi Experience: 1492 and After* (London: Thames and Hudson, 1992), p. 164; Annette B. Fromm, "Hispanic Culture in Exile: Sephardic Life in the Ottoman Balkans," in Zion Zohar, ed., *Sephardic and Mizrahi Jewry: From the Golden Age of Spain to Modern Times* (New York: New York University Press, 2005), p. 152; Stanford J. Shaw, "The Jewish Millet in the Ottoman Empire," available at www.yeniturkiye.com/display.asp?c=3012.

3. Masters, *Christians and Jews in the Ottoman Arab World,* pp. 17–18, 29, 31–34, 38; John Freely, *Inside the Seraglio: Private Lives of the Sultans in Istanbul* (London: Viking, 1999), pp. 45–46 (Selim the Grim), 50–69 (Suleyman); see generally Metin Kunt and Christine Woodhead, eds., *Süleyman the Magnificent and His Age: The Ottoman Empire in the Early Modern World* (London: Longman, 1995).

4. Masters, *Christians and Jews in the Ottoman Arab World,* pp. 18, 23, 39.

5. Levy, "Introduction," pp. 15–16, 32–34; Masters, *Christians and Jews in the Ottoman Arab World,* pp. 6, 22; Bosworth, "The Concept of *Dhimma* in Early Islam," pp. 5–9.

6. Levy, "Introduction," pp. 15, 18; Metin Kunt, "Transformation of Zimmi into Askeri," in *Christians and Jews in the Ottoman Empire,* pp. 55, 60–63.

7. Karen Barkey, *Bandits and Bureaucrats: The Ottoman Route to Civilization* (Ithaca, N.Y.: Cornell University Press, 1994), p. 31; Albert Howe Lybyer, *The Government of the Ottoman Empire in the Time of Suleiman the Magnificent* (Cambridge, Mass.: Harvard University Press, 1913), p. 167; Paul M. Pitman III, ed., *Turkey: A Country Study* (Washington, D.C.: Federal Research Division of the Library of Congress, 1987); Bosworth, "The Concept of *Dhimma* in Early Islam," pp. 11–12.

8. Levy, "Introduction," pp. 21–28; Masters, *Christians and Jews in the Ottoman Arab World,* pp. 24, 26–27, 42–47, 50–52; Robert Mantran, "Foreign Merchants and the Minorities in Istanbul in the Sixteenth and Seventeenth Centuries," in *Christians and Jews in the Ottoman Empire,* pp. 127, 132–34.

9. Paul Kennedy, *The Rise and Fall of the Great Powers: Economic Change and Military Conflict from 1500 to 2000* (New York: Vintage Books, 1989), pp. 5, 11–12; Donald Quataert, *The Ottoman Empire, 1700–1922* (Cambridge: Cambridge University Press, 2000), p. 3.

10. Kennedy, *The Rise and Fall of the Great Powers,* pp. 11–12.

11. Ibid.; Levy, "Introduction," pp. 73–74; Masters, *Christians and Jews in the Ottoman Arab World,* pp. 7–8, 129, 141–44.

12. Levy, "Introduction," pp. 74–76, 79–86.

13. On the Ottoman decline, see for example Ekmeleddin Ihsanoglu, ed., *History of the Ottoman State, Society, and Civilization,* vol. 1 (Istanbul: Research Center for Islamic History, Art, and Culture, 2001), pp. 43–44, 53–57, 95–100, 108; Charles Swallow, *The Sick Man of Europe: Ottoman Empire to Turkish Republic, 1789–1923* (London: Ernest Benn, 1973), pp. 5–6, 13–14.

On the Armenian massacre, see Vahakn N. Dadrian, "Genocide as a Problem of National and International Law: The World War I Armenian Case and Its Contemporary Legal Ramifications," *Yale Journal of International Law*, vol. 14 (1989), pp. 221, 242–45, 262–64, 272.

14. Valerie Hansen, *The Open Empire: A History of China to 1600* (New York: W. W. Norton, 2000), pp. 378–79; Kennedy, *The Rise and Fall of the Great Powers*, pp. 4–7; Gavin Menzies, *1421: The Year China Discovered America* (New York: HarperCollins, 2003), pp. 45, 52, 63, 70; Philip Snow, *The Star Raft: China's Encounter with Africa* (New York: Weidenfeld & Nicolson, 1988), pp. 21–23.

15. Edward L. Dreyer, *Zheng He: China and the Oceans in the Early Ming Dynasty, 1405–1433* (New York: Pearson Education, 2007), pp. 1–38; Hansen, *The Open Empire*, pp. 371–83; Snow, *The Star Raft*, pp. 10, 21–22; see also Julie Wilensky, "The Magical *Kumlun* and 'Devil Slaves': Chinese Perceptions of Dark-Skinned People and Africa Before 1500," *Sino-Platonic Papers*, vol. 122 (July 2002).

16. Hansen, *The Open Empire*, pp. 381–82; Snow, *The Star Raft*, pp. 21–22.

17. Hansen, *The Open Empire*, p. 379; G. F. Hudson, *Europe and China* (London: Edward Arnold & Co., 1931), pp. 195–96; Menzies, *1421: The Year China Discovered America*, p. 60; Snow, *The Star Raft*, pp. 29, 32.

18. Hansen, *The Open Empire*, pp. 383–87; Kennedy, *The Rise and Fall of the Great Powers*, pp. 7–9.

19. See J. N. Datta, "Proportion of Muhammadans in India Through Centuries," *Modern Review*, vol. 78 (Jan. 1948), pp. 31, 33. On the destruction of the mosque in Ayodhya in 1992 and the claims of Hindu nationalists, see Amartya Sen, *The Argumentative Indian* (London: Penguin, 2005), pp. 48, 209, 287.

20. My discussion of Babur and Humayun draws heavily on Abraham Eraly, *The Mughal Throne: The Saga of India's Great Emperors* (London: Weidenfeld & Nicolson, 1997), pp. 15, 22–27 (Battle of Khanua), 103–13 (Humayun); see also Richard C. Foltz, *Mughal India and Central Asia* (Karachi, Pakistan: Oxford University Press, 1998), pp. xv, 130; John F. Richards, *The Mughal Empire, The New Cambridge History of India* (Cambridge: Cambridge University Press, 1993), pp. 1–8, 12. For a discussion of the rise of Islam in India and the reign of the so-called Delhi sultanate, see Francis Watson, *A Concise History of India* (New York: Charles Scribner, 1975), pp. 87–104.

21. Akbar's letter to Philip is reproduced in Pankaj Mishra, "The First Liberal Imperialist," *New Statesman*, Mar. 24, 2003, available at www.newstatesman.com/200303240028.

22. For a general account of Akbar's reign, see Eraly, *The Mughal Throne*, pp. 114–36. On his alliances with the Rajputs, see Richards, *The Mughal Empire*, pp. 19–26; Norman Ziegler, "Some Notes on Rajput Loyalties During the Mughal Period," in Muzaffar Alam and Sanjay Subrahmanyam, eds., *The Mughal State, 1526–1750* (Delhi: Oxford University Press, 1998), pp. 168, 174–75. On religious policy during Akbar's reign, see Harbans Mukhia, *The Mughals of India* (Malden, Mass.: Blackwell Publishing, 2004), pp. 23, 47, 99; Sen, *The Argumentative Indian*, pp. 16–21; Sri Ram Sharma, *The Religious Policy of the Mughal Emperors* (Bombay: Asia Publishing House, 1972), pp. 36–52, 56–66.

23. My discussion of Jahangir and Shah Jahan is based on Eraly, *The Mughal Throne*, pp. 238–43, 304–5, 308–30; Mukhia, *The Mughals of India*, p. 20; Saiyid Athar Abbas Rizvi, *Muslim Revivalist Movements in Northern India in the Sixteenth and Seventeenth Centuries* (Agra, India: Balkrishna Book Co., 1965), p. 328. On the Peacock Throne, see K.R.N. Swamy, "As Priceless as the Peacock Throne," *The Tribune* (India), Jan. 20, 2000, available at www.tribuneindia.com/2000/20000130/spectrum/main7.htm.

24. On Aurangzeb's struggle for the throne and intolerant policies, see Eraly, *The Mughal Throne*, pp. 334–36, 370, 391–92, 401; Mukhia, *The Mughals of India*, pp. 24–26, 34–36; Richards, *The Mughal Empire*, pp. 171–84; Stanley Wolpert, *A New History of India*, 7th ed. (New York: Oxford University Press, 2004), pp. 159–60, 168.

EIGHT: THE BRITISH EMPIRE: "REBEL BUGGERS" AND THE "WHITE MAN'S BURDEN"

Epigraphs: The Voltaire quote can be found in Ole Peter Grell and Roy Porter, "Toleration in Enlightenment Europe," in Ole Peter Grell and Roy Porter, eds., *Toleration in Enlightenment Europe* (Cambridge: Cambridge University Press, 2000), p. 4. Kipling's quote can be found in Rudyard Kipling, *Plain Tales from the Hills*, H. R. Woudhuysen, ed. (London: Penguin, 1990), p. 162. Gandhi's quote can be found in Gandhi, *Young India 1919–1922* (New York: B. W. Huebsch, Inc., 1924), p. 299.

1. The comparison of Britons to "Cannibals" is from a 1648 English pamphlet, quoted in Jonathan Scott, "What the Dutch Taught Us: The Late Emergence of the Modern British State," *Times Literary Supplement*, Mar. 16, 2001, pp. 4–5. Excellent discussions of intolerance in pre-Enlightenment Britain include the scholarly essays in Ruth Whelan and Carol Baxter, eds., *Toleration and Religious Identity: The Edict of Nantes and Its Implications in France, Britain and Ireland* (Dublin: Four Courts Press, 2003), especially John Miller, "Pluralism, Persecution and Toleration in France and Britain in the Seventeenth Century," pp. 166–78.

   It is often overlooked how much Britain's transformation and rise to global dominance after 1688 was influenced by the Dutch. On this topic, see Immanuel Wallerstein, *Mercantilism and the Consolidation of the European World-Economy, 1600–1750*, vol. 2 of *The Modern World-System* (San Diego: Academic Press, 1980), pp. 67, 277–79, 285–86; Charles Wilson, *The Dutch Republic and the Civilisation of the Seventeenth Century* (New York: McGraw-Hill, 1968), pp. 240–41; Scott, "What the Dutch Taught Us," pp. 4, 6.

2. Diderot lamented that France had expatriated a "prodigious multitude of excellent people," thereby "enriching neighboring Kingdoms." Alan C. Kors, "The Enlightenment and Toleration," in *Toleration and Religious Identity*, pp. 202–3. On the Bill of Rights and Act of Toleration, see Linda Colley, *Britons: Forging the Nation, 1707–1837* (New Haven: Yale University Press, 1992), pp. 111–12; Justin Champion, "Toleration and Citizenship in Enlightenment England: John Toland and the Naturalization of the Jews, 1714–1753," in *Toleration in Enlightenment Europe*, p. 133. On the role of Jews in Great Britain, see Todd M. Endelman, *The Jews of Britain, 1656 to 2000*

(Berkeley and Los Angeles: University of California Press, 2002), pp. 15–17, 19–21, 24–25, 28–29; Jonathan I. Israel, *European Jewry in the Age of Mercantilism, 1550–1750,* 2nd ed. (Oxford: Clarendon Press, 1989), pp. 5, 57, 127–30.

3. Colley, *Britons: Forging the Nation,* pp. 24–25; Wallerstein, *Mercantilism and the Consolidation of the European World-Economy,* pp. 245–46, 248.

4. Israel, *European Jewry in the Age of Mercantilism,* pp. 123, 127–30, 132–34; Wallerstein, *Mercantilism and the Consolidation of the European World-Economy,* pp. 258, 277–81, 285; Scott, "What the Dutch Taught Us," pp. 5–6.

5. Endelman, *The Jews of Britain, 1656 to 2000,* pp. 47–49, 66; Wilson, *The Dutch Republic,* p. 240; Niall Ferguson, *Empire: How Britain Made the Modern World* (London: Allen Lane, 2003), pp. 36–38; Peter Spufford, "Access to Credit and Capital in the Commercial Centers of Europe," in Karel Davids and Jan Lucassen, eds., *A Miracle Mirrored: The Dutch Republic in European Perspective* (Cambridge: Cambridge University Press, 1995), pp. 328–29; Peter Spufford, "From Antwerp to London: The Decline of Financial Centres in Europe," Ortelius Lecture, Netherlands Institute for Advanced Study, May 18, 2005, pp. 30–31. A good treatment of the Bank of England is John Giuseppi, *The Bank of England: A History from Its Foundation in 1694* (Chicago: Henry Regnery Co., 1996).

6. Endelman, *The Jews of Britain, 1656 to 2000,* pp. 49, 66, 92–93; Spufford, "Access to Credit and Capital in the Commercial Centers of Europe," pp. 328–29; Spufford, "From Antwerp to London," pp. 30–31; Gedalia Yogev, *Diamonds and Coral: Anglo-Dutch Jews and Eighteenth-Century Trade* (Leicester: Leicester University Press, 1978), pp. 20–21. See also William J. Bernstein, *The Birth of Plenty: How the Prosperity of the Modern World Was Created* (New York: McGraw-Hill, 2004), pp. 146–49, 154–60.

7. Endelman, *The Jews of Britain, 1656 to 2000,* pp. 6, 41–44, 73, 79, 93, 153.

8. Ibid., pp. 8–9, 35–38, 79, 101–7, 127, 164, 173.

9. My discussion of the Huguenots, France's religious wars, and the Edict of Nantes and its Revocation draws heavily on R. J. Knecht, *The Rise and Fall of Renaissance France, 1483–1610* (London: Fontana Press, 1996), pp. 308–11, 322–25, 351–438, 542–47, 572–77; G. A. Rothrock, *The Huguenots: A Biography of a Minority* (Chicago: Nelson-Hall, 1979), pp. 74–75, 94–95, 97–99, chaps. 7–11; Warren C. Scoville, *The Persecution of Huguenots and French Economic Development, 1680–1720* (Berkeley and Los Angeles: University of California Press, 1960), pp. 7–21, chaps. 4 and 5; and the various essays in Raymond A. Mentzer and Andrew Spicer, eds., *Society and Culture in the Huguenot World, 1559–1685* (Cambridge: Cambridge University Press, 2002), especially at pp. 1, 10, 213–18, 224–37. See also the following Web sites: the National Huguenot Society, huguenot.net nation.com/general/huguenot.htm; and the Huguenot Society of Great Britain and Ireland, www.huguenotsociety.org.uk/history/.

10. See Carlo M. Cipolla, *Clocks and Culture, 1300–1700* (London: Collins, 1967), pp. 65–75; Scoville, *The Persecution of Huguenots,* pp. 210–52; Raymond A. Mentzer and Andrew Spicer, "Epilogue," in *Society and Culture in the Huguenot World,* pp. 224–37. For suggestions that the economic effect of the Revocation on France has been overestimated, see Rothrock,

The Huguenots, pp. 183–86; Scoville, *The Persecution of Huguenots*, pp. 434–47.

11. See Alice C. Carter, "The Huguenot Contribution to the Early Years of the Funded Debt, 1694–1714," and Alice C. Carter, "Financial Activities of the Huguenots in London and Amsterdam in the Mid-Eighteenth Century," both in *Proceedings of the Huguenot Society of London, 1952–1958*, vol. 19 (Frome, U.K.: Butler and Tanner, 1959), pp. 21–41 and 313–33, especially pp. 21–29, 37, 40–41, 313–14, 333; Wallerstein, *Mercantilism and the Consolidation of the European World-Economy*, pp. 278–80; Wilson, *The Dutch Republic*, pp. 237–40. See also the BBC's "Immigration and Emigration: The Huguenots," www.bbc.co.uk/legacies/immig_emig/england/london/article_1 .shtml.

12. My discussion of the Darien venture and the 1707 Act of Union is based largely on Arthur Herman, *How the Scots Invented the Modern World: The True Story of How Western Europe's Poorest Nation Created Our World and Everything in It* (New York: Three Rivers Press, 2001), pp. 32–37, 39–40, 42, 48–49, 53–55; and John Prebble, *The Darien Disaster* (London: Secker & Warburg, 1968), pp. 11–14, 51–52, 56–60, 90–91, 113–18, 184–85, 216, 268–69.

13. Giuseppi, *The Bank of England*, pp. 1–26; Herman, *How the Scots Invented the Modern World*, pp. 32–37, 39–40, 42, 48–49, 53–55; Prebble, *The Darien Disaster*, pp. 113–17, 184–85, 216, 314–15.

14. Colley, *Britons: Forging the Nation*, pp. 13, 116–18, 130.

15. See Colley, *Britons: Forging the Nation*, pp. 39, 119–20, 124–32, 294–95; Herman, *How the Scots Invented the Modern World*, pp. 38, 54, 59–61, 162–65, 344–47, 357–58. On the idea of the "Scottish Empire," see Duncan A. Bruce, *The Mark of the Scots* (Secaucus, N.J.: Birch Lane Press, 1996), pp. 59–60 and chap. 6; and Michael Fry's recent book, *The Scottish Empire* (Edinburgh: Tuckwell Press, 2001).

16. Bruce, *The Mark of the Scots*, pp. 102–5, 117, 192–94; Colley, *Britons: Forging the Nation*, pp. 130–32; Herman, *How the Scots Invented the Modern World*, pp. 22–27, 62–65, 165, 291–92, 310, 320–24, 337–78.

17. My discussion of Victoria and the heyday of the British Empire relies heavily on David Cannadine, *The Pleasures of the Past* (London: William Collins Sons & Co., 1989), pp. 23, 26; Ferguson, *Empire: How Britain Made the Modern World*, pp. 164–66, 240–45; Paul Kennedy, *The Rise and Fall of the Great Powers: Economic Change and Military Conflict from 1500 to 2000* (New York: Vintage Books, 1989), pp. 151–56.

18. Immanuel Wallerstein, *The Second Era of Great Expansion of the Capitalist World-Economy, 1730–1840s*, vol. 3 of *The Modern World-System* (San Diego: Academic Press, 1989), pp. 23, 122; Wilson, *The Dutch Republic*, pp. 237–38. The Bank of England quote is from Giuseppi, *The Bank of England*, p. 1.

19. Ferguson, *Empire: How Britain Made the Modern World*, p. 166.

20. Colley, *Britons: Forging the Nation*, pp. 155–64. See also, more generally, the following exceptional books by David Cannadine: *Aspects of Aristocracy: Grandeur and Decline in Modern Britain* (New Haven: Yale University Press, 1994); *The Decline and Fall of the British Aristocracy* (New York: Vintage Books, 1999).

21. Colley, *Britons: Forging the Nation*, pp. 354, 358–59.

22. See generally ibid.

23. Ibid., pp. 19–23; Colin Haydon, *Anti-Catholicism in Eighteenth-Century England c. 1714–80* (Manchester: Manchester University Press, 1993), pp. 22, 76. On John Locke and toleration, see Grell and Porter, *Toleration in Enlightenment Europe*, pp. 5–8.

24. See Colley, *Britons: Forging the Nation*, pp. 19, 22–25, 35–36, 321–24. For two excellent discussions of the Gordon Riots, see Haydon, *Anti-Catholicism in Eighteenth-Century England*, pp. 204–44 (the quote from the eyewitness is on p. 214); and Nicholas Rogers, "Crowd and People in the Gordon Riots," in Eckhart Hellmuth, ed., *The Transformation of Political Culture: England and Germany in the Late Eighteenth Century* (Oxford: Oxford University Press, 1990), pp. 39–55.

25. Colley, *Britons: Forging the Nation*, pp. 35–36, 322–34; Ferguson, *Empire: How Britain Made the Modern World*, pp. 62–64, 323–25; James Lydon, *The Making of Ireland* (London: Routledge, 1998), pp. 217, 290–91, 301–2, 336–42, 353–55.

26. Ferguson, *Empire: How Britain Made the Modern World*, pp. 29–31, 42–48, 50, 56, 180; T. A. Heathcote, *The Military in British India* (Manchester: Manchester University Press, 1995), pp. 21–36, 39–67, 70; Lawrence James, *Raj: The Making and Unmaking of British India* (London: Little, Brown and Company, 1997), pp. 5–6, 9–10, 22–24, 42–43, 63, 71, 77, 79; Stanley Wolpert, *A New History of India*, 7th ed. (New York: Oxford University Press, 2004), chaps. 12–14; David Omissi, *The Sepoy and the Raj: The Indian Army, 1860–1940* (London: Macmillan Press, 1994), pp. 1–7, 52, 62, 94–95; Heather Streets, "The Rebellion of 1857: Origins, Consequences, and Themes," *Teaching South Asia*, vol. 1, no. 1 (Winter 2000). For India population figures, see Wolpert, p. 231.

27. On India's military heritage, see Heathcote, *The Military in British India*, chap. 1. As to British strategic tolerance and the religious and ethnic diversity of the Indian army under the Raj, see Ferguson, *Empire: How Britain Made the Modern World*, pp. 136–38, 146, 173–74, 184–89; James, *Raj: The Making and Unmaking of British India*, pp. 178, 223, 227; Douglas M. Peers, *Between Mars and Mammon: Colonial Armies and the Garrison State in Early Nineteenth Century India* (London: I. B. Tauris, 1995), pp. 84–89, 93, 255, 258.

28. C. A. Bayly, *Indian Society and the Making of the British Empire*, vol. 2, sec. 1, *The New Cambridge History of India* (Cambridge: Cambridge University Press, 1988), pp. 4–10, 43, 56–58, 61, 63, 68; Ferguson, *Empire: How Britain Made the Modern World*, pp. 29–31, 42–44, 188–89.

29. Ferguson, *Empire: How Britain Made the Modern World*, pp. 45–47, 137–38, 144–45; James, *Raj: The Making and Unmaking of British India*, pp. 207, 224–28. On the "fishing fleet" and the role of British women in India generally, see Pat Barr, *The Memsahibs: The Women of Victorian England* (London: Secker & Warburg, 1976); Pran Neville, "*Memsahibs* and the Indian Marriage Bazaar," *The Tribune* (India), Jan. 19, 2003.

30. My discussion of the Indian Mutiny draws significantly on Ferguson, *Empire: How Britain Made the Modern World*, pp. 146–54; James, *Raj: The Making and Unmaking of British India*, pp. 233–40, 251–52, 262, 286; Wolpert, *A New History of India*, pp. 226–37.

31. Ferguson, *Empire: How Britain Made the Modern World*, pp. 191–203, 209, 213; Thomas R. Metcalf, *Ideologies of the Raj*, vol. 3, sec. 4, *The New Cambridge History of India* (Cambridge: Cambridge University Press, 1994), pp. 8–9, 31, 39–40, 45, 48, 59–64, 114–22, 153–54, 199–200, 211.
32. See Omissi, *The Sepoy and the Raj*, pp. 87–90, 93–102.
33. John R. McClane, *Indian Nationalism and the Early Congress* (Princeton: Princeton University Press, 1977), p. 4. Naoroji's famous essay "The Benefits of British Rule in India" is reprinted in Dadabhai Naoroji, *Essays, Speeches, Addresses and Writings* (Bombay: Caxton Printing Works, 1887), pp. 131–36.
34. Ferguson, *Empire: How Britain Made the Modern World*, pp. 196–203; James, *Raj: The Making and Unmaking of British India*, pp. 349–51; Maria Misra, *Business, Race, and Politics in British India c. 1850–1960* (Oxford: Clarendon Press, 1999), pp. 41–42; Sumit Sarkar, *Modern India, 1885–1947* (New York: St. Martin's Press, 1989), p. 22; Wolpert, *A New History of India*, pp. 242–43, 253–54.
35. Ferguson, *Empire: How Britain Made the Modern World*, pp. 204–15, 302–4; James, *Raj: The Making and Unmaking of British India*, pp. 343, 352, 359–63, 439–40, 456–58; Wolpert, *A New History of India*, pp. 248–51, 255, 265–66, 270–73, 289–91.
36. Ferguson, *Empire: How Britain Made the Modern World*, pp. 326–28; James, *Raj: The Making and Unmaking of British India*, pp. 459–63, 471–73; Misra, *Business, Race, and Politics in British India*, pp. 86, 123–24, 145–47; Wolpert, *A New History of India*, pp. 297–302.
37. On the increasingly inclusive policies of the government of India, see Misra, *Business, Race, and Politics in British India*, pp. 55, 123–24, 142–47, 163, 168–69, and on the contrasting intolerance of the Anglo-Indian business community, see pp. 5, 7–11, 123–29, 210–14.
38. Ferguson, *Empire: How Britain Made the Modern World*, pp. 112–13, 348; Kennedy, *The Rise and Fall of the Great Powers*, pp. 367–68, 423–24.
39. Ferguson, *Empire: How Britain Made the Modern World*, pp. 354–55.

PART THREE: THE FUTURE OF WORLD DOMINANCE

NINE: THE AMERICAN HYPERPOWER: TOLERANCE AND THE MICROCHIP

Epigraphs: Jefferson's quote can be found in Thomas Jefferson, *Notes on the State of Virginia*, William Peden, ed. (Chapel Hill: University of North Carolina Press, 1954), p. 159. The quote about the ENIAC computer is from *Popular Mechanics*, Mar. 1949, p. 258.
1. See Niall Ferguson, *Colossus: The Price of America's Empire* (New York: Penguin, 2004), p. 15.
2. Israel Zangwill, "The Melting Pot: Drama in Four Acts" (1908), in *From the Ghetto to the Melting Pot: Israel Zangwill's Jewish Plays*, Edna Nahshon, ed. (Detroit, Mich.: Wayne State University Press, 2006), p. 288.
3. On the approach to religion taken by the "planting fathers," see Frank Lambert, *The Founding Fathers and the Place of Religion in America* (Princeton:

Princeton University Press, 2003), chaps. 1–3, especially pp. 75–77, 101, 111–13, 121, 129; the quotes in the text are from pp. 69, 76, 96. See also Sydney E. Ahlstrom's classic, *A Religious History of the American People*, 2nd ed. (New Haven: Yale University Press, 2004), pp. 198–99, chaps. 9–11. On the Salem witch trials, see Paul Boyer and Stephen Nissenbaum, *Salem Possessed* (Cambridge, Mass.: Harvard University Press, 1974), and Peter Charles Hoffer, *The Salem Witchcraft Trials: A Legal History* (Lawrence: University Press of Kansas, 1997).

4. My discussion of the Great Awakening relies heavily on Lambert, *The Founding Fathers and the Place of Religion in America*, pp. 128–29, 136–40, 143, 145, 151, 153–58. The quote from Chancellor Hardwicke can be found on p. 133. See also W. R. Ward, *The Protestant Evangelical Awakening* (Cambridge: Cambridge University Press, 1992).

5. Jefferson, *Notes on the State of Virginia*, p. 160.

6. Adam Smith's quote can be found in Lambert, *The Founding Fathers and the Place of Religion in America*, p. 9; John Adams's quote is on p. 219. See also pp. 8–10, 160–62, 178–79, 205–7, 236, 238.

7. Ibid., pp. 239–40, 257–58, 260–61, 265–66.

8. On the large number of slaves from West Africa who originally practiced Islam, see Michael A. Gomez, "Muslims in Early America," *The Journal of Southern History*, vol. 60, no. 4 (Nov. 1994), pp. 671, 685–86, 694; see generally Michael A. Koszegi and J. Gordon Melton, eds., *Islam in North America: A Sourcebook* (New York: Garland Publishing, 1992).

9. On Franklin's transformation, see the erudite and very readable book by Doron S. Ben-Atar, *Trade Secrets: Intellectual Piracy and the Origins of American Industrial Power* (New Haven: Yale University Press, 2004), pp. 58–61, 229–30n.24. Two excellent recent biographies are Walter Isaacson, *Benjamin Franklin: An American Life* (New York: Simon & Schuster, 2003), and Edmund S. Morgan, *Benjamin Franklin* (New Haven: Yale University Press, 2002).

10. This section draws heavily on Ben-Atar, *Trade Secrets*, especially pp. 10, 12, 29–32, 52–53, 104–6, 115–18, 146. Jefferson is quoted on p. 37.

11. Ibid., pp. 159–66, 186, 197–98, 201–4.

12. Ibid., pp. xxi, 52–53, 152–53; Charles R. Geisst, *The Last Partnerships: Inside the Great Wall Street Money Dynasties* (New York: McGraw-Hill, 2001), pp. 283–85; John Steele Gordon, *An Empire of Wealth: The Epic History of American Economic Power* (New York: Harper Perennial, 2004), pp. 242–49; Cecyle S. Neidle, *The New Americans* (New York: Twayne Publishers, 1967), p. 62; Barry E. Supple, "A Business Elite: German-Jewish Financiers in Nineteenth-Century New York," *Business History Review*, vol. 31 (Summer 1957), pp. 143–50.

13. See Sean P. Carney, "Irish Race in America," and Curtis B. Solberg, "The Scandinavians: Blueprint for Americanization," in Joseph M. Collier, ed., *American Ethnics and Minorities* (Los Alamitos, Calif.: Hwong Publishing Co., 1978), pp. 143, 219. Lincoln's quote can be found in Bill Ong Hing, *Defining America Through Immigration Policy* (Philadelphia: Temple University Press, 2004), p. 21.

14. See Kristofer Allerfeldt, *Beyond the Huddled Masses: American Immigration and The Treaty of Versailles* (London: I. B. Tauris & Co., 2006), pp. 16–17; Roger Daniels and Otis L. Graham, *Debating American Immigration, 1882–*

Present (Lanham, Md.: Rowman & Littlefield Publishers, 2001), p. 93; Carney, "Irish Race in America," and Bernard Eisenberg, "The German Americans," in *American Ethnics and Minorities*, pp. 183, 219; Lance E. Davis et al., *American Economic Growth: An Economist's History of the United States* (New York: Harper & Row, 1972), pp. 126, 173; Gordon, *An Empire of Wealth*, p. 243; Hing, *Defining America Through Immigration Policy*, pp. 25, 52; Stephan Thernstrom, ed., *Harvard Encyclopedia of American Ethnic Groups* (Cambridge, Mass.: Belknap Press, 1980), pp. 481–85; Gary M. Walton and Hugh Rockoff, *History of the American Economy*, 6th ed. (San Diego: Harcourt Brace Jovanovich, 1990), pp. 373–75; Gavin Wright, "The Origins of American Industrial Success, 1879–1940," *The American Economic Review*, vol. 80, no. 4 (Sept. 1990), pp. 651, 662. On the United States' territorial expansion and military successes against Mexico and France, see Robert Kagan, *Dangerous Nation: America's Place in the World from Its Earliest Days to the Dawn of the Twentieth Century* (New York: Alfred A. Knopf, 2006), pp. 181, 224–26, 234, 301–4.

15. Roger Daniels, *Not Like Us: Immigrants and Minorities in America, 1890–1924* (Chicago: Ivan R. Dee, Inc., 1997), p. ix; Daniels and Graham, *Debating American Immigration*, pp. 12–18; Eric Foner, *Free Soil, Free Labor, Free Men* (Oxford: Oxford University Press, 1995), pp. 241–60; Neidle, *The New Americans*, p. 26. The population estimates are from Ahlstrom, *A Religious History of the American People*, pp. 564–65; and Kristofer Allerfeldt, *Race, Radicalism, Religion, and Restriction: Immigration in the Pacific Northwest, 1890–1924* (Westport, Conn.: Praeger, 2003), pp. 33–34.

16. There is a large literature on the subject of party bosses and urban politics. My discussion draws principally on Daniel Patrick Moynihan, "The Irish of New York," in Laurence H. Fuchs, ed., *American Ethnic Politics* (New York: Harper & Row, 1968), pp. 77–83; Tyler Anbinder, " 'Boss' Tweed: Nativist," *Journal of the Early Republic*, vol. 15, no. 1 (Spring 1995), pp. 109–16; Elmer E. Cornwall, Jr., "Bosses, Machines, and Ethnic Groups," *Annals of the American Academy of Political and Social Science*, vol. 353 (May 1964), pp. 27–39; Humbert S. Nelli, "John Powers and the Italians: Politics in a Chicago Ward: 1896–1921," *The Journal of American History*, vol. 57, no. 1 (June 1970), pp. 67–84. See also Adam Cohen and Elizabeth Taylor, *American Pharaoh: Mayor Richard J. Daley: His Battle for Chicago and the Nation* (Boston: Little, Brown, and Co., 2000).

17. See Kristofer Allerfeldt, *Race, Radicalism, Religion, and Restriction*, pp. 33–34. On America's "homegrown" religions, see Ahlstrom, *A Religious History of the American People*, pp. 387, 501–9, 805–24, 1020–26. For a general history of America's indigenous peoples, see Dee Brown, *Bury My Heart at Wounded Knee: An Indian History of the American West* (New York: Holt, Rinehart, and Winston, 1970); Edward Lazarus, *Black Hills, White Justice: The Sioux Nation Versus the United States, 1775 to the Present* (New York: HarperCollins, 1991).

18. Max Boot, *The Savage Wars of Peace: Small Wars and the Rise of American Power* (New York: Basic Books, 2002), pp. 39, 62, 129; Kagan, *Dangerous Nation*, pp. 302–4; Paul Kennedy, *The Rise and Fall of the Great Powers: Economic Change and Military Conflict from 1500 to 2000* (New York: Vintage Books, 1989), p. 248.

19. See Gordon, *An Empire of Wealth*, pp. 294, 310–11; William Pfaff, "Mani-

fest Destiny: A New Direction for America," *New York Review of Books*, Feb. 15, 2007, pp. 54–55.

20. Allerfeldt, *Beyond the Huddled Masses*, pp. 17, 21, 23, 109; Daniels and Graham, *Debating American Immigration*, pp. 12–18, 23–25, 27–28, 77, 129.

21. Kennedy, *The Rise and Fall of the Great Powers*, pp. 178–80, 198–202, 242–43, 277, 357–60.

22. See Ronald W. Clark, *The Birth of the Bomb* (New York: Horizon Press, 1961), pp. 1–3, 8–13; Martin J. Sherwin, *A World Destroyed: The Atomic Bomb and the Grand Alliance* (New York: Alfred A. Knopf, 1975), pp. 49–50; C. P. Snow, *The Physicists* (Boston: Little, Brown & Co., 1981), pp. 79–80.

23. On the Soviet Union's deeply contradictory "nationalities" policy, see Valery Tishkov, *Ethnicity, Nationalism and Conflict In and After the Soviet Union: The Mind Aflame* (London: Sage Publications, 1997), pp. 27, 29–31; Francine Hirsch, "The Soviet Union as a Work-in-Progress: Ethnographers and the Category *Nationality* in the 1926, 1937, and 1939 Censuses," *Slavic Review*, vol. 56, no. 2 (1997), pp. 256, 264, 276; Yuri Slezkine, "The USSR as a Communal Apartment, or How a Socialist State Promoted Ethnic Particularism," *Slavic Review*, vol. 53, no. 2 (1994), pp. 416–21.

24. On Soviet attacks on American racism and the U.S. response, see Mary L. Dudziak, *Cold War Civil Rights: Race and the Image of American Democracy* (Princeton: Princeton University Press, 2000), pp. 29–41.

25. Ibid., pp. 179–80.

26. Geoffrey Kabaservice, *The Guardians: Kingman Brewster, His Circle, and the Rise of the Liberal Establishment* (New York: Henry Holt & Co., 2004), pp. 65, 156, 174, 176, 259–60, 264, 267; Jerome Karabel, *The Chosen: The Hidden Story of Admission and Exclusion at Harvard, Yale, and Princeton* (Boston: Houghton Mifflin Co., 2005), pp. 364–67, 379, 392; Dan A. Oren, *Joining the Club: A History of Jews at Yale* (New Haven: Yale University Press, 1983), pp. 183–84, 272. On college graduation rates, see Nicole S. Stoops, *A Half-Century of Learning: Historical Census Statistics on Educational Attainment in the United States, 1940 to 2000* (Washington, D.C.: U.S. Census Bureau, Population Division, Education and Social Stratification Branch, 2006), p. 9, table 12a.

27. Samuel P. Huntington, *Who Are We? The Challenges to America's National Identity* (New York: Simon & Schuster, 2004), pp. 196, 223–25.

28. Max Boot, *War Made New: Technology, Warfare, and the Course of History: 1500 to Today* (New York: Gotham Books, 2006), pp. 318–22, 329. The quote is from Gen. Michael Dugan, cited on p. 321.

29. My discussion of American economic dominance draws on Ferguson, *Colossus: The Price of America's Empire*, pp. 18–19; Gordon, *An Empire of Wealth*, pp. 416–18. George Soros's quote can be found in Joseph Kahn, "Losing Faith: Globalization Proves Disappointing," *New York Times*, Mar. 21, 2002, p. A8.

30. My discussion of Eugene Kleiner draws on Rhonda Abrams, "Remembering Eugene Kleiner," *USA Today*, Nov. 26, 2003; "Eugene Kleiner: Obituary," *The Economist*, Dec. 6, 2003; and personal exchanges with Eugene Kleiner's sister-in-law, Dr. Sylvia Smoller. On Andrew Grove, see Tim Jackson, *Inside*

Intel: Andy Grove and the Rise of the World's Most Powerful Chip Company (New York: Dutton, 1997), pp. 18–35, 69–76; Walter Isaacson, "The Microchip is the Dynamo of a New Economy . . . Driven by the Passion of Intel's Andrew Grove," *Time*, Dec. 29, 1997/ Jan. 5, 1998, pp. 46–51.

31. Gordon, *An Empire of Wealth*, p. 418; Vivek Wadhwa, Anna Lee Saxenian, Ben Rissing, and Gary Geretti, "America's New Immigrant Entrepreneurs" (Masters of Engineering Management Program, Duke University, and School of Information, U.C. Berkeley, Jan. 4, 2007), pp. 4–5.

32. Boot, *War Made New*, pp. 421–26.

TEN: THE RISE AND FALL OF THE AXIS POWERS: NAZI GERMANY AND IMPERIAL JAPAN

1. Klaus P. Fischer, *Nazi Germany: A New History* (New York: Continuum, 1995), p. 459; William L. Shirer, *The Rise and Fall of the Third Reich: A History of Nazi Germany* (New York: Simon & Schuster, 1990), pp. 741–46; Anne O'Hare McCormick, "Europe: Hitler at Compiegne Opens Third Act of War," *New York Times*, June 22, 1940, p. 14.

2. Fischer, *Nazi Germany*, pp. 419, 431–34, 452–54; Shirer, *The Rise and Fall of the Third Reich*, pp. 5, 625, 742.

3. Theodore Abel, *Why Hitler Came into Power* (Cambridge, Mass.: Harvard University Press, 1938), pp. 30–32; Fischer, *Nazi Germany*, pp. 42–43, 62, 64–65; Gordon A. Craig, *Germany, 1866–1945* (Oxford, U.K.: Oxford University Press, 1980), pp. 424–27; Hans Mommsen, *The Rise and Fall of Weimar Germany* (Chapel Hill: University of North Carolina Press, 1998), pp. 76, 87, 94, 118; Michael Stürmer, *The German Empire* (London: Weidenfeld & Nicolson), pp. 102–4.

4. Craig, *Germany, 1866–1945*, pp. 450–55, 543, 550–51, 585, 637; Daniel Jonah Goldhagen, *Hitler's Willing Executioners: Ordinary Germans and the Holocaust* (New York: Alfred A. Knopf, 1996), pp. 86–87; Mommsen, *The Rise and Fall of Weimar Germany*, pp. 158–60, 345–46, 354–55; Roderick Stackelberg and Sally A. Winkle, eds., *The Nazi Germany Sourcebook* (London: Routledge, 2002), p. 129.

5. Craig, *Germany, 1866–1945*, pp. 550, 633–34; Stackelberg and Winkle, *The Nazi Germany Sourcebook*, p. 92.

6. Craig, *Germany, 1866–1945*, pp. 635–36; Shirer, *The Rise and Fall of the Third Reich*, pp. 943–47, 973–74.

7. See Lucy S. Dawidowicz, *The War Against the Jews, 1933–1945* (New York: Free Press, 1975), pp. 140–43; Miklos Nyiszli, *Auschwitz: A Doctor's Eyewitness Account* (New York: Arcade Publishing, 1993), pp. 37, 40; Michael Thad Allen, "The Devil in the Details: The Gas Chambers of Birkenau, October 1941," *Holocaust and Genocide Studies*, vol. 16 (Fall 2002), p. 208. On the vast bureaucracy devoted to the identification, classification, and ultimately extermination of "inferior" peoples, see generally Götz Aly and Karl Heinz Roth, *The Nazi Census: Identification and Control in the Third Reich* (Philadelphia: Temple University Press, 2004).

8. George L. Mosse, *Nazi Culture: Intellectual, Cultural and Social Life in the Third Reich* (New York: Grosset & Dunlap, 1968), pp. 198–200; Fischer, *Nazi Germany*, pp. 541–45.

9. Dawidowicz, *The War Against the Jews, 1933–1945*, p. 142; Shirer, *The Rise and Fall of the Third Reich*, pp. 939–40; "Timeline: Ukraine," BBC News, available at news.bbc.co.uk/2/hi/europe/1107869.stm.

10. Shirer, *The Rise and Fall of the Third Reich*, pp. 937–39; Stackelberg and Winkle, *The Nazi Germany Sourcebook*, pp. xxvi, 46, 214–15; Gerhard L. Weinberg, *The Foreign Policy of Hitler's Germany: Diplomatic Revolution in Europe, 1933–36* (Chicago: University of Chicago Press, 1970), pp. 6–7, 12–13.

11. Dawidowicz, *The War Against the Jews, 1933–1945*, p. 142; Shirer, *The Rise and Fall of the Third Reich*, p. 937; Stackelberg and Winkle, *The Nazi Germany Sourcebook*, pp. 294–95; Weinberg, *The Foreign Policy of Hitler's Germany*, pp. 6, 13.

12. Fischer, *Nazi Germany*, p. 446; Shirer, *The Rise and Fall of the Third Reich*, pp. 718–20, 738–46. On the Nazis' fueling resistance in France, see Sarah Farmer, *Martyred Village: Commemorating the 1944 Massacre at Oradour-sur-Glane* (Berkeley and Los Angeles: University of California Press, 1999), pp. 13–35, 39–41, 60–61; Oliver Wieviorka, "France," in Bob Moore, ed., *Resistance in Western Europe* (Oxford, U.K.: Berg, 2000), pp. 125–28, 132–34, 145.

13. John W. Dower, *War Without Mercy: Race and Power in the Pacific War* (New York: Pantheon Books, 1986), pp. 7–9, 272–81; Ramon H. Myers and Mark R. Peattie, eds., *The Japanese Colonial Empire, 1895–1945* (Princeton: Princeton University Press, 1984), pp. 124–25.

14. See Dower, *War Without Mercy*, pp. 203–5, 217.

15. Ibid., pp. 208–10.

16. Mark R. Peattie, *Nan'Yō: The Rise and Fall of the Japanese in Micronesia, 1885–1945* (Honolulu: University of Hawaii Press, 1988), pp. 113–14, 116.

17. Peter Duus, *The Abacus and the Sword: The Japanese Penetration of Korea, 1895–1910* (Berkeley and Los Angeles: University of California Press, 1995), pp. 397–98 (quoting Arakawa Gorō).

18. Duus, *The Abacus and the Sword*, pp. 402–7.

19. Dower, *War Without Mercy*, pp. 211–17.

20. Ibid., pp. 25, 36, 278–79; Mikiso Hane, *Japan* (New York: Charles Scribner's Sons, 1972), p. 453.

21. Dower, *War Without Mercy*, pp. 277–78; Naitou Hisako, "Korean Forced Labor in Japan's Wartime Empire," in Paul H. Kratoska, ed., *Asian Labor in the Wartime Japanese Empire* (Armonk, N.Y.: M. E. Sharpe, 2005), pp. 90, 95; Andrew C. Nahm, *Korea: Tradition and Transformation* (Elizabeth, N.J.: Hollym International Corporation, 1988), pp. 239, 250, 255–56.

22. Dower, *War Without Mercy*, pp. 6–7, 46; Ken'ichi Goto, *Tensions of Empire*, Paul Kratoska, ed. (Athens, Ohio: Ohio University Press, 2003), pp. 9, 44, 78; Gregory Clancey, "The Japanese Imperium and South-East Asia," in Paul H. Kratoska, ed., *Southeast Asian Minorities in the Wartime Japanese Empire* (London: Routledge Curzon, 2002), pp. 7, 10; R. Murray Thomas, "Educational Remnants of Military Occupation," in Wolf Mendl, ed., *Japan and Southeast Asia* (London: Routledge, 2001), pp. 372–78.

23. Dower, *War Without Mercy*, pp. 43–48, 296; *Asian Labor in the Wartime Japanese Empire*, pp. 129–46, 197. On the Japanese occupation of Singapore, see C. M. Turnbull, *A History of Singapore, 1819–1988*, 2nd ed. (Sin-

gapore: Oxford University Press, 1989), pp. 183–201; Shimizu Hiroshi and Hirakawa Hiroshi, *Japan and Singapore in the World Economy* (London: Routledge, 1999), pp. 7–11, 52–53, 71, 113–30; Yoji Akashi, "Japanese Policy Towards the Malayan Chinese 1941–1945," *Journal of Southeast Asian Studies*, vol. 1, no. 2 (Sept. 1970), pp. 66–89.

24. See, e.g., Anton Lucas, "Local Opposition and Underground Resistance to the Japanese in Java, 1942–1945," *Pacific Affairs*, vol. 60, no. 3 (Autumn 1987), pp. 542–43.

25. Joseph W. Ballantine, *Formosa* (Washington, D.C.: Brookings Institution, 1952), pp. 25, 33, 36–37; Myers and Peattie, *The Japanese Colonial Empire*, pp. 30–41, 279–89.

26. Gary Marvin Davison, *A Short History of Taiwan: The Case for Independence* (Westport, Conn.: Praeger Publishers, 2003), pp. 52, 54, 61–65, 67, 70; Denny Roy, *Taiwan: A Political History* (Ithaca, N.Y.: Cornell University Press, 2003), pp. 32–45.

ELEVEN: THE CHALLENGERS: CHINA, THE EUROPEAN UNION, AND INDIA IN THE TWENTY-FIRST CENTURY

Epigraphs: The Shanghainese optimist is quoted in Clyde Prestowitz, *Three Billion New Capitalists: The Great Shift of Wealth and Power to the East* (New York: Basic Books, 2005), p. 225. The Leonard quote is from Mark Leonard, *Why Europe Will Run the 21st Century* (London: Fourth Estate, 2005), pp. 3–4.

1. See, for example, "U.S. Image Up Slightly, But Still Negative," Pew Global Attitudes Project, released June 23, 2005, available at pewglobal.org/reports/display.php?ReportID=247; "U.S. Draws Negative Ratings in Poll," Associated Press, Mar. 5, 2007, available at news.yahoo.com.

2. Michael Elliott, "The Chinese Century," *Time*, Jan. 22, 2007, pp. 33–42.

3. Ted C. Fishman, *China, Inc.: How the Rise of the Next Superpower Challenges America and the World* (New York: Scribner, 2005), pp. 1–2; Prestowitz, *Three Billion New Capitalists*, pp. 19, 26, 61; Oded Shenkar, *The Chinese Century: The Rising Chinese Economy and Its Impact on the Global Economy, the Balance of Power, and Your Job* (Upper Saddle River, N.J.: Wharton School Publishing, 2005), pp. 3, 20, 59, 114; Dominic Wilson and Roopa Purushothaman, "Dreaming with BRICs: The Path to 2050," Global Economics Paper No. 99 (Goldman Sachs Group, Oct. 1, 2003), p. 6; Lester R. Brown, "China Replacing the United States as World's Leading Consumer," Earth Policy Institute Eco-Economy Update, Feb. 16, 2005, available at www.earth-policy.org/Updates/Update45.htm.

4. Elliott, "The Chinese Century," pp. 33–34, 37–38, 42; Stephen M. Walt, "Taming American Power," *Foreign Affairs*, vol. 84, no. 5 (Sept./Oct. 2005), p. 25.

5. There is a large and fascinating literature on the factors contributing to China's remarkable history of unity. For some contrasting views, see, for example, Michael Ng-Quinn, "National Identity in Premodern China: Formation and Role Enactment," James Watson, "Rites or Beliefs? The Construction of a Unified Culture in Late Imperial China," and the other excellent essays in Lowell Dittmer and Samuel S. Kim, eds., *China's Quest*

for National Identity (Ithaca, N.Y.: Cornell University Press, 1993), pp. 32–61, 80–103.

6. Lynn White and Li Cheng, "China Coast Identities: Regional, National, and Global," in *China's Quest for National Identity*, pp. 154, 163–70; Edward Friedman, "Reconstructing China's National Identity: A Southern Alternative to Mao-Era Anti-Imperialist Nationalism," *Journal of Asian Studies*, vol. 53 (Feb. 1994), pp. 67, 68, 80–85.

7. See David Yen-ho Wu, "The Construction of Chinese and Non-Chinese Identities," in Tu Wei-Ming, ed., *The Living Tree: The Changing Meaning of Being Chinese Today* (Palo Alto: Stanford University Press, 1994), pp. 148, 155–60; Dru C. Gladney, ed., *Making Majorities: Constituting the Nation in Japan, Korea, China, Malaysia, Fiji, Turkey, and the United States* (Palo Alto: Stanford University Press, 1998), pp. 115–18; Friedman, "Reconstructing China's National Identity," pp. 85–87.

8. My own book on Chinese and other "market-dominant minorities" is Amy Chua, *World on Fire: How Exporting Free Market Democracy Breeds Ethnic Hatred and Global Instability* (New York: Doubleday, 2003). The Chinese in Southeast Asia are discussed in chapter 1.

9. Asia Society, "Education in China: Lessons for U.S. Educators" (Sept. 2005), p. 6, available at www.internationaled.org; Bruce Einhorn, "No Peasant Left Behind," *Business Week*, Aug. 22, 2005, p. 102. Andrew Yeh, "China's Regional Schools Struggle to Make the Grade," *Financial Times* (Asia edition), Apr. 26, 2006, p. 2; "The Great Divide," *The Economist*, Mar. 5, 2005, p. 6.

10. Shenkar, *The Chinese Century*, pp. 72–73.

11. Ibid., p. 75; Rebecca Pollard Pierik, "Learning in China—Free Market Style," *Harvard Graduate School of Education News*, Oct. 1, 2003.

12. See, e.g., Jun Wang, "The Return of the 'Sea Turtles': Reverse Brain Drain to China," New America Media (Sept. 26, 2005), available at www.chinadaily .com.cn/english/doc/2005–09/27/content_481163.htm.

13. "Expats See Salaries Increase by 4%," *China Daily*, Dec. 8, 2005; "Westerners in Shanghai Who Are a Little Wistful for the Old Days in China When Investment and Growth Were Just Starting to Explode in the Country," Minnesota Public Radio broadcast, Jan. 19, 2006.

14. See "Expats See Salaries Increase by 4%."

15. Yen Ching Hwang, *The Overseas Chinese and the 1911 Revolution, with Special Reference to Singapore and Malaya* (New York and Kuala Lumpur: Oxford University Press, 1976), p. 149; Prasenjit Duara, "Nationalists Among Transnationals: Overseas Chinese and the Idea of China, 1900–1911," in Aihwa Ong and Donald Nonini, eds., *Ungrounded Empires: The Cultural Politics of Modern Chinese Transnationalism* (New York: Routledge, 1997), pp. 53–54.

16. Lucian W. Pye, "Erratic State, Frustrated Society," *Foreign Affairs*, vol. 69, no. 4 (Fall 1990), p. 58; Lucian W. Pye, "China: Ethnic Minorities and National Security," in Nathan Glazer and Daniel P. Moynihan, eds., *Ethnicity: Theory and Experience* (Cambridge: Harvard University Press, 1975), p. 500.

17. Wu, "The Construction of Chinese and Non-Chinese Identities," pp. 148–60; Frank Vogl and James Sinclair, *Boom: Visions and Insights for Creating Wealth in the 21st Century* (Chicago: Irwin Professional Publishing, 1996), p. 28.

18. Paul J. Bolt, "Looking to the Diaspora: The Overseas Chinese and China's Economic Development, 1978–1994," *Diaspora*, vol. 5, no. 3 (1996), pp. 467–80; Murray Weidenbaum, "The Chinese Family Business Enterprise," *California Management Review*, vol. 38, no. 4 (Summer 1996), p. 141.

19. Bolt, "Looking to the Diaspora," pp. 475–76; Nicholas R. Lardy, "The Role of Foreign Trade and Investment in China's Economic Transformation," *China Quarterly*, no. 144 (Dec. 1995), pp. 1,065, 1,067. On Shing-Tung Yau, see Sylvia Nasar and David Gruber, "Annals of Mathematics: Manifold Destiny," *The New Yorker*, Aug. 28, 2006, pp. 44–57.

20. Kathryn Kranhold, "China's Price for Market Entry: Give Us Your Technology, Too," Wall Street Journal Online, Feb. 26, 2004.

21. Ibid.

22. Timothy Garton Ash, *Free World: America, Europe, and the Surprising Future of the West* (New York: Random House), p. 52; Denis Staunton, "The Lights Go Up All Over a New Europe," *Irish Times*, May 1, 2004, p. 10; "EU Celebrates Historic Moment," BBC News, May 1, 2004, available at news.bbc.co.uk/1/hi/world/europe/3672813.stm.

23. Desmond Dinan, *Europe Recast: A History of the European Union* (Boulder, Colo.: Lynne Rienner Publishers, 2004), p. 1; John McCormick, *Understanding the European Union: A Concise Introduction*, 3rd ed. (New York: St. Martin's Press, 1999), pp. 35–38.

24. Michael J. Baun, *An Imperfect Union: The Maastricht Treaty and the New Politics of European Integration* (Boulder, Colo.: Westview Press, 1996), pp. 11–15.

25. Mark Leonard, *Why Europe Will Run the 21st Century*, pp. 13–15; Julian Brookes, Interview with Mark Leonard, Oct. 18, 2005, available at www.motherjones.com/news/qa/2005/10/mark_leonard.html.

26. T. R. Reid, *The United States of Europe: The New Superpower and the End of American Supremacy* (New York: Penguin Books, 2005), pp. 20, 145–51.

27. Ash, *Free World: America, Europe, and the Surprising Future of the West*, p. 47 (quoting and paraphrasing Jürgen Habermas and Jacques Derrida).

28. Adrian Favell and Randall Hansen, "Markets Against Politics: Migration, EU Englargement and the Idea of Europe," *Journal of Ethnic and Migration Studies*, vol. 28, no. 4 (Oct. 2002), pp. 582, 591–92.

29. "Immigration to the United States: Brains and Borders," *The Economist*, May 6, 2006, p. 53; Brian Knowlton, "EU and U.S. Face Reality of Immigration; Tides of People Spark a Trading of Ideas," *International Herald Tribune*, June 30, 2006, p. 2.

30. Carter Dougherty, "Labor Shortage Becoming Acute in Technology," *New York Times*, Mar. 10, 2007, pp. C1, C7; Fareed Zakaria, "To Become an American," *Washington Post*, Apr. 4, 2006, p. A23.

31. Jane Kramer, "Taking the Veil: How France's Public Schools Became the Battleground in a Culture War," *The New Yorker*, Nov. 22, 2004, p. 60; Robert S. Leiken, "Europe's Angry Muslims," *Foreign Affairs*, vol. 84, no. 4 (July/Aug. 2005); Lorenzo Vidino, "Dutch Get Tougher on Terror," *Washington Times*, Mar. 15, 2006, p. A17.

32. Ash, *Free World: America, Europe, and the Surprising Future of the West*, p. 53; Jens Rydgren, "Explaining the Emergence of Radical Right-Wing Populist Parties: The Case of Denmark," *West European Politics*, vol. 27, no. 3

(May 2004), pp. 474, 485; Ambrose Evans-Pritchard, "Atheist Premier Attacks Lack of Christianity in EU Constitution," Telegraph.co.uk, June 4, 2003; John Rossant, "Turkey's EU Bid: Resistance Is on the Line," *Business Week*, Feb. 9, 2004, p. 57.

33. Lindsey Rubin, "Love's Refugees: The Effects of Stringent Danish Immigration Policies on Danes and Their Non-Danish Spouses," *Connecticut Journal of International Law*, vol. 20 (Summer 2005), pp. 320, 324, 327–28; "Denmark Shifts to Right in Election Centering on Immigration," *New York Times*, Nov. 21, 2001, p. A6; "The Danish Peoples Party: History," at www .danskfolkeparti.dk/sw/frontend/show.asp?parent=3293.

34. See, for example, Ian Buruma, "Letter from Amsterdam: Final Cut," *The New Yorker*, Jan. 3, 2005, p. 26; Jane Kramer, "Comment: Difference," *The New Yorker*, Nov. 21, 2005, pp. 41–42.

35. American Council on Education, "Issue Brief: Students on the Move: The Future of International Students in the United States," Oct. 2006, pp. 4–5, 9, available at www.acenet.edu/programs/international. See also the comprehensive reports and data tables available on the Web site of the Institute of International Education, www.opendoors.iienetwork.org.

36. Prestowitz, *Three Billion New Capitalists*, p. 144.

37. Paul McDougall and Aaron Ricadela, "India Calls Its Talent Home," *Information Week*, Mar. 13, 2006, p. 24; Fareed Zakaria, "India Rising," *Newsweek*, Mar. 6, 2006, p. 32; "The Great Indian Hope Trick," *The Economist*, Feb. 23, 2006, pp. 29–31.

38. Judith E. Walsh, *A Brief History of India* (New York: Facts on File, 2006), pp. 267–68.

39. Rachel Aspden, "The Bangalore Effect," *New Statesman*, Jan. 30, 2006, p. 26; Pankaj Mishra, "The Myth of the New India," *New York Times*, July 6, 2006, p. 21; "The Great Indian Hope Trick," pp. 29–31.

40. Stephen Philip Cohen, *India: Emerging Power* (Washington, D.C.: Brookings Institution, 2001), p. 29; Mishra, "The Myth of the New India," p. 21.

41. The World Bank, *World Development Report 2006: Equity and Development* (Washington, D.C.: The World Bank, 2005), p. 278, table A1; The World Bank, *India and the Knowledge Economy: Leveraging Strengths and Opportunities*, report no. 31267-IN, Apr. 2005, p. 4; "The Great India Hope Trick," pp. 29–31.

42. Pankaj Mishra, "A New Sort of Superpower," *New Statesman*, Jan. 30, 2006, pp. 20, 22; Ziauddin Sardar, "Haunted by the Politics of Hate," *New Statesman*, Jan. 30, 2006, p. 31.

43. Amartya Sen, *The Argumentative Indian: Writings on Indian History, Culture, and Identity* (New York: Farrar, Straus & Giroux, 2005), pp. 18, 32, 47, 274, 303–4.

44. Cohen, *India: Emerging Power*, p. 120; Walsh, *A Brief History of India*, pp. 276–77, 281; Human Rights Watch, *World Report 2003*, available at hrw .org/wr2k3/asia6.html.

45. Karol Zemek, "India by Numbers," *New Statesman*, Jan. 30, 2006, p. 22.

46. Neha Bhayana, "Bright Young Lights," *New Statesman*, Jan. 30, 2006, p. 36; Gurcharan Das, "The India Model," *Foreign Affairs*, vol. 85, no. 4 (July/ Aug. 2006), p. 9; Edward Luce, "One Land, Two Planets," *New Statesman*, Jan. 30, 2006, pp. 23–25.

47. See, e.g., Yasheng Huang and Tarun Khanna, "Can India Overtake China?," *Foreign Policy*, July/Aug. 2003, p. 74.
48. "Great Indian Hope Trick," p. 290.

TWELVE: THE DAY OF EMPIRE: LESSONS OF HISTORY

Epigraph: The quoted passage is from "Four Quartets: Little Gidding," in T. S. Eliot, *The Complete Poems and Plays, 1909–1950* (New York: Harcourt, Brace & World, Inc., 1971), p. 145.

1. See Francis Fukuyama, *The End of History and the Last Man* (New York: Avon Books, 1992); Thomas L. Friedman, *The Lexus and the Olive Tree* (New York: Anchor Books, 2000), pp. ix, xvi, 12.
2. See Josef Joffe, *Überpower: The Imperial Temptation of America* (New York: W. W. Norton, 2006), pp. 38–39, 43–44.
3. Office of the President, "The National Security Strategy of the United States of America," Sept. 2002, available at www.whitehouse.gov/nsc/nss.pdf.
4. See Thomas L. Friedman, "Axis of Appeasement," *New York Times*, Mar. 18, 2004, p. 33; Christopher Hitchens, "Against Rationalization," *The Nation*, vol. 273, no. 10 (Oct. 8, 2001), p. 8; Bill Van Auken, "Friedman on Iraq: The 'Thinking' Behind the *New York Times* Debate," Oct. 25, 2005, available at www.wsws.org/articles/2005/oct2005/frie-o25.shtml.
5. See Niall Ferguson, *Colossus: The Price of America's Empire* (New York: Penguin, 2004), pp. 3, 301–2; Deepak Lal, *In Praise of Empires: Globalization and Order* (New York: Palgrave Macmillan, 2004), p. 215; Irving Kristol, "The Neoconservative Persuasion," *Weekly Standard*, Aug. 25, 2003, pp. 23–25; Max Boot, "The Case for American Empire," *Weekly Standard*, Oct. 15, 2001, p. 27.
6. See, e.g., Kenneth M. Pollack, "Spies, Lies, and Weapons: What Went Wrong," *The Atlantic Monthly*, Jan./Feb. 2004, pp. 78–92.
7. Jeffrey M. Jones, "Bush Approval Rating Remains Low," Gallup News Service, Mar. 6, 2007; "Poll: Iraq Going Badly and Getting Worse," CBS News, Dec. 11, 2006, available at www.cbsnews.com/stories/2006/12/11/opinion/polls/printable2247797.shtml.
8. Pierre Briant, *From Cyrus to Alexander: A History of the Persian Empire*, Peter T. Daniels, trans. (Winona Lake, Ind.: Eisenbrauns, 2002), p. 193.
9. Craige B. Champion, *Roman Imperialism: Readings and Sources* (Malden, Mass.: Blackwell Publishing, 2004), pp. 30–33, 50–51, 164–70; Michael Grant, *The History of Rome* (London: Faber and Faber, 1979), p. 237.
10. See C. R. Boxer, *The Dutch Seaborne Empire: 1600–1800* (New York: Alfred A. Knopf, 1965), pp. xxv, 188, 190, 194, 198, 220.
11. Immanuel Wallerstein, *Mercantilism and the Consolidation of the European World-Economy, 1600–1750*, vol. 2 of *The Modern World-System* (San Diego: Academic Press, 1980), pp. 45, 63–64.
12. Max Boot, *The Savage Wars of Peace: Small Wars and the Rise of American Power* (New York: Basic Books, 2002), p. 55.
13. Niall Ferguson, *Colossus: The Price of America's Empire*, p. 33.
14. John Steele Gordon, *An Empire of Wealth: The Epic History of American Economic Power* (New York: HarperPerennial, 2004), pp. xiv–xv.
15. Niall Ferguson, *Empire: How Britain Made the Modern World* (London:

382

NOTES

Allen Lane, 2003), pp. 164, 302, 325, 341; Lawrence James, *Raj: The Making and Unmaking of British India* (London: Little, Brown and Company, 1997), pp. 352, 439, 456.

16. Briant, *From Cyrus to Alexander*, p. 868.

17. See Joffe, *Überpower: The Imperial Temptation of America*, pp. 77–78; Thomas Olmstead, Bay Fang, Eduardo Cue, and Masha Gessen, "A World of Resentment," *U.S. News & World Report*, Mar. 5, 2001, p. 32.

18. Stephen M. Walt, "Taming American Power," *Foreign Affairs*, vol. 84, no. 5 (Sept./Oct. 2005), p. 105; Survey Results: "America's Image Further Erodes, Europeans Want Weaker Ties," Mar. 18, 2003, available on the Pew Foundation Web site.

19. "U.S. Draws Negative Ratings in Poll," Associated Press, Mar. 5, 2007, available on Yahoo.news.

20. Olmstead, Fang, Cue, and Gessen, "A World of Resentment," p. 32.

21. Samuel P. Huntington, *Who Are We? The Challenges to America's National Identity* (New York: Simon & Schuster, 2004), pp. 20, 69, 75; Transcript of "Lou Dobbs Tonight," aired Mar. 31, 2006, available at transcripts.cnn.com/TRANSCRIPTS/0603/31/ldt.01.html.

22. Anita Kumar and Vanessa de la Torre, "Work Here, Send Money Home," *St. Petersburg Times*, May 10, 2006, p. 1A

23. Kevin Allison, "Visa Curbs Are Damaging Economy, Warns Gates," *Financial Times*, Mar. 8, 2007, p. 7; Testimony of Laszlo Bock, Vice President, People Operations, Google, Inc., before the House Judiciary Subcommittee on Immigration, Citizenship, Refugees, Border Security, and International Law, June 6, 2007, available at 64.233.179.110/blog_resources/Laszlo_Bock_immigration_testimony.pdf.

INDEX

Railroad of death, 282
Raja Birbal, 185
Rajputs, 185, 213
Rasmussen, Anders Fogh, 307
Ray, John, 159
Reformation, the, 144
Religious tolerance/intolerance
  of Alexander the Great, 24–25
  British Empire, 194–200, 208–12,
    237
  Byzantine Empire, 76–77
  Dutch Republic, 142–43, 147–49,
    155, 167
  European Union, 304–8
  India in twenty-first century, 313–15
  India under British rule, 215–16,
    219, 220–21
  Mongol Empire, 90, 95, 96, 101–2,
    106, 109, 111, 112, 118–19, 121,
    122
  Mughal Empire, 185–88, 189–90
  Ottoman Empire, 169–73, 174–75,
    176, 177
  Persian Empire, 8–10, 11, 12, 14, 20
  Roman Empire, 38, 48–52, 53–55
  Spain, 129–36, 173
  Tang Empire, 70–71, 76, 84, 85–86
  Umayyad Empire, 76
  United States, 234–40, 248, 250–51
  See also specific religions
Rembrandt, 162
Reynst, Gerrit, 155
Riady, James, 298
Risley, H. H., 218–19
Roberts, Lord, 220
Robertson, William, 204
Rogers, Guy MacLean, 23–24
Roman Empire, xxiii–xxiv, 322, 323
  Antoninus Pius's rule, 38–39
  assimilationist policies, 47–48
  Christianity and, 51–52, 53–55
  citizenship rights, 31, 35, 37, 45–46
  civilizing mission, 47–48
  conquered peoples' attraction to Ro-
    man culture, 43–46
  cultural achievements, 30–31
  decline related to intolerance, 52–58
  economic conditions, 35, 39–40
  ethnic and racial tolerance/intoler-
    ance, 32–33, 41–43, 44, 55–57

  European Union and, 302
  founding of Rome, 34–35
  gladiator games, 34
  "glue" for holding empire together,
    xxx–xxxi, 330
  Greek civilization and, 44
  Hadrian's rule, 37–38
  High Empire period, 31, 37
  hyperpower status, xxi–xxii
  as idea, 29–30
  Jews and, 38, 50–51, 54, 55
  linguistic and cultural diversity, 44
  local authority, preservation of, 32,
    34, 35, 36
  Marcus Aurelius's rule, 39
  military conditions, 35, 46
  religious tolerance/intolerance, 38,
    48–52, 53–55
  slavery, 34
  social mobility, 40–41
  socioeconomic divisions, 44
  strategic tolerance, 33–34, 35–36
  territorial expansion, 35–37
  Trajan's rule, 37
  United States and, 327
  women's status, 34
  world domination as goal of, 30
  See also Byzantine Empire
Romania, 301
Romulo, Carlos, 282
Romulus and Remus, 34–35
Rosenberg, Alfred, 273–74
Rousseau, Jean-Jacques, 301
Roxane, 26
Ruisdael, Jacob van, 162
Russia/Soviet Union, 261, 327
  ethnic and racial tolerance/intoler-
    ance, 255–57
  Mongols and, 107, 108, 122
  Nazi-Soviet war, 272–74

Sabines, 35
Salem witch trials, 236
Samarkand, 103–4
Schama, Simon, 149, 158, 160
Schwab, Klaus, 311
Scotland, 41, 200–202. See also British
    Empire
Scott, Sir Walter, 205
Scylax, Adm., 17

ALSO BY AMY CHUA

*"A riveting and original book that challenges key
tenets of American political faith."*
—The Baltimore Sun

WORLD ON FIRE

*The How Exporting Free Market Democracy Breeds
Ethnic Hatred and Global Instability*

The reigning consensus holds that the combination of free
markets and democracy will transform the third world and
sweep away the ethnic hatred and religious zealotry associated with underdevelopment. In this investigation of the
true impact of globalization, Yale Law professor Amy
Chua explains why many developing countries are in fact
consumed by ethnic violence after adopting free market
democracy. Chua shows how free markets have often concentrated starkly disproportionate wealth in the hands of a
resented ethnic minority. These "market-dominant minorities"—Chinese in Southeast Asia, Croatians in the former
Yugoslavia, whites in Latin America and South Africa,
Indians in East Africa, Lebanese in West Africa, Jews in
post-communist Russia—become objects of violent hatred.
At the same time, democracy empowers the impoverished
majority, unleashing ethnic demagoguery, confiscation,
and sometimes genocidal revenge. She also shows how this
dynamic helps explain the rising tide of anti-Americanism
around the world. Chua is a friend of globalization, but she
urges us to find ways to spread its benefits and curb its most
destructive aspects.

Current Affairs/978-0-385-72186-8

ANCHOR BOOKS
Available at your local bookstore, or visit
www.randomhouse.com